WINNER OF THE 2017 DAVID O. SEARS BOOK AWARD, INTER-
NATIONAL SOCIETY OF POLITICAL PSYCHOLOGY

MORE PRAISE FOR

Democracy for Realists

"The best book to understand the 2016 campaign."

—MATTHEW YGLESIAS, *VOX*

"A comprehensive analysis that lays the foundation for a discussion
of necessary reforms and how they can be achieved."

—*Kirkus Reviews* (starred review)

"[A] provocative book." —EDWARD LUCE, *Financial Times*

"For decades, political scientists have blasted away at electoral
models based primarily on the idea of rational choice. In the most
recent and sophisticated entry in the field, *Democracy for Realists*, Christopher Achen and Larry Bartels argue that even well-
informed and politically engaged voters mostly choose candidates
based on their social identities and partisan loyalties. Judging from
the 2016 polls, that theory looks pretty good."

—E. J. DIONNE, *Washington Post*

"*Democracy for Realists* is essential reading for 2016, an empirically
and theoretically rigorous political science treatise that debunks
traditional defenses of democracy as a way to reflect the 'will of
the people' or allow well-informed and rational voters to guide
the country. In their place, Christopher Achen and Larry Bartels
advance a theory of democracy grounded in group identities and
social psychology." —JASON FURMAN, *Bloomberg*

"One of the most bracing books of political science to arrive in a long time.... An impressively comprehensive statement on the limits of electoral democracy, a book that can both explain the emergence of Trump and potentially charts a new course for the field."
—LEE DRUTMAN, *Chronicle of Higher Education*

"The folk theory of American democracy is that citizens deliberate on the issues and choose a candidate. That is false. The truth, as political scientists Christopher Achen and Larry Bartels describe in *Democracy for Realists: Why Elections Do Not Produce Responsive Government*, is that voters are tribalistic."
—JAMELLE BOUIE, *Slate*

"Their writing is clear, concise, and appropriately whimsical on occasion. Certain to become a classic."   —*Choice*

"*Democracy for Realists* is essential reading for anyone interested in the problem of voter ignorance, and the future of democracy more generally. It illuminates a dangerous problem that may well bedevil democracy for a long time to come."
—ILYA SOMIN, *History News Network*

"It will confirm much that you may already have intuited—issues do not much matter—and it may make you want to jump out of a window, if you didn't already."
—KEVIN WILLIAMSON, *National Review*

"The most clear-eyed take on American democracy I have read in a long time."   —DANIEL W. DREZNER, Tufts University

"The 2016 election cycle has confounded a good deal of scholarship and punditry so far. But one book that's coming out smelling like a rose is Christopher Achen and Larry Bartels' new book *Democracy for Realists: Why Elections Do Not Produce Responsive Government*. This book's novel argument is that we've been thinking about democracy all wrong." —SETH MASKET, *Pacific Standard*

"Not since the work of Walter Lippmann, David Truman, Philip Converse, and Robert Dahl have empirical democratic theorists made us think so deeply. Achen and Bartels demolish the folk theory of democracy in which politicians obtain mandates from rational voters. Instead, they propose an exciting new agenda that wrestles with the real democratic process in which political parties and interest groups fashion public policies to appeal to people's basic identities."

—HENRY E. BRADY, coauthor of *The Unheavenly Chorus: Unequal Political Voice and the Broken Promise of American Democracy*

"It is common in the history of science for scholars to bark up the wrong trees. Achen and Bartels make a strong case that spatial models of mass elections and the theory of retrospective voting are examples of wrong trees. Scholars, they argue, should now reorient toward group attachments as the foundation of democratic politics. All in all, this is a broad, deeply thoughtful, and courageous book."

—JOHN ZALLER, University of California, Los Angeles

"It is impossible to overstate the significance of this magnum opus on democracy and democratic theory. Achen and Bartels lay waste to the folk theory of democracy through dazzling logic and rigorous empirical analysis. *Democracy for Realists* will become an instant classic, shaping our thinking on democracy for decades to come."

—THOMAS E. MANN, Brookings Institution and the University of California, Berkeley

"*Democracy for Realists* is the single most important treatise on American democracy published in several decades. Achen and Bartels challenge just about every existing school of thought about electoral politics, policymaking, and government performance. They do not conclude with a counsel of despair for the future of American democracy, but they give no quarter to any notion that responsive government is possible without a more responsible citizenry."

—JOHN DIIULIO, University of Pennsylvania

"Two of America's smartest political scientists bid fair to transform our understanding of democracy. In our season of democratic discontent, this unsettling book could hardly be more timely. Must-reading for anyone interested in democratic theory and American politics."

—ROBERT D. PUTNAM, author of *Bowling Alone: The Collapse and Revival of American Community* and *Our Kids: The American Dream in Crisis*

"*Democracy for Realists* has the potential to become a classic. It raises questions that every democratic theorist and practitioner should take seriously. It is certain to provoke significant discussion."

—JANE MANSBRIDGE, Harvard University

"*Democracy for Realists* is a terrific book. It takes on big questions, is brimming with smart analysis and crisp argumentation, and the writing is elegant. There is pleasure and provocation on nearly every page. Achen and Bartels have made a major contribution to modern social science."

—DONALD R. KINDER, coauthor of *The End of Race? Obama, 2008, and Racial Politics in America*

DEMOCRACY FOR REALISTS

PRINCETON STUDIES IN
Political Behavior

Edited by Tali Mendelberg

DEMOCRACY
FOR
REALISTS

Why Elections Do Not Produce
Responsive Government

With a new afterword by the authors

CHRISTOPHER H. ACHEN
LARRY M. BARTELS

PRINCETON UNIVERSITY PRESS
PRINCETON AND OXFORD

Published by Princeton University Press,
41 William Street, Princeton, New Jersey 08540
In the United Kingdom: Princeton University Press,
6 Oxford Street, Woodstock, Oxfordshire OX20 1TR

press.princeton.edu

Seventh printing, and first paperback printing,
with a new afterword by the authors, 2017
Paperback ISBN 978-0-691-17824-0
Cloth ISBN 978-0-691-16944-6

Library of Congress Control Number 2016930927

British Library Cataloging-in-Publication Data is available

This book has been composed in Garamond Premier Pro

Printed on acid-free paper. ∞

Printed in the United States of America

11   13   15   17   19   20   18   16   14   12

For Monica, who will understand.
—C.A.

For Denise, the love of my life, at last.
—L.B.

Contents

Contents

Illustrations

FIGURES

TABLES

List of Illustrations

Preface

This book is the result of a long conversation. The authors first met in 1974, when Achen was a beginning assistant professor and Bartels was an even younger freshman in college. But the conversation did not begin in earnest until a quarter century later, after years of teaching and writing about public opinion, electoral politics, political representation, and public policy had left us similarly, but mostly separately, deeply uneasy about the significant tensions we saw between the findings of empirical social science and the familiar textbook portrait of democracy.

In 1998, discussion of a then-unpublished paper (Bartels 2003) and an undergraduate course Achen was teaching revealed a good deal of overlap in our evolving perspectives and concerns. We began to think and talk about potential research projects that might shed new light on the performance of democracies and on the relationship between democratic ideals and realities. By 2000 we thought of ourselves as writing a book, though its scope and thrust would obviously hinge on the results of our empirical work.

On good days, we envisioned a two-volume study of democratic politics and government. Our rate of progress to date makes it unlikely that we will complete the projected second volume focusing on democratic policy-making processes; nevertheless, we still hope to add to our existing down payment on that work (Achen 2006a, 2006b). In the meantime, even this first volume has turned out to be a much more open-ended book than we imagined, raising many crucial issues that it does little to resolve. We can only hope that colleagues and students in the years to come will find our ideas and evidence sufficiently intriguing to push further.

When we began this work, we thought about democracy in much the same way that most democratic citizens do. The gap we perceived between conventional democratic ideals and the all-too-visible realities was troubling precisely because we took the ideals seriously. Nevertheless, we believed that if the realities failed to match the ideals, we (and others seeking to vindicate contemporary democracy) still had intellectually powerful back-up defenses to bolster our convictions. Chapters 3 through 7 record the depressing failures of all those defensive positions. At that point, we knew that we had to start over from a completely different foundation, and the remainder of the book makes a start on that task.

Thus, the book resulted in a kind of intellectual conversion experience for us. Much of what we had believed and trusted turned out to be false. To be faithful to the evidence and honest with ourselves, we had to think very differently. In consequence, we have become used to listening to our colleagues and neighbors talking about this subject and feeling that their entire framework for thinking about democracy is really quite different from ours. In consequence, many readers may find this book irritating—or worse. We can only say that we sympathize; we would once have thought it quite irritating, too.

When we began our active collaboration, Achen taught at the University of Michigan and Bartels at Princeton University. As we finish the book, Achen is at Princeton and Bartels is at Vanderbilt University. We are grateful to special colleagues and students at all three institutions for the many stimulating discussions and debates that we have enjoyed. These three universities also provided timely leaves from teaching, generous funding for research and travel, and substantial infrastructure and administrative assistance, all of which were indispensable to the long process of discussion, research, and writing reflected in this book. Michigan's Political Science Department and its Center for Political Studies, Princeton's Politics Department, Woodrow Wilson School, and Center for the Study of Democratic Politics, and Vanderbilt's Political Science Department and its Center for the Study of Democratic Institutions have all provided congenial settings in which to pursue our studies. Barb Opal, Diane Price, Michele Epstein, Helene Wood, Jayne Cornwell, and Shannon Meldon-Corney have been unfailing sources of both logistical assistance and moral support.

Over the past dozen years we have taught a variety of graduate and undergraduate courses drawing on the material presented here—sometimes separately, sometimes jointly, and sometimes in collaboration with political theorists Arlene Saxonhouse at Michigan and Steve Macedo at Princeton. We thank Arlene and Steve most warmly for broadening our theoretical horizons and for demonstrating the great value of serious, thoughtful contact between political philosophy and empirical evidence. We also thank our students for providing a great deal of helpful feedback on our arguments and exposition, and Jim Kuklinski for sharing equally helpful comments and advice on a draft of the manuscript from his graduate students at the University of Illinois. We are indebted, too, to Dorothy McMurtery, who talked with us about her life and helped us understand how identities evolve.

Most of chapters 3, 5, 6, 7, and 10 and parts of chapters 4 and 9 are based on unpublished papers originally presented at annual meetings of the American Political Science Association and the Midwest Political Science Association. These and other chapters have also been presented by one or both of us in numerous seminars from Madrid to Taipei. Although we cannot acknowledge individually the many hosts, discussants, and audience members who made these events so stimulating and instructive, their contributions are very much woven into the fabric of the book. We are especially grateful to friends at Yale, Stanford, and UCLA for providing helpful reactions to overviews of the entire project, and to Jon Bendor, Walter Dean Burnham, Emilee Chapman, Josh Clinton, Barbara Geddes, John Geer, Marc Hetherington, John E. Jackson, Karen Long Jusko, Orit Kedar, Melissa Lane, Skip Lupia, David Mayhew, Emily Nacol, Bing Powell, Bob Putnam, Andrew Sabl, Phil Shively, Richard Sinnott, Paul Sniderman, Jim Snyder, Jim Stimson, Sue Stokes, Lynn Vavreck, Stephen Walker, and Alan Wiseman for advice and encouragement along the way. We also thank our editor at Princeton University Press, Eric Crahan, and our colleague and series editor, Tali Mendelberg, for their assistance and their generous encouragement.

We owe a special debt of thanks to the terrific colleagues who traveled to Nashville to provide detailed help to us on our penultimate draft: Henry Brady, Alan Gerber, Jim Kuklinski, Mike MacKuen, Jenny Mansbridge, Ben Page, Arlene Saxonhouse, Kay Schlozman, and John Zaller. Mansbridge, Zaller, Patrick Fournier, Don Kinder, and Steve Rogers provided detailed written comments on multiple chapters at various stages. Our gratitude for the collegial assistance we have received from these and many other friends and colleagues is magnified by the fact that some of them have done their best to help us formulate and defend views that they themselves have considered quite wrongheaded. For this reason, if no other, we wish to emphasize that we alone—and very much jointly—are responsible for the remaining errors and misjudgments.

Achen's daughters, Monica and Sasha, and Bartels's daughters, Ellie and Meghan, now grown and on their own, have been warmly tolerant of our occupations and preoccupations. Our spouses, Tena Achen and Denise Bartels, have been unfailingly supportive through decades of late-night writing marathons, piles of books in the house, innumerable absences from home while we attended conferences and seminars, and the inevitable vicissitudes of academic life. Our book would have been impossible without our families' support and forbearance, and our lives would have been impoverished without their love.

DEMOCRACY FOR REALISTS

Democratic Ideals and Realities

The democratic idealists of practically all schools of thought have
managed to remain remarkably oblivious to the obvious facts.
—Reinhold Niebuhr, *The Children of Light and
the Children of Darkness* (1944, 40)

In the conventional view, democracy begins with the voters. Ordinary people have preferences about what their government should do. They choose leaders who will do those things, or they enact their preferences directly in referendums. In either case, what the majority wants becomes government policy—a highly attractive prospect in light of most human experience with governments. Democracy makes the people the rulers, and legitimacy derives from their consent. In Abraham Lincoln's stirring words from the Gettysburg Address, democratic government is "of the people, by the people, and for the people." That way of thinking about democracy has passed into everyday wisdom, not just in the United States but in a great many other countries around the globe. It constitutes a kind of "folk theory" of democracy, a set of accessible, appealing ideas assuring people that they live under an ethically defensible form of government that has their interests at heart.[1]

Unfortunately, while the folk theory of democracy has flourished as an ideal, its credibility has been severely undercut by a growing body of scientific evidence presenting a different and considerably darker view of democratic politics. That evidence demonstrates that the great majority of citizens pay little attention to politics. At election time, they are swayed by how they feel about "the nature of the times," especially the current state of the economy, and by political loyalties typically acquired in childhood. Those loyalties, not

---

1 We thank Jane Mansbridge for emphasizing the centrality of this concept in our argument.

the facts of political life and government policy, are the primary drivers of political behavior. Election outcomes turn out to be largely random events from the viewpoint of contemporary democratic theory. That is, elections are well determined by powerful forces, but those forces are not the ones that current theories of democracy believe should determine how elections come out. Hence the old frameworks will no longer do.

We want to persuade the reader to think about democracy in a fundamentally different way. We are not in the business of encouraging liberals to become conservatives or vice versa. Books of that kind are plentiful enough. Rather we show both liberals and conservatives that the mental framework they bring to democratic life, while it may once have seemed defensible, can now be maintained only by willful denial of a great deal of credible evidence. However disheartening the task, intellectual honesty requires all of us to grapple with the corrosive implications of that evidence for our understanding of democracy. That is what this book aims to do.

TWO CONTEMPORARY APPROACHES TO DEMOCRACY

What are the conventional notions of democracy that we argue have outlived their time? We consider two main types of theory, one popular with broad swatches of democratic society and a second whose appeal is largely confined to scholars specializing in the study of elections.[2]

The first model, which we refer to as the *populist* ideal of democracy, emphasizes the role of ordinary citizens in "determining the policies" of democratic communities (Dahl 1998, 37–38). As we will see, this populist notion of popular sovereignty has inspired a good deal of sophisticated academic thinking derived from Enlightenment concepts of human nature and the political views of 19th-century British liberalism. In its less rarified forms it has

---

2 These two models by no means exhaust the variety of meanings of democracy around the world, or even within the United States. For example, the (overlapping) traditions of *participatory democracy*, *face-to-face democracy*, and *deliberative democracy* have received a great deal of attention from academic theorists (Pateman 1970; Barber 1984; Habermas 1994; Fishkin 1995; Benhabib 1996; Gutmann and Thompson 1996; Sanders 1997; Macedo 1999; Cohen 2003), and they have been implemented with more or less success in a variety of settings, especially in small groups and local communities (Mansbridge 1980; Mendelberg and Oleske 2000; Fung 2004; Karpowitz 2006). However, notwithstanding some creative attempts to employ small-scale deliberative exercises as simulations of how mass publics *would* decide controversial issues in a deliberative fashion (Fishkin 1991; 2009), these models seem to us to be less relevant for understanding democratic politics on a national scale than those we consider here.

also undergirded the folk theory of democracy celebrated in much Fourth of July rhetoric. As the homespun poet of democracy Carl Sandburg (1936) proclaimed, "The People, Yes."

But *how* precisely shall the people govern according to the populist theory? In subsequent chapters, we shall examine two different accounts of how populist democracy might work. In one, the public "decide[s] issues through the election of individuals who are to assemble in order to carry out its will," as an unsympathetic critic of this account put it (Schumpeter 1942, 250). In the other, the people rule through "direct democracy," choosing policies themselves via initiative and referendum procedures. Both representative democracy and direct democracy loom large in popular understanding of democratic self-government. But as we shall see, the assumptions undergirding both versions of populist democracy are highly unrealistic.

The second contemporary model in defense of democracy is less widely popular, though more persuasive to most political scientists. This model focuses on elections as mechanisms for *leadership selection*. In contrast to the populist model, which he characterized as "the classical doctrine of democracy," Joseph Schumpeter (1942, 269) famously defined the democratic method as "that institutional arrangement for arriving at political decisions in which individuals acquire the power to decide by means of a competitive struggle for the people's vote."[3] Dispensing with the notion that "the people itself decide issues" by electing those who will "carry out its will," Schumpeter (1942, 284–285) insisted that "democracy does not mean and cannot mean that the people actually rule in any obvious sense of the terms 'people' and 'rule.' Democracy means only that the people have the opportunity of accepting or refusing the men who are to rule them."

Schumpeter gave little attention to the criteria by which voters would—or *should*—choose among potential rulers. However, subsequent scholars have fleshed out his account. The most influential model of democratic selection in contemporary political science is the *retrospective theory of voting*, which portrays "the electorate in its great, and perhaps principal, role as an appraiser of past events, past performance, and past actions" (Key 1966, 61).

---

3 Pateman (1970, 3–5, 16–20) correctly pointed out that no such "classical theorists" exist; but she acknowledged that "one could extract something which bears a family resemblance to Schumpeter's definition of the 'classical' theory" from the 19th-century works of Jeremy Bentham and James Mill, among others. Some popular writers in the Progressive Era, such as William Allen White (1910), nicely exemplify the viewpoint that Schumpeter criticized. The high hopes for public opinion surveys as a guiding force for democratic policy-making reflect the same Progressive logic (Gallup 1940/1968).

In this view, election outcomes hinge not on ideas, but on public approval or disapproval of the actual performance of incumbent political leaders. This model of democratic accountability appeals to skeptical scholars because it puts much less pressure on the voters to have elaborate, well-informed policy views. Ordinary citizens are allowed to drive the automobile of state simply by looking in the rearview mirror. Alas, we find that this works about as well in government as it would on the highway. Thus, we will argue that this second model of democracy, like the first, crumbles upon empirical inspection.

Hence we must think again. The concluding part of this book shows why a dramatically different framework is needed to make sense of how democracy actually works. We will argue that voters, even the most informed voters, typically make choices not on the basis of policy preferences or ideology, but on the basis of who they are—their social identities. In turn, those social identities shape how they think, what they think, and where they belong in the party system. But if voting behavior primarily reflects and reinforces voters' social loyalties, it is a mistake to suppose that elections result in popular control of public policy. Thus, our approach makes a sharp break with conventional thinking. The result may not be very comfortable or comforting. Nonetheless, we believe that a democratic theory worthy of serious social influence must engage with the findings of modern social science. Subsequent chapters attempt to do just that.

BUT ISN'T DEMOCRACY DOING JUST FINE?

At this point, the reader may be wondering whether all this is just some arcane academic dispute of no consequence to the health of actual democracies. After all, the very idea of democratic government carries enormous prestige in contemporary political discourse. For example, the World Values Survey asked ordinary people in dozens of countries around the world, "How important is it to you to live in a country that is governed democratically?" Majorities in many countries said "absolutely important"—a score of ten on a one-to-ten scale. Figure 1.1 shows the average responses on the one-to-ten scale for the 34 most populous countries in the survey.[4] Americans may be surprised to see that the United States (with an average rating of 8.4) is unremarkable in its enthusiasm for democracy. Adherence to the ideal is nearly universal.

---

4 These data are from the sixth (2010–2014) wave of the World Values Survey (accessed July 4, 2014). The data and additional documentation are available online at http://www .worldvaluessurvey.org/wvs.jsp.

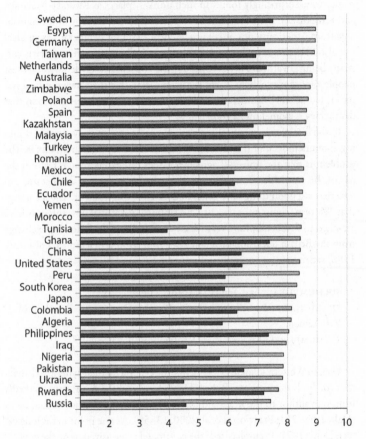

Figure 1.1. Democratic Aspirations and Perceptions, 2010–2014

Perhaps for this reason, nearly all contemporary political regimes, no matter how repressive, claim to be democracies of some sort. What is more surprising is that their citizens mostly believe them. Respondents in the World
Values Survey were also asked, "And how democratically is this country being governed today?" Again, figure 1.1 summarizes their responses. In every

country there was a gap between attachment to democracy as an ideal and perceptions of democratic reality. Nevertheless, perceptions of democratic reality were surprisingly robust in such unlikely places as Rwanda, Malaysia, and Kazakhstan. Even the Chinese respondents were virtually indistinguishable from Americans, not only in their enthusiasm for democracy as an ideal but also in their assessment of how democratically their own country is currently being governed. However various the conceptions of democracy, most people almost everywhere accept the proposition that their own political system is (somehow) democratic—and even more accept the proposition that democracy is (somehow) a good thing.

In the face of this universal acclaim, why tamper with conventional thinking about democracy? If it ain't broke, the reader may think, don't fix it. The problem is that the universal agreement does not extend much beyond the use of the word "democracy" itself. *What* makes a country democratic and *why* that is a good thing have generated much less agreement. The meanings that Western, communist, fascist, and tinhorn dictatorial governments have attached to democracy have very little in common, as the following exchange from the British television program *Yes, Prime Minister* (season 1, episode 6, 1986) satirized:

> SIR HUMPHREY: East Yemen, isn't that a democracy?
> SIR RICHARD: Its full name is the People's Democratic Republic of East Yemen.
> SIR HUMPHREY: Ah I see, so it's a communist dictatorship.[5]

Even in Western scholarly treatments, the criteria for qualifying as a democracy (or "polyarchy," to use Robert Dahl's less freighted term) vary markedly from one author to the next, and may extend to half a dozen or more items (Dahl 1989, 221; Przeworski et al. 2000, 13–55). At one point in his long career, Dahl (1971, 1) emphasized "the continued responsiveness of the government to the preferences of its citizens, considered as political equals." Decades later, he elaborated by specifying criteria for a democratic process—"effective participation," "voting equality," "enlightened understanding," "control of the agenda," and "inclusion of adults"—arguing that "each is necessary" if citizens are to be "politically equal in determining the policies of the association" (Dahl 1998, 37–38).

---

5 We are indebted to Patrick Fournier for this reference.

Unfortunately for democratic theory, how all this is to be achieved remains frustratingly vague. No existing government comes close to meeting all of Dahl's criteria; in our view, no possible government could. What then is the value of such an unattainable definition? Dahl (1998, 42) himself acknowledged that "no state has ever possessed a government that fully measured up to the criteria of a democratic process"—and, indeed, "none is likely to." But he went on to write, "Yet as I hope to show, the criteria provide highly serviceable standards for measuring the achievements and possibilities of democratic government. . . . They do provide standards against which to measure the performance of actual associations that claim to be democratic. They can serve as guides for shaping and reshaping concrete arrangements, constitutions, practices, and political institutions. For all those who aspire to democracy, they can also generate relevant questions and help in the search for answers." Other democratic theorists routinely follow Dahl on this point. Even if reality necessarily fails to correspond to the ideals, they argue, the ideals are valuable and should serve as the basis for modifying or reconstructing the reality. But for this argument to make sense, it must at least be the case that the ideals are not *too* unrealistic. More than a century ago, Graham Wallas (1908, 127) skewered the logic of unrealizable ideals:[6] "No doctor would now begin a medical treatise by saying, 'the ideal man requires no food, and is impervious to the action of bacteria, but this ideal is far removed from the actualities of any known population.' No modern treatise on pedagogy begins with the statement that 'the ideal boy knows things without being taught them, and his sole wish is the advancement of science, but no boys at all like this have ever existed.'"

If conventional democratic ideals amount to fairy tales, then we are left with no assurance that all the scholarly definitions and all the popular endorsements are of any use in making government contribute to human welfare. Hopelessly naive theories are a poor guide to policy, often distracting reformers from attainable incremental improvements along entirely different lines. As Walter Lippmann (1925, 39) put it, the unattainable ideal of "the omnicompetent, sovereign citizen" is bad in just the same sense that "it is bad for a fat man to try to be a ballet dancer."

---

6 Wallas is worth reading for his early advocacy of psychology as a tool for understanding politics, but his scholarship is sometimes less than reliable. In the passage quoted here, Wallas was disputing a remark due to Bryce, but taken out of context, and he got the title of Bryce's famous *American Commonwealth* wrong as well.

The views of ordinary citizens themselves provide intimations that not all is well with democratic theory. Despite their conventional obeisance to the civic religion, significant doubts and qualifications emerge. The gaps between democratic aspirations and perceptions of democratic reality summarized in figure 1.1 are indicative. In the United States, for example, 46% of the respondents in the World Values Survey said that it is "absolutely important" to them "to live in a country that is governed democratically," but only 7% said that the country is actually being governed in a "completely democratic" manner.[7] Other surveys have exposed a good deal of schizophrenia about the meaning of democracy. For example, a substantial majority of Americans say that democratic government is a very important factor in the nation's success;[8] but most also believe that "the government is pretty much run by a few big interests looking out for themselves."[9] On one hand, we are a free people controlling our own special form of government, the envy of the world. At the same time, we are badly governed by incompetent and untrustworthy politicians beholden to special interests. We are simultaneously dreamily idealistic and grimly pessimistic.

Prominent intellectuals, too, have embodied both these contradictory impulses. In "The Democratic Spirit" (1847), a bombastic Walt Whitman exalted "democracy with its manly heart and its lion strength," from which "we are to expect the great FUTURE of this Western World! a scope involving such unparalleled human happiness and rational freedom, to such unnumbered myriads, that the heart of a true *man* leaps with a mighty joy only to think of it!" But a quarter century later, in the midst of a wrenching period

7 These results are from the World Values Survey (http://www.worldvaluessurvey.org /WVSOnline.jsp). "Absolutely important" and "completely democratic" refer to responses of 10 on the 1–10 scales employed in both questions.

8 In a 2011 survey by the Pew Research Center for the People and the Press, 72% of Americans rated democratic government as a "very important" factor in America's success— below natural resources (82%) and military strength (77%) but above the free market system (70%) and religious faith and values (63%). In the same survey, 48% of the respondents said that America is "the greatest country in the world," while an additional 42% said it is "one of the greatest countries in the world" (http://www.people-press.org/2011/11/03/section-4 -views-of-the-nation/).

9 An item included in most American National Election Studies surveys conducted over the past half century asks, "Would you say the government is pretty much run by a few big interests looking out for themselves or that it is run for the benefit of all the people?" In 2008, 69% of the respondents chose "run by a few big interests" and 29% chose "for the benefit of all the people." In 16 separate surveys conducted from 1974 through 2008, respondents chose "run by a few big interests" by an average margin of 65% to 29% (http://www.electionstudies .org/nesguide/2ndtable/t5a_2_1.htm).

of democratization—the incorporation of millions of former slaves and the reintegration of millions of former rebels into the American polity following the Civil War—Whitman (1871, 4) addressed a prophetic essay, *Democratic Vistas*, to "him or her within whose thought rages the battle, advancing, retreating, between Democracy's convictions, aspirations, and the People's crudeness, vice, caprices."

Whitman promised readers of *Democratic Vistas* that he would "not gloss over the appalling dangers of universal suffrage in the United States," and he acknowledged that the American politics and society of his day were "cankered, crude, superstitious, and rotten. . . . The spectacle is appalling." Nevertheless, he expressed "unshaken faith in the elements of the American masses" and confidence that "the fruition of Democracy, on aught like a grand scale, resides altogether in the future," to come to "its flower and fruits in manners, in the highest forms of interaction between men, and their beliefs—in Religion, Literature, colleges, and schools—Democracy in all public and private life" (Whitman 1871, 4, 11, 15, 33). Like many citizens of modern democracies, Whitman clung to the belief that democracy could and would be perfected, despite the "appalling" spectacle of democracy in practice.

Thus, popular thinkers and scholars alike have combined enthusiasm for democracy, however vaguely defined, with a clear-eyed realization that democratic practice is, by the standards of the folk theory, dispiriting almost everywhere. In most cases, they have simply ignored the conceptual contradictions or attributed the failings of democracy to corrupt leaders or faulty institutions. Occasionally, though, the ideal itself has come under suspicion, and it is to that line of democratic thought that we now turn.

THE CRITICAL TRADITION

The folk theory of democracy celebrates the wisdom of popular judgments by informed and engaged citizens. The reality is quite different. Human beings are busy with their lives. Most have school or a job consuming many hours of the day. They also have meals to prepare, homes to clean, and bills to pay. They may have children to raise or elderly parents to care for. They may also be coping with unemployment, business reverses, illness, addictions, divorce, or other personal and family troubles. For most, leisure time is at a premium. Sorting out which presidential candidate has the right foreign policy toward Asia is not a high priority for them. Without shirking more immediate and more important obligations, people cannot engage in much well-informed, thoughtful political deliberation, nor should they.

Recognizing that actual people are far from the unrealistic ideal citizens of the folk theory, disappointed observers have often adopted a judgmental tone, implicitly assuming that the folk theory provides the appropriate moral standard for citizens, which few meet. At the end of the 19th century, for example, James Bryce (1894, 250) observed "how little solidity and substance there is in the political or social beliefs of nineteen persons out of every twenty. These beliefs, when examined, mostly resolve themselves into two or three prejudices and aversions, two or three prepossessions for a particular leader or party or section of a party, two or three phrases or catchwords suggesting or embodying arguments which the man who repeats them has not analyzed." He might have added that the remaining one in twenty exhibit the limits of rationality, too. Nevertheless, however unaware of his own human limitations Bryce may have been, in our view he was not wrong about the fact of widespread citizen inattention. Indeed, the past century of political science has done remarkably little to alter the basic outlines of his portrait of public opinion. Even in the midst of the Progressive Era, the fundamental veracity of that portrait and its troubling implications for folk democratic theory were clear enough to those willing to see them. The great political scientist and Harvard University president A. Lawrence Lowell (1913, 233), for example, noted with respect to democracy that "there has probably never existed a political system of which men have not tried to demonstrate the perfection," but he dismissed as "fallacious" all theories "based on the assumption that the multitude is omniscient" and "all reforms that presuppose a radical change in human nature."

Three other distinguished scholars of the era also saw the tension between conventional democratic ideals and dreary reality. Schumpeter (1942, 262) acidly observed that citizens are especially prone "to yield to extra-rational or irrational prejudice and impulse" in the political sphere. By comparison with other realms of life, he argued (Schumpeter 1942, 261), "the typical citizen drops down to a lower level of mental performance as soon as he enters the political field. He argues and analyzes in a way which he would readily recognize as infantile within the sphere of his real interests."

Walter Lippmann (1914; 1922; 1925) faced more squarely than other commentators of his time the inevitable limits of human cognitive ability in politics. "Once you touch the biographies of human beings," he wrote (1914, 215), "the notion that political beliefs are logically determined collapses like a pricked balloon." He saw that the cherished ideas and judgments we bring to politics are stereotypes and simplifications with little room for adjustment as the facts change (1922, 16): "For the real environment is altogether too big, too complex, and too fleeting for direct acquaintance. We are not equipped to deal with so much subtlety, so much variety, so many permutations and combinations. And although we have to act in that environment, we have to reconstruct it on a simpler model before we can manage it." Lippmann remains the deepest and most thoughtful of the modern critics of the psychological foundations of the folk theory of democracy.

Reinhold Niebuhr (1932; 1944) noted that human judgment is not just overwhelmed by the complexity of the political world, as Lippmann emphasized, but in addition is profoundly warped by self-interest and the will to power. And he perceived clearly that the idealistic justification of democracy as human rationality in pursuit of the common good serves only too well to provide cover for those who profit from the distortions and biases in the policy-making processes of actual democracies: "The will to power uses reason as kings used courtiers and chaplains to add grace to their enterprise" (Niebuhr 1932, 44).

These and other critical thinkers struggled to put democracy on an intellectually respectable foundation, taking account of human nature as they knew it. But in the era in which they wrote, few could hear. It was all too easy and convenient to dismiss the entire intellectual lineage as elitist and cynical, a mere literary tradition based on nothing but jaundiced interpretations of personal experience. Subsequent scholarly generations have also disliked the various racial and religious prejudices of the time, which these men sometimes shared. By the 1950s and 1960s, skeptical writers like Wallas, Lowell, John Dickinson (1930), and even Lippmann and Niebuhr were no longer much read by students of politics.

Meanwhile, however, new tools emerged for investigating political behavior, most notably scientific survey research, whose findings were much harder to glibly dismiss. The pioneering survey research of Paul Lazarsfeld and his colleagues at Columbia University (Lazarsfeld, Berelson, and Gaudet 1948; Berelson, Lazarsfeld, and McPhee 1954), of Angus Campbell and his colleagues at the University of Michigan (Campbell et al. 1960), and of other early analysts of electoral choice produced a rather bleak portrait of habitual, socially determined political behavior, once again calling into question whether citizens could perform the role that the folk theory of democracy seemed to require of them.

Philip Converse (1964) extended this seminal work, building a new, more formidable case for skepticism regarding the idealized image of democratic citizens, this time substituting random national samples for the insightful but less systematic observations of Bryce, Lippmann, Niebuhr, and Schumpeter. Converse's essay set off a vibrant decades-long critical discussion of his methodology and the inferences he drew from his findings, but few public opinion scholars disputed the central point he made—that judged by the standards of the folk theory, the political "belief systems" of ordinary citizens are generally thin, disorganized, and ideologically incoherent.

In chapter 2 we will argue that Converse's argument is, if anything, even better supported a half century later than it was when he wrote. A vast amount of supporting evidence has been added to his dispiriting comparison of actual human political cognition with the expectations derived from the folk theory of democracy. Well-informed citizens, too, have come in for their share of criticism, since their well-organized "ideological" thinking often turns out to be just a rather mechanical reflection of what their favorite group and party leaders have instructed them to think. Faced with this evidence, many scholars in the final chapters of their books continue to express idealistic hope that institutional reform, civic education, improved mass media, more effective mobilization of the poor, or stronger moral exhortation might bring public opinion into closer correspondence with the standards of the folk theory. But in sober moments most acknowledge the repeated failures of all those prescriptions.

Thus, scholars, too, persist uneasily in their schizophrenia, recognizing the power of the critical arguments but hoping against hope that those arguments can somehow be discredited or evaded, allowing the lackluster reality of democratic practice to be squared with conventional idealistic democratic thinking. Often, their attempts to bolster the tattered theoretical status quo bring them back to Winston Churchill's claim that "democracy is the worst form of government except all those others that have been tried from time to time."[10] But that is a distinctly un-idealistic defense of democracy—and no defense at all of the folk theory of democracy.

THE PLAN OF THIS BOOK

Our view is that conventional thinking about democracy has collapsed in the face of modern social-scientific research. This book first documents the

---

10 The authors of *The American Voter* adopted this view (Campbell et al. 1960, 545). An updated version of Churchill's argument is that democracy promotes freedom, human development, and material well-being (Dahl 1989; Mueller 1999; Przeworski et al. 2000). Demonstrating causal effects in this domain is very hard, but even if they exist, this line of argument generally does not speak to *how* democracy matters and how it should be organized to work better.

collapse, then points toward more reliable foundations that could support a vigorous rebuilding.

Our treatise on democracy does not begin with ideal boys. And while it does begin with democratic ideals, we *test* those ideals, not merely explicate and affirm them. We hope to contribute both to the improvement of democratic theory and to the improvement of democracy. After all, as Dahl (1956, 52) recognized, "There is a great variety of empirical facts that one needs to know, or have some hunches about, before one can rationally decide on the kinds of political rules one wants to follow in the real world."

Our empirical facts are drawn predominantly from the democratic system we know best, that of the United States. However, we refer frequently to other democratic systems as well, and we believe that our findings are likely to be of considerable relevance even in countries that differ from the United States—and from each other—in many important historical, institutional, and cultural respects. While history, institutions, and culture surely shape specific democratic practices in important ways, they do not, as best we can tell, lead to fundamentally different conclusions about the central issues we raise in this book.

Our analyses range over the past century of American political history, from the reelection of Woodrow Wilson in 1916 to that of Barack Obama in 2012. We consider the great New Deal realignment of the 1930s, the political transformation of the South during and after the civil rights struggles of the 1960s, the ramifications of the Watergate scandal in the 1970s, and the interplay of politics and religion in shaping baby boomers' views regarding the fraught issue of abortion over the course of their adult lives. Each of these case studies is intended to assess or illustrate specific aspects of our general account of democratic politics; but each is also intended to contribute to a broad portrait of the workings of democracy in America and elsewhere.

In chapter 2 we take up the subject of popular sovereignty. As Donald Kinder has observed, "if ordinary citizens were to reason ideologically, as political elites presumably do, then the prospects for democratic control would be enhanced." Thus, "the extraordinary interest in the possibility of ideological reasoning was and still is an expression of concern for the quality and very possibility of democratic forms of government" (Kinder 1983, 391). For example, the influential "spatial model" of electoral competition (Downs 1957; Enelow and Hinich 1984) has provided an elegant theoretical account of how ideological reasoning by ordinary citizens could enhance the prospects for democratic control over political elites.

Unfortunately from this perspective, Converse (1964) found that "the vast majority of Americans" are "thoroughly innocent of ideology" (Kinder 1983, 391)—and that finding has been "largely sustained" by subsequent scholarship (Kinder 1983, 401). The available evidence suggests that citizens of other advanced democracies are similar to Americans in this respect. Thus, Converse's work raises a significant challenge not only to the spatial model, but to a great deal of scholarly and popular thinking about how policy decisions might be justified on democratic grounds.

In chapter 2 we survey a substantial body of scholarly work demonstrating that most democratic citizens are uninterested in politics, poorly informed, and unwilling or unable to convey coherent policy preferences through "issue voting." How, then, are elections supposed to ensure ideological responsiveness to the popular will? In our view, they do not. The populist ideal of electoral democracy, for all its elegance and attractiveness, is largely irrelevant in practice, leaving elected officials mostly free to pursue their own notions of the public good or to respond to party and interest group pressures.

In chapter 3 we turn our attention from electoral representation to "direct democracy," a medley of institutional reforms intended to enhance the role of ordinary citizens (and minimize the role of professional politicians) in processes of democratic decision-making. Reforms of this sort have been a common response to the perceived failings of existing democratic procedures in the United States and elsewhere—a simplistic reflection of the Progressive faith that "the cure for the ills of democracy is more democracy."[11] However, in light of our portrait of ordinary citizens in chapter 2, it should not be surprising that naive efforts to let them directly manage the machinery of democracy often go badly astray. People are just too busy with their own lives to measure up to the standards that conventional democratic theory sets for them.

Those who doubt the practical importance of the folk theory of democracy will find its influence arising repeatedly in the history of American political reform. For example, reformers of the Democratic Party's presidential nominating process in the 1970s echoed the Progressive adage that "the cure

11 Jane Mansbridge pointed out to us that the Progressive reformer Jane Addams (1902, 11–12) used this phrase in her book on *Democracy and Social Ethics*. John Dewey (1927, 146) is more often quoted by devotees of populist democracy, but his version of the argument was more nuanced than they have generally recognized, emphasizing "the *interest* of the public" (our emphasis) and the difficulty of "enabl[ing] the public to form and manifest its purposes ... more authoritatively" rather than simply advocating a more direct translation of existing public preferences into policy.

for the ills of democracy is more democracy" (Commission on Party Structure and Delegate Selection 1970, 14). The resulting proliferation of direct primaries ultimately made both major parties' presidential nominations "more democratic" in crude populist terms while diluting the influence of political professionals, whose firsthand knowledge of the competing candidates' strengths and weaknesses had helped to weed out amateurs and demagogues (Polsby 1983).[12]

Similarly, we argue in chapter 3 that the adoption of initiative and referendum processes in many states has mostly empowered "millionaires and interest groups that use their wealth to achieve their own policy goals" (Broder 2000, 1). And when they do allow ordinary citizens to shape policy, the results can be distinctly counterproductive. For example, the most careful study we know of the impact of direct democracy on public services found that voters in Illinois seized the opportunity to curtail fire district budgets, dangerously degrading the quality of their fire protection—and possibly costing themselves more in insurance rate increases than they saved in taxes by doing so (Tessin 2009).

If popular sovereignty is so difficult to achieve—and such a mixed blessing in any case—then what is the point of having elections? One idea that has gained considerable currency among scholars in the past 50 years is that voters can control elected officials by assessing their performance in office and voting to reelect or replace them accordingly. In chapter 4, we outline this logic of *retrospective voting* and its implications for democracy and for democratic theory.

Then in chapter 5 we focus on how well citizens are able to assess responsibility for changes in their own welfare. Since there are many realms of politics, economics, and society in which leaders' responsibility for good or bad outcomes is far from clear, we consider cases in which leaders are clearly *not* responsible for good or bad outcomes—droughts, floods, and shark attacks. We find that voters punish incumbent politicians for changes in their welfare that are clearly acts of God or nature. That suggests that their ability (or their inclination) to make sensible judgments regarding credit and blame is highly circumscribed. In that case, retrospection will be *blind*, and political accountability will be greatly attenuated.

12 The most detailed recent study of the presidential nominating process argued that professional politicians subsequently regained much of their control, so that primary voters now mostly ratify the choices made by party elites in the "invisible primary" preceding the public campaign (Cohen et al. 2008).

If voters are not very good at assessing responsibility for changes in their own welfare, neither are they very good at *recognizing* those changes. Chapter 6 provides a detailed analysis of the most prominent and politically significant example of retrospective accountability, economic voting in U.S. presidential elections. There, we find that voters do indeed reward or punish incumbents for real income growth. However, the voters are *myopic*, focusing almost entirely on income growth in the months just before each election. The performance of the economy over the course of a president's entire term—which provides a better measure of changes in voters' welfare, and presumably provides a more reliable benchmark of the incumbent's competence as well—is almost entirely discounted by voters when they go the polls.

In chapter 7 we focus on voting behavior in the midst of the most severe economic crisis in American history, the Great Depression of the 1930s. Here, one might think, was an emergency that would focus voters' minds on momentous policy choices, shaping the course of government and public policy for decades to come. The stakes were indeed momentous. Yet we find that voters in the 1930s behaved much as they do at other times—punishing their leaders at the polls when economic conditions worsened and rewarding them when economic conditions improved, with short memories and little apparent regard for ideology or policy.

The primary implication of our analyses of retrospective voting is that election outcomes are mostly just erratic reflections of the current balance of partisan loyalties in a given political system. In a two-party system with competitive elections, that means that the choice between the candidates is essentially a coin toss. Thus, the picture that emerges is not "a portrait of citizens moved to considered decision as they play their solemn role of making and unmaking governments" (Key 1966, 4). Rather, elections are capricious collective decisions based on considerations that ought, from the viewpoint of the folk theory, to be largely irrelevant—and that will, in any case, soon be forgotten by the voters themselves. We conclude that the retrospective model of democracy simply will not bear the normative weight that its proponents want to place on it.

If voters are not good at retrospective voting, what is left? In the final part of the book, we point toward a quite different way of thinking about democracy. In chapter 8 we lay out a third model of democracy, which we refer to as the *group theory* of democracy. This model portrays citizens first and foremost as members of social groups, with (no doubt numerous and complex) social identities and group attachments figuring crucially in their political loyalties and behavior. We argue that this model provides a surer foundation for democratic theory than either populism or retrospective voting.

In chapter 9 we present evidence in support of this third model. We consider three significant examples of partisan change. First, we demonstrate the powerful role of religious identities in shaping responses to John Kennedy's presidential candidacy in 1960. Second, we explore the partisan realignment of the South over the past half century. The demise of the Democratic "Solid South" has typically been interpreted as an instance of "issue evolution" in response to the momentous partisan policy conflicts of the civil rights era (Carmines and Stimson 1989); but we interpret it as primarily a matter of social identity, as white southerners—even those with moderate racial views—increasingly came to feel that the Democratic Party no longer belonged to people like them.

Next, we examine the evolution and impact of citizens' views regarding the highly charged issue of abortion. As the Democratic and Republican parties took increasingly clear, opposing stands on the issue through the 1980s and 1990s, partisan identities often came into conflict with gender identities. We show that this conflict was resolved in quite different ways for women and for men. A substantial number of women gravitated to the party sharing their view about abortion, reflecting the deep significance of the issue for women. Men, on the other hand, more often changed their view about abortion to comport with their partisanship—in effect, letting their party tell them what to think about one of the most contentious moral issues in contemporary American politics. In both cases, identity was politically powerful in ways that the folk theory of democracy obscures or ignores.

Now it may be thought that, for all the apparent defects of the folk theory, when one listens to ordinary citizens they often sound quite coherent. Democrats generally espouse judgments and policy views supporting their preferred candidates; so do Republicans. Maybe all is well somehow. In chapter 10 we take up this possibility. We show that citizens' perceptions of parties' policy stands and their own policy views are significantly colored by their party preferences. Even on purely factual questions with clear right answers, citizens are sometimes willing to believe the opposite if it makes them feel better about their partisanship and vote choices. We illustrate this phenomenon by examining beliefs about a highly salient and significant political fact—the size of the federal budget deficit. The deficit had decreased by more than half during Bill Clinton's first term as president; yet most Republicans in a 1996 survey managed to convince themselves that it had increased. Even many Democrats and Independents had too little real information to get the facts right, but for Republicans the lack of information was compounded by a partisan desire to see a Democratic administration in a negative light. Indeed, moderately well-informed Republicans had *less* accurate beliefs than the least informed; a modicum of information was sufficient to discern what they should *want* to be true, but not enough to discern what was in fact true. They sounded like they were thinking, but no one should be fooled. Democrats behaved in much the same way on other issues.

We conclude that group and partisan loyalties, not policy preferences or ideologies, are fundamental in democratic politics. Thus, a realistic theory of democracy must be built, not on the French Enlightenment, on British liberalism, or on American Progressivism, with their devotion to human rationality and monadic individualism, but instead on the insights of the critics of these traditions, who recognized that human life is group life.

Our focus in this book is primarily on empirical analysis rather than on prescription. Nonetheless, we recognize an obligation, both intellectual and civic, to consider the implications of our analysis for democratic practice. What are the tangible costs of attempting to live by an unrealistic theory of democracy? And what would a more realistic theory of democracy imply about the appropriate structuring of political processes and institutions? In chapter 11 we trace the implications of our analysis for the question of what it would mean to have "more"—and better—democracy.

THE CHALLENGE: TAKING ON THE DIVINE RIGHT OF THE PEOPLE

The task before us is not easy. Democracy is the justifying political ideology of our era. It is inevitably very difficult for any of us to recognize the intellectual constraints and contradictions entailed by our own preconceptions and normative commitments to it. As one of the preeminent contemporary scholars of American politics, James Stimson (2004, 170), wrote, "The word 'democracy' is bound up with symbolism, belief, patriotism, and a quasi-religious commitment. It is imbued with our self-identity as Americans. Democracy is the civil religion of America." Dahl (1961, 317) put it even more bluntly: "To reject the democratic creed is in effect to refuse to be an American."

Some useful perspective on this aspect of contemporary thinking about democracy may be provided by recalling political thought in early modern times regarding the divine right of kings. The idea that kings were divinely anointed had a long history in human thought, and not just in the West;

Chinese emperors, too, needed "the mandate of heaven." The idea was highly functional, providing a sturdy basis for political stability—as many astute observers recognized. However, the chronic gap between kingly ideals and realities was a source of severe ideological strain.

The doctrine of "The King's Two Bodies" (Kantorowicz 1957) provided useful leeway for understanding and accommodating the fact that mortal rulers were often manifestly less than divine in bearing and behavior. On this view, the king always intended to rule well and justly, but he was sometimes misled. As Edmund Morgan (1988, 30) described the situation in 17th-century England, "A host of ambitious schemers, according to the Commons' view, continually caught the king's natural ear and misinformed him in order to procure benefits to themselves. But the king in his body politic always wanted what was best for his subjects, all his subjects, and surely no subject could know better what that was than the combined representatives of all his subjects. 'If anything fall out unhappily,' said Sir Robert Phelips, 'it is not King Charles that advised himself, but King Charles misadvised by others and misled by misordered counsel.'" In their time, these ideas were widely credited among thoughtful people and important scholars. But of course, genuine political progress depended on abandoning this entire way of thinking.

In our view, the ideal of popular sovereignty plays much the same role in contemporary democratic ideology that the divine right of kings played in the monarchical era. It is "a quasi-religious commitment," in Stimson's terms, a fiction providing legitimacy and stability to political systems whose actual workings are manifestly—and inevitably—rather less than divine. The fiction feels natural within the Enlightenment mind-set of rationality and human perfectibility. Thoughtful people and important scholars believe it. And its credibility is bolstered by the undeniable practical successes of many of the political systems that invoke it.

The fiction of popular sovereignty is so much the sturdier—and more useful to our own ambitious schemers and powerful interests who profit from its fallacies—for being notoriously hard to pin down. As Henry Maine (1885, 185) wrote long ago, "the devotee of Democracy is much in the same position as the Greeks with their oracles. All agreed that the voice of an oracle was the voice of a god; but everybody allowed that when he spoke he was not as intelligible as might be desired." Thus, policies and practices that are unjust or simply unsuccessful can always be attributed to some mistranslation or temporary deflection of the people's will, with "special interests" trotted out to play the role played by "ambitious schemers" in 17th-century England. We even have our own "two bodies" doctrine: when majorities go seriously astray, it is not the people that "advised themselves," but rather the people misadvised by others and misled by misordered counsel. "The people are never corrupted," said Rousseau, "but sometimes deceived."

In all these ways, conventional thought has avoided the painful task of grappling seriously with all the evidence undermining the standard versions of democratic theory. "Well, yes, there are problems," we say, and then we turn back to the impossible dream. In consequence, cheerful illusions and wish fulfillment have dominated both popular and scholarly thought about democracy for two centuries. Democratic theory has sailed along as if no iceberg had struck and the engine room were not taking on water. But the damage to the intellectual structure is very real.

Both the allure and the cost of romanticism in this domain were eloquently described by political philosopher John Dunn (1999, 342–343) in an essay on democratic political accountability:

> To be ruled is both necessary and inherently discomfiting (as well as dangerous). For our rulers to be accountable to us softens its intrinsic humiliations, probably sets some hazy limits to the harms that they will voluntarily choose to do to us collectively, and thus diminishes some of the dangers to which their rule may expose us. To suggest that we can ever hope to have the power to make them act just as we would wish them to suggests that it is really we, not they, who are ruling. This is an illusion, and probably a somewhat malign illusion: either a self-deception, or an instance of being deceived by others, or very probably both.

Dunn went on to say that "a political science that did justice to democracy (in all its ambiguity) would have to be one in which the presence of these perceptions and sentiments was recognized and explained, and their consequences accurately assessed, not one in which their existence was denied or dismissed as irrational in the first instance."

The history of democratic thought—including much contemporary political science—is marked by an addiction to romantic theories. As with any addiction, the first step toward recovery is to admit that we have a problem. Thus, our first aim in this book is to document the gap between democratic ideals and realities. Then we will make a start toward the more sober understanding of democracy advocated by Dunn.

The Elusive Mandate: Elections and the Mirage of Popular Control

> A good deal of traditional democratic theory leads us to expect
> more from national elections than they can possibly provide. We
> expect elections to reveal the "will" or the preferences of a major-
> ity on a set of issues. This is one thing elections rarely do, except
> in an almost trivial fashion.
>
> —Robert A. Dahl, *A Preface to Democratic Theory* (1956, 131)

Robert Dahl (1956, 1) began *A Preface to Democratic Theory* by acknowledging that "there is no democratic theory—there are only democratic theories."
Nevertheless, he noted (1956, 34–35) that "running through the whole history of democratic theories is the identification of 'democracy' with political
equality, popular sovereignty, and rule by majorities"—a notion of "Populistic Democracy" he associated with such diverse thinkers as Aristotle, Locke,
Rousseau, Jefferson, de Tocqueville, and Lincoln.

Dahl's notion of "Populistic Democracy" corresponds closely with what
we have called the "folk theory" of democracy. In particular, its emphasis on
popular sovereignty requires that "whenever policy choices are perceived to
exist, the alternative selected and enforced as governmental policy is the alternative most preferred by the members" of the relevant political community
(Dahl 1956, 37). But how might popular sovereignty in this sense actually
come about? Theorists in this tradition and practitioners alike have focused
on two primary mechanisms—electoral competition and "direct democracy"
in the form of popular initiatives or referenda. We consider these two mechanisms in this and the following chapter, respectively.

As the Gilded Age of the late 19th century came to an end, aristocratic
English observer James Bryce (1894, 923) portrayed Americans marching

"with steady steps" toward a new stage in the evolution of government—"Government by Public Opinion"—in which "the will of the people acts directly and constantly upon its executive and legislative agents." Populism as a political movement crested in the United States in the 1890s; but the Progressive Era that followed was also characterized by high enthusiasm for popular democracy as a broad political ideal. Historian Charles Beard (1912, 14), who could be clear-eyed and even cynical about the political motives of the Founders, nevertheless expressed the conviction that "every branch of law that has been recast under the influence of popular will has been touched with enlightenment and humanity." He argued that the era's new political institutions—including the initiative, referendum, and recall—would surely produce still better government in the future through greater democratization. In the same spirit, John Dewey (1927, 146) insisted that it was no "mystic faith" but "a well-attested conclusion from historic facts" that government can serve the people only when "the community itself shares in selecting its governors and determining their policies." Even the famously acerbic journalist and political observer H. L. Mencken (1916, 19) expressed his skepticism about democracy in colorfully populist terms, defining it as "the theory that the common people know what they want, and deserve to get it good and hard."

By the middle of the 20th century the populist ideal was firmly established in both American political culture and scholarly understanding of democracy. Political thinkers who resisted "the identification of 'democracy' with political equality, popular sovereignty, and rule by majorities" felt compelled to explain why. As we noted in the previous chapter, Joseph Schumpeter (1942, 250) prefaced his own theory of democracy with a scathing critique of the unrealism of a "classical doctrine" in which democracy "realizes the common good by making the people itself decide issues through the election of individuals who are to assemble in order to carry out its will." Dahl (1956) was less dismissive of "populistic" democracy, but emphasized the importance of alternative "Madisonian" and "polyarchal" conceptions. Even William Riker, who would later castigate populism as a "totalitarian sleight-of-hand . . . used to justify coercion in the name of temporary or spurious majorities" (1982, 13–14), wrote in a mid-century American government textbook (1953, 91–92) that "truly responsible government is only possible when elections are so conducted that a choice of men is a decision on policy." He added that plebiscites in the Soviet Union "are a façade . . . because the structure of government does not permit elections to influence policy making."

Ironically, the decades in which Schumpeter and the early Dahl and Riker wrote also gave rise to two major intellectual challenges to the folk theory. One of these was a logical challenge stemming from the theoretical work of economists studying collective choice. Duncan Black (1948; 1958), Kenneth Arrow (1951), and Anthony Downs (1957) all made fundamental contributions to a theory of democracy focusing on the translation of individual preferences into collective choices through voting. While their work gave the populist ideal a much clearer and more definite form than it had previously had, it also revealed unexpected difficulties in the very notion of popular sovereignty—difficulties severe enough to provoke Riker's subsequent rejection of "coercion in the name of temporary or spurious majorities."

The second formidable mid-century challenge to the populist ideal came from sociologists and political scientists harnessing the new technology of survey research to the study of public opinion and electoral politics. Time and time again, they found that the opinions and behavior of ordinary citizens comported poorly with expectations derived from democratic theory as they understood it—that is, from the folk theory. For example, a team from Columbia University conducted pathbreaking empirical studies of voting behavior in the 1940 and 1948 presidential elections (Lazarsfeld, Berelson, and Gaudet 1948; Berelson, Lazarsfeld, and McPhee 1954). They produced a long list of contrasts between democratic ideals and their own findings regarding voters' motivations, knowledge, and reasoning. "The democratic citizen is expected to be well informed about political affairs," they wrote (Berelson, Lazarsfeld, and McPhee 1954, 308). "He is supposed to know what the issues are, what their history is, what the relevant facts are, what alternatives are proposed, what the party stands for, what the likely consequences are. By such standards the voter falls short." As we will show, subsequent research by a great many other scholars has come to very similar conclusions.

In the remainder of this chapter we take up both these challenges to the folk theory of democracy. We begin with the logical challenge, then turn to the empirical challenge.

THE "SPATIAL MODEL" OF VOTING AND ELECTIONS

The most systematic and sophisticated instantiation of the populist ideal is the "spatial model" of voting and elections. Although the model has been a mainstay of political science for the past half century, it was originally formulated primarily by economists—perhaps because the intellectual framework of economics meshed naturally with "the liberal view" that "the aim of democracy is to aggregate individual preferences into a collective choice in as fair and efficient a way as possible," as David Miller (1992, 55) put it. Miller acknowledged in a footnote that some readers might object to the limited focus on "one strand of liberalism—the importance it attaches to individual preferences and their expression"; however, he argued that that strand "prevails in contemporary liberal societies, where democracy is predominantly understood as involving the aggregation of independently formed preferences." Thus, in effect, the goal of the spatial model was to give mathematical form to the folk theory of democracy.

In the canonical version of the spatial model, due primarily to Anthony Downs (1957), the political "space" consists of a single ideological dimension on which feasible policies are arrayed from left to right.[1] Each voter is represented by an *ideal point* along this dimension reflecting the policy she prefers to all others. Each party is represented by a *platform* reflecting the policy it will enact if elected.[2] Voters are assumed to maximize their ideological satisfaction with the election outcome by voting for the parties closest to them on the ideological dimension.[3] Parties are assumed to maximize their expected payoff from office-holding by choosing the platforms most likely to get them elected.

In the simplest case, where there are just two parties, this framework is sufficient to derive a striking and substantively important prediction: both parties will adopt identical platforms corresponding to the median of the distribution of voters' ideal points.[4] This so-called *median voter theorem* is a special case of a

---

1 Downs (1957, 115) attributed the spatial "apparatus" to Harold Hotelling, who briefly sketched a political application in the course of his spatial analysis of economic competition (1929, 54–55).

2 Downs wrote of *parties* rather than *candidates*, but rendered the distinction irrelevant by assuming "complete agreement on goals among the members of an office-seeking coalition" (1957, 26).

3 In multiparty systems, voters may maximize their satisfaction with the outcome by voting "strategically" for a party further from their ideal point, depending on other voters' choices. Downs recognized this fact and worried that "if each attempts to take into account the diversity of preferences, and therefore votes only after calculating how others will vote, the process of calculation becomes too complicated for him to handle" (1957, 154). Kedar (2005) argued that the calculations need not be very demanding. But in any case, this complication does not arise in the simple two-party case considered here.

4 Under the assumption that everyone votes for the party closer to her, a party located at the median will defeat any alternative located to the left of the median (by winning the median voter and everyone to her right) or to the right of the median (by winning the median voter and everyone to her left). Downs (1957, 116–117) barely acknowledged this result before turning to an "improved" version of the model in which "elastic demand" and the threat of abstention by extremists induce the parties to offer distinct platforms. In that case,

more general result regarding collective choice with single-peaked preferences (Black 1948).[5] Since a platform (and resulting government policy) located at the median of the distribution of voters' ideal points has a smaller average distance from all voters' ideal points than any other feasible policy, the median voter theorem seems to imply that the mere fact of electoral competition will ensure that voters' preferences are as well satisfied in a utilitarian sense as they possibly can be. Thus the voters enjoy responsive government regardless of which party wins any given election.

In addition to being elegant and normatively attractive, the spatial theory seemed to provide a compelling explanation for the ideologically muted politics of mid-20th-century America: candidates and parties were moderate and (to a casual observer) largely indistinguishable, apparently due to the natural centripetal tendencies of a smoothly running majoritarian system. And when more extreme candidates emerged on the political scene—Barry Goldwater in 1964, George McGovern in 1972—they were trounced at the polls, just as the theory suggested they should be. By the 1980s, it seemed apparent to many scholars that "the spatial theory of voting provides important insights into real-world voting," and more specifically that "the center of voter opinion exerts a powerful force over election results" (Enelow and Hinich 1984, 217, 221).

Subsequent work has elaborated the canonical spatial model in a variety of important ways—for example, by allowing for probabilistic voting behavior, nonspatial "valence" factors such as charisma and incumbency, parties motivated by policy as well as office seeking, constraints on parties' platforms (for example, due to historical legacies), and uncertainty in voters' perceptions of parties' platforms.[6] For our purposes here, the most important elaboration replaced the unidimensional ideological spectrum with a multidimensional policy space (Davis and Hinich 1966; 1967). Reducing all of politics to a single ideological dimension was plainly at odds with empirical evidence suggesting that most citizens in the 1950s had distinct—indeed, virtually uncorrelated—views about economic, social, and foreign policies (Stokes 1963, 370). Thus, as

the predictions of the model are quite sensitive to the distribution of voters' ideal points and to auxiliary assumptions regarding the bases of abstention (Downs 1957, 117–122), as much subsequent research confirmed.

5 In the context of the spatial model, a voter's preferences are "single-peaked" if she prefers any platform to the left of her ideal point to any other platform further to the left, and any platform to the right of her ideal point to any other platform further to the right. The symmetric case considered here, in which voters' preferences are a simple monotonic function of distance, satisfies this condition.

6 Enelow and Hinich (1984), Austen-Smith and Banks (1999), and Grofman (2004) have provided useful syntheses and reviews.

Otto Davis, Melvin Hinich, and Peter Ordeshook (1970, 429) acknowledged, "if spatial models are to retain descriptive and predictive value, they must allow for more than one dimension of conflict and taste."

In his critique of Downs's spatial model, Donald Stokes (1963, 370–371) referred to the axiom of unidimensionality as its "most evident—and perhaps least fundamental" point of unrealism, suggesting that "it might well be dispensed with." From a purely technical standpoint Stokes was right; within a few years of his writing, the assumption of unidimensionality *was* dispensed with. Unfortunately, this technical advance turned out to generate considerable conceptual difficulties for a model doing double duty as an empirical theory of electoral politics and a normative theory of populist democracy.

One of the most striking virtues of the canonical one-dimensional spatial model is that it identified a unique, normatively attractive and seemingly feasible solution to the problem of aggregating individual preferences into a "democratic" policy choice—the policy located at the "ideal point" of the median voter. However, in their influential "expository development" of the spatial theory, Davis, Hinich, and Ordeshook (1970, 427, 428) noted "an important distinction between the unidimensional and multi-dimensional cases": positions preferred by a majority of voters to every alternative position, "in general, do not exist for a multi-dimensional world." As they observed, "The possibility that such a paradox exists poses a problem for majority decision-making." Thus, even if voters' preferences in every issue domain are single-peaked, as the spatial model assumes, there may be no policy platform with a logical claim to represent "the will of the majority," much less "the will of the people."

Davis, Hinich, and Ordeshook (1970, 438) described "conditions that guarantee the dominance of a single position for *any* number of dimensions"— the symmetry and unimodality of the electorate's preference density in multidimensional space (Plott 1967). However they carefully noted "the eminent restrictiveness of these conditions" and concluded that "one should not presume the existence of dominant positions" in multidimensional models. Subsequent analyses along similar lines (Kramer 1973; McKelvey 1976; Schofield 1983) richly justified that caution by producing a series of so-called chaos theorems demonstrating with increasing mathematical generality that the sufficient conditions are exceedingly fragile; once the distribution of voters' ideal points deviates from multidimensional symmetry, it is very likely that *any* feasible policy will be beatable by some other feasible policy in a straight majority vote.[7]

7 The nonobvious nature of these results is underlined by Brian Barry's (1970, 138) cheerful assumption that identifying equilibrium strategies in a multidimensional setting

This "problem for majority decision-making," as Davis, Hinich, and Ordeshook called it, is a manifestation of the "paradox of voting" explored by a long line of social choice theorists, including the Marquis de Condorcet in the 18th century and Charles Dodgson (Lewis Carroll) in the 19th century. Kenneth Arrow's (1951) much broader *general possibility theorem* demonstrated that *any* collective decision-making process satisfying certain reasonable-sounding conditions—not just majority rule—must be subject to similar difficulties. Arrow's theorem demonstrated with mathematical rigor that what many people seemed to want—a reliable "democratic" procedure for aggregating coherent individual preferences to arrive at a coherent collective choice—was simply, logically, unattainable. One commentator, Charles Plott (1976, 511–512), referred rather melodramatically to Arrow's theorem and related theoretical work as "a gigantic cavern into which fall almost all of our ideas about social actions. Almost anything . . . anyone has ever said about what society wants or should get is threatened with internal inconsistency. It is as though people have been talking for years about a thing that cannot, in *principle*, exist, and a major effort is needed to see what objectively remains from the conversations." Of course, Arrow's theorem and the multidimensional spatial model are specific formulations of the problem of collective choice within the narrow framework of the folk theory of democracy, not the sum total of what "anyone has ever said about what society wants or should get." Nonetheless, the remarkable fact that the populist ideal turned out to be logically incoherent within this simple, seemingly congenial theoretical framework *did* spur "a major effort" to reassess processes of preference aggregation in democratic politics.

Subsequent work by political scientists (Shepsle 1979; Riker 1980; Calvert 1995) has attempted to specify and explain how specific political institutions shape collective choices in the absence of "equilibria of tastes" (Riker 1980) derivable directly from individual preferences. For example, germaneness rules, committee specialization, and conference procedures in legislatures may simplify policy choices sufficiently to ensure the existence of stable equilibria even in settings where the distribution of preferences alone would leave any outcome potentially susceptible to being overturned through agenda manipulation and multidimensional log-rolling.

---

would prove to be straightforward: "Without an even distribution of voters the solution is more difficult, but it is still clear that the parties would come together where they divide the votes between them equally." The problem is that no such convergent strategy is an equilibrium; at least one party could increase its vote share by deviating from it.

In the realm of electoral politics, Richard Johnston and colleagues (1992, 3) acknowledged that "the image of the electorate which dominates popular discussion" is one of "the people as a free-standing body, with its own indomitable collective opinion." But, in an election, the collective opinion of the people can be expressed only with reference to a very limited menu of alternative party platforms—in effect, a restriction analogous to the institutional rules facilitating the avoidance of disequilibrium in the legislative realm. As E. E. Schattschneider (1942, 52) famously put it, the electorate is "a sovereign whose vocabulary is limited to two words, 'Yes' and 'No.'" Thus, Johnston and his colleagues argued for a broader view of the electoral process encompassing not only "how voters choose" but also "how parties and leaders shape the alternatives from which the choice is made."

Empirical scholarship on agenda-setting processes and institutions has been stimulating and fruitful; but it has done little to fill the gaping hole identified by Plott in the normative logic of popular sovereignty. If collective choices depend crucially on "how parties and leaders shape the alternatives from which the choice is made," and on the detailed workings of political institutions that are themselves ultimately created by collective choices, in what sense can those choices be said to reflect popular will? The choice of institutional structures is subject to Arrow's theorem, too. So far, the spatial modeling tradition has produced no satisfactory solution to this conundrum.

Some democratic theorists have attempted to sidestep the logical incoherence revealed by Arrow's theorem by supposing that *deliberation* rather than formal agenda-setting procedures might reduce complex multidimensional decisions to a single dimension or to a sequence of unidimensional decisions, conveniently satisfying the technical assumptions for the existence of a majoritarian equilibrium.[8] For example, Miller (1992) suggested that democratic deliberation might mitigate incoherence by generating widespread consensus about how to locate the various alternatives along a single dimension, or about

8 For example, Mackie (2003, 191) argued that voting on issues one dimension at a time would produce an outcome corresponding to "the intersection of medians," which he characterized as "a normatively attractive point of aggregate subjective welfare." However, the identification of that point hinges on an arbitrary choice of axes in the multidimensional issue space; alternative decompositions of the same multidimensional preferences into different, presumably equally valid packages of separate issues will in general result in different, presumably equally attractive outcomes. In any case, strategic voters will often want to logroll across dimensions, exchanging their votes on issues they care little about for support on more important issues. That brings Arrow's theorem back in, making Mackie's proposal untenable in practice even if the structure of the issue space is taken as given.

how to separate the issue into independent unidimensional components. Writing two decades later, Jack Knight and James Johnson (2011, 149) observed that "it is by now a commonplace among interpreters of social choice theory that *political argument* might well work precisely to induce just such constraints . . . by allowing relevant constituencies to sort out, and hopefully reduce, the dimensions over which they disagree."

Christian List and his colleagues (2013) used before-and-after comparisons of opinion from "deliberative polls" (Fishkin 2009) to provide some empirical support for this suggestion. On a variety of issues, participants were somewhat more likely to express single-peaked (unidimensional) preferences after participating in deliberation than before. However, whether that should be reassuring would seem to depend crucially on the quality of deliberation leading to the reorganization of opinion, and on how frequently such reorganization actually occurs in more typical political settings.

The closest Knight and Johnson came to a concrete example of how deliberation might "induce . . . constraints" on the dimensionality of collective choice was to suggest (2011, 163) that "the parties to some controversy might agree that what is at stake is a matter of national defense rather than, say, facilitating interstate commerce (e.g., as in the argument over the U.S. interstate highway system)." But on what *basis* might they come to that agreement? And why should we be reassured if they do, since the agreement is patently mistaken? The interstate highway system is clearly a matter of *both* national defense *and* interstate commerce.

Just as with formal rules for simplifying collective choices, informal agreements struck in the course of democratic deliberation may be more or less sensible and broadly accepted. But, just as with formal agenda-setting procedures, *any* particular agreement to divide an inherently multidimensional issue into unidimensional pieces will shape the outcome of collective choice in some way that is, from a purely populist standpoint, fundamentally arbitrary. Thus, deliberation provides no easy escape from the theoretical challenge posed by Arrow's theorem.

Formal theories of collective choice thus turned out to be a mixed blessing for the folk theory of democracy. On one hand, the simple unidimensional spatial model proposed by Downs provided an elegant and largely comforting account of the political significance of electoral competition. As John Zaller (2012, 623) put it, "The economic theory of democracy has great curb appeal: The rationally ignorant median voter gets what he wants without much effort." On the other hand, the multidimensional spatial model—and the theory of social choice more generally—has no curb appeal at all: even a perfectly rational, highly informed median voter does not get what she wants. That result raised fundamental logical problems for the populist ideal by calling into question how *any* sort of electoral process could reliably aggregate potentially complex individual preferences into a coherent "will of the people."

PUBLIC OPINION AND POLITICAL IDEOLOGY

Zaller's allusion to the "rationally ignorant median voter" fused two distinct aspects of Downs's "economic theory of democracy." One is the unidimensional spatial model of electoral competition, in which parties have strong incentives to converge on the ideological "ideal point" of the median voter. The other is Downs's analysis of political information costs, which led him to conclude that, because of "the infinitesimal role which each citizen's vote plays in deciding the election," the returns to acquiring political information "are so low that many rational voters [will] refrain from purchasing any political information *per se*" (Downs 1957, 258). Thus, "A large percentage of citizens—including voters—do not become informed to any significant degree on the issues involved in elections, even if they believe the outcomes to be important" (Downs 1957, 298).

Unfortunately, for the spatial model of electoral competition to work, "rationally ignorant" voters do need *some* political information. In particular, if they are to succeed in voting for the party closest to them they need to know their own preferences and the platforms of the competing parties regarding "the issues involved in elections." The voters' own preferences, especially, are often simply taken for granted in the populist theory of democracy. But what if voters don't really know what they want? In that case, the folk theory of democracy, and the spatial model in particular, loses its starting point.

One telling indication that this foundation of the folk theory may be shakier than it appears is the fact that expressed political attitudes can be remarkably sensitive to seemingly innocuous variations in question wording or context. For example, 63% to 65% of Americans in the mid-1980s said that the federal government was spending too little on "assistance to the poor"; but only 20% to 25% said that it was spending too little on "welfare" (Rasinski 1989, 391). "Welfare" clearly had deeply negative connotations for many Americans, probably because it stimulated rather different mental images than "assistance to the poor" (Gilens 1999). Would additional federal spending in this domain have reflected the will of the majority, or not? We can suggest no sensible way to answer that question.

It seems tendentious to insist that "welfare" and "assistance to the poor" denoted *different* policies, and that Americans carefully opposed the former while supporting the latter. However, even if that distinction is accepted, qualitatively similar framing effects appear in cases where the substantive distinction between alternative frames is even more tenuous. For example, in three separate experiments conducted in the mid-1970s, almost half of Americans said they would "not allow" a communist to give a speech, while only about one-fourth said they would "forbid" him or her from doing so (Schuman and Presser 1981, 277). In the weeks leading up to the 1991 Gulf War, almost two-thirds of Americans were willing to "use military force," but fewer than half were willing to "engage in combat," and fewer than 30% were willing to "go to war" (Mueller 1994, 30). Framing more abstract quantitative choices in different but mathematically equivalent ways also produces predictable—and sometimes dramatic—differences in results (Pruitt 1967; Tversky and Kahneman 1981).

The psychological indeterminacy of preferences revealed by these "framing effects" (Kahneman, Slovic, and Tversky 1982) and question-wording experiments calls into question the most fundamental assumption of populist democratic theory—that citizens have definite preferences to be elicited and aggregated through some well-specified process of collective choice (Bartels 2003). In this respect, modern cognitive psychology has sharpened and reinforced concerns about the quality of public opinion raised by critics of democracy from Plato to the pioneering survey researchers of the 1940s and 1950s.

The first rigorous scientific portrait of the American voter, by Bernard Berelson and his colleagues at Columbia University, found that "the voter falls short" of displaying the motivation, knowledge, and rationality expected by "traditional normative theory" (Berelson, Lazarsfeld, and McPhee 1954, 308, 306). "On the issues of the campaign," the Columbia scholars found (Berelson, Lazarsfeld, and McPhee 1954, 309, 311), "there is a considerable amount of 'don't know'—sometimes reflecting genuine indecision, more often meaning 'don't care.'" Voters consistently misperceived where candidates stood on the important issues of the day and exaggerated the extent of public support for their favorite candidates. And vote choices were "relatively invulnerable to direct argumentation" and "characterized more by faith than by conviction and by wishful expectation rather than careful prediction of consequences."

Several years later, in a landmark study of *The American Voter*, Angus Campbell and his colleagues at the University of Michigan described "the general impoverishment of political thought in a large proportion of the electorate." They acknowledged that "many people know the existence of few if any of the major issues of policy," much less how the competing parties and candidates might address them (Campbell et al. 1960, 543, 168, 170). Shifts in election outcomes, they concluded, were largely attributable to defections from long-standing partisan loyalties by relatively unsophisticated voters with little grasp of issues or ideology.

Philip Converse's (1964) essay on "The Nature of Belief Systems in Mass Publics" provided an even more devastating and influential portrait of the political thinking of ordinary citizens.[9] Employing the growing store of data collected by the Michigan Survey Research Center, Converse concluded that many citizens "do not have meaningful beliefs, even on issues that have formed the basis for intense political controversy among elites for substantial periods of time" (Converse 1964, 245).

Converse's evidence was of three kinds. First, he scrutinized respondents' answers to open-ended questions about political parties and candidates for evidence that they understood and spontaneously employed the ideological concepts at the core of elite political discourse. He found that about 3% of voters were clearly classifiable as "ideologues," with another 12% qualifying as "near-ideologues"; the vast majority of voters (and an even larger proportion of nonvoters) seemed to think about parties and candidates in terms of group interests or the "nature of the times," or in ways that conveyed "no shred of policy significance whatever" (Converse 1964, 217–218; also Campbell et al. 1960, chap. 10).[10]

Second, Converse assessed the degree of organization of political belief systems, as measured by statistical correlations between responses to related policy questions. Could respondents give consistently liberal or consistently conservative responses? He found only modest correlations (averaging just .23) among domestic policy views (regarding employment, aid to education, and federal housing), similarly modest correlations among foreign policy views

---

9 Kinder and Kalmoe (n.d., chaps 1–2) noted that "The Nature of Belief Systems in Mass Publics" had been cited almost 700 times in 2013 alone, its 50th year in print.

10 We see this classification of citizens in less hierarchical terms than Converse did. As we show in chapter 10, the well-informed people who disproportionately occupy the top rungs of his scale are "ideologues" in some of the unfortunate senses of that term as well.

(regarding foreign economic aid, soldiers abroad, and isolationism), and virtually *no* correlation between views across these two domains. Nor were specific policy views strongly correlated with party preferences (averaging just .07). In each case, the corresponding correlations were much higher for a sample of congressional candidates responding to related but more specific policy questions. Converse (1964, 228) interpreted these results as providing strong support for the hypothesis that "constraint among political idea-elements begins to lose its range very rapidly once we move from the most sophisticated few toward the 'grass roots.'"

Converse himself recognized that "constraint among political idea-elements"—especially across issue domains—was primarily a matter of social learning rather than logical reasoning. Critics at the time and since have pointed out that there may be nothing particularly sophisticated about parroting the specific combination of issue positions defining a conventional ideology or party line. Perhaps ordinary citizens' issue preferences lacked "constraint" because they had thoughtfully constructed their own personal political belief systems transcending conventional ideologies and party lines?

Alas, this argument ran aground on Converse's third set of analyses, which assessed the *stability* of their attitudes regarding specific issues. Converse gauged "the stability of belief elements" by tracking the same people's responses to the same questions across three separate interviews conducted at two-year intervals between 1956 and 1960. Successive responses to the same questions turned out to be remarkably *in*consistent. The correlation coefficients measuring the temporal stability of responses for any given issue from one interview to the next ranged from a bit less than .50 down to a bit less than .30, suggesting that issue views are "extremely labile for individuals over time" (Converse 1964, 240–241).[11] In marked contrast, expressions of party

11 Some of this temporal instability no doubt reflects measurement error due to the inevitable vagueness of survey questions (Achen 1975). Moreover, people may bring different relevant considerations to bear in answering the same question in successive interviews, producing unstable responses even as their underlying stores of relevant considerations remain unchanged (Zaller 1992). In the first years after Converse wrote, the responses of sophisticated people (as measured by formal education) seemed to be almost as unstable as those of less sophisticated people, suggesting that the inevitable noise in survey questions was at fault. However, later studies using better measures of political sophistication (based on respondents' demonstrated factual knowledge about politics) have generally found the opinions of more sophisticated people to be a good deal more stable. For example, Kinder and Kalmoe (n.d., ms. 70) calculated that the average stability of responses to five issue questions in the 1992–1996 American National Election Studies panel survey ranged from .60 among the best-informed quintile of respondents down to .25 in the bottom information quintile. Again, we

identification were much more stable, with correlations from one survey to the next exceeding .70. Converse (1964, 241) inferred that parties "are more central within the political belief systems of the mass public than are the policy ends that the parties are designed to pursue."

Converse's essay set off a very substantial debate about his methodology and interpretations. Perhaps no single argument he advanced was fully persuasive. But even most critics agreed with his conclusion: the political "belief systems" of ordinary citizens bore little resemblance to the ideal embodied in the folk theory of democracy. As Kinder and Kalmoe (n.d., ms. 13) summarized current scholarly understanding, "Genuine ideological identification—an abiding dispositional commitment to an ideological point of view—turns out to be rare. Real liberals and real conservatives are found in impressive numbers only in the higher echelons of political society, confined to the comparatively few who are deeply and seriously engaged in political life." For most ordinary citizens, ideology is—at best—a byproduct of more basic partisan and group loyalties. Thus, as Kinder and Kalmoe (n.d., ms. 12) noted, "Americans are much more resolute in their identification with party than they are in their identification with ideology."

Research in other countries has generally produced similar portraits of democratic citizens. Their ideological self-placements are often driven more by partisanship than by policy positions (Inglehart and Klingemann 1976). Indeed, left-right terms are sometimes meaningful primarily as alternate names for the political parties—often, names that the parties themselves have taught the voters (Arian and Shamir 1983). Even in France, the presumed home of ideological politics, Converse and Pierce (1986, chap. 4) found that most voters did not understand political "left" and "right." When citizens do understand the terms, they may still be uncertain or confused about where the parties stand on the left-right dimension (Butler and Stokes 1974, 323–337). Perhaps as a result, their partisan loyalties and issue preferences are often badly misaligned. In a 1968 survey in Italy, for example, 50% of those who identified with the right-wing Monarchist party took left-wing policy positions (Barnes 1971, 170).

Lest younger readers be tempted to suppose that this sort of confusion is a remnant of an older and less sophisticated political era (or an artifact of older and less sophisticated scholarly analysis), we note that careful recent studies

---

want to emphasize that it is a mistake to view people at the top of the information scale as sophisticated independent thinkers, as we demonstrate in the remainder of this book. The point is simply that they are more consistent in the positions they espouse from one survey to the next.

have repeatedly turned up similar findings. For example, Elizabeth Zechmeister (2006, 162) found "striking, systematic differences . . . both within and across the countries" in the conceptions of "left" and "right" offered by elite private college students in Mexico and Argentina, while André Blais (personal communication) found half of German voters unable to place the party called "Die Linke"—the Left—on a left-right scale.[12]

This rather bleak portrait of public opinion has provoked a good deal of resistance among political scientists, and a variety of concerted attempts to overturn or evade the findings of the classic Columbia and Michigan studies.[13] In the 1970s, for example, some scholars claimed to have discovered *The Changing American Voter*, a much more issue-oriented and ideologically consistent specimen than the earlier studies had portrayed (Nie, Verba, and Petrocik 1976). Unfortunately, further scrutiny revealed that most of the apparent change could be attributed to changes in the questions voters were being asked rather than to more elevated political thinking. When 1970s voters were asked the old questions, their responses displayed little more consistency or sophistication than they had in the 1950s (Bishop, Oldendick, and Tuchfarber 1978a; 1978b; Brunk 1978; Sullivan et al. 1979).

Other scholars have argued that overarching ideological convictions are unnecessary because citizens can derive meaningful policy preferences from somewhat narrower "core values" such as equal opportunity, limited government, or traditional morality (Feldman 1988; Goren 2001). Citizens' allegiances (or antipathies) to these values do tend to be somewhat more stable than their specific policy preferences. However, they are a good deal less stable than the phrase "core values" would seem to imply, being significantly colored by party identification and even by short-term vote intentions (Goren 2005; McCann 1997).

Since the 1980s, the American political system has seen a substantial increase in partisan polarization, with Democratic elites becoming more clearly and consistently liberal and Republican elites more clearly and consistently

12 Even among professional politicians and intellectuals, the meaning and salience of ideology sometimes vary greatly with the political context. For example, the specific policy preferences of Latin American legislators typically explain less than 10% of the variance in their left-right self-placements (Zechmeister 2010, 105–110). In France, Converse and Pierce (1986, 129–132) found that "left" sounded good even to rightist deputies. Terms like "left" and "right" or "liberal" and "conservative," when they make sense at all, often turn out to represent partisan commitments as much or more than issue positions. Thus, ideological language need not have much genuine ideological content, even among elites.

13 Bartels (2010) summarized these and other developments in the scholarly study of American electoral behavior.

conservative (Poole and Rosenthal 2007; Theriault 2008; Mann and Ornstein 2012). As a result, rank-and-file partisans have increasingly come to adopt ideological labels consistent with their partisanship (Layman, Carsey, and Horowitz 2006; Hetherington 2009; Levendusky 2009). Has this solved Converse's problem? Alas, voters' policy preferences seem to have become only modestly more "ideologically coherent" as a result, with the average correlation between pairs of policy preferences increasing from a paltry .16 in 1972 to a slightly less paltry .20 in 2012. Not much has changed.[14]

Similarly, when a group of scholars half a century later painstakingly replicated many of the specific analyses presented in *The American Voter* using survey data from 2000 and 2004, they found no change in most respects, and only glacial improvements in the remainder (Lewis-Beck et al. 2008). Voters, it seems, are what they are, and not what idealistic proponents of popular sovereignty might wish them to be. The folk theory is of little use in understanding actual democratic politics.

Thus, most contemporary scholars of public opinion have come to accept, at least in broad outline, Converse's portrait of democratic citizens. Kinder and Kalmoe (n.d., ms. 61–62) conclude that "Converse's conclusion of ideological innocence still stands. . . . Educational transformation, party polarization, revolutionary changes in information dissemination, fundamental alterations in gender and race relations: impressive as these changes have been, equally impressive is how little visible effect they have had on how the American electorate understands politics."[15]

POLITICAL IGNORANCE, HEURISTICS, AND "THE MIRACLE OF AGGREGATION"

Confusion regarding political ideology is just the tip of a large iceberg of political unawareness. Michael Delli Carpini and Scott Keeter (1996) surveyed responses to hundreds of specific factual questions in U.S. opinion surveys over the preceding 50 years to provide an authoritative summary of

14 Kinder and Kalmoe (n.d., ms. 45–46) helpfully calculated that if "ideological constraint continues to increase into the indefinite future" at the same modest rate, "the American public's views on policy would eventually come to approximate the degree of structure shown by partisan elites today"—in about 300 years.

15 Converse's own subsequent assessments of these issues (1990; 2000; 2006) were broadly consistent with Kinder and Kalmoe's. (The last of these assessments appeared as part of an extensive symposium in *Critical Review* on "democratic competence," which also reprinted Converse's original essay.)

What Americans Know about Politics and Why It Matters. In 1952, Delli Carpini and Keeter found, only 44% of Americans could name at least one branch of government. In 1972, only 22% knew something about Watergate. In 1985, only 59% knew whether their own state's governor was a Democrat or a Republican. In 1986, only 49% knew which one nation in the world had used nuclear weapons (Delli Carpini and Keeter 1996, 70, 81, 74, 84). Delli Carpini and Keeter (1996, 270) concluded from these and scores of similar findings that "large numbers of American citizens are woefully underinformed and that overall levels of knowledge are modest at best." Robert Luskin (2002, 282) put the same conclusion rather more colorfully, observing that most people "know jaw-droppingly little about politics."

Here, too, it is striking how little seems to have changed in the decades since survey research began to shed systematic light on the nature of public opinion. Changes in the structure of the mass media have allowed people with an uncommon taste for public affairs to find an unprecedented quantity and variety of political news; but they have also allowed people with more typical tastes to abandon traditional newspapers and television news for round-the-clock sports, pet tricks, or pornography, producing an increase in the *variance* of political information levels but no change in the *average level* of political information (Baum and Kernell 1999; Prior 2007). Similarly, while formal education remains a strong predictor of individuals' knowledge about politics, substantial increases in American educational attainment have produced little apparent increase in overall levels of political knowledge. When Delli Carpini and Keeter (1996, 17) compared responses to scores of factual questions asked repeatedly in opinion surveys over the past half century, they found that "the public's level of political knowledge is little different today than it was fifty years ago. Given the ample reasons to expect changing levels of knowledge over the past fifty years, this finding provides the strongest evidence for the intractability of political knowledge and ignorance." Ilya Somin (2013, 192) concluded from a more recent survey along similar lines that "widespread political ignorance is a serious problem for democracy," and questioned "whether the modern electorate even comes close to meeting the requirements of democratic theory."

Some critics of this perspective have supposed that opinion surveys significantly underestimate people's political knowledge by providing insufficient motivation for them to answer questions correctly (Prior and Lupia 2008; Bullock et al. 2013). Unfortunately, insufficient motivation is endemic to mass politics, not an artifact of opinion surveys; we do not doubt that voters would be better informed if they were paid to learn political facts, but that seems impractical (and, judging by the results of these studies, extremely expensive). Others imagine that "visual political knowledge"—recognizing the faces of political figures but not their names—provides "a different road to competence" (Prior 2014); but adding photographs to the ballot would raise significant additional problems of voter bias (Todorov et al. 2005; Lawson et al. 2010; Olivola and Todorov 2010; Lenz and Lawson 2011).

Most attempts to "redeem" the electorate have taken a different tack, acknowledging that voters are generally inattentive and uninformed but denying that the quality of their political decisions suffers much as a result. For example, formal theorists have proposed versions of the spatial model of elections in which the usual postulate that voters are fully informed is loosened somewhat. Unfortunately, even "uninformed" voters in these models know a great deal more than most real voters do. For example, one influential spatial model of elections with "uninformed" voters (McKelvey and Ordeshook 1985; 1986) posited that all voters know the distribution of voters' ideal points, informed voters know the candidates' positions exactly, and uninformed voters know the levels of "informed" support for candidates (from poll data) and the left-right order of the candidates' positions, from which they then proceed to *infer* the candidates' positions on the basis of spatial theory. Alas, as we have seen, most voters do not know what political "left" and "right" mean, much less know what informed voters think. Thus, few if any of these cheery assumptions are likely to hold in practice.

In the early 1990s, a spate of books with such reassuring titles as *The Reasoning Voter* (Popkin 1991), *Reasoning and Choice* (Sniderman, Brody, and Tetlock 1991), and *The Rational Public* (Page and Shapiro 1992) argued that voters could use "information shortcuts" or "heuristics" to make rational electoral choices even though they lacked detailed knowledge about candidates and policies. These shortcuts could take a variety of forms, including "cues" from trusted individuals or groups, inferences derived from political or social stereotypes, or generalizations from personal experience or folk wisdom.

Sociologists and political scientists have long recognized that citizens sometimes take "cues" from better informed friends, relatives, neighbors, or coworkers (Katz and Lazarsfeld 1955; Huckfeldt and Sprague 1995; Mutz 2006). The writer Calvin Trillin once had such an arrangement. "Mrs. Trillin, Alice, gave Cyprus to Mr. Trillin for his birthday; for the next 12 months, she would think about Cyprus and he wouldn't have to. Mr. Trillin, for Christmas, gave Mrs. Trillin Iran. Neither of them was willing to take over thinking about the SALT [disarmament] talks" (Leonard 1982). The very humor of the story points to one limitation of this defense of democracy: while

Mr. and Mrs. Trillin were sufficiently well informed (and, we hope, politically compatible) to make such a division of labor feasible and efficient, most citizens don't have a Cyprus watcher in the house and would not know what to make of advice about Cyprus if they had it.

The literature on "heuristics" in political science is an odd stepchild of the corresponding literature in psychology. Psychologists have devoted exhaustive attention to the biases in judgment produced by reliance on specific, identifiable heuristics. For example, the classic collection of essays edited by Daniel Kahneman, Paul Slovic, and Amos Tversky (1982) included reports on "belief in the law of small numbers," "shortcomings in the attribution process," "egocentric biases in availability and attribution," "the illusion of control," and "overconfidence in case-study judgments," among other topics. It also included a series of essays on "corrective procedures" intended to mitigate the effects of these various biases and shortcomings.

Political scientists, by comparison, have typically been much more likely to view "heuristics" as a boon to democracy. We suspect, along with James Kuklinski and Paul Quirk (2000, 154), that that enthusiasm has much to do with the fact that "the notion of a competent citizenry is normatively attractive. It buttresses efforts to expand citizen participation and credits the citizenry for some of American democracy's success."

When students of political heuristics have defined the tasks of citizens sufficiently clearly for concrete performance benchmarks to be meaningful, they have tended to present those tasks in such highly simplified form that all of the difficulties of real political inference are abstracted away (Lupia and McCubbins 1998). More often, observed preferences and behavior are deemed "rational" simply because they look reasonable or seem to be influenced by plausibly relevant considerations. In one of the most colorful examples of a political "information shortcut," Samuel Popkin argued that Mexican-American voters had good reason to be suspicious of President Gerald Ford when he made the mistake, during a Texas primary campaign appearance, of trying to down a tamale without first removing its cornhusk wrapper. According to Popkin (1991, 3), "Showing familiarity with a voter's culture is an obvious and easy test of ability to relate to the problems and sensibilities of the ethnic group and to understand and care about them." An obvious and easy test, yes. An accurate basis for inferring Ford's sensitivities toward Mexican-Americans? We have no idea.

Lacking any objective standard for distinguishing reliable political cues from unreliable ones, some scholars have simply asked whether uninformed citizens—using whatever "information shortcuts" are available to them—

manage to mimic the preferences and choices of better informed people. Alas, statistical analyses of the impact of political information on policy preferences have produced ample evidence of substantial divergences between the preferences of relatively uninformed and better informed citizens (Delli Carpini and Keeter 1996, chap. 6; Althaus 1998). Similarly, when ordinary people are exposed to intensive political education and conversation on specific policy issues, they often change their mind (Luskin, Fishkin, and Jowell 2002; Sturgis 2003).

Parallel analyses of voting behavior have likewise found that uninformed citizens cast significantly different votes than those who were better informed. For example, Bartels (1996) estimated that actual vote choices fell about halfway between what they would have been if voters had been fully informed and what they would have been if everyone had picked candidates by flipping coins.[16] Richard Lau and David Redlawsk (1997; 2006) analyzed the same elections using a less demanding criterion for assessing "correct" voting. (They took each voter's partisanship, policy positions, and evaluations of candidate performance as given, setting aside the fact that these, too, may be subject to errors and biases.) They found that about 70% of voters, on average, chose the candidate who best matched their own expressed preferences. Lau and Redlawsk (2006, 88, 263) wondered, "Is 70 percent correct enough?"

Answering that question requires a careful assessment of the extent to which "incorrect" votes skew election outcomes. Optimism about the competence of democratic electorates has often been bolstered (at least among political scientists) by appeals to what Converse (1990) dubbed the "miracle of aggregation"—an idea formalized by the Marquis de Condorcet more than 200 years ago and forcefully argued with empirical evidence by Benjamin Page and Robert Shapiro (1992). Condorcet demonstrated mathematically that if several jurors make independent judgments of a suspect's guilt or innocence, a majority are quite likely to judge correctly even if every individual juror is only modestly more likely than chance to reach the correct conclusion.

---

16 The phrase "fully informed" is a misnomer here, since Bartels's imputations of "fully informed" voting behavior were based on observed variations in voting behavior across a five-point summary measure of survey respondents' general level of information about politics and public affairs. It seems safe to assume that even respondents at the top of this information scale were, in reality, far from being "fully informed." Thus, the effects of low political knowledge on voting behavior were almost certainly underestimated. Bartels (1990) provided a more detailed discussion of political interests, political enlightenment, and the logic and potential applications of the imputation strategy.

Applied to electoral politics, Condorcet's logic suggests that the electorate as a whole may be much wiser than any individual voter.

The crucial problem with this mathematically elegant argument is that it does not work very well in practice.[17] Real voters' errors are quite unlikely to be statistically independent, as Condorcet's logic requires. When thousands or millions of voters misconstrue the same relevant fact or are swayed by the same vivid campaign ad, no amount of aggregation will produce the requisite miracle; individual voters' "errors" will not cancel out in the overall election outcome, especially when they are based on constricted flows of information (Page and Shapiro 1992, chaps. 5, 9). If an incumbent government censors or distorts information regarding foreign policy or national security, the resulting errors in citizens' judgments obviously will not be random.[18] Less obviously, even unintentional errors by politically neutral purveyors of information may significantly distort collective judgment, as when statistical agencies or the news media overstate or understate the strength of the economy in the run-up to an election (Hetherington 1996).

Bartels (1996) estimated how well the overall outcomes of six presidential elections matched what they would have been if every voter had been "fully informed." The average discrepancy between the actual popular vote and the hypothetical "fully informed" outcome of each election amounted to three percentage points—more than enough to swing a close contest. Related analyses of voting behavior in Sweden (Oscarsson 2007), Canada (Blais et al. 2009), Denmark (Hansen 2009), and many other countries (Arnold 2012) have found similar effects of information on aggregate election outcomes. Thus the lack of political knowledge matters—not only for individual voters, but also for entire electorates, the policies they favor, and the parties they elect.

THE ILLUSION OF "ISSUE VOTING"

The spatial theory of voting cast "issue proximity" as both the primary determinant of voters' choices and the primary focus of candidates' campaign

17 Formal theorists have also raised questions regarding the logical underpinnings of the argument, which typically hinge on the assumption that voters behave "sincerely" rather than strategically (Austen-Smith and Banks 1996; Feddersen and Pesendorfer 1998).

18 What we have in mind is that voters' errors can be correlated and thus not independently distributed—not the random white noise that Condorcet assumed. At the same time, voters' judgments typically depend on irrelevancies that do not reflect incumbent competence, so that election outcomes are not predictable by rational considerations—elections are "random" in that sense. Thus "nonrandom" (correlated) voter errors can lead to "random" (unpredictable from rational considerations) election outcomes.

strategies. Over the course of the 1960s and 1970s, this theoretical development was gradually but powerfully translated into empirical analyses of voting behavior. In the authoritative American National Election Studies conducted by the University of Michigan, questions regarding issues of public policy were increasingly recast as seven-point "issue scales" directly inspired by spatial theory. Survey respondents were invited to "place" themselves, candidates, and parties on each issue dimension. The proliferation of issue scales provided ample raw material for naive statistical analyses relating vote choices to "issue proximities" calculated by comparing respondents' own positions on these issue scales with the positions they attributed to the competing candidates or parties.

The causal ambiguity inherent in statistical analyses of this sort was clear to scholars of voting behavior by the early 1970s. Richard Brody and Benjamin Page (1972; Page and Brody 1972) outlined three distinct interpretations of the positive correlation between "issue proximities" and vote choices. The first, *policy-oriented evaluation*, corresponds to the conventional interpretation of issue voting in the folk theory of democracy: prospective voters observe the candidates' policy positions, compare them to their own policy preferences, and choose a candidate accordingly. The second, *persuasion*, involves prospective voters altering their own issue positions to bring them into conformity with the issue positions of the candidate or party they favor. The third, *projection*, involves prospective voters convincing themselves that the candidate or party they favor has issue positions similar to their own (and perhaps also that disfavored candidates or parties have dissimilar issue positions) whether or not this is in fact the case. In both the second and third cases, "issue proximity" is a *consequence* of the voter's preference for a specific candidate or party, not a *cause* of that preference.

Brody and Page (1972, 458) wrote, "We need some means for examining the potential for 'persuasion' and for 'projection' and of estimating them as separate processes. . . . If the estimation of policy voting is important to the understanding of the role of the citizen in a democracy—and theorists of democracy certainly write as if it is—then any procedure which fails to control for projection and persuasion will be an undependable base upon which to build our understanding." Brody and Page's clear warning was followed by some resourceful attempts to resolve the causal ambiguity they identified (Jackson 1975; Markus and Converse 1979; Page and Jones 1979; Franklin and Jackson 1983). Unfortunately, those attempts mostly served to underline the extent to which the conclusions drawn from such analyses rested on fragile and apparently untestable statistical assumptions. Perhaps most dramatically, back-to-back articles by Markus and Converse (1979) and by Page and Jones (1979) in the same issue of the *American Political Science Review* estimated complex simultaneous-equation models relating partisanship, issue proximity, and assessments of candidates' personalities using the same data from American National Election Studies surveys, but came to very different conclusions about the bases of voting behavior. If two teams of highly competent analysts asking essentially similar questions of the same data could come to such different conclusions, it seemed clear that the results of such exercises must depend at least as much on the analysts' theoretical preconceptions and associated statistical assumptions as on the behavior of voters.

In light of this apparent impasse, many scholars of voting behavior have preferred to sidestep the causal ambiguity plaguing the relationship between issue positions and votes by reverting to simple single-equation models in which issue positions can affect vote choices but not vice versa. In effect, they have relied on the assumptions of the folk theory of democracy rather than empirical evidence to resolve the problem raised by Brody and Page.[19] For example, Stephen Ansolabehere, Jonathan Rodden, and James Snyder (2008) cumulated responses to dozens of specific issue questions in American National Election Studies surveys into just two broad ("economic" and "moral") issue positions, discarding all of the remaining variation in specific issue responses as attributable to "measurement error." They imputed issue positions for voters who had none, or simply dropped them from the analysis. Then they imposed a model in which the observed relationship between issue positions and vote choices (net of partisanship and ideology) was attributed entirely to issue voting, with no allowance for persuasion or group identity effects. Unsurprisingly, they reported finding "stable policy preferences" and "strong evidence of issue voting" (Ansolabehere, Rodden, and Snyder 2008, 229).[20]

---

19 Some analysts have mitigated the resulting problem of bias due to *projection* by substituting sample average perceptions of the candidates' issue positions for individual respondents' own perceptions (e.g., Aldrich, Sullivan, and Borgida 1989; Erikson and Romero 1990; Alvarez and Nagler 1995). While this approach has the considerable virtue of reducing bias due to projection, it does nothing to mitigate bias due to *persuasion*; to the extent that voters adopt issue positions consistent with those of parties or candidates they support for other reasons, they will still (misleadingly) appear to be engaging in issue voting. Moreover, substituting sample average perceptions of the candidates' issue positions for respondents' own perceptions sacrifices a good deal of theoretical coherence, since it is very difficult to see how or why voters would compare their own issue positions to *other people's* perceptions of the candidates' positions, ignoring their own perceptions.

20 Freeder, Lenz, and Turney (2014) provided a reinterpretation of this evidence more consistent with Converse's (1964) view and our own.

Subsequent work by Gabriel Lenz (2009; 2012) provided substantial additional grounds for skepticism regarding inferences of this sort. Lenz used repeated interviews with the same individuals to show that *persuasion* plays a large role—and *policy-oriented evaluation* remarkably little role—in accounting for observed associations between issue positions and votes. That is, candidate choices determine issue positions, not vice versa.

In the 2000 presidential campaign, for example, candidate George W. Bush advocated allowing individual citizens to invest Social Security funds in the stock market, thereby catapulting a previously obscure policy proposal into the political limelight. Much of the news coverage and advertising in the final month of the campaign focused on the candidates' contrasting stands on the issue; in a typical "battleground" media market, the two candidates together ran about 200 ads touching on Social Security privatization just in the final *week* before Election Day (Johnston, Hagen, and Jamieson 2004, 153–159). And, sure enough, the statistical relationship between voters' views on Social Security privatization and their preferences for Bush or Al Gore (holding constant party identification) more than doubled over the course of the campaign.

This is exactly the sort of shift we might expect if voters were attending to the political debate, weighing the competing candidates' policy platforms, and formulating their vote intentions accordingly. However, Lenz's more detailed analysis employing repeated interviews with the same people demonstrated that this substantial increase in the apparent electoral impact of views about Social Security privatization was almost entirely illusory—due not to changes in vote intentions, but to Bush and Gore supporters *learning* their preferred candidate's position on the issue and then adopting it as their own. As Lenz (2012, 59) put it, "the increase in media and campaign attention to this issue did almost nothing to make people whose position was the same as Bush's more likely to vote for Bush than they already were."

On issue after issue—ranging from support for public works in 1976 and defense spending in 1980 to European integration in Britain to nuclear power in the Netherlands in the wake of the Chernobyl reactor meltdown—Lenz's analyses provided substantial evidence of *vote-driven* changes in issue positions but little or no evidence of *issue-driven* changes in candidate or party preferences. As John Zaller (2012, 617) put it, "Partisan voters take the positions they are expected as partisans to take, but do not seem to care about them." Lenz (2012, 235) characterized these findings as "disappointing" for "scholars who see democracy as fundamentally about voters expressing their views on policy," noting that the "inverted" relationship between issue positions and votes seemed to leave politicians with "considerable freedom in the policies they choose."

ELECTIONS AND PUBLIC POLICY

Almost all of the scholarly evidence we have considered thus far regarding public opinion and electoral behavior focuses on the attitudes and votes of individual citizens. Fortunately, we are not limited to individual-level analyses of public opinion and voting behavior. We can also attempt to assess directly how elections shape democratic politics. Does issue voting compel both parties to adopt policy positions close to those of the median voter, as the spatial theory of elections implies?

As we have seen, U.S. presidential elections in the post–World War II era—and especially the landslide defeats suffered by Barry Goldwater in 1964 and George McGovern in 1972—seemed to comport rather well with the predictions of the spatial theory. However, more systematic research on U.S. presidential elections has suggested that Goldwater and McGovern's losses had less to do with their issue positions than with election-year economic conditions; ideological "extremism" probably cost them just a few percentage points of the popular vote (Bartels and Zaller 2001; Cohen and Zaller 2012). More generally, the impact of candidates' policy stands on election outcomes—at least over the range of policy stands observed in modern presidential elections—seems to be quite modest. As Zaller (2012, 616) put it, "the penalty for extremism, if real, is not large."

The broad analysis of U.S. public policy in Robert Erikson, Michael MacKuen, and James Stimson's *The Macro Polity* (2002, 303–311) similarly underlines the failure of issue voting to discipline politicians in the manner suggested by the spatial theory of elections. Erikson, MacKuen, and Stimson measured the ideological tenor of policy activity in each branch of Congress and the White House over more than 40 years. They found that policy outcomes shifted substantially when partisan control shifted from Democrats to Republicans or from Republicans to Democrats. The public's "policy mood" (Erikson, MacKuen, and Stimson 2002, 194–205) also influenced policy regardless of which party was in control, but that effect was small by comparison. For example, the estimated impact on White House policy activity of moving from the most conservative "policy mood" recorded in four decades to the most liberal "policy mood" was only about one-third as large as the estimated impact of replacing a typical Republican president with a typical Democrat. The estimated effects of partisan control on congressional policy activity were even larger. The implication is that citizens affect public policy—insofar as they affect it at all—almost entirely by voting out one partisan team and replacing it with another.

If the election of a Republican or Democratic president itself provided a reliable signal of the public's "policy mood," the resulting swing to right or left in policy outcomes might be characterized as a reflection of "majority rule" (though not in the sense suggested by the median voter theorem). The authors of *The Macro Polity* argued that presidential election outcomes *are* strongly affected by the public's "policy mood" (Erikson, MacKuen, and Stimson 2002, chap. 7). However, their statistical analyses required delicate controls for the prevailing balance of partisan loyalties in the electorate and the (inferred) ideological positions of the competing candidates. Subsequent analyses have found the apparent impact of "policy mood" evaporating once election-year economic conditions are taken into account (Cohen and Zaller 2012, table 3). Meanwhile, scholars attempting to forecast presidential election outcomes (e.g., Abramowitz 2012; Erikson and Wlezien 2012; Hibbs 2012) have generally been content to ignore "policy mood," issue preferences, and ideology—a telling indication that these factors are of relatively little importance in determining who wins.

Studies of Congress likewise find that the policy preferences of citizens in a given state or district are only modestly predictive of election outcomes—and that Democrats and Republicans routinely take very different stands once they are elected, even when they represent states or districts with very similar political views. Both of these points are clear in figure 2.1, which relates the overall roll call voting record of each member of the House of Representatives in the 112th Congress (2011–2013)[21] to the policy preferences of his or her constituents.[22] (Republican members are denoted by diamonds

21 We summarize each representative's entire roll call voting record using an index developed by Keith Poole and Howard Rosenthal (2007). Their (first-dimension) DW-NOMINATE scores represent "ideal points" that account as accurately as possible for each representative's entire roll call voting record under the assumption of spatial voting. The scale on which the ideal points are measured is arbitrary, but they are conventionally normalized to run from −1 for the most liberal member of the House to +1 for the most conservative member. However, due to constraints imposed by the DW-NOMINATE algorithm on the movement of each representative on the scale from one Congress to the next, the range of actual scores in figure 2.1 is from −0.729 to 1.376.

22 These data are from surveys conducted in 2010 and 2012 by the Internet survey firm YouGov as part of the Cooperative Congressional Election Study (CCES). There were a total of 52,464 respondents in 2010 and 51,661 in 2012. The combined sample size in each congressional district ranged from 88 to 515 and averaged 239. YouGov employs opt-in recruiting, but uses matching and weighting to produce representative samples of adult U.S.

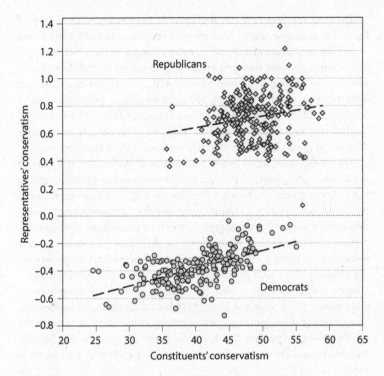

Figure 2.1. District Opinion and Representatives' Roll Call Votes, 2011–2013

and Democrats by circles.) District preferences are measured using a 12-item scale including liberal-conservative self-identification, beliefs about climate change, and support for the Affordable Care Act, domestic spending, the Iraq War, gays in the military, gun control, affirmative action, environmental protection, defense spending, a path to citizenship for illegal immigrants, and abortion.[23] The scale runs from 0 (most liberal) to 100 (most conservative), but the range of district averages is much narrower, from 24.5 to 59.0.

---

citizens (Vavreck and Rivers 2008). Additional information regarding the CCES surveys is available at http://projects.iq.harvard.edu/cces/home.

23 Factor analysis produced a single dimension with factor loadings ranging from .78 for liberal-conservative self-identification to .50 for abortion. The resulting weights of the individual survey items are .176 for liberal-conservative self-identification, .161 for beliefs about climate change, .104 for domestic spending, .083 for support for the Affordable Care

The most liberal congressional districts in the country, at the far left of figure 2.1, invariably elected Democrats to the House in 2010. (These were overwhelmingly urban and mostly majority-minority districts.) At the opposite extreme, the most conservative districts almost all elected Republicans. However, for districts in the broad middle of the political spectrum, election outcomes were a rather unreliable reflection of citizens' policy preferences. Moderately liberal districts (in the second quartile of the national distribution) elected Republicans 46% of the time, while moderately conservative districts (in the third quartile) elected Democrats 25% of the time.[24]

The modest correlation between constituents' preferences and election outcomes implies substantial variation in representation, given the gulf in roll call voting behavior between Republicans and Democrats representing similar districts in figure 2.1. Nor is it the case that representatives won election in what looked like uncongenial districts by catering closely to citizens' preferences at the expense of their own (or their parties') convictions. The dotted lines in figure 2.1 summarize the separate linear relationships between the conservatism of each party's representatives and their constituents' preferences. Within each party, there is a modest positive relationship between constituents' preferences and House members' roll call votes. However, the magnitudes of those relationships are dwarfed by the distance between the two lines, which represents the expected difference in conservatism between Republican and Democratic members representing districts with identical public opinion.

Clearly, Republican and Democratic members of Congress representing constituents with similar preferences behaved in very different ways. Whether these differences were produced by differences in the representatives' personal ideological convictions or party pressures or other factors is, for our purposes here, irrelevant. The key point is that representatives' voting behavior was not strongly constrained by their constituents' views.[25] Elections do *not* force

---

Act, .076 for environmental protection, .072 for affirmative action, .067 for gun control, .059 for the Iraq War, .058 for defense spending, .054 for gays in the military, .051 for abortion, and .039 for a path to citizenship for illegal immigrants.

24 The corresponding relationship between U.S. Senate election outcomes and constituents' policy preferences is even weaker. The difference may reflect the fact that Senate elections tend to involve more publicity and campaign spending than House elections, making voters more susceptible to being swayed by candidate-specific factors unrelated to policy (Krasno 1997).

25 Since the analysis presented in figure 2.1 employs incommensurate measures of representatives' voting behavior and constituents' preferences, we are not able to say whether

successful candidates to reflect the policy preferences of the median voter, as Downsian logic implies.

The pattern of partisan polarization evident in figure 2.1 is not a fluke attributable to a particular congressional session or opinion survey.[26] Indeed, a historical analysis of every Congress going back to the 1870s (using presidential election returns as proxies for constituents' preferences) suggests that similar differences in expected roll call voting patterns between Republicans and Democrats representing similar constituencies have been fairly common in the past 140 years (Bartels, Clinton, and Geer forthcoming).[27]

Scholars of comparative politics sometimes argue that the pattern of alternating partisan extremism that has characterized the American political system through much of its history is absent or attenuated in multiparty systems where legislative seats are allocated through proportional representation. According to G. Bingham Powell (2000, 243), for example, "proportional systems are more successful in getting governments (and even more so the influential policymakers) close to the median citizen." However, assessments of this sort depend on untested assumptions about how parties' positions get translated into policies under different institutional arrangements. More direct assessments of patterns of responsiveness have found little consistent difference between proportional and majoritarian systems in their extent of correspondence between median voters' preferences and actual policy outcomes (e.g., Kang and Powell 2010; Bartels 2015). Perhaps some other institutional arrangement would work better; we do not know. But at present, there is little evidence to suggest that changes in electoral institutions will be sufficient to ensure popular control of public policy through electoral competition.

CONCLUSION

The folk theory of electoral democracy—the notion that elections can "reveal the 'will' or the preferences of a majority on a set of issues," as Dahl (1956,

---

Republican representatives were more conservative than their constituents or Democratic representatives were more liberal or both.

26 For example, Bartels (2008, 256) documented a qualitatively similar pattern for the U.S. Senate in the late 1980s and early 1990s, and Joshua Clinton (2006, 401) did the same for the U.S. House of Representatives in 1999–2000.

27 Bartels, Clinton, and Geer's (forthcoming) analysis suggests that the intense partisan polarization of congressional roll call voting since 1994 (above and beyond what could be accounted for by differences in district preferences) was matched in the period from 1874 through 1920. By comparison, the period from the mid-1930s through the mid-1970s was one of consistently low partisan polarization by this measure.

131) put it—has played a central role in both political science and popular thinking about politics. Scholars have elegantly codified the populist ideal in the "spatial theory" of elections. The behavior it enshrines as normative, "issue voting," is widely regarded as a hallmark of good citizenship. Indeed, a conscientious voter nowadays can choose among a variety of websites inviting her to answer a series of policy questions and be told which candidates to support—apparently on the assumption that nothing other than the candidates' policy positions (and just these policy positions) should matter to her.[28] The social science theorizing and the cultural norm are both derived directly from the folk theory of democracy.

Unfortunately, as we have seen, this populist ideal in both its scientific and popular incarnations suffers from grave logical and practical problems. Both the remarkable theoretical insights of Arrow (1951) and his successors and the seminal empirical research of Converse (1964) and many others punched significant holes in the romantic populist notion of democracy. Although a great deal of subsequent scholarly effort has been devoted to recasting, circumscribing, or rejecting their claims, repeated attempts to sidestep the theoretical and empirical deficiencies of the populist ideal have failed, leaving the "strong challenge to democratic hopes" (Kinder 2003, 15) posed by modern social science fundamentally intact.

These scientific findings have had little effect on practical politics. Joseph Schumpeter (1942, 250) argued—perhaps wishfully—that "today it is difficult to find any student of social processes who has a good word for" the simplistic notions of the folk theory. Nevertheless, he added, "action continued to be taken on that theory all the time it was being blown to pieces. The more untenable it was being proved to be, the more completely it dominated official phraseology and the rhetoric of the politician" (Schumpeter 1942, 249). More than seven additional decades of demolition work have done little to alter that picture.

Indeed, periodic frustration with the apparent failure of elections to faithfully translate "the will of the people" into public policy has prompted repeated attempts to wrench American political practice into closer accordance with the folk theory. The principal goal of these efforts has been to constrain or even bypass those whom the reformers blamed for their disappointments—professional politicians. Perhaps most radically, reformers in the Progressive

28 See, for example, http://votesmart.org/voteeasy/, http://www.ontheissues.org, http://www.votehelp.org/, http://selectsmart.com/politics.html, http://www.quizrocket.com/political-party-quiz.

Era attempted "to restore the absolute sovereignty of the people" (Bourne 1912) by circumventing the traditional electoral process altogether, instituting "direct democracy" via initiatives and referendums. We turn next to the promise and pitfalls of these repeated attempts to impose an idealistic theory on the recalcitrant reality of American democracy.

Tumbling Down into a Democratical Republick: "Pure Democracy" and the Pitfalls of Popular Control

> Critics of the magistrates are also responsible. Their argument is, "The *people* ought to decide": the people accept that invitation readily; and thus the authority of all the magistrates is undermined.
>
> —Aristotle, *The Politics* (1958, 168–169)

The Founders of the American political system had a complex understanding of the role of the people in a republican government. As they proclaimed in the Declaration of Independence, governments are instituted to secure the "unalienable Rights" of "all men," and they derive "their just powers from the consent of the governed." However, the Founders also believed that direct popular control of government would be dangerous and undesirable. Thus, James Madison famously argued in Federalist Number 10 that the system of representation they proposed would "refine and enlarge the public views, by passing them through the medium of a chosen body of citizens, whose wisdom may best discern the true interest of their country, and whose patriotism and love of justice will be least likely to sacrifice it to temporary or partial considerations. Under such a regulation, it may well happen that the public voice, pronounced by the representatives of the people, will be more consonant to the public good than if pronounced by the people themselves, convened for the purpose."

The judgments and worries of the Founders regarding "the people themselves" seem rather distant in the 21st century. Living in a proudly "democratic" country that has come to unchallenged wealth and international power, most

Americans today would be hard-pressed to define the difference between a democracy and a republic, much less to defend a preference for one over the other.[1] For most contemporary Americans, democracy means rule by the people, democracy is unambiguously good, and the only possible cure for the ills of democracy is more democracy. The set of ideas that we have referred to as "the folk theory of democracy" is triumphant.

This striking evolution in our popular understanding of democracy reflects—and has probably also contributed to—a long history of periodic frustration with governmental performance. Whenever existing political institutions have seemed to fail, Americans have cast about for "reforms." But in a political culture dominated by a naive view of popular sovereignty, plausible "reforms" must be construed and defended as "more democratic" than the existing institutions they are intended to supplant. As Bruce Cain (2015, 7) put it, "The general drift of American political reform has been to try to fix the problems of representative democracy by creating more opportunities for citizens to observe, participate in, and control their government's actions. There is in American political culture a strong implicit faith in popular sovereignty as the remedy to government corruption, misrepresentation, and incompetence."[2]

This tendency has been reinforced by a paucity of respectable alternative political theories. (It has also been bolstered by self-interested politicians happy to turn the rhetoric of popular sovereignty to their own ends.) Thus, power has repeatedly been withdrawn from political parties and elected politicians and "bestowed" directly on voters. American political history has come to be celebrated as a long battle between ordinary people and a series of grasping oligarchies thwarting the popular will. And the story is inevitably told with a happy ending—a triumph of ever-expanding self-government and popular control.[3]

In this chapter, we scrutinize that self-congratulatory tale by examining how and why some of America's key political institutions have become "democratized," and with what effects. In chapter 2, we surveyed a variety of

1 Fashionable insistence on the distinction in some conservative intellectual circles has probably made little difference in this respect, although the association of republicanism with Republicanism may have added an extraneous partisan coloration to the debate.

2 Cain's study of "America's political reform quandary" assessed these issues and a variety of others—including campaign finance, election administration, redistricting, government transparency, and lobbying regulations—from a perspective quite similar in spirit to ours.

3 Efforts to expand the scope of popular control have sometimes gone hand in hand with efforts to extend enfranchisement, but the two aims are logically distinct. In our view, any defensible definition of democracy, regardless of the precise role it assigns to voters, entails universal adult suffrage.

formidable challenges to realizing the populist ideal in the realm of electoral politics. It would be surprising if a centuries-long process of expanding popular control and "direct democracy" did not entail some substantial pitfalls and unintended consequences stemming from the same underlying difficulties. In our telling, it has.

In the 1950s and 1960s, for example, many American towns and cities decided whether to add fluoride compounds to their drinking water. The scientific evidence that fluoride reduced tooth decay was compelling, and cities whose administrators or city councils made the decision without a referendum overwhelmingly adopted fluoridation. However, when the measure went to the voters, 60% of the time the electorate voted it down. Nor were the losses confined to less educated parts of the country. Cambridge, Massachusetts, home to Harvard and MIT, voted three times, defeating it, then passing it by the narrowest of margins, and then defeating it decisively on the third try (Crain, Katz, and Rosenthal 1969, 4, 48).

Around the country, voters who rejected fluoridation saved themselves a few pennies in taxes per year in return for many unpleasant visits to the dentist and substantial dental bills. Thus, the "more democracy" they had, the more likely they were to harm their finances and their children. Why the self-defeating choices? The simple answer is that the voters were confused. Crackpots, rogue doctors, and extreme right-wing interest groups all fought fluoridation, and many voters, including a substantial fraction of those with college educations, could not sort out the self-appointed gurus from the competent experts.[4]

The same sort of popular confusion has arisen in recent years with respect to childhood immunizations. Parents getting their medical information from unreliable sources have sought to exempt their children from inoculation. In states that have responded to public pressure for easy exemptions, outbreaks of long-suppressed diseases like measles and pertussis have resulted (Centers for Disease Control and Prevention 2015).

In this chapter we consider the two most significant attempts to bring the actual practice of American politics into closer alignment with the folk theory of democracy—the periodic movement to "democratize" party nominations, and the proliferation of initiative and referendum procedures at the

---

4 In this period, the television comedian Jack Paar once had a studio audience consisting mostly of dentists attending a local convention. He asked all those who favored fluoridation to raise their hands. Nearly every hand went up. Those opposed? No hands were raised. "Gee," exclaimed Paar in mock surprise, "I thought it was a controversial issue" (Mueller 1966, 64).

state and local levels.[5] In both these domains, "reforms" have been motivated by a populist desire to increase the influence of ordinary citizens on governmental decision-making. In both domains, reformers have believed that they could increase the influence of ordinary citizens by *reducing* the influence of professional politicians—elected officials and party managers. In this chapter we summarize the history of these "populist" reforms and their all-too-predictable pitfalls. But first, we provide a brief sketch of their intellectual and political roots in the dramatic long evolution of Americans' popular understanding of democracy.[6]

THE TRIUMPH OF POPULAR SOVEREIGNTY IN AMERICAN POLITICAL CULTURE

America was founded in an era in which respectable political thought took a firmly antidemocratic line. In the wake of the English Civil War a century earlier, the Earl of Shaftesbury had argued in parliament that monarchy could be sustained only with the support of an army or the nobility. "If you will not have one, you must have the other, or else the Monarch cannot long support itself from tumbling down into a Democratical Republick." Historian Edmund Morgan (1988, 103) added, "It went without saying that no one wanted England to tumble down there."

When 18th-century political theorists wrote of popular sovereignty, they often had in mind a kind of virtual popular consent that imposed no practical limitations on kings, churches, or the few nascent aristocratic representative bodies. Such theoretical circumspection was wise. Algernon Sidney had been hanged in 1683 for unpublished notes "in which he assigned the origin and limitation of government to the people, with a right to depose rulers who betrayed their trust" (Morgan 1988, 104–105). Even Rousseau, the apostle of democracy writing just a decade before the adoption of the U.S. Constitution, argued that democracy was possible only in small states. His theories posed no direct threat to the French absolutism of his day.

But popular sovereignty in colonial America had a muscular reality that would have shocked and frightened circumspect theorists of virtual popular

5 We do not take up a much older instance of direct democracy—New England town meetings. The available evidence about them is much thinner than that for party reforms and referendums, and scholarly opinion about their performance is mixed (Mansbridge 1980, chaps. 9–11; Bryan 2004).

6 For a more detailed history of American thought regarding populist democracy and its limitations, see de Grazia (1951, chaps. 5 and 6).

consent. In the most "democratic" of the colonies, Rhode Island, "elections were bitterly fought, and fraud—stuffing the ballot box, for example—was not uncommon. . . . The Assembly itself was frequently the scene of disorder: shrill charges, deals, and undignified squabbles. Most Rhode Islanders apparently enjoyed and valued all this political smoke, and the politicians played their parts with enthusiasm if not aplomb. But not everyone found the spectacle of brawling politicians and a large and apparently unstable electorate to his liking" (Middlekauff 1982, 97).

In the run-up to the American Revolution, prosaic grievances such as the Townshend Duties and the Stamp Act were transmuted into occasions for popular resistance to British oppression. Political theory put a glossy sheen on the customary human reluctance to pay taxes. Colonial elites eager to resist British rule exploited popular discontent to bolster their own political standing. Resistance turned to violence. During the agitation over the Stamp Act, Massachusetts representatives of the Crown had their homes burned and their lives threatened by thugs chanting popular political slogans. Local militias were unwilling or unable to stop them. Throughout the colonies, other officials fearing similar fates resigned their offices (Middlekauff 1982, 89–96).

To many respectable observers, the experience of democracy in colonial America simply reaffirmed the lesson of theory and history: the common people were not a reliable foundation for government. Rhode Island's tumultuous populist politics were frequently cited, in the Federalist Papers and elsewhere, as a prime example of unstable democracy.[7]

The understanding of democracy reflected in the U.S. Constitution was shaped by the Founders' intellectual heritage and political experiences. They wanted a stable government with a constitution that would protect prosperous landowners like themselves, as Charles Beard (1913) famously argued. Even Thomas Jefferson, often remembered as a dedicated democrat in a republican age, was anxious to limit the influence of the urban masses (Hofstadter 1973, chap. 1). Thus, the Constitution provided for significant limitations

7 Perhaps fittingly, then, ratification of the Constitution itself became entangled in Rhode Island's contentious debtor-versus-creditor politics. The state held out for three years before finally ratifying, the last state to do so, after several referendums and elections. Adroit maneuvering by Rhode Island politicians to let the legislature decide, together with progress on state debts and the fortuitous absences of key legislative opponents, was necessary to achieve ratification despite substantial opposition among ordinary citizens who could not grasp the momentous implications of remaining outside the new confederation (Conley 1988; Kaminski 1989).

on popular rule, including a separation of powers among largely independent branches of government, federalism, and indirect election of the president and the Senate. Central to the Constitution was a balance between popular forces and experienced leadership. Benjamin Franklin famously called it "a republic, Madam, if you can keep it"—thus suggesting that even a republic with limited democratic elements might be subject to fatal instability.

The American Revolution had been justified in the Declaration of Independence and in much other rhetoric of the time as a legitimate uprising of a sovereign people against a tyrannical king—just the sort of hypothetical possibility envisaged in European theory, though not one that respectable opinion in Britain at the time was prepared to take seriously as a practical possibility. Yet as Morgan (1988, 306) noted, "From its inception in the England of the 1640s the sovereignty of the people has been filled with surprises for those who invoked it."

The revolution brought social turmoil along with political upheaval. The colonial governors and military officials who had been prominent members of upper-crust society in the colonies were gone. Citizen loyalists, too, were discredited; many had fled. The quasi-aristocratic Federalist Party, often frankly contemptuous of ordinary citizens, constructed and then dominated the new government; but their role would prove to be short-lived. By the early 19th century they, too, were gone.

The Federalists' bitter opponent, Thomas Jefferson, became president in 1801, and politics for the next quarter century would be dominated by the proudly self-proclaimed "Democratic Republicans." In that period, American culture and society underwent dramatic change. According to Stanley Elkins and Eric McKitrick (1993, 5), "It can probably be said that the principal components for a structure of norms and social values most appropriate to the working of a capitalist, democratic, equalitarian culture were fully in place by about 1830, though not very much before then."

Arthur Schlesinger, Jr. characterized this period of American history as "the age of Jackson," in honor of the man whose mixed moral character and forceful presidency redefined American politics. Coming to the nation's highest office from a frontier background and military fame in the War of 1812, Andrew Jackson took additional steps toward democratizing the country. Certainly his inauguration, with frontiersmen traipsing through the White House and leaving mud on the carpets, seemed to his countrymen to have begun not just a new administration, but a new era in American politics. Jackson's position in the momentous battle over the National Bank was bolstered by the fact that "everyone, from right to left, believed, with more or fewer qualifications, that sovereignty belonged to the people" and that the behavior of the banks "violated the national faith in popular rule" (Schlesinger 1945, 123). As Elkins and McKitrick noted, when Tocqueville arrived in America it was this new structure of norms and social values that he so memorably described: "The people reign over the American political world as God reigns over the universe," he wrote (Tocqueville 1848, 60). America was tumbling down into a new experiment in large-scale democracy.

Popular rule had become more consequential due in part to the expansion of the franchise. Increasingly, the states modified or eliminated property requirements for voting. Jefferson's party, now known simply as the Democrats, had every incentive to enfranchise immigrants and the poor by reducing property qualifications. The Whigs, the competing party in this era, often moved in the same direction to avoid blame for obstructing the inevitable (Keyssar 2000, chap. 2), even as they bemoaned the fact that "*the Republic has degenerated into a Democracy*" (Wilentz 2005, 425).

The franchise extensions were a significant, if limited, step forward. "Rule by the people," which in practice had often been limited to a minority of white males, now increasingly came to include non-native-born white men and those without property. (Women and African-Americans were, of course, still excluded in Jackson's era and for decades thereafter.)

The convulsion of the Civil War swept away slavery in the South and created yet another set of democratizing reforms. More than any American war before or since, this momentous conflict fought on native soil engulfed the entire country. For many northerners, the long war gradually came to represent a moral crusade, and military victory made the morality of the Union cause a politically irresistible idea. African-Americans were constitutionally enfranchised and increasingly allowed in practice to vote. Though the South would take a long step backward after Reconstruction was ended in the 1870s, and the substance of legal racial equality was tenuous everywhere, nonetheless the principle that all adult males were eligible to vote had become established in most of the country.

The war stimulated the further development of northern manufacturing and Republican political loyalties. Over the next half century, a laissez-faire Republican ascendancy and an industrial jump-start set off a period of nation building and economic expansion. Steamship lines, gold, silver, and copper mines, oil, railroads, lumbering, steel manufacture, banking—all added to the national wealth and created vast personal fortunes. Fabulously wealthy "robber barons," unimpeded by government regulation or income taxes, alienated large numbers of ordinary farmers, miners, and workingmen by their rapacious pricing, abusive labor relations, and bribery of elected officials. State legislatures frequently fell under their control, particularly in the western states. Standard Oil in California, the Anaconda Copper Mining Company in Montana, and several others achieved near strangleholds on their state governments (Olin 1968; Clinch 1970).

The periodic economic contractions that punctuated the development of the industrial United States in the second half of the 19th century enhanced the appeal of third parties. Farmers, facing the most volatile conditions and some of the worst monopoly exploitation by the railroads, were a particular source of political agitation and third-party movements (Hofstadter 1955; Goodwyn 1976). Combining with western miners and southern cotton farmers, the rural protestors coalesced into a broad-based popular movement under the banner of Populism, mounting a third-party presidential campaign in 1892 and becoming a major party in several states. Because they saw themselves in bondage to Eastern monopolies, their platform was antimonopoly. Because they saw themselves in bondage to big-city political machines, their platform was also anti–political party and pro–direct democracy. As before in American history, extension of popular control was seen as the solution to contemporary evils.

During the Panic of 1893 economic distress became widespread. William Jennings Bryan's fusion campaign in 1896, uniting Democrats and Populists, roared through the western states, the South, and parts of the Midwest. Bryan received 80% of the vote in Montana, for example, and the fusion ticket swept Republicans from the state government that year. The campaign frightened the centers of Republican dominance, but William McKinley held the East, the Pacific Coast, and the upper Midwest, and Bryan ultimately fell well short of the electoral votes needed for election. Though he was to run twice more as the Democratic nominee, the Populists and their economic grievances declined rapidly in political importance. With little understanding of the need for party organization and broad coalition building, their political naiveté had proven costly.

The next period of extensive democratization, in the first decades of the 20th century, left a more significant institutional legacy. Heavy immigration was changing the character of American cities, and urban political machines were powerful players in both political parties. Reformers saw boss control, big-city Catholics, and crooked party machines as an unholy coalition that formed the chief obstacle to national political and social progress. Occasional splits in the GOP ranks produced "progressive" candidates running against both Democrats and Republicans. The Progressives eventually became a third-party force in many states, albeit with a distinctly antiparty inclination. The resulting tensions between ideology and organizational needs were to bedevil the Progressives' attempts to displace the two major parties; ultimately the Progressives went the way of the Populists. However, the progressive wings of the two main parties, under the leadership of Theodore Roosevelt and Woodrow Wilson, took a page from the Populists, enacting very limited versions of "trust-busting," labor rights, the income tax, and direct primaries, all of which had their initial legislative successes in this period. Without third-party competition, however, the two principal parties soon lapsed back into political quietism.

The democratic theory animating the Populists and Progressives was the folk theory of democracy. Those ideas directed their reform efforts along a particular path, providing a script for American reform movements that was to have fateful consequences for them and their successors down to the present era. Their allegiance to the folk theory hindered both their theorizing and their practical political efforts. However, to be fair to them, the central theoretical and practical dilemmas they faced remain thorny ones: What is the appropriate role of political parties in a democracy? And when parties stray from that role, how are they to be reformed? We now turn to those conundrums.

"A SIMPLE FAITH IN DEMOCRACY": PARTY REFORM

The internal workings of political parties pose puzzling challenges for democratic theory. Even under the most optimistic assumptions, elections can reflect "the will of the people" only within the limited compass of a fixed choice among candidates, generally those put forward by viable party organizations. Who gets to choose those candidates?

The Founders did not foresee the rise of political parties. To find a doctrine of parties paralleling their view that popular opinion and elite judgment need to be balanced, one must look to later eras. One view, put forth most forcefully by E. E. Schattschneider (1942, 60), is that the role of ordinary citizens in selecting nominees is and can only be highly indirect: "The sovereignty of the voter consists in his freedom of choice just as the sovereignty of the consumer in the economic system consists in his freedom to trade in a competitive market. . . . Democracy is not to be found *in* the parties but *between* the parties."

Like other aspects of the Founders' quest for balance, however, Schattschneider's conception of parties as private associations of political elites, disciplined only by the competitive market of general elections, has fared poorly over the course of American history. Indeed, as V. O. Key, Jr. (1964, 395) noted in a textbook summary of procedural reforms over 150 years, "Each major step in the development of the nominating process has marked a further obeisance to the doctrine that the will of the rank and file of party membership should prevail." According to Austin Ranney (1975, 105), for example, "the earliest party reforms were intended to make parties more representative of their supporters. For the nomination of candidates for statewide offices, the legislative caucuses replaced mass meetings in the capital cities—mainly to better represent, it was said, the party faithful living in other areas. The legislative caucuses then generally gave way to 'mixed' caucuses to better represent party members in districts with no party legislators."

A further step was taken when Andrew Jackson was nominated for his second term by the country's first national party convention, thus removing presidential nominations from congressional caucuses and (putatively) from elite control. Jackson himself profited politically from the arrangement, of course, but the rationale was democratization; as A. Lawrence Lowell (1913, 234) wrote, "the convention was adopted because the legislative caucus was thought undemocratic."

The convention system was considered suitably "democratic" for some 80 years following its adoption, until it was superseded by "the most radical of all the party reforms adopted in the whole course of American history" (Ranney 1975, 121), the direct primary. The direct primary represented an unprecedented attempt to impose the folk theory of democracy on the nominating process. In making the adoption of the direct primary a centerpiece of his 1900 Wisconsin gubernatorial campaign, Robert La Follette appealed to "the sovereign right that each citizen shall for himself exercise his choice by direct vote, without the intervention or interference of any political agency." "No longer," La Follette promised, "will there stand between the voter and the official a political machine with a complicated system of caucuses and conventions, by the easy manipulation of which it thwarts the will of the voter and rules official conduct" (quoted by Ranney 1975, 124–125). La Follette was eventually the 1924 Progressive candidate for president, but the antiparty spirit of that movement is already apparent in these remarks two dozen years earlier. As Key (1942, 373–374) put it, "The advocates of the direct primary had a simple faith in democracy; they thought that if the people, the rank and file of the party membership, only were given an opportunity to express their will through some such mechanism as the direct primary, candidates would be selected who would be devoted to the interests of the people as a whole."

Some canny political scientists were immediately skeptical. For example, Henry Jones Ford (1909, 2) noted that

> one continually hears the declaration that the direct primary will take power from the politicians and give it to the people. This is pure nonsense. Politics has been, is, and always will be carried on by politicians, just as art is carried on by artists, engineering by engineers, business by businessmen. All that the direct primary, or any other political reform, can do is to affect the character of the politicians by altering the conditions that govern political activity, thus determining its extent and quality. The direct primary may take advantage and opportunity from one set of politicians and confer them upon another set, but politicians there will always be so long as there is politics.

Experience with the direct primary system soon confirmed Ford's view. By 1910, an Iowa journalist complained that "the politicians already control the machinery more than they did under the old caucus system, and they are only kindergartners in the business as yet" (Horack 1910, 185). More than three decades later, the leading scholarly observer of political parties noted that "whatever the nature of the nominating process, a relatively small, cohesive group tends to take the lead in organizing support for candidates.... Under the direct primary the party organization remained and changed its methods so as to adapt them to the new machinery of nominations" (Key 1942, 390). But as we will see, the resulting indirect methods of party control were not always successful. The "relatively small, cohesive group" that controlled nominations has often turned out to be a set of unelected, intense minorities or well-heeled private interests. They learned to play the primary nomination game, too, and the simple, honest citizens envisaged by the folk theory were no match for them. The system produced nominees very far from the reformers' expectations.

From the beginning, experience with the primary system has been disheartening. In the early period, the machines learned to herd voters to the polls. The resulting overrepresentation of the lower classes appalled some observers (Millspaugh 1916, 715–716). According to Reynolds (2006, 227–228),

> Like many electoral reforms past and those to come, the direct primary proved to be a disappointment to its most avid supporters.... Low voter turnout mocked the reformers' image of a public-spirited John Q. Citizen impatient to make his voice heard.... By World War

I, enthusiasm for direct nominations had burned itself out across the country. During the 1920s, when political exposés denounced the enormous sums required to win a primary, a brief backlash induced three states to return to the convention system. Despite the disappointment and negative publicity that it aroused, the direct primary remained a fixture of American politics. A cohort of politicians had come to power through its mechanisms and they had no incentive to return to the convention system. If direct nominations chastened those who placed so much confidence in the electorate, the system did address the needs of the hustling candidates who placed it on the statute books.

Whether for these reasons or through simple institutional inertia, the direct primary has remained the predominant mechanism for nominating candidates at most levels of the American political system throughout the past century.

The failures of the folk theory as a guide to party reform became particularly clear in the wake of the remarkably contentious 1968 Democratic presidential nomination contest, which saw the rise of antiwar insurgent Eugene McCarthy, the withdrawal under pressure of incumbent president Lyndon Johnson, riots sparked by the assassination of civil rights leader Martin Luther King, Jr., and the assassination on the final night of the primary season of one of the leading contenders, Robert Kennedy. Despite this tumult, the Democratic convention delegates—most of whom had actually been selected before any of these events occurred—settled on Johnson's political heir, Hubert Humphrey, as their nominee. He lost the general election.

Perhaps unsurprisingly, the apparent unresponsiveness of the delegate selection process to the dramatic events of 1968 provoked demands for democratization. Advocates of reform echoed their predecessors in the Progressive Era, asking "the American people whether or not they will demand a greater voice in decisions affecting the world in which they live or whether they will leave such decisions to professional party elites, officeholders, bureaucrats, or others" (Saloma and Sontag 1972, 352). The Democratic Party's McGovern-Fraser Commission itself announced that "popular control of the Democratic Party is necessary for its survival" (Commission on Party Structure and Delegate Selection 1970, 49).

One consequence of the McGovern-Fraser reforms was to dramatically increase the share of convention delegates selected in primaries, from 40% in 1968 to about 60% in 1972 and more than 70% by 1976—a dramatic change in the mixed system of primaries, caucuses, and conventions that had persisted since the Progressive Era. This consequence seems not to have been intended, or even foreseen, by the reformers themselves. According to Ranney (1975, 205), himself a member of the McGovern-Fraser Commission, "most of the commissioners strongly preferred a reformed national convention to a national presidential primary or a major increase in the number of state presidential primaries. And we believed that if we made the party's nonprimary delegate selection processes more open and fair, participation in them would increase greatly and consequently the demand for more primaries would fade away. But quite the opposite happened."

In his textbook summary of American party reform through the early 1960s, Key (1964, 393) had noted that the direct primary "came in on a wave of belief that here was a means by which the 'people' might rule without much interposition by 'politicians.'" Nevertheless, Key claimed, "Second thoughts have tended toward the view that ways and means should be found by which party organization might play a legitimate and effective role in nominations, a recognition of the elemental necessity for organized leadership in a democratic politics." If so, those second thoughts about the legitimate role of organized leadership turned out to be fleeting; just a few years later, in the pressure of the next political crisis, they were readily set aside in one more attempt to invent "a means by which the 'people' might rule."

The result of the McGovern-Fraser Commission reforms was indeed to produce a more "open" presidential nominating process, with less effective control by party elites and a good deal of instability and unpredictability generated by the complex dynamic interaction among candidates, journalists, the public, and voters in specific primary states (Bartels 1988).[8] In 1972, Democratic insiders overwhelmingly favored Senator Edmund Muskie as their nominee, but Muskie's candidacy collapsed in New Hampshire and the nomination went to liberal maverick McGovern. In 1976, the primaries produced an even more audacious choice, Jimmy Carter—a candidate with such negligible party credentials that a Gallup poll in December 1974 had failed to list him among 31 potential candidates for the Democratic nomination. Meanwhile, on the Republican side, conservative insurgent Ronald Reagan mounted the strongest challenge in living memory to a sitting president—a challenge fueled by a string of primary victories, notwithstanding Gerald Ford's four-to-one advantage in endorsements by party insiders (Cohen et al. 2008, 176). And in 1980 and 1984, endorsement leaders Carter, Reagan, and

8 Although the reforms were initially limited to the Democratic Party, Republicans soon followed suit; by 1976, 70% of Republican convention delegates were selected in primaries.

Walter Mondale all had to survive substantial primary challenges in order to win their nominations.

In their detailed study of "presidential nominations before and after reform," Marty Cohen and coauthors (2008) argued that the disruptions of the nominating process stemming from the McGovern-Fraser Commission reforms were temporary, and that "by the 1980s, both parties were back on an even keel and effectively controlling the nomination process" (Cohen et al. 2008, 159). The effectiveness of that control may be cast in some doubt by the fact that party elites have conspicuously failed to coordinate in three of the four most recent nomination contests.[9] Nevertheless, the preponderance of Republican endorsements for Mitt Romney in 2012 was very much in keeping with Cohen and his colleagues' (2008, 3) emphasis on the efforts of party insiders to "scrutinize and winnow the field before voters get involved, attempt to build coalitions behind a single preferred candidate, and sway voters to ratify their choice."[10]

Of course, popular sovereignty in the presidential nominating process is greatly circumscribed if primary voters merely "ratify" the choices made by party elites. But even with party elites to "scrutinize and winnow the field before voters get involved," the complexity of the choices facing primary voters can be daunting. The most systematic assessment of how well they manage that complexity is Richard Lau's study of "correct voting" in the 2008 primary campaign. According to Lau (2013, 331), "voters in U.S. nominating contests do much worse than voters in general election campaigns, often barely doing better than chance in selecting the candidate who best represents their own values and priorities." For example, in January 2008, in the earliest stage of a three-way race for the Democratic nomination, "barely 30% of Democratic voters managed to select the candidate who, as far as I could tell, best represented

9 In 2004, a record low 5% of Democratic governors endorsed any candidate before the start of the primaries, and eventual nominee John Kerry trailed Richard Gephardt and Howard Dean in weighted endorsements (Cohen et al. 2008, 177). Unpublished tabulations provided by Hans Noel indicate that Republican endorsements in 2008 were split among John McCain (35%), Rudy Giuliani (32%), and Mitt Romney (27%), while Democratic endorsements were split between Hillary Clinton (44%) and John Edwards (43%), with Barack Obama far behind (9%).

10 Noel and his colleagues have not yet tabulated 2012 endorsement data, but blogger Nate Silver and others reported that Romney secured the lion's share of early endorsements (http://fivethirtyeight.blogs.nytimes.com/2011/11/25/romney-dominating-race-for -endorsements/?_r=0). Rick Perry, Herman Cain, and Newt Gingrich all led in the polls at one time or another during 2011, but only Perry garnered significant support from party leaders, and that support dried up after he faltered on the campaign trail.

their own interests"; later in the primary season, with only two remaining candidates (Hillary Clinton and Barack Obama), and after months of additional media coverage of the campaign, that proportion had increased to 56%—"at least now better than chance—but not by much" (Lau 2013, 339).

How has greater popular influence in the presidential nominating process affected the quality of the candidates selected? We know of no authoritative answer to that question. However, historians' ratings of presidents suggest that the quality of *winning* candidates has not improved—and has probably declined—with the advent of a more "open" system in the 1970s.[11] The average quality of presidents was distinctly lower in the first quarter century following reform (from Jimmy Carter through Bill Clinton) than in the preceding quarter century; and early assessments of George W. Bush and Barack Obama suggest that their presidencies will not significantly boost the post-reform average.[12] By this rough test, at least, "obeisance to the doctrine that the will of the rank and file of party membership should prevail" (Key 1964, 395) has entailed real costs.

We have told the story of the extension of the primary system as though it were a battle of ideas. But of course, throughout American history, debates about desirable democratic procedures have not been carried out in the abstract. They have always been entangled with struggles for substantive political advantage. In 1824, "politicos in all camps recognized" that the traditional congressional caucus system would probably nominate William Crawford; thus, "how people felt about the proper nominating method was correlated very highly indeed with which candidate they supported" (Ranney 1975, 66). In 1832, "America's second great party reform was accomplished, not because the principle of nomination by delegate conventions won more adherents

---

11 We thank Kay Schlozman for suggesting a comparison of this sort. Our summary measure of history's judgment of each president is based on the average of four distinct rankings compiled by (1) historian Arthur Schlesinger, Jr. in 1996, (2) the *Wall Street Journal* in 2005, (3) the C-SPAN cable television network in 2009, and (4) Siena College in 2010. Rating presidents is a challenging business, and we are well aware of the inevitable limitations of these four sets of ratings.

12 The average rating of pre-reform presidents since World War II (Harry Truman, Dwight Eisenhower, John Kennedy, Lyndon Johnson, and Richard Nixon) on a 40-point summary scale combining the judgments of numerous historians and other experts is 25.6. The average rating of post-reform presidents (Jimmy Carter, Ronald Reagan, George H. W. Bush, and Bill Clinton) is 19.7. Including Gerald Ford (who won a primary-dominated nomination in 1976, but as an unelected incumbent) in the post-reform group would lower its average rating, increasing the disparity between the two groups. Early ratings of George W. Bush are consistently poor, while those of Barack Obama are somewhat above average (though assessments of recent presidents often alter significantly with the passage of time).

than the principle of nomination by legislative caucuses, but largely because the dominant factional interests . . . decided that national conventions would make things easier for them" (Ranney 1975, 69).

Similarly, Ranney (1975, 122) noted that the most influential champion of the direct primary, Robert La Follette, was inspired "to destroy boss rule at its very roots" when the Republican Party bosses of Wisconsin twice passed him over for the gubernatorial nomination. And in the early 1970s, George McGovern helped to engineer the Democratic Party's new rules for delegate selection as cochair of the party's McGovern-Fraser Commission, and "praised them repeatedly during his campaign for the 1972 nomination"; but less than a year later he advocated repealing some of the most significant rules changes. Asked why McGovern's views had changed, "an aide said, 'We were running for president then'" (Ranney 1975, 73–74).

Group conflict also played a role in reform efforts in every period, perhaps most obviously in the Progressive Era. As with other elements of the Progressive reform agenda, enthusiasm for direct primaries was based in part on the reformers' expectations that the new system would work to the advantage of people like them—typically well-established, prejudiced Protestants appalled by Catholic immigrants and big-city corruption. According to John Reynolds (2006, 160), "The reform element appealed for greater participation in the nominating process, particularly by those commonly referred to as 'the respectable element.' They condemned the influence of those they branded 'the worst class of citizens' at the caucuses and primaries."

Thus no knowledgeable scholar will deny the powerful influence of party strategy and group conflict on the history of American party reform. Yet these battles were not raw power politics. Invocations of the folk theory have always given the proponents of "democratization" a considerable advantage. Hence with a few fits and starts, American history has proceeded steadily away from the sophisticated notions of balance enshrined in the Constitution and inexorably toward a larger direct popular control as envisaged in the simplistic folk theory.

To a lesser extent, the same process has played out in other democratic political systems with equally mixed results. For example, Spies and Kaiser (2014, 585–586) noted that "many Western European parties have reformed their procedures for candidate selection" in ways that produced "more inclusive nomination procedures," but that these reforms "have come along with some unintended and undesired consequences." Systematic comparisons of "inclusive" and "centralized" parties have found that greater "transparency, participation and accessibility of intra-party decisions" makes parties slightly *less* representative of voters than in "centralized" systems where party elites choose the candidates (Hazan and Rahat 2010; Spies and Kaiser 2014).

"THE ABSOLUTE SOVEREIGNTY OF THE PEOPLE": THE INITIATIVE AND REFERENDUM

Just as the adoption of the direct primary represented an attempt to circumvent party bosses and allow every citizen to "exercise his choice by direct vote, without the intervention or interference of any political agency," so also the contemporaneous movement to establish initiative and referendum procedures represented an attempt to circumvent elected legislatures by establishing "the power of the people to make or unmake laws." The aim was nothing less than "to restore the absolute sovereignty of the people—to make this in fact as well as in name, a government of, for and by the people," as one of the leading proponents of direct democracy, Senator Jonathan Bourne, Jr. (1912, 4, 3), put it.

Perceptive observers recognized the initiative and referendum movement as a reflection of dissatisfaction with the day-to-day realities of legislative politics at the turn of the 20th century. For example, A. Lawrence Lowell's study of *Public Opinion and Popular Government* (1913) proceeded directly from a chapter on "Loss of Confidence in Representative Bodies" to one on "Direct Popular Action." According to Lowell (1913, 131), "The growing distrust of legislative assemblies is due partly to the actual defects they have displayed, and partly to popular exaggeration of their faults." Henry Jones Ford (1912, 72) was less measured in his assessment, arguing that "the American people despise legislatures, not because they are averse to representative government, but because legislatures are in fact despicable."

Certainly there was much to despise about the legislatures of the Gilded Age, which were often severely malapportioned in favor of rural interests, heavily influenced by party machines, and directly or indirectly controlled by powerful corporate interests. The head of the Direct Legislative League (quoted by Broder 2000, 32) argued in a 1900 pamphlet that "representative government has been tested on these shores for over a century. In many cases it is better than the older forms. It has been acclaimed a finality. But it has borne its legitimate fruits, and they are the dead sea apples of corruption and insidious injustice. Representative government is a failure. . . . Interest coincides with justice, not in government, but in self-government; not in any form of rule by others, but in pure democracy, where the people rule themselves."

While some proponents of "pure democracy" viewed corruption and injustice as the "legitimate fruits" of representative government, others viewed representative government as legitimate in principle and direct democracy as an extraordinary expedient for addressing the current political crisis. For example, Ford (1912, 70) argued that the leaders of the initiative and referendum movement in Oregon "do not seek to destroy representative government; they want to get rid of a base imitation and introduce the real thing. When they accomplish the reorganization of public authority that they intend, they expect to drop the initiative and referendum out of ordinary use. They will then be kept in reserve simply for emergency use." Presumably Ford would be surprised to learn that the "emergency" afflicting Oregon's representative government has now lasted for more than a century; between 2000 and 2012, Oregon voters considered 107 statewide ballot measures (including initiatives and constitutional amendments referred by the state legislature).

Political scientists of the Progressive Era recognized that it might be "wiser . . . to confine the referendum to questions involving general principles alone, and to the class of matters where the public is normally familiar with the facts required for a decision, than to extend it promiscuously to questions where a rational opinion can be formed only by a knowledge of details with which the ordinary man does not readily become acquainted" (Lowell 1913, 161). Unfortunately, they could suggest no reliable means for distinguishing matters on which ordinary citizens might be expected to have rational opinions from those that would be best left to legislatures.

Lowell (1913, 184–185) argued that "the size of the vote is a measure of public interest in the matter; and hence an indication of the extent to which the people are likely to have studied the facts necessary for a decision, and thereby formed a genuine opinion about the law. A decision by a majority of the votes actually cast upon a question is doubtless the most natural method to pursue in the case of a popular vote, but that such a result expresses public opinion may sometimes be a political fiction rather than a fact." In extreme cases, this sort of "political fiction" might be obvious to all; Lowell (1913, 188) pointed to cases in Massachusetts and Michigan where constitutional amendments were adopted despite being approved by fewer than 3% of those who went to the polls. However, that sort of judgment could be made only in retrospect, and in any case an initiative procedure justified as a way "to restore the absolute sovereignty of the people," as Senator Bourne had it, could not easily be reconciled with any systematic recognition of the possibility that "public opinion may sometimes be a political fiction rather than a fact."

Ironically, the institutions of direct democracy themselves were often established on the basis of less than overwhelming popular support. Table 3.1 provides a summary of statewide votes on measures establishing initiative and referendum procedures, popular recall of public officials, and related Progressive institutional reforms from 1904 through 1912; these measures were culled from Lowell's (1913) complete list of statewide initiatives and referendums during this formative period. In each case, the table shows the yes and no votes as percentages of the total election turnout, as well as the "roll-off"—the percentage of voters who went to the polls but did not vote on the specific measure listed.

It is clear from the results presented in table 3.1 that direct democracy almost always garnered plurality support when put to the voters. Indeed, in 16 of the 17 cases in the table, yes votes outnumbered no votes; the sole exception was a 1910 effort to expand the role of initiatives, referendums, and recall in Oregon, which had already accumulated extensive experience with those institutions.[13] On the other hand, it is also striking that a third or more of voters failed to vote on many of these measures, and most of the measures that were adopted actually failed to win support from a majority of those who showed up at the polls. For example, proposals for a general initiative procedure and recall of public officers on the 1912 Nevada ballot garnered pluralities of eight- and ten-to-one among those who cast votes, but still failed to win absolute majorities because almost half the voters who went to the polls declined to support or oppose them. Maine and Colorado had similar experiences. The Progressive stronghold of Minnesota, however, required an absolute majority at the polls to approve a constitutional amendment to establish the initiative and referendum. Despite very large pluralities in favor at two successive attempts, roll-off doomed the measure. The effort to establish the initiative and referendum in Minnesota then went into abeyance for more than half a century (Achen and Bartels 2007).

The record of voting behavior on "direct democracy" measures in the early 20th century may seem to suggest that initiatives and referendums only rarely registered what Lowell referred to as "genuine opinion." However, it is instructive to contrast the parallel record of voting behavior in a domain in which public interest seems to have been a good deal higher. Table 3.2 presents the results of all 15 statewide initiative and referendum votes between 1904 and 1912 pertaining to prohibition, local option, and liquor licensing and

---

13 Lowell (1913, Appendix B) lists two statewide initiatives in Oregon in 1904, 11 (including constitutional amendments) in 1906, 19 in 1908, and 32 in 1910.

Table 3.1. Referendum and Initiative Votes on Direct Democracy, 1904–1912

	Yes (%)	No (%)	Roll-off (%)
Direct primary law, Oregon, 1904	56.6	16.5	26.9
For direct legislation on local affairs, Oregon, 1906	49.4	17.3	33.3
Act instructing legislators to vote for U.S. senator receiving highest popular vote, Oregon, 1908	59.7	18.1	22.1
To make all public officials subject to recall, Oregon, 1908	50.1	26.6	23.4
To extend the initiative, referendum, and recall, Oregon, 1910	30.8	36.9	32.3
Direct primary law, Maine, 1911	46.7	15.4	37.9
To extend the recall to all public officers, Arizona, 1912	68.6	15.6	15.8
To provide for the recall of all elective officials, Arkansas, 1912	42.4	34.6	23.0
To provide for recall of public officers, Colorado, 1912	20.4	15.0	64.6
To provide that ballots at elections shall not contain party lists of candidates, Colorado, 1912	16.5	15.0	68.5
To provide for recall by the people of judicial decisions holding laws unconstitutional, Colorado, 1912	21.1	15.5	63.4
To create direct primaries, Montana, 1912	58.2	16.1	25.6
For direct nomination of U.S. senators, Montana, 1912	57.2	15.6	27.2
For direct vote on party preferences on candidates for president, Montana, 1912	58.0	15.2	26.8
To introduce a general initiative for constitutional amendments and laws, Nevada, 1912	49.7	5.1	45.2
To subject all public officers, state and local, to recall, Nevada, 1912	48.1	5.9	46.0
Direct primary law proposed by initiative, but enacted by legislature, South Dakota, 1912	45.7	25.8	28.5
Average	45.8	18.2	35.9

Including votes on initiative and referendum, recall of public officials, nonpartisan ballots, primaries, and direct election of U.S. senators.
Tabulations based on data provided by Lowell (1913, Appendix B).

Table 3.2. Referendum and Initiative Votes on Prohibition, 1904–1912

	Yes (%)	No (%)	Roll-off (%)
Local option liquor law, Oregon, 1904	43.6	40.5	15.9
For local option, Oregon, 1906	36.6	46.7	16.7
To provide a state agency for sale of liquor, Oklahoma, 1908	41.3	47.6	11.1
To give local governments exclusive power to grant licenses for sale of liquor, etc., Oregon, 1908	33.8	44.9	21.3
For licensing, restricting, and regulating manufacture and sale of intoxicating liquors, South Dakota, 1908	34.3	36.4	29.3
Prohibition of the sale of liquor, Missouri, 1910	30.9	63.3	5.8
To introduce local option, Oklahoma, 1910	41.2	49.5	9.3
To regulate the sale of intoxicating liquors, Oregon, 1910	35.5	52.9	11.7
To prohibit manufacture and sale of intoxicating liquors, Oregon, 1910	36.2	50.9	12.9
On intoxicating liquors, South Dakota, 1910	40.1	52.3	7.6
Repeal of prohibition of the sale of liquor, Maine, 1911	42.6	43.1	14.2
Prohibition law, Arkansas, 1912	40.1	49.3	10.6
Amendment for statewide prohibition, Colorado, 1912	28.9	44.4	26.7
To enforce liquor laws by search and seizure, Colorado, 1912	24.6	30.1	45.3
To give to cities and towns the exclusive right to regulate liquor licenses, Oregon, 1912	44.3	42.2	13.4
Average	36.9	46.3	16.8

Including votes on prohibition, local option, and liquor licensing and regulation.
Tabulations based on data provided by Lowell (1913, Appendix B).

regulation. On most of these votes, more than 85% of those who went to the polls voted Yes or No; the average roll-off was less than half that in table 3.1. In Maine in 1911, repeal of prohibition failed narrowly, drawing less than 15% roll-off. In Colorado in 1912, more than twice as many voters saw fit to express their views about prohibition as about popular recall of public officers or nonpartisan ballots. Clearly, voters could be moved to vote on issues they viewed as important in their day-to-day lives; but for many, the political institutions and procedures of "direct democracy" did not rise to that level, even in an era of unusual political ferment. Citizens in the Progressive Era seem not to have been much different in this respect from the politically disengaged contemporary citizens we portrayed in chapter 2.

"THE PEOPLE THEMSELVES"?

A century after the wave of Progressive Era reforms, more than 20 U.S. states have had substantial experience with direct democracy in action.[14] What light does that experience shed on the virtues and pitfalls of "pure democracy"?

One key question is whether the establishment of initiative and referendum procedures has, in fact, shifted power from political elites and special interests to ordinary citizens, as Progressive Era reformers had hoped. From the start, skeptics claimed that "what the initiative really does is to transfer that function [of framing laws] from official lawmakers to non-official lawmakers. But every such non-official lawmaker, being self-appointed and extra-constitutional, occupies an irresponsible position very similar to that of the party machine boss who holds no public office" (Hollingsworth 1912, 38).

Indeed, it did not take long for "non-official lawmakers" to begin to exploit opportunities for political entrepreneurship under direct democracy. According to the "father and chief apostle" of Oregon's direct democracy movement at the turn of the 20th century, W. S. U'Ren, "just as soon as we got the initiative and referendum through we organized the 'People's Power League' to back up measures we wanted the people to vote on." Asked whether "the people of Oregon always vote the way you want them to," U'Ren replied, "They always have thus far" (Hollingsworth 1912, 39–40).

Concerns about behind-the-scenes influence in the initiative process have recurred throughout the century-long history of direct democracy in the

---

14 A tabulation by the Initiative & Referendum Institute listed 27 states with initiative or referendum processes (including 21 with both). All but a handful of these processes were established in the first two decades of the 20th century.

American states. For example, V. O. Key, Jr. and Winston Crouch (1939, cited by de Grazia 1951, 157) observed of California in the 1930s that "the initiators of propositions have usually been pressure organizations representing interests—commercial, industrial, financial, religious, political—which have been unable to persuade the legislature to follow a particular line of action." In a 2000 book titled *Democracy Derailed*, political journalist David Broder similarly argued that "wealthy individuals and special interests . . . have learned all too well how to subvert the process to their own purposes" (Broder 2000, 243). "Though derived from a reform favored by Populists and Progressives as a cure for special-interest influence," Broder wrote (2000, 1, 167), "this method of lawmaking has become the favored tool of millionaires and interest groups that use their wealth to achieve their own policy goals—a lucrative business for a new set of political entrepreneurs. . . . What was striking to me as I traveled the initiative states was the discovery that so many of the measures had been designed by a handful of people and were being sold with their dollars. Whether their motivations were financial or ideological, they had mounted this Populist warhorse and were riding it hell-for-leather to achieve their own purposes."

Another 15 years later, Bruce Cain—a political scientist with extensive practical experience in California politics—argued that attempting "to check or bypass representative government" via direct democracy simply empowers "a new class of election entrepreneurs" by delegating to them the tasks of "formulating policy, organizing the effort to get something on the ballot, and providing voters with the information and cues they need to make a decision." Whereas "average citizens will sporadically give input to government when something really matters to them," Cain (2015, 8–9) noted, "organized interests are a constant presence."

Pessimistic assessments of the relative influence of "average citizens" and "organized interests" are common among observers of the initiative process. However, a more systematic analysis by John Matsusaka of the policy consequences of employing the initiative process has challenged the notion "that special interests use the initiative to thwart the will of the voters" (Matsusaka 2004, 53). Comparing fiscal policies in states with and without the initiative process over a period of three decades, Matsusaka identified three significant differences:

- First, "the initiative reduces total government spending" by about 4%.

- Second, "the initiative shifts spending from state to local governments."

- And third, "the initiative shifts the sources of revenue from taxes to user fees and charges for services," allowing "fewer possibilities for redistribution of wealth" (Matsusaka 2004, 52).

Drawing on survey data from a variety of sources, Matsusaka argued that each of these policy shifts was broadly consistent with the preferences of ordinary Americans and, plausibly, with the preferences of ordinary citizens in the affected states.

Now in one sense, Matsusaka's findings are utterly unsurprising. Any policy adopted by referendum or initiative must, *by definition*, be preferred by a majority of voters—and probably, barring substantial biases in turnout, by a majority of citizens—to the status quo. However, as we noted in chapter 2, the range of policies that can be sold to a majority of the voters may be very broad indeed, leaving plenty of room for "wealthy individuals and special interests" to further "their own purposes," as Broder put it, through agenda-setting and framing. The tax reductions that Matsusaka finds in initiative states are particularly likely to disproportionately benefit the prosperous.

This sort of selective appeal to popular opinion is especially likely in narrower, complex, less salient policy domains where public preferences are unclear or nonexistent.[15] However, the fundamental indeterminacy of public preferences is sometimes evident even on highly salient issues. An unusually clear example arose when voters in a Houston referendum declined to abolish the city's affirmative action program. According to a *New York Times* report (Verhovek 1997),

> The fundamental truth that seems to have emerged from the debate here is that the future of affirmative action may depend more than anything else on the language in which it is framed. . . . Affirmative-action

15 In November 2012, for example, Californians voted on initiatives concerning tax treatment of multistate businesses, labeling of genetically engineered foods, human trafficking penalties, whether auto insurance pricing should vary with drivers' histories of insurance coverage, and State Senate redistricting, among other issues. In Oregon, voters decided whether to eliminate real estate transfer taxes, authorize a casino in Multnomah County, ban commercial salmon fishing with gillnets on the Columbia River, and change the terminology referring to the three branches of state government in the state constitution.

proponents around the nation hailed not just the result of Houston's vote, but the phrasing of the referendum as a straight up-or-down call on affirmative action, and they said that is the way the question should be put to voters elsewhere. Its opponents, meanwhile, who are already in court challenging the City Council's broad rewording as illegal, denounced it as a heavy-handed way of obscuring the principles that were really at stake.

Who is to decide what principles are "really at stake" in a policy choice like the one facing voters in Houston? If we accept, at least for the sake of argument, that a referendum employing the wording originally proposed by opponents of affirmative action would have passed, as opinion polls indicated and most observers seem to have believed, would that result have been more or less legitimate than the actual, opposite result? The doctrine of "direct democracy" provides no sensible way to answer such questions.

In any case, even policies that are unambiguously preferred by a majority of citizens to the status quo may or may not be *good* policies in the broader sense of comporting with citizens' interests. Matsusaka (2004, 71) was careful to emphasize that his evidence "does not tell us whether the initiative process is a good or bad form of government. The evidence simply shows that the initiative promotes the will of the majority." However, a broader literature review coauthored by Matsusaka and Arthur Lupia was much less circumspect in this regard, arguing that "every such study to date [assessing the impact of direct democracy on policy] points to higher-quality (or no worse) decisions when the institutions of direct democracy are available" (Lupia and Matsusaka 2004, 475).

What constitutes a "higher-quality" decision? As Lupia and Matsusaka (2004, 474) acknowledged, "it is difficult to come up with an objective definition of a good or bad policy." Thus, the evidence they offer ranges from anodyne ("in this respect, the initiative process does not lead to prima facie irrational public policies") to heroically indirect (Swiss survey researchers "find happier people in cantons with more direct democracy, after controlling for income and other demographics").

Any balanced assessment of the impact of direct democracy would have to weigh evidence of this sort against more concrete evidence from a variety of studies of specific instances of government by initiative in which "the will of the majority" has produced policies that are seemingly at odds with citizens' interests. For example, one of the more popular uses of initiatives in the modern era has been to impose term limits on elected officials. In the early 1990s, term limit measures were approved by voters in 20 of the 24 states allowing initiatives.[16] Although some of these measures were subsequently struck down by courts, voters have shown considerable persistence in supporting term limits; for example, Nebraska voters approved successive term limit initiatives in 1992, 1994, 1996, and 2000.[17]

Supporters of term limit initiatives have displayed little regard for the cautions of political scientists regarding the likely unintended consequences of these measures. For example, in the run-up to the vote on California's term limit initiative, political scientist Nelson Polsby (1990) argued that "term limitations just shift power from elected officials to the relatively inaccessible officials, bureaucrats and influence peddlers who surround them." Polsby's assessment is broadly consistent with subsequent evidence from surveys of state legislators in states with and without term limits, which found that legislative leaders lost significant influence in the term-limited states, while governors, legislative staffs, and bureaucrats gained influence (Carey, Niemi, and Powell 1998).

Thad Kousser's (2005) detailed examination of the impact of term limits documented a variety of negative implications for legislative performance—as Kousser's title summarized it, a "dismantling of state legislative professionalism." For example, legislative committees received less deference in states with term limits, presumably because "shortened time horizons reduce the incentives of members to specialize in a policy area" (Kousser 2005, 206). In addition, "term-limited legislatures play a diminished role in crafting the state's budget," a pattern Kousser (2005, 207) attributed to "less politically canny" legislators "giving up more ground to the executive branch" in budget negotiations. Finally, term-limited legislatures "produce less innovative policies," as gauged by their lesser utilization of flexibility in federal program guidelines and by their lower receipt of innovation awards from the Council of State Governments (Kousser 2005, 207). Meanwhile, contrary to the expectations of proponents, "term limit initiatives have not filled legislatures with citizen members" (Kousser 2005, 205); instead, experienced professional politicians

16 Our tabulation is based on the list of statewide initiatives on the website of the Initiative & Referendum Institute, www.iandrinstitute.org.

17 In 1995 the U.S. Supreme Court invalidated state-mandated term limits for federal office holders. State courts have overturned a variety of successful term limit initiatives on narrower grounds. Courts have also overturned "informed voter laws" designed to pressure members of Congress to institute federal term limits (for example, by printing the phrase "disregarded voters' instructions on term limits" on the ballot if they failed to support a constitutional amendment imposing term limits).

have mostly been replaced by less experienced professional politicians moving up the career ladder from local government positions.

More recently, proponents of electoral reform have turned from term limits back to the nominating process. A century ago, the establishment of direct primaries marked the triumph of "the doctrine that the will of the rank and file of party membership should prevail," as Key (1964, 395) put it. But why, recent reformers ask, if popular sovereignty is our paramount value, should the choice of nominees be left to "the rank and file of party membership" rather than to the public as a whole?

In some states, "open primaries" have long allowed nonmembers to participate in the choice of party nominees. In 1996, California voters adopted a constitutional amendment instituting a "blanket primary" in which primary voters could choose on a race-by-race basis which party's primary to participate in. Although blanket primaries were subsequently declared unconstitutional by the U.S. Supreme Court, the short-lived experiment provided an opportunity to gauge the impact of more "open" primary rules. The result, according to a study by Will Bullock and Joshua Clinton (2011, 916), was that elected officials "move[d] away from the ideological extremists in their own party after the adoption of the blanket primary," but only in "the most moderate districts—of which there are increasingly fewer." Thus, "simply allowing more registered voters to participate in primaries is unlikely to be the panacea for elite polarization in legislatures that many believe." A broader study by Eric McGhee and his coauthors likewise suggested that "the openness of a primary election has little, if any, effect on the extremity of the politicians it produces" (McGhee et al. 2014, 337).

Not to be deterred, California voters in 2010 adopted another formula for instituting a more "open" primary process, the so-called top two primary system. The top two system takes the logic of popular sovereignty one step further by replacing separate party primaries with a single ballot listing all the candidates for a given office regardless of their party affiliations; primary voters vote for any one, and the top two vote-getters, regardless of party affiliation, advance to the general election. According to one prominent proponent, replacing party primary elections with the top two system would be "a direct, simple fix" for the "hyper-partisanship and legislative dysfunction now gripping American politics."[18]

---

18 Phil Keisling, "To Reduce Partisanship, Get Rid of Partisans," *New York Times*, March 21, 2010.

In its first test, in 2012, the California top two primary seemed no more effectual than previous reforms; the *Los Angeles Times* headlined, "Few Centrists Advance in California's New Primary System."[19] A survey experiment comparing vote choices under the old and new ballot rules (Ahler, Citrin, and Lenz 2013, 33) helped to explain why: "Voters need fine-grained knowledge of candidates' positions to vote as advocates of electoral reform predict they will upon the adoption of open primaries. Voters in the 2012 California primaries struggled to distinguish between candidates from the same party and were especially unfamiliar with challengers' positions. As a result, although voters tended to be moderate and a sizeable portion were willing to break party ranks, the average voter was ill-equipped to do so in a way that led them to select more centrist candidates in contests for House and state Senate."

Of course, to say that the top two primary has (so far) been ineffective in achieving the stated aim of its proponents is not to prove that it is a bad policy. More experience and broader analysis will be necessary to weigh its advantages and disadvantages. However, it does seem clear that the simplistic hopes of its backers were torpedoed by voters' lack of "fine-grained knowledge"—a lack that has loomed large in many criticisms of direct democracy more generally. As Cain (2015, 6) noted, "populist" reform is likely to fail "when it overestimates citizen capacity and commitment and when it ignores the critical role that intermediaries inevitably play in any large democracy."

CITIZEN COMPETENCE AND THE PRICE OF POPULAR CONTROL

In *The Age of Reform*, Richard Hofstadter (1955, 260–261) explicated the Progressives' enthusiasm for the folk theory of democracy by describing the mythical "Man of Good Will" at "the core of their conception of politics": "It was assumed that somehow he would really be capable of informing himself in ample detail about the many issues that he would have to pass on, and that he could master their intricacies sufficiently to pass intelligent judgment. Without such assumptions the entire movement for such reforms as the initiative, the referendum and recall is unintelligible." As we saw in chapter 2, contemporary political scientists have found little evidence of ordinary citizens mastering the intricacies of political issues. Nonetheless, some political scientists, at least, have expressed considerable confidence in the ability

19 Michael J. Mishak and Anthony York, "Few Centrists Advance in California's New Primary System," *Los Angeles Times*, June 7, 2012.

of ordinary citizens to exercise effective popular sovereignty via initiatives and referendums through the same sorts of heuristic processes we considered there. For example, Lupia and Matsusaka's (2004, 467) literature review highlighted "a frequent finding in new studies of direct democracy . . . that voters are competent to make the kinds of policy decisions with which direct democracy confronts them." Sometimes, of course, the issues underlying an initiative are simple or consensual, and the voters get it right. But can they do so when genuine policy complexities are involved?

The primary empirical evidence cited in support of the optimistic view came from Lupia's (1994) own exit poll of 339 Los Angeles voters on a series of five 1988 auto insurance initiatives. Lupia measured both detailed knowledge of the provisions of the various initiatives and knowledge of the insurance industry's position on each initiative. He found that "respondents who possessed relatively low levels of factual (or encyclopedic) knowledge about the initiatives used their knowledge of insurance industry preferences to emulate the behavior of those respondents who had relatively high levels of factual knowledge" (Lupia 1994, 72). According to Lupia and Matsusaka (2004, 468), this finding "demonstrated that voters can use simple pieces of information as substitutes for the detailed information that political surveys show them to lack."

Alas, as James Kuklinski and Paul Quirk (2000, 158) pointed out, "being *relatively* well informed falls far short of being well informed."[20] Lupia's *relatively* well-informed voters overwhelmingly supported a proposal mandating a 20% rollback of auto insurance rates—a superficially appealing but shortsighted (and, as it turned out, unworkable) attempt to repeal the law of supply and demand.[21] Thus, "the evidence from the California referendum

20 Lupia's knowledge measure was based on 20 questions with binary responses. The median knowledge score was 12, only slightly better than chance; almost 30% of the respondents scored below 10, worse than they should have by guessing randomly. Moreover, the main effects of knowledge on vote choices on most of the propositions were modest in magnitude (and quite imprecisely estimated), suggesting that the information captured by the knowledge scale was probably of rather limited relevance even to those who possessed it.

21 According to law professor Stephen Sugarman (1990, 683), "in the two years since its adoption Proposition 103 has primarily provided employment for lawyers, actuaries and expert witnesses in the field of insurance. Many of its key provisions have yet to be implemented, and, looking down the road, there is good reason to doubt that any of its substantive goals will be achieved absent additional changes in the law." A decade later, a consumer watchdog group noted that "most insurance rates in California remained frozen" for five years "pending conclusion of the legal challenges and final compliance by insurance companies with the rollback requirement." In 1995, a new insurance commissioner "lifted the rate freeze and has since stirred controversy by refusing to implement or enforce many of 103's statutory requirements, including the 'prior approval' process, despite excessive premium levels in the state."

suggests that even relatively well informed citizens responded heavily to extraneous factors—dislike of insurance companies and wishful thinking about their rates, for example—rather than making an informed assessment of the merits" of the five proposals on the ballot (Kuklinski and Quirk 2000, 158).

The only other empirical evidence cited in support of the claim "that voters are competent to make the kinds of policy decisions with which direct democracy confronts them" (Lupia and Matsusaka 2004, 467) came from Shaun Bowler and Todd Donovan's book, *Demanding Choices: Opinion, Voting, and Direct Democracy*. Lupia and Matsusaka (2004, 469) quoted Bowler and Donovan's (1998, 168) conclusion that voters "appear able to figure out what they are for and against in ways that make sense in terms of their underlying values and interests. . . . Just as legislators do, these voters make choices purposefully, using available information."

In most domains, making choices on that basis would be considered a very low standard of competence. One would not want to engage a surgeon or fly with a pilot who proposed to "make choices purposefully, using available information." Indeed, Donovan and Bowler's evidence is by no means uniformly optimistic in its implications for the quality of policies adopted via direct democracy. For example, Broder (2000, 219) cited Donovan and Bowler in support of the view that "the tax limitation measures (like Prop. 13) that pass so readily when presented to the voters often have the perverse effect of reducing expenditures on popular public services—like parks and libraries—below what the public wants."

Oddly, Lupia and Matsusaka's survey of the effects of direct democracy made no mention of California's Proposition 13, which set off a national "tax revolt" by sharply limiting and redistributing the state's property tax burden. In ignoring the single most consequential policy adopted by initiative in the modern era, Lupia and Matsusaka also overlooked the single most detailed empirical analysis of voters' decision-making under direct democracy, David Sears and Jack Citrin's book-length study of Proposition 13 and related tax and spending issues. Sears and Citrin (1985, 217) found

> little evidence that voters reasoned very carefully from their basic preferences about taxation and spending and the effects they forecast of these tax-reform measures, to a vote decision. Nor did the rationalizations

---

See "Background on Insurance Reform—A Detailed Analysis of California Proposition 103" (http://www.consumerwatchdog.org/feature/background-insurance-reform-detailed-analysis-california-proposition-103).

for self-interest, however logically "appropriate," always direct people to the equally appropriate vote decision. For example, it was not primarily the public employees' self-protectiveness toward their own wages that led them to oppose the tax revolt, nor did parents' preferences about school spending affect their votes on Proposition 13 any more strongly than non-parents' preferences affected theirs. Throughout our data the voters seem to respond to symbols in an affectively consistent but not necessarily logical or reasoned way.

Sears and Citrin (1985, 217) grappled with the apparent irrationality of voters wanting "something for nothing," as the subtitle of their book put it:

> Throughout most of the tax revolt period the electorate wanted "smaller government" but also the same or increased spending on specific services. . . . But this combination quite clearly involves a logical tension, and there were no other beliefs that we could add into that particular equation that would render that combination more sensible. We thought that perhaps voters believed services could be maintained, and government shrunk, as well, if only waste were eliminated. Or perhaps the inconsistency held primarily among unsophisticated voters, who might not realize the two goals were incompatible; or that voters equated "big government" with some especially unpopular services (such as welfare), and wanted to cut those but maintain others thought to be more essential (such as police and fire protection). Or perhaps voters were indulging a wish-fulfilling mood when responding to surveys, and only confront the hard tradeoffs between taxes and services when faced with them explicitly at the ballot box. But none of these escape routes succeeded in explaining away this basic anomaly: it prevailed even among people believing in small amounts of waste, the most sophisticated voters, and both liberals and conservatives.

When voters insist on getting "something for nothing," the cost is likely to be higher than they realize. One striking example of perverse consequences comes from an unusually careful empirical study of the impact of direct democracy on the actual quality of government services, Jeff Tessin's (2009) analysis of fire protection services in Illinois.[22] In the early 1990s, some

---

22 The findings presented in Tessin's 2009 Princeton University dissertation have not been published. Thus, with his permission, we summarize them in some detail here.

counties in Illinois began requiring local governments to obtain voter approval for increases in property tax levies exceeding the rate of inflation. The referendum requirement was instituted in five suburban counties bordering Chicago in 1991, in Cook County (including Chicago) in 1994, and (on the basis of county-wide referendums initiated by county boards) in 34 downstate counties over the subsequent 13 years. Tessin exploited both geographical and temporal variation in this institutional requirement to examine the impact of tax referendums on the quality of fire protection services provided by Illinois fire districts—special districts akin to school districts that operate largely independent of county governments.

As Tessin (2009, 87–88) noted, there is relatively little political disagreement regarding the desirability of high-quality fire protection, and a good deal of consensus among experts about "how to measure the quality of fire services in practice." Moreover, local idiosyncrasies in proposing and adopting referendum requirements meant that affected and unaffected downstate fire districts were similar in many key respects. (Tessin excluded Chicago districts from his analysis due to lack of a comparable area with different laws.) Thus, this seemingly narrow case allows for an unusually compelling empirical assessment of the impact of popular control on the quality of an important public service.

As might be expected based on Matsusaka's (2004) findings, Tessin found that fire districts affected by the referendum requirement experienced slower growth in tax revenues. With a variety of potentially important demographic and political characteristics statistically controlled, Tessin found that districts with referendum requirements experienced average annual revenue growth of 3.9%, as compared with 6.2% in districts without referendum requirements. As a result, the typical household's property tax bill increased by 43 cents less per year in districts with referendum requirements ($1.07 versus $1.50).

What would those additional 43 cents annually have bought? According to a retired fire chief interviewed by Tessin, the referendum requirement significantly constrained the resources of affected fire districts, causing them to reduce training and defer maintenance and replacement of capital equipment. The result was a measurable degradation in the quality of fire protection services. Using data recorded in the National Fire Incident Reporting System, Tessin showed that the average response time across all Illinois fire districts during the period covered by his analysis was 11.5 minutes—far above the widely accepted 4- to 5-minute adequate response standard. But in fire districts with referendum requirements, average response times were almost one minute (about 7%) higher than in comparable districts without referendum requirements. He noted (2009, 94–95) that this difference is "substantively large based on widely-accepted fire safety standards" and "represents a serious decline in public safety." Moreover, the impact of the referendum requirement on average response times appeared to increase the longer the requirement was in force, from about 45 seconds in the first four years following implementation of the referendum requirement to 80 seconds thereafter, presumably reflecting the cumulative effect on training and equipment maintenance and replacement of smaller tax increases over several years.

Tessin (2009, 96–97) considered the possibility that "voters rationally traded lower taxes for higher response times." However, he noted that "most citizens want to maintain or improve fire services, even when survey questions draw attention to the trade-off between services and spending," and that, in any case, "the tax savings that voters enjoyed may have been smaller than what they would have saved on their homeowners insurance policies with better fire protection." Thus, he concluded that "given more power over policy inputs, voters produced worse outcomes than those produced by the counterfactual institutions, in which public officials had more independence from public opinion."

The risks of inadequate fire protection were seen in graphic form during the 1991 Oakland Hills Firestorm in California. This terrifying fire "destroyed more than 3000 homes, killed 25 people and seriously injured more than 150 others during a 24 h[our] period" (Simon and Dooling 2013, 1415). According to the Federal Emergency Management Agency (FEMA), longstanding drought conditions and high winds made the firefighting difficult, but the 1978 passage of the Proposition 13 tax-cutting initiative exacerbated the difficulties. The proposition eliminated a number of firefighting companies and reduced the staffing of those that remained. Funds for removal of dead trees were also cut drastically. When the fire began, the result was an uncontrollable conflagration for many hours. Although detailed voting data for the fire-stricken area itself seem to be unavailable, the sad irony is that the victims had probably voted heavily for Proposition 13: the Piedmont area of Oakland, at the edge of the fire, had voted 73% in favor (Simon and Dooling 2013, 1420). Direct democracy had overruled the judgment of fire professionals, with horrific results.

Of course, most results of direct democracy are less dire. Tessin found cases in which provisions increasing direct public control of policy produced no discernible decline in the quality of government services. For example, laws requiring voter approval of bonds to pay for sewers and prisons had no apparent ill effects on the frequency of sewer overflows or prison overcrowding. Yet even this seemingly good news for the folk theory turned out to be illusory. The voters continued their self-defeating votes in these elections. But they were saved by public officials who quietly created work-arounds to keep the voters from harming themselves, using "a variety of tools, such as user fees and unguaranteed bonds, to adopt their preferred policies over the median voter's objection" (Tessin 2009, 196). However, "the elite discretion needed to maintain performance is not always cost-free. . . . Because unguaranteed bonds typically have higher transaction costs, due to higher interest rates and the need for more services from banks and bond lawyers, voters pay a price for a largely symbolic form of popular control. The quality of prisons and sewers are no different under direct and representative democracy, but public officials must spend significant time, effort, and tax dollars to compensate for voter-imposed spending cuts" (Tessin 2009, 198).

Whereas Tessin's analysis focused on the impact of more direct public control on government spending and performance, Michael Sances's (2015) analysis of property tax assessments in New York towns focused on the impact of electoral accountability on the equity and efficiency of governments' tax policies. Gradually over a 25-year period, hundreds of New York towns switched from electing to appointing their property assessors.[23] Comparing assessments in the same towns before and after the switch (allowing for persistent differences across towns and statewide fluctuations from year to year), Sances found that direct election of assessors reduced the probability of conducting an assessment in any given year by 9 percentage points, increasing the average time between reassessments from about five years to nine years. The main effect of less frequent assessments was to benefit affluent homeowners at the expense of others; Sances estimated that directly electing assessors increased the average advantage in effective tax rates for the most expensive homes (relative to the least expensive homes) by 26 percentage points. In this instance, greater "electoral accountability" mostly seems to have involved catering to the interests of an affluent (and probably more attentive) minority of the electorate.

The lesson we draw from these studies is not that some direct popular control of policy-making is always undesirable. Rather, it is often costly, sometimes frighteningly costly—and a political culture that uncritically equates "good government" with "more democracy" will be ill equipped to sensibly weigh the benefits of greater popular control against the costs.

---

23 These institutional changes, which cut against the broader trend toward more popular oversight or even direct involvement in the making of public policy, were adopted under pressure from the state government.

CONCLUSION

As a blueprint for government, the folk theory is hopelessly flawed. Primaries and referendums with no admixture of party or legislative influence exemplify the failure. Overlooking "the elemental necessity for organized leadership in a democratic politics" (Key 1964, 393) has produced a mishmash of heightened responsiveness to popular impulses, behind-the-scenes elite influence, and self-defeating choices stemming from the limited political expertise and attention of ordinary citizens. Something different is needed to break the cycle of blind plebiscitary reforms and ensuing political dysfunction.

That is not to suggest that every aspect of American politics has been sufficiently democratized. For example, we suspect that American government would function better if the poor were better organized and more economically secure, if turnout in elections were higher and more equal, and if campaigns were financed with public funds rather than with contributions from billionaires, ideologues, and special interest groups. In Cain's (2015) terms, these are instances in which "populist" and "pluralist" reform impulses point in the same direction. But contemporary thinking about democracy is too often simplistic in its understanding of the role of the public in the democratic process. In consequence, it provides little help in creating political institutions that would make ordinary people's interests more effective in government decision-making.

As we have emphasized, the Founders believed that popular preferences needed to be tempered by political experience and judgment. That is, they believed in both political leadership and popular influence—neither would be right all the time, but balance would help correct the flaws of each. Thus they opposed both kingship and majoritarianism.

Nowadays, we often cloak our political practices in the Founders' authority while downplaying or even rejecting the importance of leadership in their political thinking. In this regard, Charles Beard did us a great favor. By reminding us of the wealth and conservatism of the Founders, Beard's classic *Economic Interpretation of the Constitution* (1913) made the tensions between contemporary thinking about popular rule and the logic of the revered Constitution psychologically manageable. The republican principles of the Founders are now conveniently dismissed as the elitist and aristocratic trappings of a bygone era. Hence, coping with the deep differences between their sophisticated ideas and our simplicities, which would not be easy, becomes happily unnecessary.

This conceptual laziness has consequences. Faced with the inevitable occasional failures of our political institutions, we cast about for curative measures. But we have only one cure we trust. Throughout American history, calls for "political reform" have nearly always entailed calls for greater "democratization." But the medicine has rarely been applied thoughtfully. It is as if we prescribed powerful antibiotics for every illness. Sometimes they have cured, sometimes they have been a harmless waste, and sometimes they have caused organ damage, seizures, or psychosis.

In their influential early study of primary elections, Charles Merriam and Louise Overacker alluded to criticisms of the then-still-new mode of popular participation in the nominating process. "Most of the objections raised against primaries," they wrote in the conclusion of their book (1928, 355), "apply to elections as well as to universal suffrage, and to the whole plan of democracy. Disbelievers in popular government are constantly asserting that many are incompetent, that many are indifferent, that many are lax, lazy, and drifting, that nothing can come from this mediocre mass of yokels and boobs, that the mass should abdicate in favor of the few and kiss the rod that condescends to rule them, thanking God that they are allowed to live and be cared for by their betters—these are common charges among those to whom modern democracy is unwelcome."

Merriam and Overacker's shrill dismissal of the critics of primary elections betrays a moral certitude regarding the nature and value of "modern democracy" that is perhaps even more common now than it was when they wrote, in the immediate wake of the Progressive Era.[24] Now, as then, standing up for "popular government" in opposition to "the few" conveys an immediate and more or less automatic rhetorical advantage. Even writers whose professional expertise will not let them pretend that people are attentive or well informed find it helpful to wrap themselves in the flag in their uplifting conclusions. We have argued in this chapter for a quite different understanding of American democratic history, one in which simplistic faith in "popular government" has often outpaced its usefulness as a practical mechanism for policy-making.

In America, as elsewhere, the movement toward greater power for ordinary citizens began as an overdue corrective against centuries of domination by military, economic, religious, and cultural elites. For centuries, "more democracy" was a good idea as well as an appealing ideal. But nothing that simple is a defensible all-purpose theory of government. In time, democratization

---

24 Their dismissal of concerns about citizen competence also seems at odds with their own qualms about voters, expressed earlier in the same book (Merriam and Overacker 1928, 288): "Simple comments often seem astonishing to the electors, who appear not to know in what world they are living."

cured many of the evils that had initially animated the demand for popular control. Despotic governments, corrupt aristocracies, and restrictions on suffrage were swept away. But because popular understandings of democracy provided no clear recipe for reconciling popular control with competent leadership, the cure of "more democracy" went on being applied in every crisis. The adoption and expansion of direct primaries, initiatives, and referendums demonstrate the influence of this view on American political thought and practice in the Progressive Era and since.

On this "populist" view, representative institutions are, at best, unfortunate substitutes for direct democracy, necessitated by the inconvenience and expense of frequent plebiscites. When we must have representation, the representative should be an *instructed delegate*, someone who goes off to the legislature to mechanically vote the preferences of her district as recorded in opinion polls. However, modern technology is swiftly reducing the inconvenience and expense of frequent plebiscites in ways even the Progressives could not have imagined. Recently, a congressional staffer turned technology entrepreneur launched Capitol Bells, a smartphone application that lets constituents "vote" in real time on bills being considered on the House floor. According to one enthusiastic commentator, "It's like the Holy Grail of civic engagement: Letting Americans participate in the process of legislating." Eventually, the developer promised, "lawmakers will be able to gauge how well they're representing their most engaged constituents by looking at differences in the last 20 or 30 votes."[25]

We see little reason to think that letting lawmakers' "most engaged" constituents "participate in the process of legislating" every time their phones chime would improve either the process of legislating or the product. Edmund Burke and James Madison, among many others, favored a very different model of representation, the *trustee model*. On this view, elected officials ought to use their own judgment to look out for the best interests of their district and their country, regardless of what their constituents believe. But this perspective flies in the face of the simplistic enthusiasm for "more democracy" in modern American political culture. As the majority of respondents in one recent survey had it, "The will of the people on most issues is pretty clear, and politicians should just follow it."[26]

25 Brian Fung, "You Can Now Cast Votes Alongside Your Congress Member, in Real Time," *The Switch* blog, *Washington Post*, July 29, 2013 (http://www.washingtonpost.com/blogs/the-switch/wp/2013/07/29/you-can-now-cast-votes-alongside-your-congress-member-in-real-time/).

26 YouGov survey, May 2012; 55.6% of the respondents agreed with the statement (23.5% "strongly"), while 19.5% disagreed (3.1% "strongly").

In the wake of Warren Miller and Donald Stokes's (1963) landmark study of "Constituency Influence in Congress," political scientists, too, have largely taken to studying political representation by measuring the fidelity with which elected representatives "just follow" the preferences of their constituents, whether on broad issue dimensions of the sort analyzed by Miller and Stokes or specific roll call votes or overall liberal-conservative ideology (e.g., Miller 1964; Converse and Pierce 1986; Bartels 1991; Esaiasson and Holmberg 1996; Clinton 2006; Bafumi and Herron 2010). Even when subsequent scholars have not explicitly endorsed the instructed delegate model of representation, they have often implicitly accepted it as the appropriate benchmark for empirical analysis (as noted by Achen 1978, who ended by accepting it himself). The influence of the trustee model has declined substantially by comparison, due in no small part to the fact that "judgment" and "best interests" are much harder to measure than the constituency preferences reflected in opinion polls.

Alas, as we saw in chapter 2, empirical studies of representation grounded in the instructed delegate model have produced very mixed results. The positions of elected officials are usually no more than mildly correlated with those of their constituents. Apparent disparities are persistent and sometimes substantial, notwithstanding the pressures toward congruence arising from electoral competition. Whether those disparities are attributable to—or plausibly justifiable in terms of—a trustee model of representation is, for now, simply unknown.

Faced with that fact, and with an eye toward the manifest failures of the folk theory, many political scientists have devoted increasing attention to a different conception of the meaning of elections, closer in spirit to the trustee model. In this alternative conception, the point of elections is not to mimic the policy outcomes of "direct democracy" by constraining elected officials to pursue the policy preferences of their constituents. Ordinary citizens have too little free time for political study and thought to make that theory work well. Rather, elections are seen as a mechanism by which voters can hold elected officials accountable, after the fact, for the success or failure of whatever policies they choose to pursue.

This alternative view, which we set out in chapter 4, has seemed to many scholars to offer a more tenable and appealing model of democracy than the folk theory. In chapters 5, 6, and 7, we assess how well this alternative model of democracy works in practice.

CHAPTER FOUR

A Rational God of Vengeance and of Reward? The Logic of Retrospective Accountability

> What is more dramatic than the spectacle we have seen repeated, and doubtless long shall see—the popular judgment taking the successful candidates on trial in the offices—standing off, as it were, and observing them and their doings for a while, and always giving, finally, the fit, exactly due reward?
>
> —Walt Whitman, *Democratic Vistas* (1871, 31)

> To support the Ins when things are going well; to support the Outs when they seem to be going badly, this, in spite of all that has been said about tweedledum and tweedledee, is the essence of popular government.
>
> —Walter Lippmann, *The Phantom Public* (1925, 126)

The developments in survey research, political psychology, and social choice theory summarized in chapter 2 severely undercut the intellectual foundations of the folk theory of democracy. Fourth of July rhetoric notwithstanding, the hope that elections could ensure "the continued responsiveness of the government to the preferences of its citizens" (Dahl 1971, 1) seemed to many students of democracy increasingly hollow in light of mounting evidence regarding voters' opinions and behavior. Absent some reliable mechanism for eliciting meaningful popular preferences and aggregating them into a coherent policy prescription, what, concretely, should a "responsive" democratic government actually do?

No wonder, then, that when a less demanding version of democratic theory began to draw renewed attention in the 1960s, it was greeted with considerable enthusiasm—if not by political philosophers or ordinary citizens, at least by political scientists who spent their time studying public opinion, elections, and the policy-making process. The underlying idea was not new, but its explicit and detailed formulation as a defense of democracy brought it fresh respectability.

The key insight of this alternative theory of democracy was that voters could exert substantial control over their leaders, despite knowing little about the details of public policy, simply by assessing the *performance* of incumbent officials, rewarding success and punishing failure. In one of the first and most influential formulations of this perspective, V. O. Key (1966, 61) portrayed "the electorate in its great, and perhaps principal, role as an appraiser of past events, past performance, and past actions. It judges retrospectively; it commands prospectively only insofar as it expresses either approval or disapproval of that which has happened before."

This *retrospective theory* of political accountability seems to provide a compelling way to think about the relationship between leaders and citizens in democratic political systems. Empirically, it accounts for fluctuations in the electoral fortunes of incumbent leaders and parties much more successfully than any spatial theory of issue voting. Moreover, it rescues political leaders from their fate as hapless automatons "converging" on the policy preferences of the median voter in the spatial theory—or, perhaps more realistically, as demagogues pretending to cater to the garbled voice of the people. In Key's words (1958, 590), "the most acute ear attuned to the voice of the people can sense only the vaguest guidance for innovation to cope with the questions that must be met day by day as an Administration governs. The efficacy of self-government thus depends on party and governmental leadership with the initiative and imagination necessary to meet the public problems that develop and with the courage to assume the political risks involved." The retrospective theory gives political leadership its due, leaving initiative in the hands of elected officials to further voters' well-being by any feasible and legitimate means at their disposal.

The normative appeal of the retrospective theory stems in no small part from the fact that it seems to save voters from the charge that they are too uninformed or too disengaged to play a meaningful role in the democratic process. For example, Morris Fiorina (1981, 5) argued that retrospective voters "need *not* know the precise economic or foreign policies of the incumbent administration in order to see or feel the *results* of those policies. . . . In order to ascertain whether the incumbents have performed poorly or well, citizens need only calculate the changes in their own welfare. If jobs have been lost in a recession, something is wrong. If sons have died in foreign rice paddies, something is wrong. If thugs make neighborhoods unsafe, something is wrong. If polluters foul food, water, or air, something is wrong." By dispensing with the unrealistic notion that ordinary citizens vote on the basis of detailed preferences regarding every issue that might conceivably come before their future leaders, the theory of retrospective voting made the rather bleak portrait of poorly informed, habitual political behavior provided by the survey researchers of the 1950s and 1960s, if not quite irrelevant, at least not fatal. Voters need only monitor their own and their fellow citizens' day-to-day experiences and well-being.

The seminal works of Key (1966), Fiorina (1981), and Gerald Kramer (1971) all portrayed retrospective voting as evidence of the fundamental rationality of American voters and elections. For example, Kramer (1971, 140) characterized his analysis as demonstrating that election outcomes "are not 'irrational,' or random, or solely the product of past loyalties and habits, or of campaign rhetoric and merchandising." Fiorina (1981, 4) insisted that American democracy "functions better than one would expect, given behavioral political science's destruction of old illusions," and discerned "rough justice" in the electoral punishment meted out to incumbent politicians by American voters in the elections of 1932, 1952, 1958, 1968, and 1974. And Key (1966, 7) famously put the "perverse and unorthodox argument" of his book in a nutshell: "voters are not fools."

As often happens, a coherent account of retrospective voting within the framework of rational choice theory (Ferejohn 1986; Rogoff 1990; Banks and Sundaram 1993; Fearon 1999) came along only after considerable empirical evidence establishing the substantive importance of the phenomenon had already piled up. Nevertheless, the development of coherent accounts of why "rational" citizens might be expected to engage in retrospective voting— and might benefit from doing so—added considerably to the theory's normative appeal. In fact, two distinct accounts of that kind were produced. Much of the present chapter is devoted to summarizing them.

While we attach great importance to the realism, empirical power, and normative appeal of the retrospective theory, we believe that its implications for democracy are less unambiguously positive than existing literature tends to suggest. In particular, the theory as it stands fails to do justice to the very considerable logical and informational difficulties faced by retrospective voters attempting to assess "changes in their own welfare," as Fiorina put it, and to translate those assessments into meaningful evaluations of incumbent political leaders.

For one thing, it is by no means obvious that voters can "ascertain whether the incumbents have performed poorly or well" simply by calculating "changes in their own welfare," as Fiorina claimed. If jobs have been lost in a recession, something is wrong, but is that the president's fault? If it is not, then voting on the basis of economic conditions may be no more sensible than kicking the dog after a hard day at work.[1] An even more fundamental problem is that voters may have great difficulty accurately assessing "changes in their own welfare." Proponents of retrospective voting have routinely assumed that voters *know* when "thugs make neighborhoods unsafe" or "polluters foul food, water, or air," as Fiorina put it. But that is by no means obvious. To the extent that voters' assessments of their own well-being are erroneous, retrospective voting will succeed much less well in selecting good leaders and in disciplining them to pursue voters' interests.

We believe that these difficulties are more serious than previous scholars of retrospection have generally thought. As a result, we are left with a much more measured view of the extent to which retrospective voting justifies "a portrait of citizens moving to considered decision as they play their solemn role of making and unmaking governments" (Key 1966, 4).

EVIDENCE OF RETROSPECTIVE VOTING

Politicians and political observers have long believed that voters punish failure and reward success, especially in the management of the economy.[2] President James Buchanan blamed his party's dismal showing in the 1858 midterm election on economic distress resulting from the Panic of 1857 (Huston 1987, 166–168). And no less a politician than Benjamin Disraeli recognized the electoral significance of bad harvests in 19th-century Britain.[3] In 1879, he wrote to a colleague that "the only danger and difficulty which the present Ministry has to encounter are natural.... After four bad harvests in this country, we are apparently about to meet a fifth dearth" (Monypenny and Buckle 1929, 1347). Sure enough, in a disastrous election the following spring the Tory government fell.

The spatial model of party competition outlined in chapter 2 provides no help in understanding politics of this sort. As Donald Stokes (1963, 373)

---

1 Fiorina (1981, 202, emphasis original) noted in passing that the normative appeal of the theory of retrospective voting hinges in significant part on the assumption "that the *electorate does a passable job of attributing responsibility to government decision makers.*" However, his brief discussion of the problems raised by that assumption focused almost entirely on the issues of divided government and responsible parties, rather than on the more basic questions considered here.

2 William Keech (2013) provided a comprehensive review of theory and evidence related to "pocketbook voting."

3 We are indebted to W. Phillips Shively for this reference.

argued in his insightful critique of Anthony Downs's version of the spatial model, "throwing the rascals out is very different from choosing between two or more parties on the basis of their advocacy of alternatives of government action." Stokes insisted upon the electoral significance of "*valence*-issues ... that merely involve the linking of the parties with some condition that is positively or negatively valued by the electorate" in contrast to "*position*-issues" of the sort represented in Downs's model: "in American presidential elections of the past generation it is remarkable how many valence-issues have held the center of the stage," from depression and recovery in the 1930s and 1940s to the Korean War and corruption in 1952 to America's international prestige in 1960.

Political scientists in the subsequent half century have provided a great deal of more systematic evidence regarding the political significance of Stokes's "valence-issues." Key's evidence in *The Responsible Electorate* consisted primarily of statistical analyses of the correlates of vote-switching from one presidential election to the next. For example, in each of Franklin Roosevelt's reelections, poorer people and blue-collar workers—the presumed beneficiaries of New Deal policies—were less likely than wealthy people and those in business and professional occupations to report having switched their votes from Democrats to Republicans (Key 1966, 35, 37). Moreover, people who reported supporting specific policies of the incumbent administration—compulsory old-age insurance in 1936, the Wagner Labor Act in 1940, the Korean War in 1952—were less likely to defect than those who reported opposing those policies (Key 1966, 43, 47, 75, 97). And, most important for Key's argument, people who approved of the incumbent president's performance were more likely to "stand pat," even when the incumbent himself was not on the ballot, as in 1960 (Key 1966, 139).[4]

In *Retrospective Voting in American National Elections* (1981), Fiorina elaborated and extended Key's analyses in a variety of ways. He incorporated a wider variety of retrospective assessments—ranging from presidential

4 While Key emphasized the electoral significance of retrospective judgments of incumbent policies and performance, he clearly supposed that voters were forward-looking as well as backward-looking. Indeed, he reported even stronger statistical relationships between *prospective* judgments and vote choices than between *retrospective* judgments and vote choice. In Gallup data from 1960, for example, vote-switchers overwhelmingly rated the party they supported as "best for people like yourself," "more likely to keep the United States out of World War III," better at "keeping the country prosperous," and better at handling the "most important" specific problem facing the country (1966, 124, 125, 127, 133). Obviously, the causal status of judgments of this sort is far from clear. Did voters in 1960 support Nixon because they thought he would keep the country out of war, or did they think he would keep the country out of war because they already supported him?

performance to avoiding war to personal financial circumstances—in statistical analyses of vote choices in a dozen presidential and congressional elections (Fiorina 1981, 35–43). He used repeated interviews with the same survey respondents to document the impact of retrospective evaluations on shifts in partisan identification (Fiorina 1981, 94–102). And he examined the extent to which "mediated retrospective evaluations"—assessments of incumbent performance—were grounded in "simple retrospective evaluations"— assessments of economic and other conditions as good or bad (or improving or deteriorating) without reference to government, political parties, or the president (Fiorina 1981, 108–129).

Scholars following in the footsteps of Key and Fiorina have generated a substantial body of research relating individuals' expressed retrospective judgments to their vote choices. Most of this work focuses specifically on judgments of national economic conditions or personal economic circumstances or both (Kinder and Kiewiet 1981), rather than on the broader variety of retrospective assessments examined by Key and Fiorina. Although most of the evidence comes from the United States, similar patterns of retrospective voting have been documented in many other countries (Lewis-Beck 1988; Duch and Stevenson 2008).

Virtually all of this work is subject to much the same methodological criticism we raised with respect to empirical studies of "issue voting" in chapter 2: observed cross-sectional relationships between retrospective evaluations (for example, assessments of incumbent performance or perceptions of the economy) and vote choices may reflect the electoral impact of retrospective evaluations, but they may also reflect the extent to which retrospective evaluations are constructed to *rationalize* vote intentions whose real causes lie elsewhere.[5] Indeed, as Kramer (1983) pointed out, in a single snapshot survey *real* national economic conditions are a constant, so *all* of the observed variation in *perceived* national economic conditions must reflect partisan bias,

---

5 Key clearly recognized this possibility, but downplayed its practical importance on grounds that seem distinctly tangential. The "relationship between policy outlook and vote," he wrote (1966, 45–46), "doubtless reflected to a degree the tendency of a voter on a specific question to improvise policy views that seem to be consistent with the way he planned to vote for other reasons entirely. A steadfast Democratic partisan might have been expected to opine that the 'Roosevelt administration has done a good job in handling the farm problem,' if the question were put to him in that form. Yet, however such opinions come into being, their supportive function in the political system should be the same." While it is true that even "rationalizing" retrospective judgments may have a "supportive function," the fact that they are not genuine *causes* of voting behavior seems to us to be the key point.

overgeneralization from personal experience or local conditions, and other vagaries of individual perception.

As in the case of issue voting, it is possible to get some traction on this possibility by analyzing data from repeated surveys of the same individuals. Gabriel Lenz's analyses along these lines provided a striking contrast between the apparent causal impact of voters' policy preferences on one hand and their performance evaluations on the other. As we noted in chapter 2, Lenz (2012, 216) found "surprisingly little evidence" that policy preferences "carried much weight in voters' judgments" once he allowed for the reciprocal impact of vote intentions on policy preferences. However, his parallel analyses of performance evaluations provided "further evidence of the importance of performance-related issues, such as the economy. Although politicians, journalists, and scholars often interpret elections ideologically," Lenz concluded (2012, 225), "a growing body of evidence suggests that it is the economy and other performance domains, not ideology, that largely explain election outcomes. My results support this view."

In the case of economic voting, the ready availability of objective economic data provides additional leverage for disentangling the causal relationship between retrospective assessments and vote choices. While economic perceptions and evaluations may be colored by politics, income and unemployment statistics have an independent reality that may (or may not) be manifested in voting behavior. Insofar as it is, the connection cannot simply be a matter of voters rationalizing choices unrelated to the actual condition of the economy. Thus, systematic analyses of the aggregate-level relationship between economic conditions and election outcomes may complement and bolster analyses showing that individual voters' economic perceptions shape their electoral behavior.[6]

Harold Gosnell and various coauthors produced a series of remarkably sophisticated and politically acute studies of the relationship between economic conditions and election outcomes in the New Deal era (Gosnell and Gill 1935; Gosnell and Schmidt 1936; Gosnell and Pearson 1939; Gosnell

---

6 Of course, the aggregate-level relationship between objective economic conditions and election outcomes need not be attributed solely to retrospective voting. For example, economic growth may inspire wealthy campaign donors to contribute to the incumbent's re-election campaign, providing resources to buy votes without the voters themselves knowing or caring about the state of the economy (Bartels 2008, 116–122). However, the strength of the relationships between economic conditions and aggregate economic perceptions and between economic perceptions and voting behavior leaves little doubt that most of the aggregate-level relationship is indeed attributable to retrospective voting of one sort or another.

and Cohen 1940; Gosnell and Coleman 1940; Gosnell 1942). Using an impressive variety of economic and political data from Chicago, Iowa, Pennsylvania, and Wisconsin, and statistical tools that would not come into general use in the social sciences until a quarter century later, they demonstrated that voters' recent economic circumstances did indeed appear to influence election outcomes.

The line of research advanced by Gosnell made little further progress over the next few decades, as scholars of electoral politics turned their attention to the exciting new possibilities for detailed individual-level analysis offered by the advent of scientific opinion surveys. However, the study of economics and elections was reinvigorated by the publication of Kramer's 1971 article on "Short-Term Fluctuations in U.S. Voting Behavior, 1896–1964." Whereas Gosnell and his colleagues had focused on single states or localities over relatively short periods of time, Kramer analyzed the relationship between national economic conditions and the national congressional vote across 34 biennial elections.[7] He examined the electoral relevance of a variety of economic indicators, including real income, unemployment, and inflation, as well as the effects of congressional incumbency and presidential coattails. He concluded that economic fluctuations—most notably, election-year changes in real per capita income—"are important influences on congressional elections, . . . account[ing] for something like half the variance of the congressional vote, over the period considered" (Kramer 1971, 140–141).

Scores of scholars following in Kramer's wake have examined the impact of economic conditions on election outcomes in the United States and elsewhere.[8] While various aspects of the relationship—including the magnitude and timing of electoral responses to specific economic conditions, the psychology linking economic conditions to voters' choices, and the implications of institutional and contextual variation—are far from settled, a virtual

---

7 Kramer (1971, 135) regarded congressional elections as providing the clearest possible test of retrospective theory, "since of the races for national office, House contests come closest to the Downsian case of relatively anonymous candidates competing as members of a common party team." His statistical analysis suggested that presidential elections "are substantially less responsive to economic conditions" (Kramer 1971, 141). However, subsequent analyses—most of which have focused on the post–World War II era—have consistently found larger effects of economic conditions in presidential elections than in congressional elections (for example, Erikson 1989; 1990).

8 Lewis-Beck and Stegmaier (2007) provided a broad survey of relevant literature. For U.S. presidential elections, Bartels and Zaller (2001) compared a variety of alternative measures of economic performance and probed the robustness of the statistical results to variations in model specification.

consensus has emerged that the electoral impact of economic conditions is real and substantial.

RETROSPECTIVE VOTING AS A MECHANISM FOR SELECTING COMPETENT LEADERS

The most straightforward way to interpret retrospective voting is as an attempt by voters to select the best available team of political leaders. In this view, there are consequential differences among the competing parties in any given election—differences in motivation, competence, ideology, or some combination of these and other factors. These differences imply differences in future personal or collective well-being, at least in expectation.[9] The voters' problem is to forecast future well-being under each of the competing parties and choose the one offering the most favorable prospects.

This interpretation of retrospective voting portrays voters as rational and forward-looking; but their *prospective* choices are rendered *retrospective* through the auxiliary assumption that the parties' past performance in office can generate rational expectations about future performance. In the influential formulation of Anthony Downs (1957, 106, 39), "rational behavior is impossible without at least some way of forecasting future events. . . . Since one of the competing parties is already in power, its performance in period *t* gives the best possible idea of what it will do in the future, assuming its policies have some continuity."

While the basic logic of retrospective selection is straightforward, the precise implications for voting behavior depend on the nature of the presumed relationship between past performance and future prospects. Assuming for the sake of argument that the voter's well-being under the incumbent party in the most recent period provides "the best possible idea" of its future performance, how informative is that? And how informative is earlier experience with the incumbents, or with the "out" party? Does the diagnostic value of past experience vary with turnover in personnel or changes in social conditions?

The appendix to this book sets out a simple mathematical model of retrospective selection providing a framework for addressing questions of this

9 Political scientists have generated a substantial literature focusing on the distinction between "sociotropic" assessments of the national economy and "pocketbook" assessments of personal economic well-being (Kinder and Kiewiet 1981; Kramer 1983; Markus 1988). For our purposes, it does not matter whether voters define well-being individually or collectively; any consistent desideratum will suffice to ground a retrospective theory of democracy.

sort. The model assumes that a representative voter's *electorally relevant subjective well-being* under the incumbent is determined by a simple combination of the incumbent's intrinsic competence and random factors outside the incumbent's control—good or bad luck.[10] The problem, from the voter's perspective, is to infer as much as possible about the incumbent's intrinsic competence, and thus about her likely performance in the next period if she is reelected.

If the incumbent's intrinsic competence does not vary over time, or varies purely randomly with no correlation across time periods, the best available estimate of her competence is simply the average well-being experienced under her leadership in the current and previous periods. An important implication of this fact is that a rational voter's assessment of the incumbent's competence will take into account performance in every relevant period, not just in the current period. In Fiorina's (1981, 84) felicitous phrase, the rational voter maintains a "running tally" of subjective well-being under the incumbent, updating it continually on the basis of good or bad experience. Thus, retrospection provides a basis not only for vote choices in a given election but also for more or less durable partisan preferences—what Fiorina (1977) called "a political theory of party identification."

If we relax the assumption that the incumbent's competence is constant over time, then our voter should form his forecast of the incumbent's future competence somewhat differently, depending upon exactly how competence is supposed to evolve over time (Gerber and Green 1998; Achen 2012). In general, however, the possibility of changes in competence makes previous experience less relevant, leading voters to attach relatively more weight to more recent experience.

The efficacy of the voter's effort to select a competent incumbent in this framework obviously depends on the quantity and quality of evidence provided by prior experience. If the continuity of party leadership is minimal, a party's past performance may have little bearing on how well it will perform in the future. If voters' subjective well-being is determined more by extraneous

---

10 We focus here on a single representative voter. More generally, one might posit a parallel relationship for each voter, with individual-specific well-being determined by individual-specific incumbent competence and individual-specific doses of luck. Doing so would add empirical plausibility at the cost of considerable strategic complexity. As Hibbs (2006, 570) noted, if voters' retrospective judgments are heterogeneous, "incumbents could pursue a divide and rule strategy by exploiting distributive conflicts in the electorate, and thereby mitigate, or perhaps avoid completely, the discipline of having to satisfy a minimal standard of macroeconomic performance augmenting aggregate welfare."

events such as droughts or oil price shocks than by the quality of the incumbent's policies and management, electoral rewards and punishments may often be misdirected. However, to the extent that voters' past political experience does shed light on the likely quality of future leadership, they can and should weigh that experience when they go to the polls.

RETROSPECTIVE VOTING AS A MECHANISM FOR SANCTIONING LEADERS

The logic of retrospective voting as a mechanism for selecting competent leaders is fairly straightforward. However, it may be more surprising that retrospective voting can promote voters' well-being even when there are *no differences in competence* among potential leaders. As long as incumbents (or their parties) desire reelection, the knowledge that voters at the next election will reward them for success or punish them for failure provides incentives for leaders to maximize voters' well-being as best they can. As Fiorina (1981, 11) put it, "Given political actors who fervently desire to retain their positions and who carefully anticipate public reaction to their records as a means to that end, a retrospective voting electorate will enforce electoral accountability, albeit in an *ex post*, not an *ex ante*, sense."

To explicate this logic, the appendix sets out a second model of retrospective voting in which variation in incumbent competence plays no role (Ferejohn 1986). Incumbents and challengers are assumed to be identical; the issue of political accountability is a simple matter of "moral hazard" of the sort familiar from economic models of principal-agent relationships (Laffont and Martimort 2002). The current incumbent may be tempted to focus on other goals besides maximizing voters' subjective welfare,[11] and voters cannot directly monitor how diligently the incumbent is working on their behalf. However, they can tell when they experience pain or pleasure, and they know that their pain or pleasure is attributable, in part, to the incumbent's efforts.

In contrast to the retrospective selection model, the *sanctioning* model assumes that each voter's electorally relevant subjective well-being depends solely on the amount of effort expended by the incumbent leader on the

---

11 In the theoretical literature, this is often labeled "shirking." We think the image conjured up by that label, of politicians sitting around with their feet up on their desks, is inapt; however, models of this sort can be used to explore the implications of a much broader class of competing goals that might tempt incumbent leaders to deviate from doing whatever will maximize their prospects for reelection—including graft, courageous leadership on behalf of their constituents' long-term welfare, or anything in between.

voter's behalf and on the net effect of random forces beyond the incumbent's control. "Luck" plays much the same role in this model as in our model of selection on the basis of incumbent competence, representing the impact on the voter's well-being of factors unrelated to the incumbent's effort. However, we assume that the voter cannot directly observe the incumbent's expenditure of effort or distinguish the effects of effort and luck; thus, his decision whether or not to return the incumbent leader to office for the next period is governed by the sum of both factors.

In this second model, the incumbent knows that her probability of reelection depends in part on how much effort she exerts on the voters' behalf. However, she also knows that her fate depends in part on good or bad luck. Moreover, since effort devoted to increasing the voter's subjective well-being is presumed to be costly—it may require foregoing graft, ideological goals, or the esteem of future historians—incumbents weigh the opportunity cost of exerting effort on the voters' behalf against the potential benefit of reelection.

For their part, voters cannot directly control or even observe the incumbent's exertion of effort. However, they can decide whether or not to reelect the incumbent based on good or bad outcomes attributable, in part, to the incumbent's level of effort. They want to choose a standard for reelection that will elicit as much effort as possible from incumbents. Intuitively, one might think that they should set the standard as high as possible, since their expected well-being is always higher when incumbents exert more effort on their behalf. However, setting the standard too high actually discourages effort; if incumbents know they are unlikely to get reelected whatever they do, they are more likely to shirk. Indeed, in equilibrium, it turns out that voters should always set the standard for reelection so that the incumbent's *ex ante* probability of reelection will be .5, regardless of whether that standard turns out to induce incumbents to exert a little or a lot of effort on their behalf. Thus, an interesting implication of the model is that we should expect incumbents to be reelected half the time.[12]

Nevertheless, the voters' expected well-being is greater when their assessment of the incumbent's performance depends less on luck and more on incumbent effort, since in that case the incumbent can expect a closer correspondence between exertion and reward (in the form of reelection). In that

12 David Mayhew (2008) has noted that, historically, incumbent U.S. presidents running for reelection have succeeded approximately two-thirds of the time. That success rate can be derived formally from a model that allows for differences in perceived competence between incumbents and challengers (Achen 2016), unlike the model we discuss here.

respect, the primary implication of the model focusing on variation in incumbent effort parallels that of the model focusing on variation in incumbent competence: Retrospective voting can be a powerful mechanism for electoral accountability, but only insofar as voters can discern and set aside irrelevant factors contributing to their subjective well-being.

CHALLENGES TO THE EFFECTIVENESS OF RETROSPECTIVE ACCOUNTABILITY

Jonathan Bendor, Sunil Kumar, and David Siegel (2010, 31) have argued that "it is important to start with a model of retrospective voting that is consistent with the strongest patterns uncovered by empirical students of voters: what voters know and how they think." We heartily agree, and the models of retrospective voting set forth in the appendix do just that. They focus (as voters mostly do) on ends rather than means, and they allow for the fact that voters' assessments of individual and collective well-being will only imperfectly reflect the competence and effort of political leaders.

The positive implication of these models is that retrospective voting can promote democratic accountability in two distinct ways—by selecting good leaders and by inducing leaders to exert effort on voters' behalf.[13] In that sense, our analysis validates the informal logic of Key, Fiorina, and other proponents of retrospective voting. However, our analysis also underlines the fact that the likely effectiveness of retrospective voting in promoting democratic accountability hinges crucially on the magnitude of random forces influencing voters' electorally relevant subjective well-being. While this is a common feature of formal models of retrospective voting, previous analysts have given it little attention. We explore it briefly here, and more expansively in chapters 5 to 7.

In the simplest version of our model of retrospective selection, which assumes that the competence of the incumbent is constant over time, the un-

---

13 We have presented separate models explicating the logic of these two distinct mechanisms of accountability. Extending our analysis to deal simultaneously with differences in intrinsic competence and incentive effects within a unified model would make the analysis more complicated and the results sensitive to arbitrary choices of assumptions regarding how the various moving parts fit together. James Fearon (1999) provided an insightful examination of the interaction of "selecting" and "sanctioning" processes. In his framework, "*any* variation in politicians' attributes or propensities relevant to their performance in office" gives voters incentives "to focus *completely* on choosing the best type when it comes time to vote" (Fearon 1999, 77); thus, the dual model reduces in practice to a model of selection. Jane Mansbridge (2009) provided a broader discussion of the history and implications of the "selection model" of political representation.

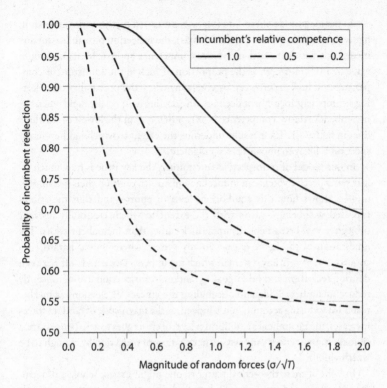

Figure 4.1. Blind Retrospection Impairs Voters' Judgment of Good Incumbents

certainty of the voter's assessment of that competence depends upon the magnitude of discrepancies between competence and subjective well-being and (inversely) upon the extent of the voter's relevant experience.[14] The implications of that uncertainty are illustrated in figure 4.1, which shows the probability of incumbent reelection as a function of competence and uncertainty.

14 Having proposed a model in which voters' "party difference in benefits" is assumed to be constant, Achen (1992, 200) specified that the model was intended to apply "*within* realignments" of the party system. With major realignments typically occurring every 30 or 40 years (Sundquist 1983), this suggests that a typical voter will have a handful of terms of experience on which to base his estimate of party performance. Allowing performance to vary over time makes the voter's prior experience less informative than in the simplest version of the model; the implications of randomness in that case are qualitatively similar, but more severe.

As the magnitude of random forces (represented on the horizontal axis in figure 4.1) shrinks to zero (at the left axis), the reelection probability for any incumbent with greater-than-average competence approaches its maximum value of 1.0.[15] However, as the proportion of luck in the admixture of competence and luck experienced by voters increases, the probability of reelecting a competent incumbent declines. The decline is especially rapid when the incumbent's relative competence is only modest, as in the lowest of the three lines in figure 4.1. These results underline the extent to which random retrospection is likely to impair voters' judgment.

In our model of retrospective sanctioning, the key issue is how much effort retrospective voters can induce incumbents to exert on their behalf. Figure 4.2 shows how this equilibrium level of effort—and thus the voter's expected well-being—varies with the extent to which electorally relevant subjective well-being depends upon luck rather than incumbent effort. The implication of the figure is that, in any system where "moral hazard" is a concern—that is, in any system in which incumbents face a trade-off between desiring reelection and other goals—random retrospection can significantly reduce incumbents' diligence, degrading the efficacy of elections as mechanisms for inducing accountability. Indeed, as the magnitude of random forces increases, the incumbent's equilibrium level of effort goes to zero (since no feasible exertion of effort can increase her chances of reelection by enough to be worthwhile).

In light of these theoretical patterns, one might expect scholars of retrospective voting to have devoted substantial effort to assessing the magnitude of randomness in the perceptions and behavior of voters and to exploring the bases of that randomness. However, that has not been the case. Although allusions to the potential difficulties faced by retrospective voters appear with some frequency, they are usually made in passing and are often remarkably brief and vague.

Downs, one of the first and most influential theorists of rational retrospective voting, clearly recognized the problem. He wrote (1957, 45–46),

> we have glibly spoken of voters computing their party differentials and performance ratings without pointing out how difficult such com-

15 Reelection probabilities for incumbents with negative (less than average) competence are a mirror image of those shown in figure 4.1. As the magnitude of random forces shrinks to zero, the probability of reelecting an inferior incumbent shrinks to zero; but increasing randomness increases the probability of reelecting an inferior incumbent, especially when her relative competence is only modestly negative.

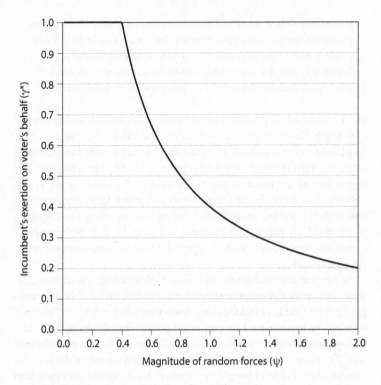

Figure 4.2. Blind Retrospection Erodes Incumbents' Diligence

putation is. In order to find his current party differential, a voter in a two-party system must do the following: (1) examine all phases of government action to find out where the two parties would behave differently, (2) discover how each difference would affect his utility income, and (3) aggregate the differences in utility and arrive at a net figure which shows by how much one party would be better than the other. This is how a rational voter would behave in a world of complete and costless information—the same world in which dwell the rational consumer and the rational producer of traditional economic theory.

In the real world, uncertainty and lack of information prevent even the most intelligent and well-informed voter from behaving in precisely the fashion we have described. Since he cannot be certain what his present utility income from government is, or what it would be if an opposition party were in power, he can only make estimates of both. . . . When we open the door of our model to uncertainty, we must also admit such undesirables as errors, false information, and ignorance.

Having admitted the possibility of "errors, false information, and ignorance" in voting behavior, Downs had little more to say about their likely nature, magnitude, or consequences. In similar fashion, Key (1966, 110) acknowledged but then devoted little further attention to the importance of "the impressions of the march of affairs that exist in the minds of the voters. Differences in voters' interest, in their range of information, in the orientation of their attention, in their first-hand experience, and in their exposure to communications produce enormous variation in their perceptions of events and, consequently, in their appraisals of the alternatives posed by the electoral system."

Subsequent analysts have mostly followed suit, ignoring or dismissing substantial potential challenges to effective retrospective voting. Take, for example, Fiorina's (1981, 5) striking claim that retrospective voters can "ascertain whether the incumbents have performed poorly or well" simply by "calculat[ing] the changes in their own welfare." Of course, this claim is not literally true. If our voter slips on the ice and breaks his leg on the way to the polls, his own welfare has clearly changed for the worse, but we would not expect him to infer from his misfortune that the president has performed poorly. Fiorina's claim makes sense, however, if we assume that voters know a good deal about *which* "changes in their own welfare" are plausibly attributable in some part to the incumbents' performance. That is, they need to monitor indices of incumbent performance that contain a lot of honest signal and not too much noise. For some voters, domains of evaluation, and political contexts, that assumption may be a useful starting point; for others, not.

How are Fiorina's retrospective voters supposed to monitor the extent to which "polluters foul food, water, or air"? Few of the most serious threats to environmental well-being are immediately evident to the senses. Indeed, when the staff of the U.S. Environmental Protection Agency compared public perceptions of the relative significance of various environmental threats with those of experts, they found little correlation. The agency's Office of Policy Analysis (1987, 95) noted that public misperceptions of environmental threats seemed to be skewing the EPA's priorities, inspiring the EPA's Science Advisory Board to recommend that the agency "should work to improve public understanding of environmental risks" (Science Advisory Board 1990).

Nor do voters seem to be very good at discerning the extent to which "thugs make neighborhoods unsafe." Public perceptions of the prevalence of crime seem to be more strongly related to local media coverage of crime—largely a product of broadcasters' commercial incentives—than to official crime rates (Graber 1980). Thus, Gallup polls typically find majorities of respondents saying that crime is increasing, and pluralities saying that crime *in their area* is increasing, even though recent actual "rates of violent crime as well as property crime have generally leveled off at extremely low numbers" (Saad 2007). Misperceptions of this sort are probably common in domains where voters have very limited personal experience, even (and perhaps *especially*) when, as in the case of crime, they care a lot about the true state of the world.

Even perceptions of economic well-being—a domain in which objective measures of social conditions are extraordinarily well-developed and salient—are subject to considerable vagaries. Prospective voters' economic perceptions are powerfully shaped by partisan biases, rationalization, and sheer randomness (Kramer 1983; Conover, Feldman, and Knight 1987; Bartels 2002a; Erikson 2004). Scholars who recognize that fact often assume nonetheless that *the electorate as a whole* responds sensibly and sensitively to actual economic experience under the incumbent administration. As James Stimson (2004, 165) put it, "The net perception of the economy, neither biased nor ignorant, is . . . right on the mark."

In our view, Stimson's reassuring formulation significantly exaggerates the reliability of economic retrospections. Aggregate economic perceptions are far from perfectly correlated with objective economic indicators.[16] And discrepancies between objective economic conditions and the public's economic mood can be politically consequential, as they probably were in 1992, when

---

16 In support of his claim, Stimson (2004) cited the analysis of Erikson, MacKuen, and Stimson (2002, 98) reporting a correlation of .54 between "Business Retrospections" (the economic assessment most similar to those employed in most studies of retrospective economic voting) and the previous year's income growth rate; but a correlation of .54 means that just under 30% of the variance in economic perceptions was explained by income growth, leaving plenty of room for bias and ignorance. Erikson, MacKuen, and Stimson's more elaborate regression analyses predicting aggregate economic expectations and perceived good or bad "economic news" on the basis of leading economic indicators, inflation, and unemployment produced stronger correlations, but the strongest predictors in those analyses were not objective economic indicators but lagged *perceptions* (2002, 94). That gives people credit for having the same bad judgments this period that they had last period; it is not evidence that voters are "right on the mark."

misleadingly negative media coverage of an improving economy contributed to widespread economic pessimism and the defeat of incumbent president George H. W. Bush (Hetherington 1996).

Moreover, even when aggregate economic perceptions do track real changes in economic conditions, they may provide a misleading basis for assessing voters' genuine well-being, and thus for selecting or sanctioning incumbents. For example, in chapter 6 we shall show that American voters focus inordinately on *recent* economic conditions, forgetting or ignoring most of their relevant experience under the incumbent and voting solely on the basis of how they feel about what has happened lately.

It does not seem unreasonable to imagine that a party's recent past performance might provide voters with a useful clue about its likely future performance. However, in light of the crucial importance of this assumption for the whole notion of retrospective selection, it is striking that it has never, as far as we know, been subjected to any systematic empirical examination. Most theorists of retrospective voting have simply *assumed* that there are real, persistent differences in competence between competing teams of political elites, and that voters (consciously or unconsciously) evaluate incumbents on the basis of criteria that do, in fact, systematically predict future performance.[17] In chapter 6, we put those assumptions to the test.

LEADERSHIP AND PANDERING

One of the most attractive features of theories of retrospective accountability is that they free elected officials from subservience to the policy preferences of ordinary citizens—preferences that are often likely to be vague, uninformed, or incoherent. As Fiorina (1981, 201) put it, retrospective voting "lays no policy constraint on the governing administration; rather, the government is free to innovate, knowing that it will be judged on the results of its actions rather than their specifics. In a word, the accountability generated by a

17 We note in passing that the entire notion of retrospective accountability also hinges critically on the assumption that there are, in fact, competing teams of political elites willing and able to seek reelection. In his classic study of southern politics in the Jim Crow era, Key (1949, 302–305) observed that an absence of party competition, stringent term limits, and disorganized "kaleidoscopic" factional competition within the dominant Democratic Party often left voters with no one to reward or punish: "The candidates are new and, in fact, deny any identification with any preceding administration. Without continuing groups, there can be no debate between the 'ins' and 'outs' on the record." The resulting "atomized and individualistic politics," he argued, frustrated political accountability while placing "a high premium on demagogic qualities of personality that attract voter-attention."

retrospective voting electorate and reaction anticipating politicians provides latitude for political *leadership*."

The theories of retrospective voting we have considered assume that voters base their choices at the polls entirely on assessments of how much the incumbent party has contributed to their own or the nation's well-being. However, when voters have their own ideas about good policy, sensible or not, they may be tempted to vote for candidates who share those ideas, as in the spatial model of voting discussed in chapter 2. In that case incumbent politicians may face a dilemma: should they implement the policies voters want or the policies that will turn out to contribute to voters' welfare?

The strategic implications of this dilemma are nicely captured in the formal model of "leadership and pandering" developed by Brandice Canes-Wrone, Michael Herron, and Kenneth Shotts (2001). They posited a world in which an elected official has some private information regarding which of two alternative policies would serve the voters' interest. The elected official chooses a policy that may or may not comport with the preferences of voters, who do not have access to the elected official's private information.[18]

The impact of the elected official's policy choice on voters' welfare may or may not be revealed before the next election. If it is, voters revise their beliefs regarding the elected official's quality accordingly, and an incumbent who is revealed to have chosen the right policy is more likely to be reelected than one who is revealed to have chosen the wrong policy.[19] However, if the impact of the policy is not revealed before the next election, voters may still condition their support on whether the incumbent chose the policy that they believe (but do not yet know) will better serve their interests.

If the incumbent's private information suggests that the policy the voters prefer will, in fact, maximize their welfare, then her choice is straightforward. However, if her private information suggests that the voters are mistaken, then she may have to choose between the risk of being punished for flaunting their will (if she chooses the policy she thinks is right, but its impact is not revealed before the next election) and the risk of being punished for choosing

18 The assumption that voters are relatively but not completely uninformed is crucial to the analysis. If voters knew as much as their leaders about the likely consequences of policy choices, there would be no need for leadership. On the other hand, if voters paid no attention to policy (as in the purely retrospective models we have outlined in this chapter), leaders would have no incentive to "pander."

19 The model assumes—unrealistically—that voters, having observed the impact of only one of the two alternative policies, will know whether it was the right choice or the wrong choice.

the wrong policy (if she chooses the policy they think is right, but the negative consequences become evident before the next election).[20]

Canes-Wrone, Herron, and Shotts's analysis identifies the circumstances under which an incumbent may be tempted to "pander"—implementing the policy preferred by the voters even though her private information suggests that it will not serve their interests.[21] In their basic model, pandering occurs when the probability is not too high that the inferiority of the voters' preferred policy will be revealed before the next election (and if the expected quality of a prospective challenger is strong enough that the incumbent has to worry about her public standing at election time).[22]

Alexander Hamilton argued in Federalist Number 71 that politicians' temptation to pander depends in part on the length of their terms in office, with longer terms encouraging politicians "to be the guardians of those [genuine] interests to withstand the temporary delusion." Canes-Wrone, Herron, and Shotts's analysis has the same implication: the more distant in time is the next election, the more likely bad policies are to be revealed as such by the time the voters go to the polls. An intuitive recognition of this fact may help to account for the fact that American governors' terms have been steadily lengthened since the late 18th century, when one-year terms were most common.

For lower-level offices, however, a good deal of variation in term lengths remains, and it seems to have just the sort of consequences suggested by Hamilton and by Canes-Wrone, Herron, and Shotts's analysis. For example, elected officials facing the issue of fluoridating drinking water in the 1950s and 1960s were significantly less likely to pander to their constituents' ungrounded fears when longer terms gave them some protection from the "sudden breezes of passion" that Hamilton associated with public opinion. Figure 4.3 shows the dramatic difference that longer terms made to mayoral

20 In a detailed study of politics and policy-making in Latin America, Stokes (2001) underlined the tension between populist campaign promises and "neoliberalism by surprise" once the winners took office.

21 Technically, elected officials in Canes-Wrone, Shotts, and Herron's model are of two types. "High-quality" incumbents know with certainty which policy will maximize voters' welfare, and it is never in their electoral interest to act contrary to their own judgment. The dilemma of whether to "lead" or "pander" arises for "low-quality" incumbents, whose private signals are informative but not perfect.

22 Canes-Wrone, Herron, and Shotts also consider a more complicated model in which some policy options are more likely than others to be revealed as good or bad before the next election. In that case, additional strategic possibilities arise, including such perverse strategies as "fake leadership"—choosing a policy that is both unpopular and (probably) inferior in hopes of convincing voters that the incumbent must know best.

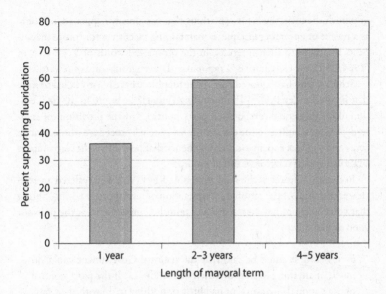

Figure 4.3. American Mayoral Terms and Support for Fluoridation

support for fluoridation.[23] Many political leaders, not caring deeply about the topic, ducked; but those with longer terms had more political leeway to do what was right, and a significant fraction of them used it.

RATIONAL CHOICE OR KICKING THE DOG?

So far, we have examined the logic of retrospective voting on the *assumption* that voters, however uninformed they may be, are at least behaving rationally. As Achen (1992, 199) put it, following Downs (1957, 106): " 'Retrospective voters' . . . choose at least partly on the basis of the past, even though they cannot hope to change it and its lessons may have long ceased to be relevant. For the rational voter, however, bygones are bygones, and only the future matters. . . . As standard decision theory teaches, the rational chooser looks forward, not backward. The rational voter is a prospective voter, and the past is useful only for its clues about the future." By this logic, voters may use the past to learn about the incumbent's likely future behavior, or they may reward

23 The data were reported by Crain, Katz, and Rosenthal (1969, 179–183). The percentages shown in the figure are based on 11, 75, and 54 cases, respectively.

or punish the incumbent for something that has already happened, but only as a means of enforcing discipline, maintaining incentives for future incumbents to attend to their interests. In the oft-quoted words of V. O. Key, Jr. (1964, 568), the electorate is "a rational god of vengeance and of reward."

Scholars who have quoted Key's colorful phrase have mostly failed to note that he used it derisively. "The Founding Fathers," he wrote in the final edition of his influential textbook on party politics, "by the provision for midterm elections, built into the constitutional system a procedure whose strange consequences lack explanation in any theory that personifies the electorate as a rational god of vengeance and of reward."

In the first edition of the same textbook, Key (1942, 628) offered an even clearer dismissal of the rational interpretation of retrospective voting, noting that voters seem to have rewarded and punished incumbents at the polls for good or bad times

> even before it could be said that the national Government could do much of anything to improve their condition. . . . If the party control of the national Government had little or nothing to do with their fate, how is this behavior to be explained? Is it to be considered as a rational seeking to better one's status by the ballot or is it merely blindly striking a blow at a scapegoat? To throw out the "ins" probably had about the same effect on economic conditions as evangelical castigation of Satan has on the moral situation. Perhaps the swing against the "ins" can best be described as a displacement of economic resentment on political objects. By this catharsis discontent was dissipated and the peace kept.

Readers whose only exposure to Key's work is to *The Responsible Electorate*, or (especially) to simplistic summaries of that book, will be surprised to find Key characterizing retrospective voting in such bleak terms.[24] However, the apparent irrationality of the electorate's vengeance and reward has been remarked by many political observers over the years. Indeed, in both of the 19th-century examples we cited earlier, the prominent politician on the losing end of the electorate's vengeance wrote feelingly of its illogic. President Buchanan, whose party was stung by the effect of the Panic of 1857, protested

---

24 This passage disappeared from the second (1947) and subsequent editions of Key's textbook, replaced by more detailed analysis of New Deal voting patterns. It is unclear whether this alteration reflects a change in Key's view or merely routine updating, of which there was a good deal from one edition of Key's text to the next.

that "the administration are as responsible for the motions of the Comet as for the low price of iron" (Huston 1987, 167). For his part, Prime Minister Disraeli complained (Monypenny and Buckle 1929, 1395), "Never was so great a discomfiture with a cause so inadequate. I think, as far as I can collect, 'hard times' was the cry against us. The suffering want a change—no matter what, they are sick of waiting." Presumably, voters in Victorian Britain did not imagine that their government controlled the weather, but that did not prevent them from exacting vengeance at the polls in the wake of a wrenching succession of bad harvests.

In the post-Keynesian era, governments are thought to have real influence on the course of their national economies. Economists tell us that competent policy-makers can reduce the likelihood of recessions and ameliorate their effects when they occur; and practicing politicians take their assessments and advice seriously. Thus, the strong tendency for voters to reward incumbents for good economic times and punish them for bad times is readily interpretable as reflecting rational retrospective voting along either or both of the lines we have sketched in this chapter.

However, the fact that voters rewarded and punished incumbents for economic booms and busts well before Keynes taught governments how to exercise (at least partial) control over their economies represents a significant embarrassment to the rational interpretation of retrospective voting. Moreover, the rational basis for economic voting even in modern industrial economies is murky at best, especially in small countries highly vulnerable to global economic tides. The economy may flourish or falter, but political leaders may or may not be responsible. Moreover, whatever they did right or wrong may or may not be relevant in the circumstances, possibly quite different, that prevail after the election.

Does it really matter whether retrospective voting is thought of as "a rational seeking to better one's status by the ballot" or "merely blindly striking a blow at a scapegoat"? Debating whether a given pattern of behavior is or is not "rational" is largely a tedious matter of definition. Largely, but not entirely. Insofar as we think of retrospective voting as reflecting conscious, conscientious efforts by voters to further their future individual and collective well-being, we should expect them to overcome—as best they can, given inevitable constraints on their attention and information—the challenges to effective retrospection surveyed in the preceding section. However, if retrospective voting represents "a displacement of economic resentment on political objects," as Key put it, then there is no particular reason to expect that displacement to be bound by careful thinking about cause and effect.

Some previous studies have attempted to gauge the "rationality" of retrospective voting by focusing specifically on the electoral impact of forces beyond incumbents' control. For example, Justin Wolfers (2002) showed that U.S. governors in oil-producing states were rewarded and punished by voters for economic fluctuations traceable to changes in world oil prices. He concluded that the "simplest explanation" of his results was that "voters are quasi-rational" and "make systematic attribution errors" (Wolfers 2002, 16–17). Similarly, Daniela Campello and Cesar Zucco (2013) found that the fortunes of political leaders in Latin America could be predicted on the basis of international commodity prices and U.S. interest rates, a result that they suggested "should prompt democracy enthusiasts to engage in some soul-searching." And Bartels (2014) found that incumbent parties in a variety of affluent democracies were punished at the polls for declines in their national economies in the wake of the Great Recession, regardless of how they fared relative to other OECD economies at the time.

While these studies and others in the same vein shed useful light on electoral behavior and political accountability, they shed little light on the underlying psychology of retrospection. Were voters swayed by world oil price shocks doing "a reasonable, albeit imperfect job of disentangling variation in the economy due to competence from variation due to other factors" (Wolfers 2002, 17), or were they punishing their leaders out of mere frustration?

Rather than quibble about which specific economic conditions can or cannot sensibly be attributed to incumbent politicians, in chapter 5 we focus on events that even "reasonable, albeit imperfect" rational voters ought to recognize as clearly outside any incumbent's control—droughts, floods, and shark attacks. We argue that voters respond to those events in much the same way that they respond to ordinary economic downturns, and thus that most retrospective voting of all kinds is more a matter of kicking the dog than of rationally assessing blame or credit. However, that debate makes little difference for democratic theory. Even if the voters are doing the best they rationally can manage, the result of their efforts is sadly unimpressive, as we shall show. Hence, no matter how we interpret voters' responses to bad times, the "blindness" of retrospection poses a significant challenge to democratic accountability.

CONCLUSION

In this chapter we have examined a stylized world in which ordinary voters think quite differently about politics than they are supposed to do in the conventional spatial model of voting outlined in chapter 2. These "retrospective" voters have no policy preferences representable as "ideal points" in multidimensional space. They may know little or nothing about the policies any government has actually enacted. They only know whether things have gone well or badly under the incumbents, and they vote on the basis of that retrospective evaluation. As Key (1966, 7) insisted, such "voters are not fools"—but they are woefully ignorant about much of what is typically taken to be at the heart of democratic politics.

The theory of retrospective accountability demonstrates that, in principle, voters in this stylized world can select competent leaders and discipline those leaders to pursue the voters' well-being, even though they cannot distinguish "politically relevant" pain and pleasure—aspects of well-being plausibly attributable to the policies of the incumbent government—from everything else going on in their lives. However, the *effectiveness* of retrospective accountability depends significantly on the precision with which voters can discern the contributions of the incumbent government to their well-being. Indeed, the implication of the formal models set out in this chapter and summarized in figures 4.1 and 4.2 is that even relatively small amounts of randomness in the relationship between incumbents' actions and voters' subjective well-being can significantly degrade the efficacy of elections as mechanisms for selecting and sanctioning political leaders.

The theory of retrospective voting promises a realistic account of democratic politics. But like any theory, it is a proposal, not a settled finding. How well can the voters manage what the theory of retrospective voting asks them to do? In the next three chapters we provide a more detailed assessment of how, and how well, retrospective voting works in actual elections.

Blind Retrospection: Electoral Responses to Droughts, Floods, and Shark Attacks

> And Moses stretched forth his rod over the land of Egypt, and the Lord brought an east wind upon the land all that day, and all that night; and when it was morning, the east wind brought the locusts. And the locusts went up over all the land of Egypt, and rested in all the coasts of Egypt: very grievous were they; before them there were no such locusts as they, neither after them shall be such. For they covered the face of the whole earth, so that the land was darkened; and they did eat every herb of the land, and all the fruit of the trees which the hail had left: and there remained not any green thing in the trees, or in the herbs of the field, through all the land of Egypt.
>
> Then Pharaoh called for Moses and Aaron in haste; and he said, I have sinned against the Lord your God, and against you.
>
> —Exodus 10:13–16 (King James Version)

When collective misfortune strikes a society, someone must be blamed. For ancient Israel, disasters were God's punishment for sin—perhaps the ruler's sin, perhaps the people's. Theology did not single out the guilty party, but it structured the search and set limits on what counted as a credible explanation.

In the theology of classical Egypt, pharaohs were divine beings responsible for making the Nile flood annually. Some scholars believe that when it failed to do so, as happened repeatedly in the First Intermediate Period (ca. 2200 BCE), the resulting famines and political disorder shortened the pharaoh's reign, and perhaps his life as well (Bell 1971; Hassan 1994). Not surprisingly, there are records of Egyptian court officials wishing their pharaoh a good Nile flood.

Through the centuries, rulers and their potential challengers have been well aware of the potential political significance of natural disasters. Poor weather and bad harvests have been given substantial credit for the rise of the Populists in Kansas (Miller 1925) and Nebraska (Dixon 1898, 637; Barnhart 1925) in the 1890s. More recently, one Republican presidential campaign official said in 1992 that "it wouldn't be so bad" if Hurricane Andrew left Florida and instead "blew on up to Kentucky and the rust-belt states" where incumbent George H. W. Bush had less chance to win electoral votes (Schneider 1995, 96).

When disasters take on truly catastrophic dimensions, not just the ruler but the entire regime may face a crisis of legitimacy. Islamic missionaries in Java and Sumatra successfully blamed Dutch rule for the 1883 volcanic explosion on Krakatoa (Winchester 2003, 317–338). An earlier catastrophic eruption in 11th-century Arizona apparently triggered social upheavals among the people living nearby; their Hopi descendants still preserve folk memories of the event, which they interpret as retribution for their ancestors' "morally imbalanced and corrupt" culture (Gidwitz 2004, 52). Similarly, the European famine of the early 14th century led to outbreaks of heresy and heretic burning in Silesia (Jordan 1996). Later in the 14th century the Black Death, which may have killed one-third or more of the population of Europe, generated numerous spontaneous religious and political movements to threaten church and government (Herlihy 1997, 64): "The plague also discredited the leaders of society, its governors, priests, and intellectuals, and the laws and theories supported by them. These elites were obviously failing in their prime social function, the defense of the common welfare, in the name of which they enjoyed their privileges."

The argument that natural disasters threaten rulers and regimes is not new. However, the base of evidence on which it rests, while impressively broad historically, is also uncomfortably thin. In this chapter we take up the challenge of providing more precise and comprehensive evidence about the political impact of natural disasters. We focus on modern history and electoral politics, where the data are sufficiently detailed and reliable to trace the political consequences of hard times.

Contemporary democratic rulers have little aura of divinity about them, nor have they faced epic famines or medieval plagues. Nonetheless, we find that when election time comes, the electorate continues to hold rulers responsible for calamities and disasters that are clearly beyond their control. We go beyond that simple correlation, however, to argue a deeper point. While voters' reactions to natural disasters are of importance in their own right, our interest here is in what they can tell us about democratic accountability more broadly. From that perspective, electoral responses to natural disasters are just particularly illuminating instances of the broader phenomenon of retrospective voting.

Our assertion is that voters' retrospections are blind, not just in natural disasters but in hardships of all kinds. When they are in pain they are likely to kick the government, so long as they can justify doing so with whatever plausible cultural constructions are available to them. Only if no such constructions are available, or if no ambitious challengers emerge to articulate them, will people take out their frustrations on other scapegoats, or just suffer. In most cases, incumbents will pay at the polls for bad times, whether or not objective observers can find a rational basis for blame.

Our analysis begins with the unjustly neglected electoral impact of shark attacks.

SHARK ATTACKS IN NEW JERSEY: THE VOTERS BITE BACK

On the four-day Fourth of July weekend in 1916, the beaches of New Jersey were packed with crowds happy to escape the summer heat of nearby cities.[1] On Saturday, July 1, a young Ivy League graduate from Philadelphia, Charles Vansant, was swimming just beyond the breakers in four feet of water at Beach Haven when he was attacked by a shark. Skillful lifeguards managed to get him to shore, but he died soon after from blood loss. Five days later, a young Swiss bellhop named Charles Bruder, a strong swimmer like Vansant, ventured out past the lifelines at Spring Lake beach, some 45 miles north of Beach Haven. He, too, was attacked by a shark. Though rescued by lifeguards in a small boat, he died of his wounds before reaching shore.

In the days after the two deaths, nearly all of the diminished numbers of Jersey Shore swimmers stuck close to shore. However, no one worried about boys swimming in a creek on July 12 in the town of Matawan, about two miles from open water. Yet one was attacked and killed by a shark, as was

---

1 Unless otherwise noted, our historical account follows that of Fernicola (2001); we also draw upon Capuzzo (2001).

a young man from the town who dove in to recover the boy's body. Downstream, another group of boys were swimming at the same time in ignorance of the attacks. Within half an hour, one of them had his leg mauled by a passing shark. However, he was quickly pulled from the water, reached the local hospital, and survived.

By this time, the mounting panic reached a crescendo. Even the distant *San Francisco Chronicle* trumpeted the shark attacks in a July 14 front-page headline: "EAST COAST BEGINS WAR ON RAVENOUS MAN-EATERS" (Fernicola 2001, 87). Steel mesh was being installed at beaches. Bounties were offered, and sharks were killed in sizable numbers along the shore. Finally, one great white shark was hauled in near Matawan Creek with what appeared to be human bones in its stomach. Perhaps for that reason, the attacks stopped, ending the most serious string of shark-related fatalities in American history.

Before the attacks, no arm of government had patrolled for sharks or set up barriers against them in New Jersey, since there had never been a recorded shark attack in the history of the state. Indeed, prominent American scientists doubted that unprovoked shark attacks on human beings ever occurred, certainly not as far north as New Jersey (Fernicola 2001, 22).[2] The general climate of skepticism led the *New York Times* to bury its article about the first attack on page 18, headlined "Dies after Attack by Fish"—no doubt a consolation to the New Jersey resort owners, who were anxious to avoid publicity.[3]

In the aftermath of the attacks, the federal government was called on for help. The resorts were losing money rapidly, with $250,000 in reservations cancelled within a week. Some resorts had 75% vacancy rates in the midst of their high season (Capuzzo 2001, 274). Losses may have amounted to as much as $1 million for the season altogether, a sizable sum in 1918 (Fernicola 2001, 174). Letters poured into congressional offices from the affected communities demanding federal action, though there was little any government agency could do. Fernicola (2001, 70) described the atmosphere, as the shark attacks entered popular imagery and became a metaphor for other political crises as well: "Newspaper cartoons now portrayed Wilson's chances for reelection in November, using the shark fin as the symbol for his potential loss.

---

2 Indeed, two scientists who were later called in to investigate the attacks, Dr. John T. Nicols, an ichthyologist and director of the Fishes Wing of the American Museum of Natural History, and Dr. Frederick Lucas, director of the museum, had recently coauthored with a third scientist an article arguing that unprovoked sharks never attack human beings.

3 Parallels to the film *Jaws* and its sequels are no accident. Peter Benchley, the author of the novel on which the film was based, was a New Jersey resident, and the film version, though set on Long Island, New York, included a reference to the 1916 New Jersey attacks.

The black fin labeled 'defeat' was shown slicing through shark-infested northeast regions. Other political cartoons of the day showed lawyers, represented by sharks heading toward a beleaguered sailboat, embossed with 'Union Bank.' At the stern of the bank boat, a chewed and legless victim dangled over the gunnel depicting 'deposits.' "

As it happened, the Secretary of the Treasury, William McAdoo, had a summer home in Spring Lake and was in residence at the time of the second attack. Joseph Tumulty, Wilson's powerful aide for political affairs, had a summer home in Asbury Park, about five miles north of Spring Lake. President Wilson himself, a former president of Princeton University and former governor of New Jersey, had been looking for a summer White House in New Jersey as well, and chose a hotel in Asbury Park, moving there shortly after the attacks ended. Thus the attacks received immediate federal attention. Wilson held a cabinet meeting to discuss the attacks (Fernicola 2001, 70), but the Bureau of Fisheries could suggest nothing beyond killing sharks at random and warning bathers. "No certainly effective preventive measure could be recommended," they said (Capuzzo 2001, 277). The president could only direct the Coast Guard to inspect the beaches and patrol the water. However, the shark attacks ended and autumn arrived before much could be done.

By election time in November, Wilson was back at his Asbury Park headquarters, but other election issues, notably potential U.S. entry into World War I, took over the headlines (Link 1954, 247–251). In the end, Wilson lost nearly all the northeastern and Great Lakes states, including New Jersey, but managed to squeak out his reelection by adding most of the Great Plains, Mountain States, and West to the Democrats' customary Solid South.

Did the shark attacks influence the presidential election in the affected areas of New Jersey? Hitherto, sharks have not been suspects in any electoral analysis. Nonetheless, if our argument is correct, they should have reduced Wilson's vote. First, the attacks caused several deaths plus considerable emotional and financial distress to shore communities. Second, the election occurred just a few months after the summer's events, increasing the likelihood that they would be fresh in the minds of the voters as they went to the polls. Third, high federal officials were present at the scene from the beginning, reinforcing the notion that the federal government should have done *something* to deal with the crisis. The fact that no government has any influence over sharks would, from our perspective, have been irrelevant to the voters.

The evidence for a shark effect turns out to be rather strong. We now turn to the first piece of that evidence, using election returns from New Jersey counties.[4] The Wilson vote in 1916 is the outcome to be explained. Our key explanatory factor is an indicator for "beach counties," defined as Monmouth, Ocean, Atlantic, and Cape May counties. These were, and are, the classic "Jersey Shore" counties listed in the guidebooks, whose beach areas are heavily dependent upon summer tourism. They are the places in which the shark attacks would have had the most pronounced economic effects. The attacks themselves took place in Monmouth (three deaths) and Ocean (one).

We include two additional factors in our county-level analysis. The first is the Wilson vote in 1912, a measure of both partisanship and candidate appeal, including favorite son effects. Wilson's 1912 vote predicts his 1916 showing well, despite the fact that 1912 was a three-way race with former president Teddy Roosevelt running as a Progressive.[5] By contrast, the four presidential elections prior to 1912 (and their mean) were less correlated with the 1916 vote, and they added nothing to the accuracy of the statistical analysis once 1912 was included.[6]

One other control variable is needed to capture an important change in New Jersey politics between 1912 and 1916. Having supported Wilson for governor in 1910, the New Jersey bosses turned against him shortly after his election.[7] They initially opposed his nomination for president in 1912, but fell in line once it became inevitable (Link 1947, chaps. 8–9 and 427–428). After he became president, however, Wilson's control of the New Jersey Democratic Party, once nearly complete, slipped away (Blum 1951, 39, 76; Link 1947, 288). For example, the infamous Jersey City political boss Frank Hague supplanted a progressive Wilson ally during this period (McKean 1940, chap. 3; Connors 1971, chap. 3). To take account of Wilson's reduced power over the

4 New Jersey electoral data are from the official reports published in the *Legislative Manual of the State of New Jersey*, various years.

5 Throughout the Northeast, the Roosevelt vote from 1912 returned almost entirely to Charles Evans Hughes, the Republican candidate, in 1916. (Socialist and other minor candidates, including Prohibition advocates, were also running in both years, but of course only Roosevelt was a serious third-party contender for the presidency.) Wilson gained less than a percentage point statewide in New Jersey in 1916 from his 1912 totals, and similar results held in other northeastern states. Wilson's 1912 vote is an excellent predictor of his 1916 vote across New Jersey counties, and even at the township level.

6 Adding the Roosevelt proportion of the vote from 1912 generated a small positive, statistically insignificant coefficient. Keeping the Roosevelt variable made no difference in subsequent analyses, and so it was dropped.

7 For this reason, Wilson's vote for governor in 1910 is poorly correlated with his showing in both presidential elections and was not used as a statistical control in our analysis of his 1916 vote.

bosses in 1916, we include a control variable for "machine counties," defined as those counties with at least 30,000 voters in 1916 and 60% or more "foreign" citizens in the census of 1910.[8] The counties so defined are Bergen, Hudson, Essex, and Union, adjacent to each other and just across the state line from New York City.

Two of these machine counties, Hudson (Jersey City) and Essex (Newark), were particularly well known for boss control. In fact, alone among New Jersey's counties, Wilson never did get so much as partial control of the Essex Democratic machine, which was under the thumb of James Smith, Wilson's bitter political enemy, throughout this period (Blum 1951, 39–40; Link 1947, 288, 424). For that reason, Wilson's 1912 vote in Essex was so low relative to its electoral history that the county becomes a substantial outlier in predicting the 1916 vote, even beyond its status as a machine county. Simply put, Essex County in this electoral period does not act like the rest of New Jersey at the polls; we therefore excluded it from our analysis. The other 20 New Jersey counties make up our sample.

Table 5.1 presents the results of a statistical analysis estimating the difference in Wilson's 1916 presidential vote share between beach counties and non-beach counties, controlling for machine counties and for Wilson's 1912 vote share. All of the parameter estimates are substantively significant and sensibly sized, and each of them is statistically significant beyond the .01 level. The analysis accounts for Wilson's 1916 vote share with an average error of just 1.7 percentage points, and the correlation between actual and predicted 1916 vote shares is .97.[9]

The estimated negative effect on Wilson's vote in the beach counties is a little more than three percentage points, with a 95% confidence interval confined between 1.3 and 5.2. The shark attacks indeed seem to have had an impact. The statistical significance of the estimate is due to the very consistent effect across the beach counties, as may be seen from figure 5.1. This figure shows the statistical relationship between Wilson's 1916 vote share and his 1912 vote share with the machine county variable controlled. The linear relationships are estimated separately for beach and non-beach counties, with Essex excluded. As the graph shows, the beach counties are each depressed

8 "Foreign" here means that the citizen was foreign-born or had at least one foreign-born parent (the so-called hyphens in the vernacular of the time).

9 None of the residuals from this regression analysis falls more than two standard deviations from zero, and only one of them (Salem's) is near that level, about what would be expected by chance. By contrast, the excluded Essex County observation has a residual 4.6 standard deviations from zero in this analysis, amply justifying its exclusion from the sample.

Table 5.1. The Effect of Shark Attacks on the 1916 New Jersey Presidential Vote

Beach county	−3.2
	(1.0)
Machine county	−5.7
	(1.1)
Wilson 1912 vote (three-way fraction)	0.95
	(0.06)
Intercept	4.5
	(2.8)
Standard error of regression	1.7
Adjusted R^2	.94
N	20

Parameter estimates from ordinary least squares regression analysis (with standard errors in parentheses) of Woodrow Wilson's vote share (two-party %) in New Jersey counties, 1916.

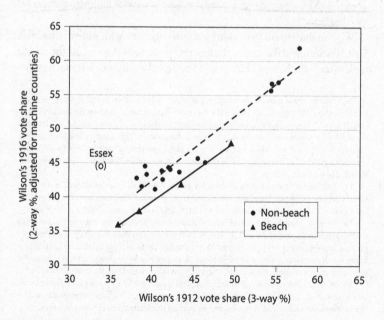

Figure 5.1. Support for Woodrow Wilson in New Jersey Counties, 1916 versus 1912

nearly the same amount from their expected 1916 vote, and the consistency of the effect bolsters the plausibility of the specification visually while tightening the standard errors statistically.[10]

We explored a variety of other statistical specifications using different measures of partisanship. None worked as well as Wilson's 1912 vote share, and the estimated effect of the shark attacks remained fairly constant—two to four percentage points—so long as the 1912 vote share was included. We also tried including measures of the proportion German, the proportion Irish, and the total proportion "foreign," since speculation was rampant at the time of the 1916 election that these communities would be unhappy with Wilson over his potential entry into World War I on the British side or over the British suppression of the 1916 Easter Rising in Dublin. We found no effects of this sort, which is consistent with the conclusions of analysts of the national vote at the time.[11] Similarly, weighting the counties by their total 1916 turnout, or using the change in Wilson's vote share from 1912 to 1916 as the dependent variable, or both, never reduced the estimated impact of the sharks by more than a tenth of a percentage point. In fact, all the turnout-weighted estimates were larger by a few tenths of a percentage point. Thus the shark effect stands up well under a variety of alternative statistical specifications.[12]

We also undertook two additional investigations with different samples. First, we examined the vote in the first two shore townships where the attacks took place.[13] Both Beach Haven and Spring Lake were small, stable commu-

10 If the machine counties were counted as beach counties, they would fit nicely on the regression line. They are themselves on the water or adjacent to the Hudson River. Capuzzo (2001, 270–273) noted that fear extended well beyond the Jersey Shore counties, up through the machine counties and onto New York State beaches, where the economy was also harmed. One shark was killed with a revolver near a yacht club in machine-controlled Hudson County (Fernicola 2001, 27). Thus it is possible that some of the negative "machine county" effect is, in fact, due to the sharks.

11 Two days after the election (November 9), the *New York Times* headlined "Both Candidates Got Hyphen Vote." For subsequent treatments reaching the same conclusion, see Link (1954, 232–251) on the Germans and Leary (1967) and Cuddy (1969) on the Irish.

12 Another possibility we considered was that Roosevelt might have run worse in the beach counties than in the rest of the state, leaving Wilson fewer voters there to pick up from Progressive Republicans in 1916. This would have created an artificial drop in Wilson's 1916 vote in the beach counties. To the contrary, however, Roosevelt ran *better* along the shore than in the rest of the state, so that the shark attack effect is, if anything, slightly underestimated in table 5.1.

13 Matawan Township and Matawan Borough, where the final two shark deaths occurred in a river, were excluded from this analysis since they are not beach resort communities and thus suffered no widespread economic loss from their shark attacks or anyone else's. In any

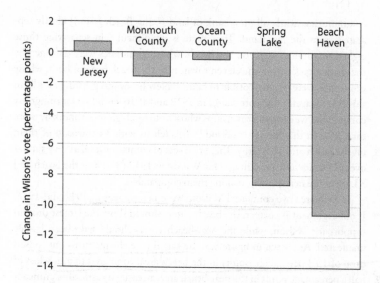

Figure 5.2. Change in Woodrow Wilson's Vote Share (1912–1916) in Counties and Townships with Shark Attacks

nities, making comparison sensible.[14] Figure 5.2 shows the vote change for Wilson between 1912 and 1916 in these two communities, and compares it with the change in their respective counties and in New Jersey as a whole. Both townships show remarkable drops in Wilson's support, 11 points in Beach Haven and 9 in Spring Lake—far more than the modest decline in the Wilson vote in their counties. It is apparent that something drastically reduced enthusiasm for Woodrow Wilson in these two townships.

We also investigated whether Beach Haven and Spring Lake were typical of beach areas. To answer this question, we examined the townships in Ocean County near the water. Ocean was chosen because it has many beach

---

case, the rapid growth in the number of voters in both places between 1912 and 1916 makes reliable comparison impossible; more than a quarter of the 1916 voters in Matawan Township had not been there in 1912.

14 Beach Haven cast 112 votes for president in 1912 and 119 in 1916. The corresponding numbers for Spring Lake are 271 and 265.

communities, nearly all on a bank of land (Long Beach Island) clearly separated from the mainland. Thus there is no difficulty in separating those eight communities right on the beach, whose economies were damaged by the shark attacks, from the eleven towns near the beach but not on it, whose economies were less susceptible to harm.[15] New Jersey was growing rapidly in this era; to ensure that vote shares in 1912 and 1916 would be meaningfully comparable, we dropped townships whose vote totals grew or shrank by more than 25% in this four-year period.[16] This left us with 14 towns, 4 of them on the beach and 10 nearby. These two sets of communities had very similar overall Democratic percentages for Wilson in 1912 (37.1% at the beach and 33.5% in the near-beach), making them comparable.

In each area, we compared Wilson's vote percentages in 1912 and 1916. If our argument is correct, the beach voters should show the largest drop in support for Wilson, while the near-beach voters should have been largely unaffected. As shown in figure 5.3, the actual vote change turns out to be a drop of 13.3 percentage points in the beach area, compared to a tiny loss of half a percentage point in the near-beach area, an easily statistically significant difference.[17] Again, we find that disaffection for Wilson was widespread in the beach areas where livelihoods were most directly affected by the shark attacks, far different from the otherwise comparable areas next door, where Wilson's vote was nearly constant.

In summary, then, every indication in the New Jersey election returns is that the horrifying shark attacks during the summer of 1916 reduced

15 The western border of the near-beach area was set to the current Garden State Parkway, which runs within a few miles of the shore in Ocean County.

16 One beach township, Sea Side Park, apparently split into two between 1912 and 1916 and jointly nearly doubled in size; we dropped it from the analysis.

17 The simplest approach is a differences-in-differences regression model weighted by the 1916 total vote (to take account of the wide range of electorate sizes in these boroughs). Thus, with the change in the Democratic vote percentage from 1912 to 1916 as the dependent variable and beach township as the explanatory variable, we obtain a coefficient of -12.8 percentage points, with a standard error of 4.4 (and a t-statistic of 2.9). Alternately, a weighted regression with the Democratic vote in 1916 as the dependent variable, and with beach township and the 1912 Democratic vote as explanatory variables, yields a beach effect of -11.1 percentage points with a standard error of 3.2 (and a t-statistic of 3.5). Unweighted regressions, though arguably substantively inappropriate, yield even larger beach coefficients. Finally, if we eliminate two townships with fewer than 50 voters in 1916, the differenced regression produces a beach coefficient of -8.4 percentage points, while the second regression version yields -8.8, both with t-statistics exceeding 2.5. In short, alternate versions of the beach versus non-beach comparison lead to precisely the same substantive conclusion, which we summarize as a loss of about 10 percentage points in the areas most directly affected by the shark attacks.

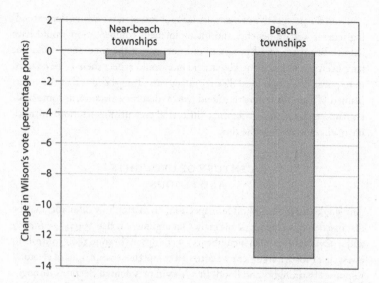

Figure 5.3. Change in Woodrow Wilson's Vote Share (1912–1916) in Ocean County Townships

Wilson's vote in the beach communities by about ten percentage points. An effect of that size may sound modest to those unfamiliar with American electoral experience, but by those standards it is a near-earthquake. (A full earthquake, the Great Depression, reduced Herbert Hoover's vote in New Jersey by 12 percentage points, from 59.8% in 1928 to 47.6% in 1932.)

In the case of the shark attacks, retrospection was surely blind. Shark attacks are random events in the purest sense of the term, and they have no governmental solution. If bathers insist on swimming in the ocean, governments then and now cannot save them, as subsequent attacks in New Jersey in 1960 and regular encounters in Florida, California, South Africa, and Australia demonstrate (Fernicola 2001, chap. 5). Nor could the aftermath of the 1916 attacks be repaired by governmental action. The truth could not be covered up. The vacationers could not be compelled to come to the beach, nor could the sharks be forced to stay away. The government was helpless. Yet the voters punished anyway.[18]

---

18 On one occasion, sharks apparently had a more direct and unfortunate impact on an incumbent political leader. On December 17, 1967, Australian Prime Minister Harold Holt

From the perspective of a century later, of course, it is obvious that extending federal welfare benefits and unemployment compensation would have helped. But these social programs did not exist at the time, they could not have been put in place quickly, and no one would expect them to be enacted in response to a single local disaster in any case. Thus the idea that the voters blamed Wilson for failing to extend federal disaster assistance, as some readers have suggested to us, is a form of historical presentism—a serious misreading of circumstances at the time.

A CENTURY OF DROUGHTS
AND FLOODS

Any single instance of blind retrospection, no matter how dramatic, may be dismissed as coincidence or anomaly. Our argument is that voters *consistently* and *systematically* punish incumbents for conditions beyond their control. To assess that broader argument we turn to a comprehensive analysis of electoral responses to droughts and floods by voters in presidential elections throughout the 20th century. We show that voters do indeed punish the incumbent party at the polls for presiding over dry or wet spells.

The data on droughts and floods employed in our analysis consist of monthly readings from 1897 to 2000 of hydrological conditions in each of 344 climate divisions covering the contiguous 48 U.S. states.[19] Each observation summarizes daily data from several weather stations within each climate division. We measure wet and dry spells using the Palmer Hydrological Drought Index (PHDI), an index of long-term moisture supply.[20] A PHDI reading of zero represents an ideal moisture level; negative values represent droughts and positive values represent wet spells.[21]

---

disappeared while swimming in shark-infested waters at Cheviot Beach near Portsea, Victoria. His body was never found.

19 The data were generated by the U.S. government and are publicly available from the National Climatic Data Center (NCDC), a unit of the National Oceanic and Atmospheric Administration in the U.S. Department of Commerce. See http://lwf.ncdc.noaa.gov/oa /climate/onlineprod/drought/readme.html; also http://ingrid.ldeo.columbia.edu/SOURCES /.NOAA/.NCDC/.CIRS/.ClimateDivision/.dataset_documentation.html.

20 We believe that the Palmer Hydrological Drought Index provides a better measure of the damage associated with droughts and floods than the Palmer Drought Severity Index, which measures the severity of dry or wet spells of weather rather than long-term moisture supplies.

21 PHDI values between 2 and 3 represent "moderate" droughts, values between 3 and 4 represent "severe" droughts, and values less than 4 represent "extreme" droughts, and similarly

We aggregate the monthly data for each climate division by computing the absolute value of the sum of monthly PHDI readings from May through October of each calendar year. For simplicity we refer to the result of this calculation as a "drought index," but it is important to bear in mind that the absolute values reflect both wet and dry spells.[22] We further aggregate the data to the level of states by computing a simple average of the annual absolute PHDI values for the climate divisions in each state.[23]

The result of these calculations is an index of climatic pain running from 0.04 to 49.08, with a mean value of 11.03 and a standard deviation of 6.29. Low values of the index are good and high values are bad for voters and thus, according to our account, for incumbent presidents. Our 4,992 observations (for each of 48 states in each of 104 years) include 649 (13%) with absolute PHDI values in excess of 18, the equivalent of a full year of "severe" drought or wetness; 203 observations (4%) have absolute PHDI values in excess of 24, the equivalent of a full year of "extreme" drought or wetness.

We investigate electoral responses to droughts and floods by conducting statistical analyses of popular support for incumbent party candidates in 26 presidential elections (from 1900 through 2000). Thus our analysis is not based on a single, possibly idiosyncratic drought or flood. Rather, we examine an entire century of wet and dry spells, relying upon the random occurrence of numerous droughts and floods to distinguish their common effects from potentially confounding specific circumstances. Our analyses employ state-level voting data and six different versions of our drought index.[24] In each

---

for positive values indicating wet spells. The distribution of PHDI values is approximately normal, with no asymmetry apparent between the severity of wet spells and dry spells.

22 This calculation assumes that equally severe droughts and wet spells are equally painful to voters. We investigated that assumption by repeating our statistical analyses using separate measures of droughts and wet spells. The estimated effects were generally similar. For example, in the simplest regression model presented in the first column of table 5.2, distinguishing between droughts and wet spells produced estimated effects of .067 (with a standard error of .047) and .066 (with a standard error of .050), respectively.

23 Most states are composed of between seven and nine climate divisions; eight states have one, two, or three divisions. The climate division boundaries sometimes reflect geographical features such as coastal areas or mountain ranges, but more often follow county lines.

24 All our statistical analyses weight each state in each year by the number of votes cast in the presidential election; thus, populous states and those with heavy turnout get more weight than those with fewer voters, and more recent elections get more weight than those earlier in the century covered by our analysis.

Table 5.2. Droughts, Floods, and Presidential Elections, 1900–2000

	Drought index			Rural drought index		
	(1)	(2)	(3)	(4)	(5)	(6)
Election-year drought index	−0.060 (0.031)	−0.052 (0.034)	—	−0.176 (0.083)	−0.140 (0.082)	—
(Election−1) drought index	—	−0.043 (0.029)	—	—	−0.116 (0.088)	—
(Election−2) drought index	—	0.016 (0.036)	—	—	0.023 (0.102)	—
(Election−3) drought index	—	−0.043 (0.040)	—	—	−0.024 (0.102)	—
Time-weighted drought index	—	—	−0.104 (0.045)	—	—	−0.273 (0.122)
Standard error of regression	3.61	3.60	3.60	3.61	3.61	3.60
Adjusted R^2	.88	.88	.88	.88	.88	.88
N	1,233	1,233	1,233	1,233	1,233	1,233

Parameter estimates (with standard errors in parentheses) from ordinary least squares regression analyses of incumbent vote (%) by state; states weighted by turnout; observations clustered by election year. Election-specific intercepts and election-specific effects of lagged incumbent vote, twice-lagged incumbent vote, % rural and South not shown.

case, we expect droughts and floods to depress the incumbent party's popular vote share. Table 5.2 presents the key results.

In order to allow for other factors affecting the incumbent party's fortunes in each state in each election, we take account of the incumbent party's vote share in the same state in each of the previous two presidential elections, the percentage of the population living in rural areas, and an indicator variable for southern states. The effects of all of these factors are allowed to vary from one election to the next, so that there are 130 coefficients in each regression model in addition to those reported in table 5.2—an intercept for each election, a coefficient for the lagged incumbent vote in each election, and so on. Only the effects of drought are assumed to be constant across elections.

The simplest version of our analysis, reported in the first column of table 5.2, employs the absolute PHDI value for each state in each election year as the primary explanatory factor. The negative estimated effect indicates that, on average, voters punished incumbent parties for droughts and wet spells; the t-statistic for this parameter estimate is -1.9, so the effect of wet and dry spells on election outcomes cannot easily "be dismissed by the dubious as a coincidence" (Barnhart 1925, 529).[25] Nor is the estimated effect trivial in magnitude. It implies that wet or dry conditions in a typical state and year (an average absolute PHDI value of 11) cost the incumbent party 0.7 percentage points, while "extreme" droughts or wet spells (absolute PHDI values of 24 or more) cost incumbents about 1.5 percentage points.

The second column of table 5.2 reports the results of a slightly more complicated analysis in which the drought index values for all four years of each president's term appear as separate explanatory factors. Here, the estimated effect of election year drought is quite similar to the estimated effect in the first column, and drought values in two of the three preceding years appear to have additional (albeit slightly smaller) negative effects. In the third column we employ a time-weighted cumulative drought index in which drought conditions in each year of a president's term get twice as much weight as those in the preceding year.[26] Once again, the effect of droughts and wet spells on the incumbent party's vote share is clearly negative (in this case with a t-statistic of -2.3) and of considerable magnitude (costing the incumbent party about 1.1 percentage points in a typical state and year).

The remaining three columns of table 5.2 repeat the analyses reported in the first three columns, but with each drought variable multiplied by the proportion of the population living in rural areas in each state and year. The resulting rural drought indices allow for the possibility that wet and dry spells

25 The observations in the regression analyses reported in table 5.2 are clustered by election year, which allows the unmeasured factors affecting incumbent party support in each year to be correlated across states. The result of clustering is to increase the estimated standard errors (and reduce the associated t-statistics) by about 35%.

26 The resulting weights attached to drought index values in the four years leading up to each election are .06667, .13333, .26667, and .53333. Deriving geometrically declining weights from the separate estimates reported in the second (or fifth) column of table 5.2 would produce roughly similar weights.

may be particularly consequential in rural areas where farming, ranching, and forestry are major economic activities. However, allowing for the difference in scales between the original and rural drought indices, the pattern of estimated effects turns out to be quite similar. For example, the estimated effect of election year rural drought in the fourth column implies that the incumbent party lost 0.6% of the vote in a typical state and year (as compared with 0.7% in the first column).

The strength and consistency of these results across a variety of analyses employing different versions of our drought index should leave little doubt that droughts and wet spells *in general* had a negative effect on electoral support for the president's party.[27] Climatic distress is a pervasive risk to the re-election chances of every incumbent, and no more controllable than the rain.

An important disadvantage of the summary results presented in table 5.2 is that they conceal a great deal of potentially interesting variation in effects across election years, some of which may be attributable to more or less effective governmental responses and some of which may reflect other factors. For example, as noted by Barnhart (1925, 536–539), insufficient rainfall has less impact on livestock ranchers than on farmers. Thus we expect that some droughts will have substantial economic and political impacts and others less so, depending on where they occurred. That variation is conveyed by figure 5.4, which presents separate estimated effects of election-year drought on the incumbent party's vote share in each election.

The estimated effects of droughts and wet spells are clearly quite variable, with almost half of the election-specific estimates more than twice as large—and a few as much as five times as large—as the corresponding overall estimates in table 5.2. A detailed examination of those varying responses might shed very useful light on the psychology and sociology of voters' attributions of responsibility for natural disasters. However, that sort of detailed examination is beyond the scope of the present study.

Rather than attempting to provide a detailed analysis of climatic retrospection in each election, we propose here merely to emphasize that our analysis of droughts and floods cannot be dismissed as a bit of Dust Bowl

---

27 In addition to the variety of regression analyses reported in table 5.2 we examined models with separate effects for droughts and wet spells, models with nonlinear variants of our drought indices, models allowing for secular trends in the magnitude of drought effects, models allowing drought effects to vary with prior partisanship, and models employing interactions between local climatic conditions and national climatic conditions. All of these models produced clear evidence of drought effects, but none added significantly—in terms of statistical fit or substantive insight—to the simpler analyses reported in table 5.2.

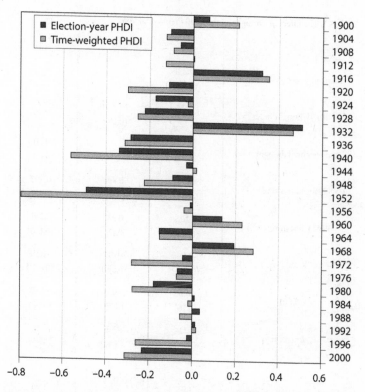

Figure 5.4. Election-Specific Estimates of Drought and Flood Effects, 1900–2000

antiquarianism. We do so by examining the electorate's response to droughts and floods in the 2000 presidential election. The 2000 election occurred under relatively unfavorable climatic conditions for the incumbent party. The average absolute PHDI value was about 10% higher than the historical average, with severe drought in parts of the South and West and excessive wetness in the Dakotas and New York and Vermont.[28]

28 Drought conditions were most severe in Arizona and Alabama, which had drought index values in excess of 20; Louisiana, Montana, Georgia, Mississippi, Texas, Utah, Wyoming, New Mexico, and Nevada also had drought values in excess of 15. At the opposite extreme, the Dakotas, Vermont, and New York had absolute PHDI values ranging from 15.8 to 20.3.

Table 5.3. The Effect of Drought on the 2000 Presidential Vote

	(1)	(2)	(3)
Election-year drought index	−0.231 (0.073)	—	—
Rural drought index	—	−0.546 (0.259)	—
Time-weighted drought index	—	—	−0.310 (0.103)
1996 Clinton vote (%)	0.915 (0.113)	0.896 (0.119)	0.802 (0.115)
1992 Clinton vote (%)	0.206 (0.121)	0.237 (0.127)	0.291 (0.120)
Rural (%)	−0.098 (0.026)	−0.032 (0.040)	−0.116 (0.027)
South	−0.60 (0.76)	−0.96 (0.79)	−1.57 (0.68)
Intercept	−0.14 (3.33)	−3.14 (3.40)	3.40 (3.86)
Standard error of regression	1.94	2.06	1.96
Adjusted R^2	.92	.91	.92
N	48	48	48

Parameter estimates (with standard errors in parentheses) from ordinary least squares regression analyses of Democratic vote (%) by state; states weighted by turnout.

Table 5.3 presents our analysis of the impact of climatic conditions on the 2000 presidential vote. We consider three different versions of our drought index, with statistical controls for previous Democratic votes, percentage rural, and an indicator variable for southern states. All three versions of the statistical analysis fit the data very well, with average errors of less than two percentage points in the predicted Democratic vote share and adjusted R^2 values in excess of .90.

The results of these analyses suggest a great deal of continuity with previous partisan voting patterns, albeit with some significant defections from the Democratic ticket in rural states. The three versions of our drought index all have strong negative estimated effects on the Democratic vote, with t-statistics ranging from -2.1 to -3.2. The magnitudes of these estimated effects suggest that the Democrats' national vote share was from 1.6 to 3.6 percentage points lower than it would have been had voters not been inclined to make the incumbent party feel their climatic pain. The aggregate effect implied by the best-fitting model, employing the simple election year drought index, falls in the middle of that range at 2.7 percentage points.

This estimate implies that 2.8 million people voted against Al Gore in 2000 because their states were too dry or too wet. As it turned out, Gore could have used those votes. Attributing them to the various states in proportion to their drought scores suggests that climatic retribution cost Gore seven states—Arizona, Louisiana, Nevada, Florida, New Hampshire, Tennessee, and Missouri—and almost three times as many electoral votes as Florida's infamous "butterfly ballot" (Wand et al. 2001). Voters responded to climatic distress in 2000, as they have repeatedly throughout the past century, by punishing the incumbent government at the polls.

HOLDING INCUMBENTS RESPONSIBLE: WHY SO MUCH PUNISHMENT?

When voters endure natural disasters they generally vote against the party in power, even if the government could not possibly have prevented the problem. In our experience, this simple fact induces in many readers a powerful urge to defend the sophistication and rationality of the electorate. Here we take up their arguments.

First, it is possible that voters did not blame the government for the disasters themselves, but did blame it for *exacerbating* or failing to *ameliorate* the damage. In that case, retrospection might not be blind. The point is not a new one. As Barnhart (1925, 540) wrote of 19th-century Nebraska,

> To suggest that the farmer held the politician responsible for the shortage of rainfall would be an unwarranted exaggeration of the thoughtlessness of the voters. But it is quite another matter to suggest that the drouth in Nebraska made a bad set of agricultural conditions worse and that the politicians were held responsible for some of the conditions. Perhaps some held them responsible for most of them. The situation of

many farmers forced them to think about the things that had brought about that situation.... They could not make it rain, but they thought they could lower railroad rates.

The difficulty with this argument is its strong policy component. If the voters learn in disasters what they had hitherto not suspected—namely that stronger government intervention in the economy is needed—then droughts ought to push electorates to the ideological left. What they actually do, however, is reduce support for incumbents regardless of their ideological commitments. "Throwing the rascals out" after droughts did lead to left-wing gains in Nebraska in the 1890s; but where left-wing governments have been in power the lack of rain has created surges of right-wing voting, as in the American Dust Bowl in the mid-1930s. Similarly in the case of the sharks, if New Jersey voters in 1916 wanted a better government social safety net enacted, then their swing from Wilson to his Republican opponent was politically quite illogical.

Moreover, whatever the voters learn in natural disasters has a very short half-life. As many scholars have noted, Populism declined rapidly as economic conditions improved in the farming states. Confirming that historical pattern, table 5.2 suggests that droughts in the first half of a president's term have no consistent influence on the voters. Similarly, by 1920 the Jersey Shore was back to its customary partisanship among New Jersey counties, and the beach areas of Ocean County that had suffered most from the shark attacks were 8 percentage points more favorable to the party of Wilson than the near-beach, just the reverse of their views at the time of the attacks four years earlier. In sum, the voters quickly forget their grievances. Short-term anti-incumbent voting without substantial policy content is the only common pattern in the electorate's response to natural disasters.

An alternative defense of voter rationality is that the electorate punishes incumbents not for the *occurrence* of natural disasters, which are clearly beyond their control, but for insufficient *responses* to those disasters. In this view, voters monitor incumbents' performances in the aftermath of disasters in much the same way, and for much the same reasons, that they monitor other aspects of incumbent performance—imperfectly, based on observed results, in order to *select* competent leaders and provide *incentives* for future performance. This sort of punishment seems wholly consistent with the logic of retrospection we set out in chapter 4.

The problem with this interpretation is that it is manifestly irrational for well-informed voters to punish incumbent politicians for droughts, floods, or other natural disasters *in general*. Any *particular* drought, flood, or other natural disaster may be an occasion for rational punishment of incumbent politicians who fail to take adequate steps to ameliorate its effects. However, a competent electorate must recognize that incumbents' preparations for, and reactions to, the substantial physical and social dislocations resulting from major disasters are, by definition, better than average about half the time. And while it may be sensible for voters to punish incumbents who perform less well than average in the wake of a disaster, punishing those who perform *better* than average is counterproductive both from the standpoint of selecting competent leaders and from the standpoint of providing proper incentives for future incumbents to do their best under difficult circumstances.

Thus, we should expect to find rational electorates *rewarding* incumbents for better-than-average responses to natural disasters as often as they *punish* incumbents for worse-than-average responses. The evidence strongly contradicts this expectation. Energetic politicians can sometimes successfully claim credit for federal disaster assistance or shift the blame to other levels of government (Abney and Hill 1966; Arceneaux and Stein 2006; Healy and Malhotra 2010; Gasper and Reeves 2011; Brader n.d.). However, the one-sided tendency for voters to punish rather than reward their leaders in times of distress is evident in our statistical results. The estimated drought effects in table 5.2 represent average effects on incumbent vote shares of all the droughts and floods of the 20th century, including effective responses as well as ineffective ones. If reward and punishment were distributed impartially, the *average* effects of droughts and floods would be zero. Instead, they are preponderantly negative. Voters are much more apt to punish their leaders than to reward them.

In human terms, the voters' behavior is understandable. They see friends and neighbors pitching in to help immediately after the disaster. They do not understand why the government cannot do the same. To citizens, government bureaucracies with their rules to prevent fraud and their accounting regulations may dispense disaster assistance with a heartless attitude and a lethargic spirit. Or, if the money is dispersed more freely, citizens may complain about waste and abuse (Schneider 1995, 70–71). Either way, in the wake of a disaster the government will look inept or uncaring to a devastated and emotionally shaken electorate. Hence, the voters will punish most of the time. But doing so can neither relieve their distress nor produce more competent or caring political leaders.

One final version of the principal-agent argument is more consistent with our evidence. On this view, voters simply punish incumbent leaders any time their own well-being falls below "normal" levels, regardless of whether the incumbents have performed well or badly. Disasters are very likely to cause hardship even when incumbents' responses are vigorous and competent, so this sort of decision rule leads to frequent punishing after disasters, thus matching the evidence. And it is "rational" in the technical sense set forth in chapter 4—if voters are incapable of distinguishing relevant from irrelevant sources of subjective well-being, the best they can do may be to respond identically to both. In that case, voters will respond in much the same way to shark attacks and droughts as they do to poor tax policies and disastrous foreign wars. Incapable of assessing causation, they will mechanically translate pain into electoral punishment. But that is just what we mean by blind retrospection.

THE SOCIAL CONSTRUCTION OF BLAME

Thus far we have written of retrospective voting as if hardship itself created electoral backlash. Like many other scholars, we have deemphasized the voters' interpretation of their plight, as if it had little causal importance. In fact, however, we believe that voters' attributions of blame are often crucial in their decisions to punish incumbents. Positive or negative events that voters themselves would recognize as politically irrelevant, such as the outcomes of local college football games, may also influence voting behavior through subconscious effects on voters' moods (Healy, Malhotra, and Mo 2010). But substantial punishment at the polls is likely to be grounded in a belief, however farfetched, that the government is somehow responsible for the voters' pain.

It is easy to overlook the need for social interpretation of hard times, since suggestions about their meaning are typically mass-produced. Political and ideological entrepreneurs have an incentive to construct explanations and solutions, often self-serving, for people's hardships. Amplified by the mass media, these ideas may increase or decrease the likelihood that citizens will attribute responsibility for social problems to the government (Iyengar 1991). In garden-variety economic recessions, the accepted stories about blame are familiar, and the process of generating common understandings occurs so smoothly and easily that its importance may go unnoticed. Natural disasters, by contrast, create deeper and unfamiliar hardships, which lead to uncertainty and even fear. The old complacent assumptions are shown to be mistaken, and a search begins for new explanations that will avoid a repetition of the disaster (Cantril 1958, chap. 1; Birkland 1997). People are ready to listen.

After disasters, the more popular attributions of blame and proposals for reform often come from widely trusted sources and appeal in a clear, simple way to broadly shared values, though not necessarily those that intellectual elites rely on for their political judgments. As Hadley Cantril (1941, 67) put it, "There are short-cut rationalizations which fire the imagination and spread because they somehow express the dissatisfactions from which people have been suffering and at the same time imply a new direction and purpose." If a single nutty or dangerous vision comes to be sufficiently widely shared, demagogues may be able to ride it to power.

Elite culture is usually (though not always) less susceptible to nutty or dangerous visions. It may even play some role in discouraging the most ignorant or vicious attributions of blame. But popular culture is never entirely under the control of the respectable. A variety of unconventional interpretations and nostrums may be available, and under the right circumstances deviant doctrines may attract considerable popular acceptance. Some medieval towns blamed the plague on Jews, prostitutes, beggars, or foreign agents (Herlihy 1997, 65–67). Some New Jersey residents in 1916 thought that German U-boats might have induced the sharks to attack (Fernicola 2001, 166–170). Some Americans in the grip of the Spanish Influenza pandemic two years later feared that "plague germs were inserted into aspirin made by the German drug company Bayer" (Kolata 1999, 3).

Different sectors of the population, immersed in distinct subcultures, may find different explanations appealing. Ideological commitments may color the plausibility of alternative explanations, as with the Federalists' and Republicans' competing accounts of the yellow fever epidemic of 1793. Physicians "divided bitterly over the cause of the epidemic," with Republicans generally attributing it to poor sanitation, climatic conditions, and the unhealthy location of Philadelphia, while Federalists blamed disembarking refugees from Haiti; in fact, "both sides were right" (Pernick 1972, 562–563). If available interpretations are sufficiently contested, and if incumbents can exploit competing explanations to exonerate themselves and blame others, they may sometimes escape blame altogether (McGraw 1991; Arceneaux and Stein 2006).

In other cases, blame may fail not because there are too many available interpretations of disaster but because there are too few. In 1874, for example, locust swarms devastated large swaths of western Nebraska and adjacent states. By fall, many farmers literally faced starvation. The Army had clothing and food supplies stored in the area, but refused to distribute the clothes until several weeks after the fall election, and did not give out food until the following February (Lockwood 2004, 80–84). Nonetheless, the incumbent Republicans sailed to victory in Nebraska in 1874, and repeated plagues of locusts throughout the mid-1870s did not notably dent their popularity in either gubernatorial or presidential elections (Nebraska Legislative Reference Bureau 1918, 436–506). The voters did not punish. The simplest explanation is probably that in the thinly populated farming areas of Nebraska at that time, communication was poor and no shared interpretation of the disaster emerged. A strong ethic of self-reliance also militated against expecting assistance from the government (Lockwood 2004, 38–39). And, perhaps most important, the Populists were not well organized until a decade later and did not mount a serious campaign for governor until 1890. At that point, farmers suddenly had a credible explanation for their troubles and a target for their frustrations—and punishment began.

If our interpretation of the cultural element in natural disasters is correct, then it should be possible to point to a major disaster for which a government was plausibly responsible, yet for which it escaped electoral blame because the case for responsibility was never constructed by political opponents. The Spanish Influenza pandemic of 1918 represents a remarkable case of just that sort. The magnitude of the disaster was epic; most estimates of the worldwide death toll range from 20 million to 40 million, with some as high as 100 million. In the United States alone, the flu killed approximately half a million people—more than the total number of American battle deaths in World War I, World War II, Korea, and Vietnam combined (Crosby 1989; Kolata 1999, 285, ix–x). This was no mere blown college football game. If voters punished the incumbent government whenever they felt significant unhappiness, the millions of people who lost friends or family members to influenza in 1918 would have produced the greatest anti-incumbent landslide in American electoral history. But electoral retribution requires voters to imagine, however plausibly or implausibly, that incumbent leaders could have prevented or ameliorated their pain. In the case of the flu pandemic, that crucial attribution of political responsibility was lacking. As a result, as best we can tell, the electorate utterly failed to respond to the greatest public health catastrophe in U.S. history.

The 1918 midterm election occurred just as the pandemic was at its peak in many parts of the country, with flu deaths numbering more than one thousand per week in some major cities. Using detailed data on influenza mortality rates from 16 states and 29 major cities (Crosby 1989; Pyle 1986, 46–47), we examined voting patterns in the 1918 midterm election, looking for evidence of electoral retribution aimed either at Democratic gubernatorial candidates or at incumbent governors regardless of party.[29] We also examined the 1920 presidential vote. In no case did we find reliable statistical evidence that voters in the worst-hit states and cities punished anyone at the polls.[30]

One important race was almost certainly affected by the pandemic—the Senate contest in New Mexico, in which President Wilson clumsily attacked Republican Albert B. Fall at the same time Fall was grieving over the deaths from influenza of two of his children. Fall was elected by fewer than 2,000 votes, and Alfred Crosby (1989, 175) quite plausibly argued that "sympathy for the bereaved Fall caused Wilson's attack to backfire." In this isolated case, the horrific effect of the pandemic became a potent political issue; but in the country as a whole, remarkably, it did not.

It is impossible to know, even in retrospect, how much could have been done to minimize the loss of life in what was, after all, a vast and virtually unprecedented tidal wave of human misery. Nevertheless, it seems clear that a rational electorate could reasonably have held its leaders accountable, in part, for the devastating consequences of this natural disaster. Even with due allowance for the less developed public health technology of 1918, there is little reason to doubt that tens of thousands of flu victims could have been saved by more effective government action. Efforts to stem the contagion, or even to track its spread, were slow and disorganized (Crosby 1989, chaps. 1, 2, esp. 49–51; Kolata 1999, 10, 19, 22–23).

So why no electoral retribution? For one thing, blaming the government was not easy: the country was at war, making criticism seem unpatriotic. Both the government and the press downplayed flu risks (Barry 2004, chap. 29). Indeed, the pandemic seems to have received remarkably little national attention. As one historian put it, "When you talk to people who lived through it,

---

29 As it happens, 13 of the 16 "registration states" for which detailed mortality data are available had Republican governors in 1918. Thus, voting patterns would look very different depending on whether voters chose to punish incumbent governors or the party of the Democratic president.

30 In most cases, we examined the impact of influenza mortality rates in the final four months of 1918; for some cities we also had more detailed data that allowed us to examine the impact of flu deaths in the weeks immediately preceding the election. Not surprisingly, given the limitations of the available data, all of our statistical results were fairly imprecise and, in some cases, quite sensitive to changes in the sample or variable definitions. On the whole, however, it seems clear that the flu pandemic had little or no political effect. Some of the estimates suggest, quite implausibly, that incumbent governors actually *gained* votes in the major cities with the highest death rates. Only the estimate for Democratic votes at the state level had the "correct" (negative) sign, and even that estimate was of very modest magnitude.

they think it was just their block or just their neighborhood" (Crosby, quoted by Kolata 1999, 8). Victims were widely scattered around the country; and since people died of influenza every year, no one could be certain that their own spouse or parent or child was one of the "excess deaths" from the epidemic, much less a death that the government might have prevented.

Most important, no thread of elite rhetoric or popular discourse seems to have suggested any attribution of responsibility to President Wilson or other public officials. As long as no one supplied a convincing argument that the government did control or should have controlled the spread of the pandemic or its horrific consequences, the pain of millions failed to have any electoral impact. President Wilson was berated for the insufficiency of his efforts to stem the tide of shark attacks in New Jersey in 1916 and taunted with editorial cartoons featuring shark fins; but there is no evidence of a comparable outcry over his handling of the flu pandemic, except in an isolated instance in which he insensitively attacked a political opponent whose children had been among the victims.

The striking absence of a broad-based electoral response to the flu pandemic dramatically illustrates the importance of voters' cultural understandings of causation and responsibility. In the language of Deborah Stone's (1989, 283) typology of causal frameworks, voters thought of the pandemic as part of the natural world ("the realm of fate and accident") rather than as part of the social world ("the realm of control and intent"). Obviously, such cultural understandings are subject to change.[31] But at the time, while hundreds of thousands of people died, no one thought to blame the pharaoh.

CONCLUSION

In most recent scholarly accounts, retrospective voting is a natural and rational feature of democratic politics. In our view it is natural, but not so obviously rational. Indeed, blind retrospection of the sort we have documented in this chapter seems to us to provide a significant challenge to the conventional understanding of political accountability in modern democracies.

We have shown that voters sometimes punish incumbent political leaders for misfortunes that are clearly beyond the leaders' control. Moreover, we have

31 Modern governments have certainly believed that the political cost of a major flu epidemic might be considerable, as witnessed by the Ford administration's aggressive—as it turned out, overly aggressive—response to the swine flu scare in the 1970s (Neustadt and Fineberg 1983).

shown that they do so with considerable regularity. The fact that American voters throughout the 20th century punished incumbent presidents at the polls for droughts and floods seems to us to rule out the possibility that they were reacting to subpar *handling* of misfortunes rather than to the misfortunes themselves. After all, it is hard to see how incumbent presidents' handling of droughts and floods could have been substantially worse than average over the course of an entire century.

Of course, voters may themselves contribute to poor disaster preparedness by insisting on low taxes and less intrusive government. In that case, government performance in response to disasters will nearly always seem poor in some absolute sense, and incumbents will be punished accordingly. But this sort of retrospective punishment is self-defeating in exactly the way we have suggested, since the randomness of the punishment from the standpoint of incumbents makes it pointless (in an electoral sense) for any incumbent to invest *ex ante* in adequate preparations for disasters (Healy and Malhotra 2009).

What, if anything, is wrong with blind retrospection? In a world of great uncertainty and costly attentiveness, perhaps this is exactly what voters should do to hold their leaders accountable—"only calculate the changes in their own welfare," as Fiorina (1981, 5) put it, and vote accordingly. Maybe there was something Woodrow Wilson could have done for the Jersey Shore, even if no informed person at the time could think of what that might be. And if a few pharaohs perish needlessly as a result of fanciful causal chains in the voters' minds, is that such a high price to pay for a system in which every incumbent has a strong incentive to do whatever she can to maximize her citizens' welfare? In short, aren't voters behaving rationally when they reward or punish incumbents for good or bad times?

In one sense, this view of retrospective voting is quite right. When voters are utterly ignorant about whether and how their leaders' actions affect their own welfare, blind retrospection may be "rational" in a narrow, technical sense. However, that does not imply that it will be sensible or prudent. Crazy beliefs can make crazy behavior "rational." But as the models presented in chapter 4 demonstrate, ignorance about reality can be quite costly in the realm of democratic politics, just as it is in other aspects of life.

Our account strikes directly at the heart of the common normative justification for the retrospective theory of political accountability. In that view, while voters may know very little, they can at least recognize good or bad government performance when they see it. Thus, they can retrospectively reward or punish leaders in a sensible way. We agree that voters operating on the basis of a valid, detailed understanding of cause and effect in the realm of public policy could reward good performance while ridding themselves of leaders who are malevolent or incompetent. But real voters often have only a vague understanding of the connections (if any) between incumbent politicians' actions and their own well-being. Even professional observers of politics often struggle to understand the consequences of government policies. Politics and policy are complex. As a result, retrospective voting is likely to produce consistently misguided patterns of electoral reward and punishment.

To sensibly translate an assessment of economic or social *conditions* into an assessment of political *performance*, citizens must find—and accept—a valid cultural understanding of the causal relationships linking the actions of public officials to changes in the public's welfare. When is one such understanding accepted rather than another? A healthy democratic culture among political elites can, no doubt, help significantly to constrain the scapegoating impulses of democratic electorates. Yet just as much or more seems to depend on the political folk culture among ordinary citizens, or on different folk subcultures for different groups.

Tracing how a specific political attribution of blame attains plausibility among inattentive citizens suddenly in want of an explanation for their troubles is a daunting task. The young and old, the rich and poor, the educated and uneducated are all swept along by the ideas popular in their groups, and sometimes all are swept along together. Certain looks, certain sounds, and certain arguments meet widespread needs in a particular culture at a particular time, nearly always for complex reasons unforeseeable in advance. The only certainty is that there is nothing very rational about the process.

Our analysis suggests that "blind" retrospection on the basis of overall well-being, with no consideration of the impact of government policies on that well-being, is very unlikely to provide much in the way of effective accountability, notwithstanding the fact that it may be "rational" in a narrow sense. Voters ignorant about evidence and causation, but supplied with a tale of incumbent responsibility, will punish incumbents whenever their subjective well-being falls below some fixed standard, regardless of whether or not their pain is in fact traceable to the incumbents' policies.

The "rough justice" (Fiorina 1981, 4) embodied in the electoral verdicts rendered by such voters is likely to be very rough indeed. And the rougher it is, the less incentive reelection-minded incumbents will have to exert themselves on the voters' behalf. As a result, voters who cannot distinguish the effects of shark attacks and droughts from the effects of tax policies and foreign wars are likely to experience more than their share of misguided tax policies and disastrous foreign wars. This sort of voting is hard to square with rosy interpretations of retrospective accountability, and even harder to square with the folk theory of democracy, in which ordinary citizens assess their public life critically, weigh the qualifications of competing candidates for public office, and then choose between the candidates in accordance with their own values.

Democracies take their electoral direction from human beings with limited capacities for self-government. Human passions remain powerful, and human understanding remains weak. Under sufficient pressure, voters sometimes lash out blindly. Such events are not quaint historical footnotes rendered irrelevant by modern education and hygiene. Indeed, in just the past century many citizens—and many prominent intellectuals—have been enthusiastic supporters of Nazis, Bolsheviks, Mao's Communist guerillas, and a host of other brutal demagogues whose policies seemed to offer attractive solutions to fundamental social problems that the previous incumbent rulers had failed to master.

Blind retrospection afflicts us all. It is the inevitable consequence of bewildering social complexity and human cognitive limitations—limitations that the rise of democratic government has not altered. The conventional account of retrospective voting, minimalist as it is, fundamentally underestimates the limitations of democratic citizens and, as a result, the limitations of democratic accountability.

Musical Chairs: Economic Voting and the Specious Present

> We endow our presidents with mythical power, holding them responsible for the health of the economy. . . . If the economy is flourishing in the final weeks of a campaign, when the music stops, the incumbent is likely to be re-elected.
>
> —Louis Uchitelle, "Beyond a President's Control" (2004)

> The longest duration which we immediately feel is what is called the "specious present."
>
> —Walter Lippmann, *Public Opinion* (1922, 90)

The most important application of the retrospective theory of democracy has been in the realm of "economic voting." Politicians and journalists have long believed that economic distress is politically damaging to incumbent leaders. As we saw in chapter 4, electoral punishment for economic hardship seems to date back to the 19th century, at least—well before Keynes taught governments how to control (at least to some extent) modern industrial economies. The contribution of modern political science has been to provide an impressive body of systematic evidence that voters reward incumbent politicians for good economic times and punish them for bad times (Kramer 1971; Lewis-Beck 1988; Markus 1988; and many others). While the details—which specific economic conditions matter, when, and why—are subject to scholarly dispute, we noted in chapter 4 that a near-consensus has emerged that the effect of economic voting is real and substantial, providing strong support for the retrospective view of elections.

If competent governments are thought to be able to control the economy, at least to some degree, then economic voting seems eminently sensible—and the impact of economic conditions on election outcomes seems to provide powerful evidence of democratic accountability. One strand of the voluminous literature on economic voting focuses on the possibility that myopic voters can be fooled by irresponsible policies that stimulate the economy around election time, leaving the costs to be borne after the votes are counted (Tufte 1978). But more often, the strong tendency of voters to reward incumbents for good economic times and punish them for bad times has been viewed as a mark of the rationality of democratic electorates.

In this chapter we examine more critically the "rationality" of economic voting within the retrospective theory of democratic accountability. As we suggested in chapter 4, it is by no means obvious that voters can ascertain how incumbents have performed simply by assessing changes in their own welfare. If jobs have been lost in a recession, something is wrong, but is that the president's fault? If it is not, then voting on the basis of good or bad economic conditions may be no more efficacious than killing the pharaoh when the Nile fails to flood or voting against Woodrow Wilson when sharks attack the Jersey shore. As professional survey researcher Andrew Kohut (quoted by Uchitelle 2004) put it, "Ordinary people don't have a good sense of what the president can and cannot do about the economy. Their perception is that he is responsible for how they are faring, and if he does not acknowledge their complaints, they judge him as indifferent and not doing a good job." Or, as Theodore Roosevelt (quoted by Goodwin 2013, 530) put it while he coped with the Panic of 1907, "When the average man loses his money he is simply like a wounded snake and strikes right or left at anything, innocent or the reverse, that presents itself as conspicuous in his mind."

An even more fundamental problem is that voters may have great difficulty accurately assessing changes in their welfare—even with respect to national economic conditions, which are highly salient and carefully monitored by professional economists in and out of government. If voters are systematically biased in their perceptions of economic conditions, retrospective accountability will suffer for the reasons we set out in chapter 4. In that case, economic voting may be little more than a high-stakes game of musical chairs.[1]

---

1 In the game of musical chairs, a group of children march around a set of chairs in which they had been seated. Music is played while one chair is removed. Then the music is suddenly stopped and everyone must try to find a seat. The child who fails to do so is out of the game. This sequence is repeated until the last round, when only one child—the winner—has a seat.

THE SPECIOUS PRESENT

Louis Uchitelle's (2004) account of economic voting in presidential elections has a disturbingly arbitrary air: "If the economy is flourishing in the final weeks of a campaign, when the music stops, the incumbent is likely to be re-elected." Even if we agree that an incumbent president's policies have some significant long-term impact on the economy, he is no more likely to control whether it is flourishing on Election Day than the children in a game of musical chairs are to control how close they are to a vacant seat at the moment the music stops. Is that really how we pick our presidents?

In this chapter, we examine voters' economic time horizons as a test of their astuteness in holding incumbent leaders accountable for economic performance. If voters are attempting to reward (or punish) incumbents for contributing (or failing to contribute) to their real incomes, or to the economic fortunes of society as a whole, they should assess economic conditions "over the incumbent's entire term of office, with little or no backward time discounting of performance outcomes," as Douglas Hibbs (2006, 570) put it. However, the striking fact is that virtually all analyses of retrospective economic voting focus on economic conditions during the election year, or even some fraction of the election year, rather than over the longer haul of an entire term.

The scholarly literature on economic voting includes surprisingly little justification—or even discussion—of this narrow temporal focus. For example, in his pioneering analysis of economic voting in congressional elections, Gerald Kramer (1971, 134) defined the relevant economic variable as "the difference between the actual performance of the incumbent party during its just-ending term in office, as measured by some index such as per capita income, and the performance 'expected' of it by the electorate." He then added the "reasonable and convenient hypothesis . . . that expectations about year t are formed on the basis of experience during the preceding year, $t-1$." That is, voters should simply compare their current income with last year's income—the most recent growth rate. Having stipulated that prior years were irrelevant, Kramer proceeded to report the results of statistical analyses relating the incumbent party's congressional vote to income growth in the election year only, rather than over the incumbent party's entire term.

Other analysts have focused on even shorter time horizons, such as the first and second (Lewis-Beck and Tien 2001) or even just the second (Campbell 2001) quarter of the election year, or have assumed that most or all of each incumbent's term matters, but with recent performance weighted more heavily than earlier performance (Hibbs 1982; Erikson 1989; Bartels and Zaller 2001). Implicitly, at least, all of these analysts, and many others, have assumed that voters attempt to ascertain whether the incumbents have performed poorly or well on the basis of a limited—and potentially misleading—assessment of changes in their own or the nation's economic welfare.

If voters are rationally forecasting the future, as Kramer stipulated, then the optimal weights for them to place on past performances are a function of how the economy and incumbent competence evolve over time, and different assumptions make a substantial difference (Achen 2012). In the simplest and most plausible case, however, in which incumbent competence is assumed to be constant over time, the best forecast voters can make of an incumbent's future performance is just the average past performance. All time periods for which the incumbent is responsible should be weighted equally. This is also the weighting that has the most intuitive ethical plausibility—and some evidence suggests that it comports with voters' own intentions (Healy and Lenz 2014).

Why, then, so much emphasis in the empirical literature on short-term performance? We suspect that analysts have simply given up on what *should* work because it *doesn't* work. With the notable exception of Hibbs (2006, 576), whose analyses imply "modest (if any) discounting over the term," the clear consensus in the literature is that recent economic performance is much more relevant at election time than earlier performance.[2] However, most analysts have failed to notice the troubling implications of this fact for democratic accountability under the retrospective voting model.

In this chapter we explore the time horizon of economic voting in U.S. presidential elections. Our economic data consist of quarterly readings of real disposable personal income per capita from the U.S. Bureau of Economic Analysis (BEA).[3] As Hibbs (2000, 149) noted, "Growth of real disposable personal income per capita is probably the broadest single aggregate measure of changes in voters' economic well-being, in as much as it includes income from all market sources, is adjusted for inflation, taxes, government transfer payments and population growth, and tends to move with changes in unemployment. For

2 Hibbs's analyses are rare in focusing on the extent of temporal discounting in voters' reactions to economic conditions. However, as we will see, both his analyses (Hibbs 1982; 2000; 2006; 2012) and others employing similar models (Erikson 1989; Bartels and Zaller 2001; Erikson, Bafumi, and Wilson 2002) have produced rather mixed evidence regarding the extent to which voters discount past economic performance.

3 The data are publicly available from the BEA website, http://www.bea.gov, table 7.1, line 12.

these reasons, it is not surprising that it is a good single-variable election predictor." Many analysts of economic voting have used GDP rather than real income to gauge incumbents' economic performance; however, direct comparison of these two indicators clearly demonstrates that real income is more relevant than GDP in accounting for election outcomes (Achen and Bartels 2004; Bartels 2008, chap. 4).

We employ data from the first quarter of 1947 through the second quarter of 2013, focusing on quarterly growth rates in real income.[4] Since our focus is on economic voting in presidential elections, it will be convenient to index quarters in relation to the four-year election cycle, with Q1 referring to the quarter in which a president is inaugurated and Q16 referring to the final quarter of the subsequent election year.

At first blush, the cumulative income growth rate from Q1 through Q16 may seem like a good summary of how voters have fared economically on the incumbent president's watch.[5] However, there are two reasons to think that a president's entire four-year term does not and should not figure in voters' assessments of his economic stewardship. First, Q16 is only one-third completed at the time of the next election, so voters may not incorporate it in their assessments. (As we will see, they seem not to do so—at least not very strongly or consistently.) Second, economic conditions in the early months of a president's term may more reasonably be associated with the policies of his predecessor than with his own policies, which take time to adopt and implement before they can alter economic conditions. Thus, voters may, and probably should, ignore the first months of a president's term in assessing his economic performance.

How long is a new president's economic grace period? Bartels (2008), citing macroeconomic research on the timing of economic responses to monetary and fiscal policy changes (Christiano, Eichenbaum, and Evans 1999; Blanchard and Perotti 2002), measured partisan control of the economy with

---

4 We analyze quarterly growth rates, defined as

$$\Delta RDI_t = 100\,[ln(RDI_t) - ln(RDI_{t-1})].$$

The natural logarithms convert gains and losses to an equivalent scale, so that they count equally. To a good approximation when changes are not large, the differences in the logs represent fractional changes. Multiplication by 100 turns the fractions into more intuitive percentage points.

5 Given our definition of quarterly growth rates, cumulative growth over any specified period is simply the sum of the relevant quarterly growth rates. For example, cumulative RDI growth over a president's entire term is

$$\Delta RDI{:}Q1\text{-}Q16 = \Sigma_{t=Q1,\ldots,Q16}\,\Delta RDI_t.$$

a one-year lag. With quarterly data we can be more flexible. Here, we treat each administration's economic responsibility as beginning five months after it takes office (that is, with economic growth in Q3) and ending five months after the next inauguration (at the end of Q18). Empirically, this definition of economic responsibility maximizes observed variability across administrations in economic outcomes. Thus, it seems attractive given our specific interest in examining voters' abilities to assess the economic performance of successive presidential administrations—and the potential for economic voting along the lines envisioned by theorists of retrospective voting. However, plausible alternative definitions (for example, assigning each administration responsibility beginning 11 months after it takes office) generally produce results similar to those reported here.

Table 6.1 presents the results of three different statistical analyses exploring the political effects of income growth over varying time horizons in presidential elections since 1952.[6] Each of these analyses focuses on the electoral success of the incumbent party,[7] as measured by its candidate's national popular vote margin (in percentage points).[8] In addition to income growth, these statistical analyses include the incumbent party's tenure in office as an explanatory factor. There is a fairly strong tendency for the incumbent party's

6 We exclude the 1948 election from our analysis because comparable measures of long-term economic performance are unavailable (our quarterly income data begin in 1947) and because the transition from a wartime economy to a peacetime economy may have skewed the economic meaning and political implications of income growth in the immediate post-war years. However, our key results would remain virtually unchanged if we included the 1948 election in our analyses involving short-term income growth. This stability is impressive in light of the fact that income grew at an annual rate of 7.7% in the second and third quarters of 1948, well outside the range observed in subsequent election years.

7 We follow the usual practice in the literature of treating would-be successors from a retiring president's party as members of the same partisan team, and thus equally affected by voters' assessments of economic conditions. This assumption greatly simplifies both the theory of retrospective voting and the empirical analysis. Of course, whether voters see it that way is another matter. Helmut Norpoth's (2004) analysis going back to 1872 casts some doubt on the notion. Our analysis below suggests that for the post–World War II era, at least, the assumption of partisan continuity is not unreasonable.

8 Most analysts focus on the incumbent party's share of the two-party vote, which is an entirely equivalent measure in two-party races but inflates the magnitude of the winning candidate's victory when there are large numbers of minor-party voters. If minor-party votes were drawn proportionally from the vote shares of the two main parties, the winner's share of the two-party vote would arguably provide a better reflection of his share of overall support. However, in most cases it seems more reasonable to suppose that minor-party votes were drawn disproportionately from the losing party (thus helping to explain why it lost). Of course, the range of possible vote *margins* is twice the range of possible vote *shares*, and our statistical results must be interpreted accordingly.

Table 6.1. Long-Term and Short-Term Economic Voting in Presidential Elections

	Long-term growth	Short-term growth	Both
Income growth: Q3–Q15	1.35 (0.49)	—	—
Income growth: Q14–Q15	—	6.37 (1.06)	7.62 (1.43)
Income growth: Q3–Q13	—	—	−0.70 (0.55)
Incumbent tenure (years)	−1.68 (0.45)	−1.78 (0.29)	−1.79 (0.29)
Intercept	6.20 (4.84)	9.45 (2.55)	12.33 (3.37)
Standard error of regression	7.40	4.82	4.71
Adjusted R^2	.54	.81	.81
N	16 (1952–2012)		

Ordinary least squares regression parameter estimates (with standard errors in parentheses) for incumbent party's popular vote margin (%); quarterly growth in real disposable income per capita (inauguration in Q1, election in Q16).

electoral fortunes to decline the longer it has held the White House; presumably this pattern reflects the cumulative effect of exhausted policy agendas, personnel turnover, and accumulating scandals on voters' desire for a change in leadership (Stokes and Iversen 1962; Abramowitz 1988; Bartels 1998). Over the course of a four-year term, these forces reduce the incumbent party's expected popular vote margin by 5 to 8 percentage points.

The statistical analysis presented in the first column of table 6.1 includes a measure of long-term economic performance, the cumulative rate of real income growth in the 13 quarters leading up to Election Day (Q3–Q15)—the entire period for which the incumbent administration might reasonably be held accountable at the polls. The impact of income growth on the incumbent party's electoral fortunes is clearly discernible in this analysis. The statistical results imply that every additional percentage point of income growth increased the incumbent party's expected popular vote margin by almost

1.5 percentage points. However, the overall fit of the statistical model is mediocre, with an average error of 7.4 percentage points in the predicted incumbent vote margins.

The analysis presented in the second column of table 6.1 focuses instead on short-term income growth in Q14 and Q15—the six months leading up to Election Day. Despite ignoring most of each president's income growth record, this version of the economic voting model clearly provides a much better explanation of election outcomes. The average error in the predicted incumbent vote margins is reduced by more than one-third and the estimated effect of income growth is almost five times as large, implying that every additional percentage point of income growth increased the incumbent party's expected popular vote margin by more than 6 percentage points. Thus, a one-term incumbent seeking reelection during a recession (Jimmy Carter in 1980) might expect to lose by about 3 percentage points, whereas a one-term incumbent seeking reelection in a boom year (Lyndon Johnson in 1964, Richard Nixon in 1972, or Ronald Reagan in 1984) might expect to win in a landslide, by from 18 to 23 percentage points.[9]

[handwritten margin note: Short term before election greater impact]

The final column of table 6.1 includes both short-term (Q14–Q15) and earlier (Q3–Q13) income growth as explanatory factors in a single statistical analysis. Here, it is even clearer that recent rather than long-term income growth is what matters to voters. Indeed, the estimated impact of short-term income growth is even larger in this specification, while the apparent effect of earlier income growth is perversely negative—though too small to be confident that there is any real long-term effect at all. As in the previous column, the average error of the predicted incumbent vote margins is about 5 percentage points, which implies that a typical error in predicting the incumbent party's vote *share* would be on the order of 2 or 3 percentage points.[10]

These results suggest that it is possible to account for recent presidential election outcomes with a fair degree of precision solely on the basis of how long the incumbent party had been in power and how much real income growth voters experienced in the six months leading up to Election Day. Economic growth earlier in the president's term seems to contribute little or nothing to the incumbent party's electoral prospects.

9 In fact, Johnson, Nixon, and Reagan all won by 18 to 23 percentage points, while Carter lost by 10 points—the second-largest residual in this version of our analysis—perhaps due to retrospective assessments of dramatic foreign policy failures in Iran and elsewhere.

10 Eisenhower's landslide reelection in 1956, a year with below-average income growth, produced the largest residual vote margins in both these analyses, 9.4 and 9.8 percentage points, respectively.

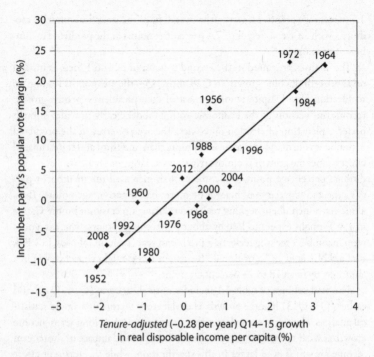

Figure 6.1. Short-Term Income Growth, Tenure, and Presidential Election Outcomes, 1952–2012

Figure 6.1 provides a graphical summary of the historical relationship between short-term income growth, incumbent party tenure, and presidential election outcomes. Election years are arrayed along the horizontal axis on the basis of growth rates in real disposable personal income per capita in the six months leading up to each election (Q14–Q15), adjusted for how long the incumbent party has held the White House.[11] The vertical axis represents the popular vote margin (in percentage points) for the incumbent party's presi-

11 The parameter estimates reported in the second column of table 6.1 imply that each additional year in the White House reduced the incumbent party's vote margin by the equivalent of $(1.78/6.37) = .28$ percentage points of short-term income growth. Thus, we calculate adjusted income growth rates by subtracting .28 from the actual income growth rate for each additional year of incumbent party tenure beyond the four-year minimum; when the incumbent party has held the White House for only one term, the adjusted and actual income growth rates are identical.

dential candidate. Although there are some significant deviations from the historical pattern in specific election years, this simple model clearly provides a powerful account of modern presidential election outcomes.

We probed the robustness of the results presented in table 6.1 by examining several additional statistical specifications relating incumbent party vote margins to income growth measured over a variety of alternative time horizons and subsets of elections. For example, we examined all of the time horizons longer than the "short-term" (2-quarter) time horizon in table 6.1 but shorter than the "long-term" (13-quarter) time horizon to see if any did better in accounting for election outcomes; none did.[12] Moreover, as the scatterplot presented in figure 6.1 suggests, the statistical relationship is quite insensitive to the inclusion or exclusion of particular elections or subsets of elections. Omitting each election in turn produced estimated effects of short-term income growth ranging from 5.5 to 6.7. Omitting all three boom years (1964, 1972, and 1984) produced an estimate of 5.2. Omitting all three years with negative short-term income growth (1980, 2008, and 2012) produced an estimate of 5.6. Omitting the three most recent elections (as we did in the original version of this analysis a decade ago) produced an estimate of 6.7.[13] Limiting the analysis to the eight elected presidents who ran for reelection produced an estimate twice as large as for the six "successor" candidates who were not themselves presidents (7.8 versus 3.7); however, this difference is too imprecisely estimated to be statistically reliable.[14]

The results presented in table 6.2 summarize a variety of additional robustness checks. The analyses presented in the first two columns of the table focus on the possibility that voters may weigh income growth over the entire course

12 The best fitting of these intermediate models, with income growth averaged over the last seven quarters before the election (Q9-Q15), produced a standard error about 6% larger than the standard error of the short-term regression reported in the fifth column of table 6.1; the standard errors for the other intermediate models ranged from 7% to 54% larger.

13 The parameter estimate for short-term income growth reported in our original working paper (Achen and Bartels 2004) implies an estimate of 5.8 using the quarterly growth rates employed here. The higher estimate of 6.7 is attributable to subsequent revisions in the BEA's income data. However, the addition of more recent elections has a counterbalancing effect, producing a parameter estimate in table 6.1 virtually identical to the one we originally reported—a reassuring indication of the robustness of our simple model of presidential election outcomes.

14 In an interactive analysis, each additional year in the White House (ranging from zero to four, with Lyndon Johnson in 1964 and Gerald Ford in 1976 as intermediate cases) increased the apparent impact of short-term income growth by .60 (with a standard error of .48), about 12%.

Table 6.2. Alternative Models of the Timing of Electoral Responses to Income Growth

	(1)	(2)	(3)
Geometrically weighted income growth	5.83 (1.36)	−0.76 (2.76)	—
Income growth: Q16		—	
Income growth: Q15		7.04 (2.69)	3.25 (0.92)
Income growth: Q14			
Income growth: Q13			
Income growth: Q9–Q12	—		2.45 (1.08)
Income growth: Q5–Q8		—	−0.02 (0.60)
Income growth: Q1–Q4			−1.11 (0.63)
Incumbent tenure (years)	−1.50 (0.37)	−1.82 (0.33)	−1.35 (0.32)
Intercept	0.73 (4.48)	10.72 (5.32)	0.52 (3.58)
Standard error of regression	6.03	5.00	4.58
Adjusted R^2	.70	.79	.83
N		16 (1952–2012)	

Ordinary least squares regression parameter estimates (with standard errors in parentheses) for incumbent party's popular vote margin (%); quarterly growth in real disposable income per capita (inauguration in Q1, election in Q16) constrained or omitted as shown.

of a president's term, but with systematic discounting of growth earlier in the term. The specific functional form adopted here is the geometric lag structure proposed by Hibbs (1982; 2000).[15]

15 The geometric lag specification allows voters to weigh income growth in each quarter by a fixed proportion λ (less than 1.0) of the weight attached to the subsequent quarter. Values of λ close to 1.0 imply that early income growth is almost as important as election-year income

The statistical analysis presented in the first column of table 6.2 uses the resulting geometrically weighted income growth rates along with incumbent tenure to account for presidential election outcomes. The analysis produces a substantial estimated effect of weighted income growth and a good statistical fit (with an average error in estimated incumbent vote margins of 6 percentage points). However, adding our measure of short-term income growth (in the second column of table 6.2) obliterates the apparent effect of geometrically weighted income growth, suggesting that Hibbs's formulation adds little or nothing to the simpler analysis presented in the second column of table 6.1.

The analysis presented in the third column of table 6.2 provides a more detailed examination of temporal fluctuations in the apparent impact of economic conditions, with separate estimates of the electoral impact of income growth in each year of a president's term. The result is a fairly smooth-looking pattern of declining weights going backward in time. However, the estimated effect of income growth in the second year of a president's term is almost exactly zero, while the estimated effect of income growth in the first year is actually *negative*. While it would be a mistake to take these results too seriously, given the limitations of the available data, they certainly suggest that the geometric lag specification understates the extent to which voters discount economic performance in the first half of a president's term. More generally, they suggest, once again, that accounting for income growth outside of presidential election years does little to improve upon the simpler analysis presented in the second column of table 6.1. While income growth in the third year of each president's term almost surely has *some* effect at the polls, incorporating that effect improves the statistical fit of the model only slightly. And income growth in the second year of each president's term seems to be utterly forgotten—or at least politically irrelevant—by the time of the next election.

None of these alternative statistical analyses clearly improves upon the simple analysis presented in the second column of table 6.1, in which voters

---

growth in voters' assessments; lower values imply greater discounting of early performance. Hibbs's estimates of λ range from .80 (Hibbs 1982, using data from 1952–1980) to .954 (Hibbs 2000, using data from 1952–1996). Other scholars employing versions of Hibbs's specification have estimated more substantial discounting, with estimates of λ ranging from .82 (Bartels and Zaller 2001) down to .53 (Erikson, Bafumi, and Wilson 2002). Our data and model specification produce an estimate of .76. However, for purposes of illustration in table 6.2 we adopt Hibbs's most recent estimate, .90 (Hibbs 2012, using data from 1952–2008), which implies an intermediate level of temporal discounting. All of these parameter estimates are based on quarterly data; thus, if λ = .90, Q15 is assumed to receive about 3.5 times as much weight as Q3.

are assumed to respond to income growth only in the last two quarters before the election. Certainly none provides empirical support for the notion that voters weigh economic outcomes equally, or even approximately equally, over the entire period for which the incumbent president and his party could plausibly be considered responsible.

CAN MYOPIC VOTERS SELECT COMPETENT ECONOMIC MANAGERS?

Our analysis of economic voting suggests that presidential elections provide significant moments of economic accountability. As Gerald Kramer (1971, 140) put it decades ago, "election outcomes are in substantial part responsive to objective changes occurring under the incumbent party." However, objective changes in economic well-being seem to matter significantly only if they occur in close proximity to Election Day. In this respect, economic accountability is seriously skewed by voters' short time horizons. Myopic voters reward their elected leaders for *some* good times and punish them for *some* bad times. Is that good enough?

We explore this question by assessing separately the two distinct rationales for retrospective voting set out in chapter 4—selection and sanctioning. In this section we consider the selection rationale, in which retrospective voters systematically improve the average economic competence of political leaders by retaining incumbents who are competent economic managers and replacing those who are not. In the next section we turn to the sanctioning rationale, in which retrospective voters induce leaders (regardless of their intrinsic competence) to strive to produce good economic outcomes by rewarding success and punishing failure.

The selection rationale requires us to assume that there are real differences in economic competence between competing political teams. If there are, it certainly seems reasonable to suppose that an administration's past economic performance might provide voters with a useful clue about its competence, and thus about its likely future economic performance. However, in light of the crucial importance of this assumption for the whole notion of retrospective selection, it is striking that it has never, as far as we know, been subjected to any systematic empirical examination. Proponents of retrospective voting have simply *assumed* that there are real, persistent differences in economic competence between competing teams of political elites, and that voters who retain or replace the incumbent administration on the basis of its past performance are likely to get more competent government in the future as a result.

In this section, we attempt to put those assumptions to the test. In particular, we explore how well an electorate voting on the basis of very recent economic performance and ignoring or discounting most of what has happened on the incumbent's watch—an electorate of the sort portrayed in our empirical analysis of economic voting in modern presidential elections—is likely to succeed in selecting competent economic managers. The answer depends not only on the behavior of voters, but also on the dynamics of real income growth.

Three important characteristics of income growth in the post-war United States are evident in figure 6.2, which shows *annualized* quarter-by-quarter changes in real disposable income per capita over the entire period covered by our analysis. First, it is hard to see any striking trends in prevailing growth rates over this period.[16] Second, there is a great deal of short-term volatility in growth; quarterly fluctuations of 5 percentage points or more in the annualized growth rates are fairly common.[17] Third, and related, there is surprisingly little temporal continuity in quarter-to-quarter growth rates, even over short periods of time. For example, relating income growth in the current quarter to income growth in the four previous quarters produces lag coefficients of .00, .06, −.00, and −.14, with an adjusted R^2 statistic of .01. Thus, current deviations from the long-run average growth rate are very unlikely to provide a good basis for forecasting future deviations—a point of crucial but little-noticed importance if retrospective voting is supposed to result in the selection of successful future leaders.[18]

The solid line in figure 6.2 represents the average income growth rate for each four-year presidential administration.[19] Here, as in the analyses reported in table 6.1, we treat each administration's economic responsibility as beginning five months after it takes office (with Q3) and ending five months after the next inauguration (at the end of Q18).

16 More elaborate statistical analysis reveals some drift over time in the average income growth rate, but the discernible trends are of modest magnitude.

17 To some extent these fluctuations presumably reflect measurement error. However, there is no strong pattern of negative association between growth rates in successive quarters, as one would expect if the *level* of income in each quarter were measured with substantial random error.

18 Simply regressing the current rate of real income growth on the previous quarter's rate produces a lag coefficient of −.03 and an adjusted R^2 statistic of −.00. More elaborate time series analyses produce similar results.

19 We ignore the midterm transitions from Kennedy to Johnson and from Nixon to Ford, since in both cases there seems to have been a good deal of continuity in economic management teams and policies.

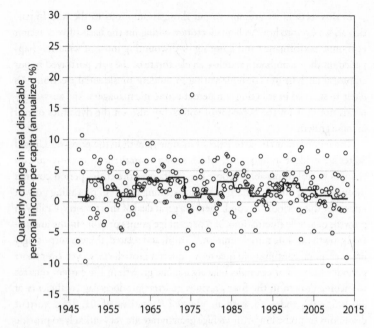

Figure 6.2. Income Growth by Presidential Administration, 1947–2013

Changes in the average level of real income growth from one administration to the next are clearly discernible in figure 6.2; but they are modest by comparison with the short-term fluctuations from one quarter to the next.[20] As a result, the correlation between each quarter's change in income and the *average* change for the corresponding administration is only .29. Allowing for the mechanical contribution of each quarter's change to the corresponding average reduces that correlation to only .16. (The correlation between quarterly and administration-average changes in GDP is only slightly more impressive.) More elaborate analyses including multiple lagged values, polynomial trends, and seasonal adjustments produce essentially similar results.

These features of the data are relevant for our analysis of retrospective voting because they suggest that voters are likely to have a good deal of difficulty discerning systematic changes in growth rates from one administration to the

20 It is not even possible to decisively reject the null hypothesis that the average income growth rates for every administration are identical; the tail probability for an *F*-test is .12.

next amid the constant short-term fluctuations in their economic well-being. Obviously, if voters cannot reliably *discern* differences in economic outcomes they cannot reliably *respond* to those differences.

The volatility of short-term income growth rates underscores the difficulty of making sensible assessments of an incumbent's economic competence on the basis of how things are going right now. Voters evaluating the economy on the basis of any one or two quarters are likely to do little better than chance at capturing the potentially meaningful differences in long-term performance represented by the administration average growth rates depicted in figure 6.2. In particular, the correlation between income growth over any two quarters and income growth over the same president's entire term is only .41, implying that more than 80% of the variance in overall economic performance is unrelated to short-term successes or failures of the sort that actually matter in the voting booth. Of course, part of the relevant overall performance in our accounting occurs *after* Election Day—but that simply underscores the extent to which any inference about the differential competence of specific administrations to produce future economic growth can be little more than a roll of the dice.

The fundamental dynamics of income growth suggest that myopic voters are unlikely to succeed in detecting genuine differences in the economic competence of specific administrations. However, suggesting that effective retrospective selection is likely to be difficult is not the same thing as establishing that it does not occur. Unfortunately, it is notoriously hard to provide a direct test of the prospective efficacy of economic voting, since the logic of the argument hinges on an inherently unobservable comparison between future economic performance under the incumbent and future economic performance under the challenger. Inevitably, the voters' choice on Election Day relegates one of those two outcomes to the realm of historical might-have-beens. Thus, we are reduced to testing the plausibility of the retrospective selection hypothesis from a variety of more or less oblique angles.

We begin with a test inspired directly by the model of retrospection set out in chapter 4. In that model, the voter's *electorally relevant subjective well-being* is represented as the sum of incumbent *competence* and random factors. In keeping with our evidence regarding myopic economic voting, we shall assume here that electorally relevant subjective well-being is indexed by observed income growth over a six-month period. In that case we can use observed economic data to directly estimate the magnitude of random factors contributing to subjective well-being. Table 6.3 presents the results of two different versions of such an analysis.

Table 6.3. Discerning the Economic "Competence" of Presidential Administrations Based on Six-Month Growth Records

	Presidencies	Parties
Competence (deviations from average income growth)	+0.26, −0.24, +1.38, +0.51, −0.89, +0.30, −1.26, +0.20, −1.16, −0.34	+0.41 (Dem), −0.28 (Rep)
Standard error of regression	2.98	2.98
Adjusted R^2	−.000	.005
N	131 (distinct six-month windows)	
Average efficiency of selection (improvement over random chance) (%)	8.3	9.1

Ordinary least squares regression parameter estimates for six-month income growth rates regressed on indicators for parties or presidencies, 1947–2012.

In the first version of the analysis, we assume that competence attaches to specific incumbents; in that case, our best guess regarding the competence of each president is represented by the average rate of income growth over that president's time in office. In the second version of the analysis, we assume that competence attaches to political parties rather than individual incumbents, and is constant over the entire post-war era; in that case, our best guess regarding the competence of each party is represented by the post-war average rate of income growth under all presidents of that party. In both cases, we assume—with unrealistic optimism—that competence is perfectly measured by the observed average rate of income growth, ignoring other aspects of competence as well as effects of good or bad luck that extend over an entire presidency or over all the Democratic or Republican presidencies of the post-war era.[21]

21 Treating observed average growth rates as *estimates* of underlying competence would clearly make retrospective voting look even less effective, since it would add another layer of uncertainty to voters' inferences based on short-term economic performance.

In keeping with these assumptions, we relate income growth in each six-month period of the post-war era—successive slices of economic experience of the sort actually relied on by myopic economic voters—to indicator variables representing the ten distinct presidencies (in the first version of the analysis) or Democratic and Republican parties (in the second version of the analysis). The results of these analyses are presented in the left- and right-hand columns of table 6.3, respectively.

In the analysis assuming incumbent-specific competence, the average (annualized) income growth rates range from 1.4 percentage points higher than the overall average (for Kennedy-Johnson) to 1.3 percentage points below the overall average (for George H. W. Bush). If we assume that voters assessing each incumbent contemplated replacing him with a challenger of average quality, these deviations from overall average growth rates directly reflect each incumbent's presumed relative competence.[22] However, the statistical analysis implies that six-month slices of short-term income growth are virtually uncorrelated with (these estimates of) underlying competence. The adjusted R^2 statistic, a measure of the signal-to-noise ratio, is slightly *less* than zero, while the average error of the regression is 3.0, implying a "noise" level (literally) off the chart of retrospective difficulty depicted in figure 4.1.[23]

In the analysis for parties, average income growth under Democratic presidents was .4 percentage points higher than the overall average, while average growth under Republican presidents was .3 percentage points lower than the overall average. Thus, our best estimate of the economic competence of Democratic presidents (relative to Republicans) is +.7, while our best estimate of the economic competence of Republicans (relative to Democrats) is −.7. Even these estimates capitalize on chance to some degree, though less than in the case of individual administrations. Nevertheless, the statistical analysis accounts for only a tiny fraction of the substantial variation in short-term income growth rates. The adjusted R^2 statistic is .005, implying that the best estimate of the signal-to-noise ratio for this model is essentially *zero*.

What do these results suggest about the likely effectiveness of retrospective selection? Clearly, the electorate's likely success in inferring the competence

22 A more complicated analysis might allow for long-term trends in income growth rates. Doing so would make the voter's problem even harder, since incumbent-specific deviations in growth rates would be (slightly) smaller in magnitude, making incumbents look (slightly) less distinct.

23 Given our scaling of variables, the standard error of the regression implies an estimated value of slightly less than 3.0 for the "noise" parameter σ in figure 4.1, well off the 0–2 scale.

of parties or specific incumbents from narrow slices of economic experience is essentially nil. Translating the estimates of relative competence and the estimated magnitudes of random factors into probabilities of reelection (as in figure 4.1), the average improvement over random chance is in each case less than 10%. That is, voters are less than 60% likely to reelect a party or candidate who is actually more competent than the available alternative, and more than 40% likely to reelect a party or candidate who is *less* competent than the available alternative.

These meager estimated success rates are partly a reflection of the fundamental difficulty of the voters' task—and it is worth reiterating that we have simplified that task considerably for purposes of our analysis by assuming that good and bad luck always cancels out over the course of a presidency, leaving average observed income growth as a perfectly reliable indicator of competence. However, the estimated inefficiency of selection is also attributable in significant part to myopia, which impels voters to judge incumbents on the basis of brief, relatively uninformative slices of economic experience.

Another way to examine the effectiveness of retrospective voting is to see what happens *after* each election. If we take seriously the notion that reelection hinges on economic competence, one implication is that we should expect to see more economic growth when the incumbent party is reelected than when it is dismissed by the voters. In the former case the incumbent party has presumably been retained because its past performance makes it a better than average bet to provide good economic management in the future.[24] In the latter case the new administration is presumably an unknown quantity, a random draw from some underlying distribution of economic competence. A secondary implication of this logic is that future economic performance should be less variable when the incumbent party is retained, since reelected administrations are a truncated subsample of the underlying distribution of economic competence (the worst economic performers having presumably been weeded out at reelection time).

These implications of the retrospective selection model are examined in table 6.4, which compares post-election economic performance in cases where the incumbent party has been reelected with the corresponding performance in cases where the incumbent party has been voted out of office. Our measures of post-election economic performance are the average rates of growth in real disposable income per capita and GDP per capita in Q19–Q34, the

24 Obviously, election outcomes are influenced by many other factors besides economic management. That fact complicates our proposed comparison, but does not alter the basic logic.

Table 6.4. Post-Election Economic Growth under Old and New Administrations

	Incumbent party retained	Incumbent party replaced	Difference
POST-ELECTION INCOME GROWTH			
Average growth	7.95 (1.73)	9.17 (1.70)	−1.22 (2.43)
Standard deviation	4.89	4.82	+0.06
POST-ELECTION GDP GROWTH			
Average growth	7.87 (2.50)	8.46 (1.43)	−0.59 (2.88)
Standard deviation	7.06	4.06	+3.00
N	8 (1948, 1956, 1964, 1972, 1984, 1988, 1996, 2004)	8 (1952, 1960, 1968, 1976, 1980, 1992, 2000, 2008)	16

Average values (with standard errors in parentheses) and standard deviations of post-election (Q19–Q34) growth in GDP per capita and real disposable income per capita (%), 1948–2008.

entire four years of the new president's economic stewardship. (We lose 2012 from this comparison because Barack Obama's full second-term post-election economic performance is not yet known; but we add 1948, giving us eight cases of reelection and eight cases of replacement.)

Expectations derived from the retrospective selection perspective fare quite poorly in this comparison. Post-election income growth was slightly more variable under reelected incumbents than in cases of partisan turnover, and post-election GDP growth was much more variable—the opposite of what one might expect if voters succeeded in weeding out poor performers. More important, the average rates of post-election income and GDP growth were *lower* in terms with reelected incumbents than in cases of partisan turnover—by 13% and 7%, respectively. Of course, with only 16 administrations to analyze, these comparisons are far from definitive.[25] However, there is

25 The estimated difference in post-election income growth between reelected administrations and those that were replaced is −1.22 percentage points (with a standard error of

clearly no support here for the notion that incumbents are retained or replaced on the basis of intrinsic economic competence.

A further, more stringent test of the retrospective selection perspective is to examine directly whether the factors that affect post-election economic performance, whatever they may be, also affect voters' decisions to retain or replace the incumbent party. If voters succeed to some extent in forecasting future economic competence, and vote accordingly—as the logic of the retrospective selection perspective implies—then we should observe more electoral support, other things being equal, for incumbents who turn out to be competent economic managers after the election than for those who turn out to be incompetent.

Of course, the context of post-election policy-making may bear little resemblance to what voters imagine on Election Day. The prospect of changes in the global economy, wars and terrorist attacks, unforeseen bouts of inflation or recession, and alterations in the makeup of the incumbent management team all produce a great deal of uncertainty about future economic performance under any incumbent. But that uncertainty is by no means irrelevant to our assessment of the likely efficacy of retrospective selection. To argue that the test of actual post-election performance is too stringent is, in effect, to concede that retrospective selection is too difficult for voters to succeed at it.

Table 6.5 presents the results of additional statistical analyses intended to search for traces of economic foresight in the outcomes of recent presidential elections.[26] Our aim in each case is to account for the reelected incumbent party's popular vote margin (in percentage points) on the basis of *post*-election income or GDP growth, measured over the entire four-year period for which the reelected administration is assumed to be responsible (Q19–Q34).

The statistical analysis reported in the first column of table 6.5 tests whether voters' support for incumbent administrations depends at all upon the *future* success of those administrations in producing income growth. The answer seems to be no; the estimated effect of future income growth is actually negative, though the estimate is quite imprecise. Of course, this statistical

---

2.43). The estimated difference in post-election GDP growth is −0.59 percentage points (with a standard error of 2.88). Going back to 1929 (using *annual* income data to approximate the quarterly data) adds four additional observations to the analysis, but leaves the results essentially unchanged.

26 By the logic of retrospective selection, new administrations are simply random draws from some overall distribution of competence—mere campaigning sheds no light on their specific competence. Thus, we limit our analyses here to the eight elections in which the incumbent party was, in fact, reelected—the instances in which pre-election economic performance should, theoretically, have provided useful insights regarding post-election performance.

Table 6.5. Economic Voting on the Basis of Post-Election Income and GDP Growth

	Post-election income growth		Post-election GDP growth	
	(1)	(2)	(3)	(4)
Post-election growth (Q19–Q34)	−0.11 (0.68)	−0.51 (0.59)	0.17 (0.46)	0.11 (0.56)
Short-term income growth (Q14–Q15)	—	6.73 (2.69)	—	4.92 (3.45)
Incumbent tenure (years)	—	−1.72 (0.61)	—	−1.80 (0.67)
Intercept	13.66 (6.19)	13.39 (4.60)	11.48 (4.76)	12.61 (5.00)
Standard error of regression	8.73	5.70	8.65	6.17
Adjusted R^2	−.16	.50	−.14	.42
N	8 (1948, 1956, 1964, 1972, 1984, 1988, 1996, 2004)			

Ordinary least squares regression parameter estimates (with standard errors in parentheses) for reelected incumbent party's popular vote margin (%), 1948–2008.

analysis would be very hard to defend as a plausible model of voting behavior, and its poor fit to the data (with an adjusted R^2 statistic of −.16) does nothing to inspire confidence.

The analysis presented in the second column of table 6.5 adds two explanatory factors that we have already shown to be strongly related to incumbent parties' electoral fortunes—short-term income growth in the two quarters preceding the election and the length of time (in years) that the incumbent party has controlled the White House. Not surprisingly, adding these factors to the analysis improves the goodness of fit substantially. The average error is reduced by more than one-third, and the adjusted R^2 statistic increases from −.16 to .50.[27] However, the key parameter estimate, for post-election income

27 The estimated effects of short-term income growth and incumbent tenure in this truncated sample are reassuringly similar in magnitude to the estimates for the full sample

growth, remains perversely negative and even increases in magnitude. In short, our analysis provides no support for the notion that retrospective voters can reliably recognize and reward competent economic management.

The third and fourth columns of table 6.5 present the results of parallel analyses focusing on post-election GDP growth. They require little by way of exposition, since the results are generally similar to those for post-election income growth. In the third column of the table, without controls, it appears that voters are no more supportive of incumbents who turn out, upon reelection, to preside over high rates of GDP growth. Adding control variables does nothing to improve the estimated effect of future GDP growth on incumbent vote margins. As with the results presented in the first two columns of table 6.5—and those presented in table 6.4—these results cast doubt on the notion that incumbents are reelected, even in part, on the basis of economic competence.

It behooves us to reiterate that the tests of retrospective selection offered here are indirect, and that their statistical power is quite limited. Thus, our results certainly do not *prove* that successful retrospective selection through economic voting is impossible. Nevertheless, it is striking how little empirical trace we have been able to find of the presumed connection between the choices of American voters in presidential elections and their subsequent economic fortunes. We eagerly await better data and more powerful tests. In the meantime, however, the efficacy of retrospective economic voting as a mechanism for selecting competent leaders must, we think, be taken as a matter of theoretical speculation, not as a matter of fact.

CAN MYOPIC VOTING PROVIDE INCENTIVES FOR SUSTAINED ECONOMIC GROWTH?

As we saw in chapter 4, even if retrospective voters are unlikely to succeed in selecting competent economic managers, they may contribute to their post-election welfare by incentivizing incumbents—regardless of competence—to do whatever they can to produce economic growth. The key idea here is that a rational electorate may have good reason to punish the incumbent party when times are bad, despite the fact that the past is past, and regardless of *why* times are bad, simply in order to discipline *future* incumbents. Whether or not voters can reliably identify variation in the competence of incumbents, their

---

of post-war elections reported in table 6.1, though of course they are much less precise due to the reductions in both sample size and variation in the dependent variable.

tendency to vote on the basis of perceived success or failure may reinforce incentives for future incumbents to do whatever they can to maximize voters' welfare.

In models of this sort, voters have no reason to expect the outcome of any particular election to have any direct impact on the course of the economy; whichever party wins will produce exactly the same post-election economic conditions. From this perspective, the empirical results presented in tables 6.3 and 6.4 are no embarrassment to an electorate whose sole aim is to establish a reputation for rewarding success and punishing failure. Retrospective voting, in this interpretation, is a simple mechanism for enforcing as much correspondence as possible between the goals of the voters and the goals *any* set of self-interested reelection-seeking politicians will actually pursue once they are in office.

For this retrospective sanctioning model to work effectively, however, voters must presumably reward (or punish) current incumbents for doing (or failing to do) what they want future incumbents to do. The usual, and quite sensible, assumption is that voters want to maximize the present discounted value of their future income stream. If we add the corollary assumption—well supported by a good deal of empirical evidence—that gains in income tend to cumulate and persist over time,[28] then the increment in voters' long-term economic welfare on any given incumbent's watch can be indexed, to a good approximation, by the average rate of real income growth throughout his term.[29] Thus, that is what rational voters implementing a retrospective sanctioning strategy should reward or punish.

It is striking, then, that the substantial empirical literature on economic voting finds voters doing no such thing. Most analysts have simply focused, without any explicit explanation or justification, on economic conditions in the year of the election. And, as we have shown here, paying more careful attention to earlier conditions clearly demonstrates that they are, to a good

28 In time series terms, income is not mean-reverting. Either a unit root or trend stationarity would imply that condition, with parameters varying by presidential administration. The voter's inference problem is somewhat different in the two cases, but the distinction makes no difference for our purposes.

29 A more exact calculation depends on the discount rate voters use to assess the present value of future income. The average rate of real income growth throughout a president's term is insensitive to differences in the timing of that income growth, which affect voter's welfare in the short run but are swamped in the long run, assuming that there *is* a long run and that voters do not discount future income too severely. To the extent that voters are impatient, they should reward early income growth more than later income growth of similar magnitude. As we have seen, they do not. In any case, for the sake of simplicity we adopt the customary assumption in the literature—that voters care about long-run average income growth.

approximation, electorally irrelevant—despite being (at least) as important as election-year conditions for voters' long-term economic well-being.

How would we expect reelection-seeking incumbent politicians to respond to the electoral incentives generated by such "myopic" retrospection? The obvious-seeming answer is that they should attempt to maximize income growth in the immediate run-up to elections, but care little about what happens to the economy at other times. A president who shirks (or, more realistically, pursues his own ideological agenda) in the months just before the election may be punished, but a president who shirks (or pursues his own ideological agenda) earlier in his term is likely to suffer little or no penalty at the polls. Thus, there is little or no *electoral* incentive for presidents to promote myopic voters' well-being during much of their time in office. Meanwhile, voters' short time horizons magnify incentives for incumbents to manipulate the economy in order to maximize economic performance around election time. The result is "a rational incentive for the party in power to manipulate the business cycle for electoral benefit" (Erikson 1989, 570).

William Nordhaus (1975) first called scholars' attention to the fact that voters' short time horizons might induce a "political business cycle" in democratic political systems, with incumbents' efforts to stimulate the economy producing regular peaks in growth around election times. The first extensive empirical analysis of political business cycles, by Edward Tufte (1978), provided statistical evidence of electoral cycles in transfer payments, income growth, unemployment, and inflation, as well as considerable qualitative evidence of specific efforts by incumbents to produce those cycles. Richard Nixon in 1972 was a particularly energetic manipulator of everything from the money supply (through his erstwhile political ally Arthur Burns, the chairman of the Federal Reserve Board) to effective dates of increases in Social Security benefits and payroll taxes; as Tufte (1978, 63) delicately put it, "The extremes of 1972 were special because Richard Nixon was special."[30]

Tufte worried that political manipulation of economic policy could generate significant social costs due to wasteful government spending and other forms of "economic instability and inefficiency" aimed at making the

---

30 According to Tufte, Nixon's enthusiasm for political manipulation of the economy arose in significant part from his unhappy experience with an *un*manipulated economy in his first presidential campaign in 1960. In a post-campaign memoir, Nixon (quoted by Tufte 1978, 6) wrote, "In October, usually a month of rising employment, the jobless rolls increased by 452,000. All the speeches, television broadcasts, and precinct work in the world could not counteract that one hard fact." Nixon lost the official national popular vote by fewer than 120,000 votes. (See Gaines 2001 for a recount.)

economy flourish around election time—"a bias toward policies with immediate, highly visible benefits and deferred, hidden costs—myopic policies for myopic voters" (Tufte 1978, 143). However, a good deal of subsequent empirical research has produced less clear-cut results. As one observer (Schultz 1995, 79) put it, "while the general logic behind the theory is quite persuasive, the empirical evidence for electoral-economic cycles is spotty at best."

We believe that a variety of problems contribute to the spotty empirical support for electoral cycles in economic outcomes. The power of statistical tests to detect pre-election fluctuations in economic conditions may be quite modest in short times series with few elections. Some studies focus on secondary measures of economic performance such as unemployment and inflation rather than income growth, which is clearly of primary electoral importance. Others are insensitive to important institutional details, such as whether the timing of elections is fixed or variable. The advent of "rational expectations" theory in macroeconomics has probably contributed to the skepticism of the scholars generating the empirical evidence, despite demonstrations that political business cycles of some form can emerge even in dynamic models with fully rational voters and politicians (Rogoff and Sibert 1988; Rogoff 1990).

We do not pretend to offer a thorough review and assessment of empirical evidence regarding political business cycles here. Instead, we provide a very simple test of whether economic performance has fluctuated in the run-ups to recent presidential elections in the way one might expect if incumbent presidents were catering to myopic economic voters. The results of this test are reported in figure 6.3, which summarizes average growth rates in real GDP per capita and real disposable income per capita in each year of the presidential election cycle, from inauguration (year 1) to reelection (year 4), from 1949 through 2012. The shaded bars represent GDP growth, while the solid bars represent income growth.

We have two distinct reasons to expect a stronger electoral cycle in real disposable income growth than in GDP growth. First, since voters are much more responsive to income growth than to GDP growth, incumbents have much more to gain from manipulating income growth. Second, as a practical matter, it is probably a good deal easier for incumbents to manipulate income growth—for example, through transfer payments and tax cuts—than to manipulate the pace of real economic output through macroeconomic policy.

As one might expect, given these considerations, the most striking aspect of figure 6.3 is the marked increase in average income growth (though not in GDP growth) in presidential election years. The changes in income growth over the course of the election cycle are impressively large, with average

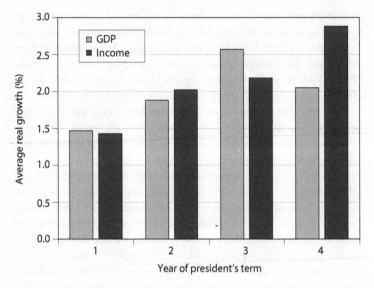

Figure 6.3. GDP and Income Growth through the Electoral Cycle, 1949–2012

income growth a full percentage point—more than 50%—higher in presidential election years than in non-election years (and substantially *lower* in the year *after* each election).[31] Moreover, the average election-year income growth rate exceeds the corresponding GDP growth rate by 40% (2.9 versus 2.0 percentage points)—just as we would expect if incumbents tailored their economic policies to appeal to an electorate that is much more attentive to election-year *income* growth than to election-year *GDP* growth. These pronounced electoral cycles of economic growth are a testament to the incentives created by a myopic electorate. As Tufte (1978, 137) insisted almost 40 years ago, "economic life vibrates with the rhythms of politics."

Another way to gauge the magnitude of election-related economic manipulation is to compare the average (annualized) rate of income growth in Q14 and Q15 with the average rate of GDP growth in Q3 through Q18—arguably the best single measure of each administration's overall economic

31 The *t*-statistic for the difference in average income growth between election years (2.9) and non-election years (1.9) is 2.8, making the difference exceedingly unlikely to be due to chance.

success or failure. Across the 16 administrations for which both numbers are available, the former exceeds the latter by an average of about 0.2 percentage points.[32] Given the estimated impact of short-term income growth on incumbent vote margins in table 6.1, this difference suggests that post-war incumbent parties have routinely padded their electoral margins by about two-thirds of a percentage point through political manipulation of the economy.

Of course, in any particular instance the difference between short-term and long-term economic performance is likely to reflect sheer good or bad luck in the timing of economic growth. We note, however, that Richard Nixon's 1972 reelection bid—Tufte's (1978) prime source of colorful examples of economic manipulation—produced one of the largest differences on record between short-term income growth and long-term GDP growth, boosting Nixon's vote margin by 7 or 8 percentage points. (Ronald Reagan in 1984 and Lyndon Johnson in 1964 probably gained 8 or 9 percentage points.) At the opposite extreme, Jimmy Carter's vote margin in 1980 was probably *reduced* by 10 or 11 percentage points—more than enough to cost him reelection—by the fact that voters judged his economic record on the basis of an election-year recession rather than on the basis of his overall economic performance.

More generally, our comparison of politically consequential short-term income growth rates with long-term GDP growth rates suggests that economic booms in the run-up to elections are not wholly a matter of good or bad luck. In the ten elections since World War II in which incumbent presidents ran for reelection, the annual rate of income growth in the run-up to the election exceeded the annual rate of GDP growth over the president's entire term by an average of almost half a percentage point, producing an estimated increase in the incumbents' average vote margin of 1.5 percentage points. However, in the six elections in which the incumbent president was retiring—giving him a less direct stake in the election outcome—the electorally crucial Q14–Q15 income growth rate was slightly *lower* than the long-term GDP growth rate, reducing the successor candidates' average vote margin by about 0.7 percentage points.[33]

---

32 This difference is primarily due to presidential elections rather than to the distinction between GDP and income growth rates. Outside of presidential election years, the average rate of GDP growth (1.94) slightly exceeds the average rate of income growth (1.77); but during presidential election years the average rate of income growth (3.03) greatly exceeds the average rate of GDP growth (2.04).

33 Omitting the 1968 election from this calculation (on the grounds that incumbent president Lyndon Johnson was eligible to run for reelection but chose not to) reduces but does

The social cost of this political manipulation of the economy is very difficult to assess. If incumbents merely shift income gains that would otherwise have occurred earlier or later into the election-year window of voter cognizance, the result is simply to add one more electoral edge to every incumbent's balance sheet.[34] On the other hand, to the extent that political manipulation of the economy generates deadweight losses due to wasteful government spending and other forms of "economic instability and inefficiency" (Tufte 1978, 143), the costs are presumably borne by the same voters whose short-sightedness generates the electoral economic cycle in the first place.

Less institutionalized, more volatile national economies may shed clearer light on the consequences of election-time pork. A director of the Turkish Treasury noted that the inflation rate was 17% in the six months preceding the November 1987 elections, and 48% in the next six months as voters paid the price for pre-election pump priming. The corresponding rates were 26% and 36% at the October 1991 elections and 24% and 46% at the December 1995 elections. "We, economy bureaucrats, do not like early and frequent elections," he said (Uras 2004).

What, if anything, can be done to mitigate political manipulation of the economy? Nordhaus (1975, 188–189) doubted "the practical possibility" of what he referred to as "the 'classical' political solution"—"improve the information available to voters so they can judge and condemn the partisan nature of myopic economic policies." He argued instead for tinkering with the frequency of elections or assigning greater control over economic policy to "persons who will not be tempted by the Sirens of partisan politics," including unelected central bankers and interest groups. In contrast, Tufte (1978, 154) concluded his analysis by asserting that "sleazier efforts at manipulating economic policy for short-run advantage cannot survive public scrutiny," and hoping that books like his might "improve the level of public understanding so that voters can evaluate and repudiate corrupt economic policies."

---

not eliminate this apparent penalty. Conversely, the apparent election-year boost for incumbents seeking reelection would be almost twice as large (increasing their average vote margin by 2.8 percentage points) if we excluded Jimmy Carter's election-year recession in 1980.

34 Of course, sensitive democrats might still consider it unfair or distasteful that the most shameless manipulators get the biggest electoral edge. And sensitive Democrats might still consider it unfair or distasteful that Republicans have generally benefited from uncharacteristically high short-term income growth when they have held the White House (gaining an average of 2 percentage points) and from uncharacteristically low short-term income growth when Democrats have held the White House (gaining an average of 1 percentage point). Bartels (2008, chap. 4) provided a more detailed analysis of the partisan implications of myopic economic voting in U.S. presidential elections.

Alas, there is little evidence to suggest that developments in the decades since Tufte wrote have done anything to increase public scrutiny of electoral economic cycles. For example, in the period from 1949 through 1976, the average income growth rate was 1.2 percentage points higher in presidential election years than in other years; since 1977 it has been 1.1 percentage points higher in presidential years than in other years.[35] Voters continue to think and act in much the same way they always have—and politicians behave accordingly.

CONCLUSION

We have argued for an understanding of retrospective voting quite different from the conventional scholarly view that we summarized in chapter 4. While we agree that voters' assessments of economic conditions play a substantial role in determining election outcomes, we part company with those who see retrospective voting as a mechanism for ensuring effective political accountability.

The evidence presented in this chapter casts considerable doubt on the view that citizens can reliably form and act upon sensible retrospective judgments at election time. While they vote on the basis of how they feel at the moment, they forget or ignore how they have felt over the course of the incumbents' term in office. Like medical patients recalling colonoscopies, who forget all but the last few minutes (Kahneman 2000; Redelmeier, Katz, and Kahneman 2003), the voters' assessments of past pain and pleasure are significantly biased by "duration neglect." Their myopia makes retrospective judgments idiosyncratic and often arbitrary.

The myopic behavior of economic voters does not seem to be a mere reflection of complex campaign environments or restless media coverage. Similar biases are evident even in simple laboratory settings where experimental subjects have (modest) material incentives to make sensible choices. For example, one such study found "evidence of three important deviations from optimal retrospection": subjects "overweighted recent performance," "allowed unrelated events that affected their welfare to influence evaluations of incumbents," and "were influenced by rhetoric" to focus on recent rather than cumulative performance (Huber, Hill, and Lenz 2012, 738). The authors concluded that their findings point to "inherent limits in citizens' ability to motivate incumbent performance" (Huber, Hill, and Lenz 2012, 739).

---

35 The *t*-statistics for the earlier and recent differences are identical, 1.9.

The result of this kind of voter behavior is that election outcomes are, in an important sense, *random*. Again, as we said in chapter 1, we do not mean to suggest that outcomes are random in the literal sense of being utterly chaotic or unpredictable. Indeed, as figure 6.1 highlighted, they are highly structured. Our point is that the most important single factor in determining who wins—myopic retrospection—is, from the standpoint of democratic accountability, essentially arbitrary. It is not much related to either ideology or incumbent performance. Thus, when electoral competition is sufficiently vigorous for the outcome to be in doubt, the choice between competing governing teams is likely to hinge on the accident of whether "the economy is flourishing in the final weeks of a campaign" (Uchitelle 2004). Usually, in effect, the voters toss a coin.

One last possibility remains, however, by which retrospective voting might be rehabilitated, at least in part. Perhaps in times of national crisis, voters can rise to the occasion, casting an ideologically sophisticated vote that changes the political system dramatically, ushering in a new majority party with a mandate for dramatic policy change (Sundquist 1983). The period from 1932 to 1936 is the strongest recent nominee for a watershed of that kind. The next chapter therefore takes up the elections of the Franklin Roosevelt years.

A Chicken in Every Pot: Ideology and Retrospection in the Great Depression

> For their part, academics have tended to dismiss campaign slogans of the past like "the full dinner pail" and "a chicken in every pot" on the grounds that something deeper must have been going on in these elections. But perhaps it wasn't.
>
> —David R. Mayhew, *Electoral Realignments* (2002, 161)

Americans are accustomed to thinking of the New Deal realignment as a triumph of both democratic responsiveness and Democratic Party ideology. The Great Depression following the stock market crash of 1929 had brought unprecedented economic catastrophe on the nation; real income per capita fell by an appalling 28% from 1929 to 1932. A rigidly conservative Republican government resisted public pressure to provide energetic relief and institutional reforms. Republicans lost heavily in the 1930 congressional elections. Then in the presidential election of 1932, voters responded with a historic repudiation of the incumbent president, Herbert Hoover. Franklin Roosevelt swept into office with 57% of the popular vote, and the Democrats—a minority party for most of the preceding 70 years—won 313 of the 435 seats in the House of Representatives.

Roosevelt's first hundred days in the White House brought a flurry of innovative policies. A robust economic recovery followed in short order. Real incomes increased by one-third over the course of Roosevelt's first term. Unemployment declined by one-third. Voters rewarded Roosevelt with a landslide reelection in 1936; he won more than 60% of the popular vote and carried 46 of 48 states. He went on to win an unprecedented four terms in the White House, and the Democratic Party enjoyed a durable reservoir of popular support that allowed it to dominate congressional elections for the next six decades. As V. O. Key, Jr. (1958, 589) summarized these events, "The election of 1936 ratified a sharp turn in public policy and successive Democratic victories clinched the reforms of the New Deal."[1]

Our aim in this chapter is to challenge this conventional interpretation of the New Deal era as a popular ratification of Roosevelt's policies. We do so primarily by analyzing American voters' reactions to the Depression, using electoral and economic data. In our account, voters in the depths of the Depression behaved in much the same myopic retrospective way as in the more ordinary times we considered in chapter 6.

We bolster our interpretation of the New Deal realignment by juxtaposing the American experience with parallel developments in several other democracies, where we find much the same results. Thus, what looks to the American eye like a triumph of folk democratic theory and ideological transformation was instead an accident produced by a specific configuration of election dates and economic vicissitudes. Policies were mostly irrelevant, and voters were their same old selves.

THE ROOSEVELT ELECTIONS

The conventional account of FDR's triumph in the presidential election of 1932 is that it represented a protest vote, a cry for help, with the electorate taking a chance on a largely unknown and cautious moderate whose principal attraction was that he was not Herbert Hoover. According to Key (1947, 268),

> The campaign gave to the public no clear-cut alternatives of policy, except with respect to prohibition. The Democrats were thoroughly wet. But no other issue of a major nature presented itself sharply and dramatically in the campaign. The times called for a great debate on measures to lift the American economy out of the morass, but a stranger might have presumed that all the fighting was about when and whether one could get a glass of legal beer. . . . It is doubtful that the rational

1 The scholarly literature focusing on this period is enormous; Katznelson (2013) provided an important recent statement with extensive references. Key (1955), Sundquist (1983), and Clubb, Flanigan, and Zingale (1990) discussed realignments generally, including this one. Mayhew (2002) offered a thorough critique of the concept of realignment and its empirical power.

appeals of either candidate had much to do with the election results. All types and classes of people had suffered deprivations; all of them were anxious for a change. Poor men, rich men, middle-class men, farmers, workers, all moved over into the Democratic ranks in sufficient number to give Roosevelt a resounding victory. All these classes could identify themselves with the "forgotten man," and they could equally feel themselves deserving of a "new deal" without necessarily insisting on exactitude in the definition of what the "new deal" was to be.[2]

By 1936, however, the character of Roosevelt's administration had become much clearer, not least to himself, and he campaigned well to the left of where he had stood in 1932. In his famous speech at Madison Square Garden in New York City two nights before the election, he attacked "organized money" for their hatred of him, and proclaimed to a thunderous ovation, "I welcome their hatred." A new political barometer, the Gallup poll, found an astounding degree of political polarization in the general public: 45% of the poll respondents, and 83% of Republicans, agreed that "the acts and policies of the Roosevelt Administration may lead to dictatorship" (Key 1961a, 246).

Despite the breadth and intensity of opposition to Roosevelt, the election result was a historic landslide for the incumbent. The voters joining in that landslide are said to have been "attracted by the Democratic program and the Rooseveltian personality and leadership" (Sundquist 1983, 214). Key, who had disparaged the importance of policy issues in the 1932 election, interpreted the 1936 election in a very different light. "The return of a party to power under circumstances [like those] of the 1936 campaign," he wrote (Key 1958, 578–579),[3] "gives such an election a special significance. Drastic innovations in public policy aroused the most bitter denunciation by the outs; the ins had to stand on their record. The electorate had before it the question whether to ratify these innovations, few of which had been clearly

2 Lest Key's emphasis on the political significance of repealing Prohibition strike modern readers as exaggerated, we note that a highly laudatory account of Roosevelt's campaign published in the early months of the new administration (Guilfoyle 1933, 218–219) suggested that the "return of beer in less than a month after the new Administration took office did more than anything else to inspire the people with confidence in the President.... Seldom, if ever before in the history of the country, has there been such a major accomplishment in such a short time.... If there was any turning point in the attitude of the people toward this depression it came simultaneously with beer."

3 The interpolated words are from a subsequent (1958) edition of Key's textbook, which repeats the quoted passage with only minor alteration.

foreshadowed in the 1932 campaign. The result could only be interpreted as a popular ratification of the broad features of new public policy."

This interpretation of the 1936 election has persisted down to the present, making it the preeminent example of a policy-based election in scholarly accounts of American electoral politics. Most scholars recognize that voters in the current era may place little emphasis on ideology and a great deal on economic conditions, as we discussed in chapters 2 and 6. However, they sometimes suppose that voting behavior was quite different in the 1930s. The continuing intense debate in the country over Roosevelt and his New Deal programs may have focused voters' minds on the practical implications of politics and public policy, making them more ideological than in normal times. As Theda Skocpol (2012, 42) put it—in contrast with the contemporary era—"back in the 1930s, American citizens could see that big, new things were being proposed and debated in Washington DC."

On this view, the dramatic economic distress of the Depression era might well have altered ordinary myopic patterns of economic voting. Millions of lost jobs and lost homes, hungry children, and ruined lives should be hard to forget. Minds would be focused on the full length of the Depression and on policy proposals for dramatic change in the government's role in the economy. In a popular textbook on *Party Politics in America*, for example, Marjorie Hershey (2011, 297) wrote,

> At critical times in American history, the parties have divided in ways that were, if not truly ideological, at least determinedly policy oriented. In the 1936 presidential election, for example, the Democrats and the Republicans offered dramatically different solutions to a nation devastated by the Great Depression. The hardships of that economic collapse probably focused voter attention to an unusual degree on the possible remedies that government could provide. Combined with a campaign centered on the pros and cons of the Roosevelt program for social and economic change, this may well have produced something close to a mandate in the election for both the president and Congress.

The conventional ideological interpretation of the voting patterns in this period requires that voters punished Hoover for his conservative ideological orthodoxy in 1930 and 1932, rewarded Roosevelt for adopting more progressive policies in the early years of the New Deal, and tapped the ideological brakes in 1938 when Roosevelt's court-packing scheme and the "second New Deal" raised concerns that policy might be drifting too far to the left. For example, in accounting for the Republican congressional gains in 1938, James Sundquist (1983, 226) supposed that "independent voters were by now rebelling against Democratic excesses and swinging to a Republican party that in many states had acquired new progressive leadership, and deviant Republicans, having chastised their party sufficiently, were returning home."

MYOPIC RETROSPECTION IN THE ROOSEVELT REALIGNMENT

The conventional accounts seem to us to greatly overstate the extent to which Depression-era voters weighed and endorsed the specific policies of the Roosevelt administration. Our alternative interpretation is that voters responded to the hardships of the economic collapse in much the same way that they respond to ordinary economic vicissitudes—by punishing incumbents when things get worse and rewarding them when things get better. In broad outline, this retrospective interpretation accounts nicely for the major political tides of the Depression era, as figure 7.1 shows. The top part of the figure charts the course of the Great Depression in the United States as measured by changes from year to year in average real personal income.[4] The bottom part charts electoral support for the incumbent president's party (Republicans from 1928 through 1932, Democrats from 1934 through 1940) in presidential and congressional elections.[5]

It should be evident that there is a good deal of correspondence between the economic and electoral patterns in figure 7.1. In 1930, the first year of widespread economic distress, the Republican Party lost both votes and seats in a midterm congressional election. Two more years of accelerating depression triggered a thoroughgoing repudiation of Hoover and the Republicans in 1932. Roosevelt and the Democrats took power in early 1933, at what

---

4 Data on per capita personal income appear in table 7.1 of the National Income and Product Accounts available from the website of the Commerce Department's Bureau of Economic Analysis (www.bea.gov). Unemployment figures tell much the same story as the real income figures, except that unemployment remained well above its pre-Depression level throughout the 1930s. According to the *United Nations Statistical Yearbook* (Statistical Office of the United Nations 1949), the unemployment rate increased from 3.2% in 1929 to 23.6% in 1932, peaked at 24.9% in 1933, declined to 14.3% in 1937, before spiking at 19.0% in 1938, then declined back to 14.6% by 1940.

5 The popular vote shares shown in figure 7.1 are taken from Rusk (2001), as are the vote and seat shifts reported in the text. Some other historical compilations are misleading because they tabulate total congressional votes without distinguishing between those cast in districts and those cast in (sometimes multiple) statewide at-large elections.

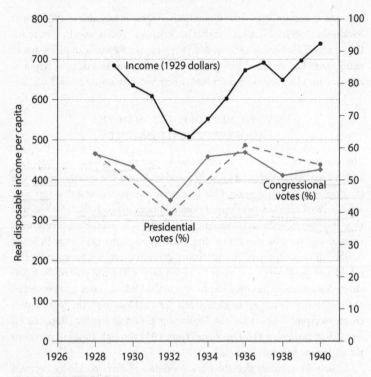

Figure 7.1. U.S. Income and Incumbent Electoral Support, 1928–1940

turned out to be almost precisely the low point of the Depression. As three years of steady economic recovery recouped most of the real income that had been lost since 1929, the Democrats made further gains in the midterm election of 1934 and again in the presidential and congressional elections of 1936. The economy continued to improve in 1937 but took a marked turn for the worse in 1938; the Democrats lost significant ground in the 1938 midterm election, leaving them well behind where they had been in 1932. In 1939 and 1940 the recovery resumed, and the Democrats regained some of that lost ground, but they still held fewer seats than they had in 1933—and fewer seats than the Republicans had held in 1929.

Of course, while the broad correlation between economic conditions and electoral tides evident in figure 7.1 is certainly suggestive of retrospective voting, it is far from definitive. Fortunately, in this period for the first time in American history, the federal government collected detailed, standardized economic data from all across the United States. The dramatic economic collapse and recovery in the Depression era were by no means uniform across the country. Thus, we can test our interpretation by examining the political behavior of voters exposed to very different local economic conditions. Year-to-year income gains and losses in specific states were very large and extremely variable. In 1936, for example, real personal income per capita increased by 18% or more in Colorado, Delaware, and Nevada. At the same time, income plunged by 8% in Iowa, 14% in North Dakota, and 23% in South Dakota. Figures for some of the other Depression years are even more variable. This variation provides ample leverage for assessing the impact of state-level economic conditions on the vote, making the Depression era an extremely fertile setting for systematic analysis of retrospective voting. The bleak economic misery of the 1930s presents an extraordinary opportunity to test our account of the nature of electoral accountability.

Given the central importance of the 1936 election in conventional ideological interpretations of the New Deal era, our analyses of economic voting focus primarily on popular support for Roosevelt in that year.[6] We confine the analyses to states that were not part of the Confederacy, since the Solid South of this era, with its suppression of the black vote and widespread racial repression, its limited two-party competition, and its low white turnout (Key 1949), provides little scope for assessing the effect of economic conditions on voting behavior.

Our primary goal is to assess the impact of economic conditions during the Roosevelt administration on the 1936 vote. Doing so is not a historical anachronism, imposing current thinking on people of a different era. To the contrary, political insiders in 1936 were well aware of the likely connection between voters' income and their choices at the polls. Indeed, during the campaign James Farley and Harry Hopkins, FDR's powerful aides, were repeatedly accused of trying to buy the election with relief funds (Sherwood

---

6 We would like to have studied economic voting in the 1932 election, but doing so is not easy. The 1928 results reflect the distinctive polarizing effect of Democratic candidate Al Smith's Catholicism, while the 1924 results are skewed by the Progressive candidacy of Robert La Follette; thus, finding an appropriate baseline to control for partisanship is challenging. Even if midterm years were used, the economic data go back only to 1929, so that the economically grounded vote deviations from partisanship in baseline years, which were no doubt considerable in some states, could not be controlled.

1948, 85).[7] That there may have been something to these charges is suggested by the fact that spending on government transfers jumped significantly in 1936 after remaining fairly steady from 1933 to 1935.[8]

The explanatory factors in our analyses parallel those in chapter 6 with minor exceptions, the principal difference being the annual character of the economic observations here.[9] (Quarterly data do not exist for this period.) We focus on real personal income rather than GDP in light of the statistical results presented in chapter 6, which suggested that voters are much more responsive to changes in income than to changes in GDP.[10]

We begin by focusing on per capita income changes in each state in the election year, 1936. Figure 7.2 summarizes the relationship across the 37 non-southern states between these election-year income changes and the change in Roosevelt's share of the two-party vote from 1932 to 1936.[11] As an aid in

7 Relief funds are included in personal income, and thus are reflected in our analyses of economic voting. We would have liked to examine them separately, since they are more directly under government control and thus might be especially consequential at the polls, but their effect proved impossible to isolate satisfactorily. In the early New Deal years, transfer payments went primarily to the states with large cities, where FDR may have done especially well for other reasons. Relief payments per person within each state were quite steady from month to month, with only a small upward drift until late 1935. At that point, relief was turned over to the states, with only partial federal subsidies. The number of people on relief and the average per-person payment both dropped dramatically in many states—sometimes due to improving economic conditions (Whiting 1942) and sometimes due to state penny-pinching. None of the drop was the fault of the federal government, at least not directly. In any case, 1936 transfer payments turn out to have had no discernible effect on Roosevelt's electoral performance over and above their contribution to overall income gains.

8 However, no such pattern appears in the corresponding data from 1937 to 1940. The recovery was much further along by then, and payments may have settled into bureaucratic routine.

9 As in chapter 6, we define income changes as differences in logged income levels from the preceding year, multiplied by 100 to express them as percentage changes.

10 All of our state-level data on per capita personal income are from the Bureau of Economic Analysis, table SA1–3. We deflate nominal income levels using the Consumer Price Index produced by the Bureau of Labor Statistics. The price index is for urban consumers only, and even for them, its accuracy during this era of widely varying and drastically changing incomes (and thus consumption patterns) is questionable. However, the relevant changes in price levels were modest, and in any case the choice of price index has little effect on our analysis (since any alternative index would simply add a constant increment to each state's logged income change in a given election year).

11 These two elections both clearly reflect a new partisan alignment quite different from the one that had prevailed in the preceding decade. The turnout-weighted correlation between states' Democratic vote margins in 1936 and 1932 is .65; the corresponding correlations between 1936 and 1928, 1924, and 1920 range from .13 to −.02. Clearly, as one would expect, the realignment mattered. Hence we cannot use an average of several prior elections to proxy for partisanship in our analyses, as we would otherwise prefer.

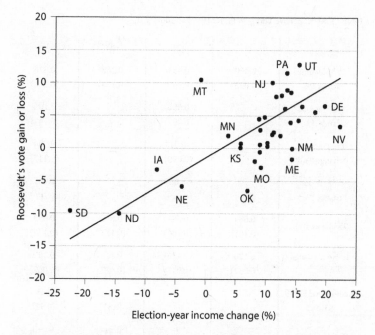

Figure 7.2. Election-Year Income Changes and Roosevelt's Popular Vote, 1936 (non-southern states)

interpreting the relationship between state income changes and vote shifts, the figure includes a turnout-weighted summary line. It is clear that there was a strong and fairly consistent tendency for Roosevelt to gain support in states that experienced significant income growth in 1936, and to lose support in states that experienced declines in income.[12] On its face, this evidence is quite consistent with our myopic, nonideological interpretation of the election outcome.

The analyses reported in table 7.1 confirm and elaborate the basic relationship evident in figure 7.2 between election-year income changes and vote shifts.

12 This relationship is not simply due to Roosevelt's vote losses in the thinly populated farm states where incomes fell. Indeed, excluding those states from the analysis would make the relationship even steeper.

Table 7.1. Retrospective Voting in FDR's 1936 Landslide

	(1)	(2)	(3)	(4)
1936 income change (%)	0.360 (0.092)	0.483 (0.166)	0.288 (0.132)	0.326 (0.208)
1935 income change (%)	—	0.080 (0.097)	—	0.105 (0.147)
1934 income change (%)	—	−0.012 (0.090)	—	0.084 (0.117)
1933 income change (%)	—	−0.065 (0.149)	—	0.067 (0.200)
1932 vote (%)	0.684 (0.101)	0.681 (0.106)	0.658 (0.127)	0.693 (0.138)
Turnout change (%)	0.120 (0.052)	0.126 (0.057)	0.117 (0.057)	0.129 (0.062)
Income level (1929 $100s)	—		1.19 (0.85)	1.19 (0.92)
Rural farm (%)	—		0.044 (0.143)	0.010 (0.153)
Foreign-born white (%)	—		−0.199 (0.167)	−0.149 (0.201)
Black (%)	—		−0.260 (0.218)	−0.174 (0.261)
Intercept	15.83 (6.32)	13.42 (6.55)	12.12 (8.30)	7.40 (10.11)
Standard error of regression	2.90	3.00	2.92	3.03
Adjusted R^2	.57	.54	.56	.53
N (non-southern states)	37	37	37	37

Dependent variable is the Democratic share of the presidential vote in non-southern states. States are weighted by turnout. Ordinary least squares regression parameter estimates (with standard errors in parentheses).

The analysis reported in the first column of the table relates Roosevelt's vote in each non-southern state in 1936 to election-year income changes. Rather than analyzing the change in Roosevelt's vote share from 1932, we include the 1932 vote share as an explanatory factor in order to allow for the possibility of erosion in his support in states that were most heavily Democratic in 1932. And since Roosevelt is said to have appealed especially strongly to new voters, we include the percentage change in turnout between 1932 and 1936 as an additional explanatory factor.[13]

The estimated impact of election-year income changes in the first column of table 7.1 suggests that every additional percentage point of state income growth boosted Roosevelt's vote share by more than one-third of a percentage point. This estimate implies differences of as much as 16 percentage points in the Democratic share of the two-party vote due to differences in election-year income growth from state to state. Moreover, this simple statistical model accounts for Roosevelt's performance in each state with an average error of less than 3 percentage points. Clearly, Roosevelt's electoral fortunes were heavily dependent on voters' local economic conditions, over and above whatever support he gained nationwide due to the overall economic recovery.

In the second column of table 7.1 we report the results of a more elaborate analysis including measures of state income growth in 1935, 1934, and 1933 in addition to the 1936 income figures. Whereas election-year income growth had a strong positive effect on Roosevelt's vote, previous income growth seems to have had little or no effect. Thus, the evidence from the 1930s is quite consistent with the evidence from more recent presidential elections presented in chapter 6 in suggesting that voters' retrospective assessments of the economy are quite myopic. These results provide a dramatic indication of the political significance of voters' myopia in a situation where the economic stakes were much larger than any observed in subsequent eras of American politics. In 1934 and 1935, Roosevelt presided over an increase of 17% in real personal income per capita, recouping more than half of the total decline in income over the preceding four years of depression. Whether he was truly responsible or not, our analysis suggests that he got little or no credit at the polls.

In all of the analyses reported in table 7.1, the estimated effect of turnout changes indicates that Roosevelt gained more support in states with large

---

13 The increase in turnout between 1932 and 1936 ranged from 2% to 22%, except in Kentucky (−6%) and Pennsylvania (+45%). Excluding these two outliers leaves the estimated effects of turnout on Roosevelt's vote virtually unchanged.

numbers of new voters than in states where turnout was relatively static. These estimates imply that Roosevelt's vote share in 1936 was 10 to 15 percentage points higher among new voters than among old voters (who were themselves giving Roosevelt almost 60% support). Thus, our findings are quite consistent with the notion that "the rising strength of the Democratic Party during the Roosevelt years probably depended heavily on new voters drawn to the polls by the Great Depression and the New Deal" (Campbell et al. 1960, 89).[14]

The analyses reported in the third and fourth columns of table 7.1 include state-level measures of a variety of demographic characteristics that loom large in historical accounts of the New Deal realignment: per capita income, the rural farm proportion of the population, the percentage of foreign-born whites, and the percentage of blacks.[15] To the extent that poor people, farmers, immigrants, and African-Americans responded more enthusiastically than other citizens to the New Deal policies implemented between 1933 and 1936, we should expect to see that states in which they were more numerous were relatively more supportive of Roosevelt in 1936 than they had been in 1932. For the most part, however, the reverse seems to be true. None of the effects is very large or very precisely estimated; but insofar as there are any patterns at all, they suggest that Roosevelt gained *less* support among these groups than in other parts of the population.[16] Of course, many, if not most, of the people in these groups were already Democrats. Our point is that unusually clear evidence of the Democrats' new ideology favoring them seems to have made no difference.

Including these demographic factors in the analysis turns out to make little difference for our conclusions regarding the nature and extent of retrospective economic voting. The estimated effects of election-year income changes in the third and fourth columns of table 7.1 remain substantial, albeit somewhat less precisely estimated. And the estimated effects of income changes earlier in

---

14 Additional statistical analyses, not detailed here, suggest that turnout gains also boosted Roosevelt's support in 1932 and 1940. Thus, the cumulative contribution of new voters to the building of a Democratic majority was even greater than is evident in the calculations reported here—probably adding about 5 percentage points to the "normal" Democratic presidential vote. Of course, Roosevelt also gained from conversion of former Republicans (Anderson 1979; Gamm 1989).

15 Data on the rural farm population, foreign-born whites, and blacks are from the Historical Census Browser developed by the University of Virginia's Geospatial and Statistical Data Center (http://fisher.lib.virginia.edu/collections/stats/histcensus).

16 We also examined statistical specifications including various subsets of these demographic variables. None produced more sensible results.

Roosevelt's first term, while also less precise, are again much smaller than those in the election year, reinforcing the impression of substantial myopia in voters' assessments of the economy even in the midst of the Great Depression. This finding is quite consistent across alternate specifications, estimation methods, and samples. Omitting notable outliers from the analysis, individually or in various combinations, improves the statistical fit of our models, but the substantive pattern is again just the same—only myopic economic considerations mattered.[17]

Our analysis thus provides strong, consistent evidence that Roosevelt's landslide reelection hinged importantly on the fact that he presided over strong income growth during the election year. The implications of that fact may be illustrated by considering what might have happened if Roosevelt had happened to stand for reelection under less favorable economic circumstances than those prevailing in 1936. For example, what if incomes had *fallen* substantially in 1936 rather than *growing* substantially? Lest this possibility seem farfetched, we note that real per capita income *did* fall by more than 6% only two years later—with dire consequences for the Democrats in the 1938 midterm election.

Table 7.2 summarizes the results of a historical simulation comparing Roosevelt's actual performance in the 1936 election with his hypothetical performance under the economic conditions prevailing in 1938. Of course, any calculation along these lines must be far from exact. Most important, the statistical estimates of the effect of state-level economic conditions in table 7.1 provide no direct evidence regarding the additional impact of *national* economic conditions on Roosevelt's vote. Voters undoubtedly attended also to the national economy, but since that does not vary across states, we have no way to directly assess its importance here. However, rough calculations based on aggregate vote shifts comport with more detailed calculations based on data from the modern era in suggesting that the impact of national economic conditions was probably similar in magnitude to the impact of state economic conditions, making the total effect of the economy twice as large

17 For example, FDR's vote increased by more than 10 percentage points in Montana despite a small decline in real income in 1936. (This unexpected enthusiasm may be attributable to an economic boom in the preceding two years driven by excellent wheat prices and abetted by Roosevelt's 1934 decision to support the price of silver, a Montana victory in a policy battle dating to the 19th century.) On the other hand, Roosevelt lost ground in 1936 in Oklahoma, Missouri, and Maine despite substantial election-year income growth. However, omitting any or all of these outliers from our analysis leaves the results essentially unchanged.

Table 7.2. The 1936 Presidential Election with a 1938 Economy

	1936 conditions (actual)	1938 conditions (simulated)
National election-year change in real income (%)	+11.2	–6.4
Roosevelt vote share, non-South (%)	58.8	46.2
States carried (including South)	46/48	29/48
Roosevelt electoral votes (including South)	523/531	258/531

as suggested by the parameter estimates in table 7.1.[18] Thus, in the absence of better evidence, we simply assume that the estimated effect of state-level income changes in 1936 in table 7.1 can be applied both to state-level changes and to the national change.[19]

The resulting calculation suggests that under the economic conditions prevailing in 1938 Roosevelt would have received only 46% of the vote outside the South in 1936. More important, he probably would have lost 17 of the 46 states he actually carried, including New York, Pennsylvania, Illinois,

18 Hoover's share of the national two-party vote dropped by 18 percentage points when real personal income per capita fell by 17% in 1932; Roosevelt's vote share increased by 3.4 percentage points when real income grew by 11% in 1936. These results suggest that a president's national popular vote share might change by roughly three-fourths of 1% with each 1% change in election-year income growth. (A disparity of 28% in income growth between the two election years was associated with a 21-point difference in the incumbent's vote gain or loss.) That total impact is approximately double the estimated effect of state-level variation in table 7.1, with the difference presumably attributable to voters' sensitivity to national economic conditions. Rough tests using data from post-war presidential elections similarly suggest a total effect about twice as large as the state-level effect—though the electoral shift attributable to each percentage point change in real income seems to be larger in the post-war period than it was in the Depression era, perhaps because the relatively small shifts in the current era draw more attention now than they would have during the Depression's tectonic income changes.

19 Specifically, we project Roosevelt's hypothetical vote share in each non-southern state by subtracting the differences between 1936 and 1938 income growth figures for both the state and the nation, each multiplied by the average estimated effect of election-year income changes in table 7.1.

Ohio, and Michigan. In that case, even with a lock on the Solid South, he would have fallen short of an Electoral College majority, bringing the New Deal realignment to an abrupt and (from the perspective of hindsight) very premature conclusion.[20]

We conclude this section by reiterating how dramatically our interpretation of the 1936 election contrasts with the conventional understanding of the New Deal realignment. In our interpretation, voters rendered no meaningful verdict on the substance of New Deal policies. Judgments about the role of the government in economic life, the value of laissez-faire economics, or specific aspects of the New Deal program were largely irrelevant. Indeed, insofar as ordinary Americans did express specific judgments about economic policy in this period of crisis, they mostly reiterated the conventional judgments of the past. As Paul Krugman (2014) noted, "the public remained wedded to economic orthodoxy: by a more than 2-to-1 majority, voters surveyed by Gallup just after the [1936] election called for a balanced budget. And F.D.R., unfortunately, listened; his attempt to balance the budget soon plunged America back into recession."

Even in the remarkable circumstances prevailing in 1936, voters were focused on concrete economic conditions that they could see and feel when they went to the polls. Specifically, they were focused on income gains or losses over the course of the election year. Income growth earlier in Roosevelt's term, which contributed as much or more to their economic well-being, had no apparent electoral effect. That was water under the bridge. Roosevelt's reelection in 1936—and the New Deal realignment—depended crucially on a positive balance of answers to the question, "What have you done for us lately?"

CONGRESSIONAL ELECTIONS AND SHORT-TERM RETROSPECTIONS

Our analysis so far sheds light on the key event of the New Deal realignment—Roosevelt's landslide reelection in 1936. But it does nothing to explain how or why that landslide produced a long-lasting alteration of the partisan balance of power. The most significant electoral legacy of the New

---

20 Although Roosevelt's projected electoral vote in table 7.2 is not far short of a majority, he would have needed substantial additional popular votes to reach that majority. The closest pivotal state in this simulation is New Jersey, with a projected popular vote for Roosevelt of 47.4%.

Deal era was the establishment of durable Democratic majorities in Congress. The overwhelming Republican congressional majorities of the 1920s were swept away by the Great Depression, and the House of Representatives remained in Democratic hands for 58 of the next 62 years. Thus, the dynamics of congressional voting in the Depression era are crucial to understanding the nature and significance of the New Deal realignment.

Many scholars have argued that this momentous partisan realignment was fundamentally ideological or programmatic. Even the authors of *The American Voter*, no friends to intellectualist interpretations of elections, wrote, "The program of welfare legislation of the New Deal and the extraordinary personality of its major exponent, Franklin D. Roosevelt, brought about a profound realignment of party strength, which has endured in large part up to the present time" (Campbell et al. 1960, 534). Similarly, the most prominent contemporary study of party identification primarily emphasized the importance of social identities in the development of partisan attachments, but cited the New Deal as an exceptional period in which "an unusually clear ideological divide between the parties, dramatized again and again . . . shaped party attachments to an unusual extent" (Green, Palmquist, and Schickler 2002, 106–107).

In contrast, we argue that the partisan realignment of the 1930s resulted in significant part from the accumulation of myopic short-term assessments of economic conditions in each successive election year. To validate this interpretation, we begin by showing that congressional election outcomes, too, were significantly affected by election-year income changes. But the fact that economic retrospections influenced current election outcomes does not in itself imply that they also influenced voters' long-term partisan loyalties. Indeed, our emphasis on the myopic nature of economic retrospections might suggest that voters are inevitably focused on the present, and thus that short-term political judgments formed in the heat of an election year are unlikely to have any long-term political ramifications. However, more careful attention to the persistence of electoral responses to short-term economic conditions suggests that retrospective judgments were indeed incorporated into durable partisan attachments, though as we will show, not in the way that some theoretical perspectives predict (Fiorina 1981; Achen 1992).

Table 7.3 reports the results of a series of statistical analyses relating the Democratic share of the two-party congressional vote to changing economic conditions through the early New Deal period.[21] The columns of the table

21 The economic data for this era are available only for states, not for specific congressional districts. Using state values as proxies for the unknown district-specific values no doubt induces

Table 7.3. Retrospective Voting in Congressional Elections, 1934–1940

	1934	1936	1938	1940
Election-year income change (%)	−0.014 (0.085)	0.498 (0.104)	0.300 (0.137)	0.462 (0.354)
Prior-year income change (%)	0.031 (0.083)	0.187 (0.066)	0.138 (0.111)	0.265 (0.199)
Previous vote (%)	0.796 (0.078)	0.858 (0.054)	1.000 (0.040)	0.808 (0.039)
Turnout change (%)	0.050 (0.039)	0.091 (0.033)	−0.025 (0.047)	0.007 (0.037)
Incumbency change (−2 to +2)	0.80 (0.45)	0.94 (0.41)	0.13 (0.48)	0.02 (0.44)
Intercept	12.34 (4.09)	−0.11 (4.23)	−4.79 (2.27)	5.13 (3.48)
Standard error of regression	5.73	4.79	4.96	4.70
Adjusted R^2	.66	.79	.82	.80
N (non-southern districts)	259	285	294	290

Dependent variable is the Democratic share of the vote in contested non-southern congressional districts. Districts are weighted by turnout. Ordinary least squares regression parameter estimates (with standard errors in parentheses); observations clustered by state.

present separate results for the 1934, 1936, 1938, and 1940 congressional elections.[22] In each case, the observations are non-southern congressional districts contested by both major parties in both the current and previous

---

non-negligible measurement error. Thus, the results of these analyses must be considered suggestive rather than definitive. However, the general similarity between our (state-level) presidential results and (district-level) congressional results provides some reassurance on this score.

22 The 1940 election provides a natural stopping point for our analysis, since thereafter politicians and voters alike were increasingly distracted from economic concerns and domestic policy debates by the coming of war.

election cycle.[23] In addition to election-year income changes and income changes in the off-year preceding the election, we include changes in turnout and the Democratic vote share in the preceding election as explanatory factors. We also take account of changes in incumbency status since the preceding election, since incumbency is likely to be the most salient local factor in most congressional elections (albeit less salient in the 1930s than in the contemporary era). Because there was substantial variation in the population (and electoral mobilization) of congressional districts in this era, we weight the districts by turnout.[24]

The results of these analyses parallel those for the 1936 presidential election in suggesting a strong effect of election-year economic conditions. Although no discernible effect appears in the 1934 midterm election, the estimated effect is sizable in each of the other three elections of the early New Deal era, and the average estimated effect across the four elections (.31) is comparable in magnitude to the estimated presidential effect reported in table 7.1. By comparison, economic conditions in the off-year preceding each election had little apparent impact, with an average estimated effect only half as large as for election-year income changes. Increasing turnout and incumbency also had significant positive effects on the Democratic congressional vote in 1934 and 1936, though these factors seem to have ebbed in importance thereafter.

The 1938 midterm election provides a convenient basis for comparison between the congressional election results presented in table 7.3 and the presidential election results presented in table 7.1. The estimated effect of election-year income changes in 1938 is of roughly average magnitude; the estimated effect of the 1936 vote is exactly 1.0, implying an essentially stable party balance; and the estimated effects of changes in off-year income, turnout, and incumbency are all modest. Thus, a simple scatterplot comparing election-year income changes and vote shifts in 1938 reflects the relationship with fair accuracy. The result is presented in figure 7.3. The figure

23 We exclude multimember and at-large elections (two seats each in Illinois, New York, North Dakota, and Ohio and one seat each in Connecticut and Oklahoma); several cases in California and Pennsylvania in which the same candidate ran on both the Democratic and Republican ballot lines (though we include cases in which either or both of the major party candidates also ran on minor party lines); and Minnesota and Wisconsin, where third parties (Farmer-Labor and Progressives, respectively) dominated state politics throughout this period. We also exclude Kentucky and Missouri in 1934 (since those states elected all representatives in multimember statewide elections in 1932).

24 To allow for the possibility that gubernatorial "coattails" and other unmeasured factors influencing congressional election outcomes in each state were correlated across districts, we cluster the observations by state and report robust standard errors.

A Chicken in Every Pot

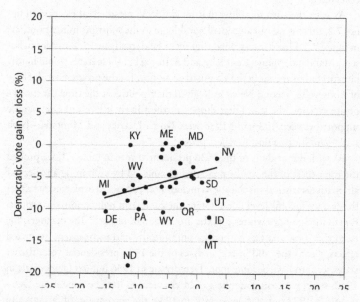

Figure 7.3. Election-Year Income Changes and Congressional Votes, 1938 (non-southern states)

is constructed so as to maximize visual comparability with figure 7.2, which presented the corresponding relationship for the 1936 presidential election. The scales for the horizontal and vertical axes are unchanged, despite the fact that there was a good deal less variation in state-level economic conditions in 1938 than in 1936, and also less variation in electoral shifts.

It is clear from figure 7.3 that economic conditions were much less propitious for the Democrats in 1938 than in 1936. Only five sparsely populated western states registered (small) gains in real income. Most states experienced real income *losses* of 5% to 10%, while Michigan and Delaware experienced losses of more than 15%. It is also clear that income gains and losses had somewhat less impact on congressional election outcomes than on presidential election outcomes; the turnout-weighted summary line in figure 7.3 is noticeably less steep than the corresponding summary line in figure 7.2. Nevertheless, the relationship is strong enough to account for differences of up to 6 percentage points in the expected Democratic vote over the range of economic conditions observed in 1938.

As with the corresponding plot for the 1936 presidential election in figure 7.2, there is no obvious ideological logic to the most prominent outliers in figure 7.3. Democrats gained slightly or held steady in 1938 in Massachusetts, Maryland, Maine, Kentucky, and Arizona; but these states would hardly be expected to appear in the vanguard of support for the progressive ideology of Roosevelt's "second New Deal," given their politics at the time. At the opposite extreme, the states that slipped furthest in their levels of Democratic support between 1936 and 1938 were North Dakota and Montana—both states hard hit by a bust in wheat prices.[25]

As with our analysis of the 1936 presidential vote in table 7.1, we probed the robustness of the results presented in table 7.3 by examining a variety of alternative statistical specifications including as additional explanatory factors the average income level in each state, the rural farm population, the proportion of foreign-born whites, and the proportion of blacks.[26] The demographic factors in these analyses had rather unimpressive and inconsistent estimated effects, just as they did in our analyses of the 1936 presidential vote. Richer states seem to have become more Democratic in 1936 but *less* Democratic in 1940; states with large numbers of blacks seem to have become more Democratic in 1938 but *less* Democratic in 1934; the percentages of farmers and immigrants seldom seemed to matter one way or the other. These results are quite puzzling in light of the prominence of these groups in conventional ideological accounts of the emergence of the Democratic New Deal coalition; as we noted earlier, these groups were already substantially Democratic, but additional ideological clarity about the Democrats' new commitment to them seems to have had no effect. And more important for our purposes, taking account of these demographic factors had very little effect on our conclusions regarding the political significance of short-term economic retrospections in congressional elections of the New Deal era.[27]

25 Wheat prices—a salient barometer of economic well-being in these states, among others—soared from $0.35 per bushel in 1932 to $1.14 per bushel in 1936, but were back down to $0.45 per bushel in 1938. Achen (2012) discussed the electoral politics of wheat prices in Montana.

26 As with our economic data, these demographic data are available only for states, not for specific congressional districts. This limitation may account for some of the apparent anomalies in our estimates of the impact of demographic factors on New Deal voting patterns.

27 The average estimated impact of election-year income changes across the four election years declined from .326 to .291 (with an average standard error of .168). The average

PARTISAN REALIGNMENT AND THE CUMULATION
OF SHORT-TERM RETROSPECTIONS

We turn next to the long-term implications of these short-term retrospections. As we saw in chapter 4, Morris Fiorina (1981, 84) described partisanship as a "running tally" of retrospective judgments of political performance, suggesting that those judgments might have persistent electoral effects over considerable periods of time. All of our analyses of congressional voting patterns demonstrate a good deal of persistence from election to election, with 80% or more of the Democratic vote share in each election carrying over to the next. This stability handsomely illustrates the significance of durable partisan loyalties in congressional elections. But are economic retrospections incorporated into those partisan loyalties, or are they merely short-term perturbations, irrelevant by the time of the next election?

We examine that question by tracking the *cumulative* impact of economic retrospections on the Democratic vote share in congressional elections from 1934 through 1940. Our statistical analysis generally parallels the separate analyses of the same four elections presented in table 7.3.[28] However, rather than considering each election separately, we assess the cumulative effect of both economic and noneconomic factors over the course of the whole decade.

As in table 7.3, we assess the electoral impact of real income changes in each election year and the preceding off-year. However, we also allow for the possibility that income changes in prior election cycles (beginning in 1933) continued to matter through their incorporation into durable partisan loyalties. In order to isolate the persistent effects of these income changes from other, noneconomic sources of change in partisan loyalties, we use the 1932 congressional vote as our baseline measure of partisanship throughout the decade and measure changes in turnout and incumbency relative to that baseline in each election year. Since we expect the persistent effects of income changes to be proportional to their original effects, we estimate a single persistence parameter reflecting the proportional impact of previous economic retrospections in each successive election cycle.

---

estimated impact of prior-year income changes declined from .153 to .085 (with an average standard error of .111).

28 As in the analysis reported in table 7.3, we exclude southern states, states dominated by minor parties, multimember and at-large elections (including states that elected their entire delegations at-large in 1932), and districts that were uncontested at any point in the decade. The resulting sample consists of 255 districts, about 10% fewer than in table 7.3. We weight each district by average turnout in the four elections.

The results of this analysis, presented in table 7.4, provide surprisingly strong statistical support for our account of partisan updating.[29] Income growth in each election year seems to have had a significant impact on Democratic fortunes at the polls, while income growth in the preceding off-year seems to have had rather little effect, just as our account of myopic retrospective voting (and the election-by-election evidence presented in table 7.3) would suggest. What is more striking is that our estimated persistence parameter implies that *all* of this myopic retrospection carried forward undiminished to subsequent election cycles, making its electoral impact extremely long-lasting.[30]

This pattern, with its odd durable emphasis on economic experience in even-numbered years, is very hard to square with conventional accounts of rational partisan updating, which imply that retrospective voters should rely on "a simple average of past benefits" to estimate parties' competence (Achen 1992, 200) or smoothly weight past experience in proportion to its current relevance (Gerber and Green 1998). However, the uneven accumulation of retrospections follows logically from the idea that elections prompt voters to engage in myopic updating of their assessments of partisan performance. The fact that times were good in 1936 had a significant impact on the 1938 congressional vote because much of the heightened Democratic support stemming from good times in 1936 carried over to 1938. The fact that times were also good in 1935 had much less effect, since 1935 was not an election year and thus was not as strongly incorporated into voters' party identifications or voting behavior in 1936 or, as best we can tell, thereafter.

These results imply that retrospective voting contributed significantly to the shifting balance of party fortunes in the Depression era, but not in a particularly sensible way. *Myopic* economic retrospections dominated not only in

---

29 To allow for correlation in the unmeasured factors influencing the results of the four elections in each district, we estimate the parameters of the model via nonlinear seemingly unrelated regression. The constrained nonlinear model fits the data less well than the separate linear models reported in table 7.3, and increasingly so in later years; but that difference reflects the fact that the model does not incorporate noneconomic sources of partisan change after 1932. (The "1932 vote" in table 7.4 is less strongly correlated with current Democratic support in each year than the more recent "previous vote" in table 7.3, and that difference increases with each successive election.)

30 The standard error of this parameter estimate is large enough to make *some* temporal discounting of past elections' economic conditions statistically plausible. However, even at the low end of the plausible range of parameter values, the extent of persistence implied by our analysis is substantial.

Table 7.4. Cumulative Retrospection in Congressional Elections, 1934–1940

	1934	1936	1938	1940
Election-year income change (%)	0.144 (0.037)			
Prior-year income change (%)	0.037 (0.028)			
Persistence of previous economic effects	—	1.02 (0.11)		
1932 vote (%)	0.821 (0.035)	0.780 (0.038)	0.873 (0.043)	0.644 (0.043)
Cumulative turnout change (%)	0.052 (0.023)	0.104 (0.022)	0.033 (0.019)	0.089 (0.026)
Cumulative incumbency change (−2 to +2)	1.01 (0.19)			
Intercept	9.30 (1.95)	8.92 (2.30)	−0.22 (2.52)	9.81 (2.78)
Standard error of regression	5.55	6.26	7.32	7.56
R^2	.69	.64	.61	.50
N (non-southern districts)	255	255	255	255

Dependent variable is the Democratic share of the vote in contested non-southern congressional districts. Districts are weighted by turnout. Nonlinear seemingly unrelated regression parameter estimates (with standard errors in parentheses).

the short run, by affecting current voting behavior, but also in the long run, through their incorporation into durable partisan attachments. The result was not quite the "running tally" described by Fiorina (1981), but more like a *skipping* tally. Only election years mattered. The New Deal realignment was due, in significant part, to this peculiar accumulation of myopic economic retrospections.

THE U.S. EXPERIENCE IN COMPARATIVE PERSPECTIVE

Our unconventional interpretation of the New Deal realignment helps to make sense of some otherwise-puzzling patterns in American electoral behavior in the Depression era. It also helps to account for a striking feature of electoral politics in other parts of the world during this period. Incumbent governments of widely varying ideological coloration were driven, willy-nilly, from office when the world economy fell into depression. But in almost every case, the short-term shift had long-term implications—the new incumbents enjoyed more or less stable electoral majorities for a decade or more. It is hard to attribute these long-term shifts to ideological judgments on the part of voters, given the remarkable diversity of principles and policies they embraced and the irrelevance of Depression-era principles and policies for dealing with the subsequent problems of world war and post-war change. It seems more straightforward to suppose that they, too, reflected "a kind of 'moving average' of reactions" (Berelson, Lazarsfeld, and McPhee 1954, 316) to the dramatic economic dislocations and recoveries of the 1930s.

Figure 7.4 summarizes the timing and magnitude of the Great Depression in the United States and seven other countries, as measured by changes in real GDP per capita (Maddison 2004). Although these data are, no doubt, subject to significant measurement error, they convey some sense of the dimensions of the depression in different parts of the industrialized world. The United Kingdom and Sweden (in the right panel of figure 7.4) experienced relatively mild declines in economic output in the early 1930s followed by substantial, steady increases through the rest of the decade (until the onset of war in 1940). Germany and France suffered somewhat steeper declines in output in the early 1930s, followed by rapid growth in the case of Germany but prolonged stagnation in the case of France. Australia (in the left panel) experienced a sharp drop in output in 1930 and 1931 followed by a fairly steady increase through the rest of the decade, while Ireland experienced rather little economic fluctuation throughout this period. Finally, the United States and Canada stand out in figure 7.4 both for the depth of the Great Depression and for its duration. Real output fell by 30% in the United States and by one-third in Canada; in both cases, the economy did not fully rebound until 1940.[31]

---

31 These trends in economic output are paralleled by trends in unemployment, which increased from 3.2% in 1929 to 24.9% in 1933 in the United States and from 4.2% in 1929 to 26.5% in 1933 in Canada (Statistical Office of the United Nations 1949).

A Chicken in Every Pot

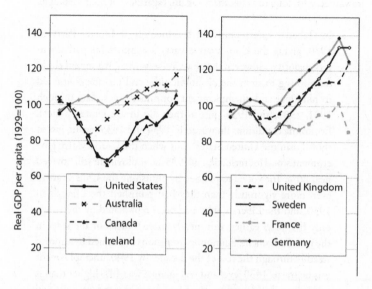

Figure 7.4. Depression and Recovery in Eight Countries, 1928–1940

In the United States, the resulting New Deal realignment replaced a profoundly conservative government with a liberal—critics would say radical—alternative. The shift seems entirely interpretable along ideological lines. Moreover, the subsequent recovery of the national economy seems to validate the efficacy of Roosevelt's dramatic policy innovations: real income per capita increased by a remarkable 46% over the years from 1932 to 1940.[32] However, the story seems a good deal less simple when we canvass the responses of electorates in other established democracies to the economic crises documented in figure 7.4.

Around the world, electoral reactions to the Depression produced momentous realignments of established party systems in a bewildering variety of configurations. Incumbent governments were deposed with impressive consistency during the worst days of the Depression, regardless of their ideologies.

32 One occasionally hears it said that "the war got us out of the Depression, not Roosevelt." We explore the appeal of factually incorrect but politically convenient beliefs in chapter 10.

And new incumbents who presided over robust economic recoveries were rewarded with long runs in office—again, regardless of their ideologies:

- In Canada, voters punished the incumbent Liberal Party in 1930, giving the Conservative Party a comfortable parliamentary majority. However, the new Conservative government could do nothing to stem the economic tide; real income continued to plummet and unemployment continued to escalate through 1931, 1932, and 1933 (just as they did in the United States). Economic conditions improved in 1934 and 1935 (again, just as they did in the United States), but when the Conservative government stood for reelection in 1935 unemployment still hovered near 20%. The voters responded by punishing the Conservatives even more vigorously than they had punished the Liberals in 1930, and the Liberals, who had been repudiated by the voters only five years earlier, won nearly three-fourths of the seats in the new Parliament. Economic conditions continued to improve steadily through the rest of the decade. By 1940, unemployment was below its 1930 level and real income was 40% higher than it had been a decade earlier. The Liberal government was returned with overwhelming parliamentary majorities in 1940, and again in 1945, 1949, and 1953 before finally falling in 1957.

- In Australia the economy declined precipitously in 1930–31, either despite or because of the "radical" policies of the incumbent Labor Party. In the general election of 1931, Labor was challenged by the newly founded United Australia Party, a coalition of conservative nationalists and Labor dissidents. Labor's vote share fell from 49% (winning 46 House seats) in 1929 to 27% (winning 14 House seats) in 1931. The United Australia Party won with 40% of the vote, the economy improved markedly, and UAP held power through three subsequent elections in the next decade.

- In Britain, a minority Labour government took office in 1929 but pursued orthodox policies and a balanced budget. By the end of 1930, unemployment had more than doubled and the value of exports had fallen by half. A plan to bolster the Exchequer through massive cuts in unemployment relief divided the Labour Party, leading Prime Minister Ramsay MacDonald to form a multiparty National Government in 1931 to impose austerity. The National Government won a general election in 1931, but with 470 of the 615 seats in Parliament held by the Conservative Party. The remnant of the Labour Party, having expelled supporters of the National Government, won only 52 seats. In 1935, following two years of fairly robust economic growth, the Conservatives again won a comfortable parliamentary majority, and they remained in power through the end of World War II a decade later.

- In Ireland, the nationalist Fianna Fáil party came to power in 1932 (following a significant decline in the production of oats and potatoes, the two most important crops) and won an electoral majority early in 1933 (following a substantial rebound in agricultural production). Fianna Fáil continued in power for the next fifteen years, and remained the dominant party in Ireland until 2011.

- In Sweden, a Conservative prime minister was replaced by a Liberal in 1930. Real GDP declined and unemployment escalated from 12% to 22% over the next two years, despite an early exit from the gold standard in 1931. Another election in 1932 brought the Social Democratic Party to power. Unemployment peaked in 1933 and began to decline in 1934; real GDP increased markedly from 1933 through 1939. The Social Democrats remained in power (sometimes in coalition with other parties, and with a brief interlude in 1936) until 1976.

- In France, accountability was greatly complicated by the political institutions and culture of the Third Republic. The incumbent center-right coalition was defeated in the general election of 1932, at the low point of the Depression; but the victorious socialists and more conservative "radicals" failed to produce a government, leaving the radicals to govern with support from the center-right. That coalition was driven from office in early 1934 by riots organized by far-right groups. The economy continued to languish under the rightist governments that followed.

In 1936 a new Popular Front combining socialists, communists, and radicals won 57% of the vote, but the resulting government was again hampered by chronic friction among the coalition partners and was dissolved by the president. In 1939, economic output finally regained its 1929 level, mostly due to increased spending on armaments.

- In Germany, the downturn stemming from the Great Crash was exacerbated by a collapse of U.S. loans to fund war reparations and rebuilding. A series of coalition governments traumatized by the hyperinflation of the 1920s responded by cutting wages and spending and raising taxes. The unemployment rate doubled (from 15% to 30%) between 1930 and 1932. Popular support for the Nazi Party doubled over the same two years (from 18% in the Reichstag election of September 1930 to 37% in July 1932 and 33% in November 1932), while support for the Communist Party also increased. The 1932 elections produced a legislative stalemate that ended with the appointment of Adolph Hitler as chancellor in January 1933. In March, the Reichstag ceded its powers to Hitler. An election in May was marred by Nazi intimidation of the Communist and social democratic parties; the former was banned shortly after the election, the latter in June, and all other parties in July. Meanwhile, unemployment fell steadily beginning in 1933 (back to 15% in 1934 and below 5% in 1937), real GDP expanded rapidly (due in large part to a massive military buildup), and Hitler led Germany on to world war.

A crucial feature of this brief litany of electoral responses to the Depression is that the ideological interpretation customarily provided for voters' reactions in the United States does not turn out to travel well. Where conservatives were in power when the Depression hit they were often replaced with liberals or socialists, as in the United States and Sweden. But where relatively leftist governments were in power during significant downturns they were often replaced with more conservative alternatives, as in Britain and Australia. Where the existing party system was oriented around noneconomic issues, as in Ireland, voters rejected the "ins" and replaced them with "outs" whose policy positions cannot even be sensibly classified in left-right terms. Where the timing of elections forced more than one major party to stand for reelection during the worst years of the Depression, as in Canada and Sweden, voters seem to have been perfectly willing to reject both in turn. Where complex coalition politics defused responsibility, as in France and Germany, discontented citizens turned to unstable coalitions, to fringe parties, or to the streets. Simply put, there is no consistent ideological logic evident in voters' responses to the Depression when we look beyond the American case. When voters got a chicken in every pot at election time, they usually liked the incumbent party's ideology just fine, whatever it happened to be. But when incomes eroded and unemployment escalated, they became ripe for defection to anyone who promised to bring home the poultry.

"A PROMISE OF SALVATION": SOCIAL CREDIT SWEEPS ALBERTA

Our brief global survey of electoral responses to the Great Depression underlines the apparent willingness of voters experiencing significant economic distress to embrace a remarkable variety of proposed solutions. In most cases, of course, those proposed solutions reflect *some* more or less respectable understanding of economic policies and their consequences. Thus, it may appear that voters in these instances were merely guilty of some ideological inconsistency—hardly surprising and plausibly sensible under the circumstances. However, we believe that the problem goes deeper than that. When the proposed solutions to economic distress happen *not* to be respectable, voters may be quite willing to embrace them nonetheless.

A remarkable example of this sort comes from the Canadian prairie province of Alberta, where voters in the midst of the Great Depression abandoned all of the province's established political parties in favor of an improbable, totally untried alternative, the Social Credit Party. We have nothing to add to existing scholarship on the meteoric rise of Social Credit, most notably John Irving's (1959) detailed account of *The Social Credit Movement in Alberta*. Nevertheless, we review the case in some detail, since it seems to us to shed considerable light on the combustible potential of blind retrospection under conditions of economic distress.[33]

---

33 Similar economic nostrums were embodied in the Townsend Plan, which attracted substantial support in California and other parts of the United States in the same period (Cantril 1941, chap. 7).

"In 1935," according to W. L. Morton (1950, 286), "the rural electors of Alberta refused to listen to their former leaders. They closed their ears to reason; in their despair, they sought only a promise of salvation." Although Social Credit embodied a certain "reforming impulse" (Finkel 1989, 40), careful analysis of the party's electoral support suggests that it was a catch-all party whose appeal had less to do with conventional economic cleavages or policies than with voters' desire for "a strong-willed, dauntless leader who would take them out of the wilderness" (Irving 1959, 340). The result was a colorful and unnerving episode in the history of modern democratic politics.

As we have seen, the national government of Canada had been in Liberal hands before passing to the Conservative Party in 1930. At the provincial level, an agrarian populist party, the United Farmers of Alberta (UFA), had been in power since 1921. In 1933, UFA leaders played a prominent role in the creation of a national farm-labor socialist party, the Co-operative Commonwealth Federation, which in turn supported the UFA provincial government of Alberta. Thus, Alberta entered the first provincial election campaign of the Depression era with what was, in effect, an agrarian socialist governing party. The Liberals were the largest mainstream opposition party, having received about 25% of the vote in each of the previous two provincial elections.

Alberta's Social Credit Party emerged from a social movement led by William Aberhart, a charismatic preacher, educator, and radio broadcaster. Though he had earlier dismissed the Social Credit philosophy as "crazy," he was won over by a highly popularized version he encountered in a book borrowed from a colleague in the summer of 1932. He "decided that Social Credit was exactly what the people of Alberta needed to redeem their province from the depths into which the bankers and financiers had plunged it" (Irving 1959, 48–49)—and he proceeded to give it to them.

Aberhart's crusade on behalf of Social Credit drew upon the resources and prestige of the Calgary Prophetic Bible Institute, a powerful religious institution which he had built and directed in the 1920s. "Under his leadership," Irving (1959, 50, 259) wrote, "the Social Credit movement glided almost imperceptibly from a religious to an educational to a social to a political movement, but throughout that evolution the people's perception of Aberhart as a Man of God was never dimmed and was one of the principal factors in inspiring them with loyalty and devotion to the Social Credit movement." Until just a few months before the 1935 provincial election, Social Credit retained the character of a social movement rather than a political party. However, "Social Credit speakers did not hesitate to whip up the people's resentment at the government's seeming indifference to their sufferings. Small-town week-lies began to suggest in their editorial columns that thousands of people were persuaded that Aberhart was the Moses of a new economic deal. It followed that the Social Credit movement should enter politics without further delay" (Irving 1959, 121).

Aberhart and his followers employed an impressive variety of organizational and propaganda techniques, including study groups, parades, and open-air meetings. Aberhart's radio broadcasts spread the Social Credit gospel throughout the province. Often the broadcasts featured a "Man from Mars" who personified the confusion of ordinary Albertans in the face of economic chaos: "The 'Man from Mars' . . . could not understand why people were not receiving enough food and clothing in a land where food and clothing were being needlessly destroyed. Why were some people driving around in big cars, well-fed and prosperous, while others did not have even the barest necessities of life? Aberhart informed the Martian visitor that, if he could stay for the meeting, he would learn that Social Credit was the only way out of the present financial chaos, the only solution of the paradox of 'poverty in the midst of plenty'" (Irving 1959, 113).

The Social Credit platform called for the distribution of $25 monthly Basic Dividends to every citizen, the establishment of Just Prices on all goods and services, and a suspension of foreclosures pending the issuance of interest-free loans by the provincial government. Critics charged that "'basic dividends' could not be issued in Alberta because of constitutional limitations, and that, if they could be initiated, inflation would result. The prevailing attitude of educated people in the small towns to such arguments was aptly summed up by a local editor: 'The hope of the people, long deferred, has made hearts sick. Desperate diseases require desperate remedies. Perhaps people cannot be blamed for accepting unconstitutional and unintelligent prescriptions when constitutional and rational ones are platitudinous'" (Irving 1959, 121). According to Irving (1959, 256), "interviews are replete with admissions of a lack of understanding of the technical mechanisms or procedures that would be involved in carrying out monetary reform or in the provision of basic dividends and the just price. All such matters, people constantly insisted, could safely be left to Aberhart and the experts he would call in to implement his Social Credit programme." Editorialists railed in vain against "the uncritical belief of Aberhart's followers in Social Credit as a magic formula" (Irving 1959, 86). One pro-business interest group complained that "the whole Social Credit scheme is impracticable. It can be defended only by those who close their eyes to simple reasoning or those who are utterly cynical and reckless in what they say to electors. The religious atmosphere of Social Credit blinds people to these dangers" (Irving 1959, 362).[34]

The appeal of Social Credit no doubt stemmed in part from the fact that "in 'explaining' the causes of the depression it did not run counter to, but rather accentuated, the extremely hostile attitudes towards the existing economic system that had arisen in a period characterized by 'poverty in the midst of plenty'" (Irving 1959, 334). The electoral potential of the Social Credit movement was further enhanced by the weakness of voters' attachments to the existing political parties.[35] Most important, the incumbent UFA was, as Morton (1950, 287) put it, "old in the sense that it had been tried."

The UFA election manifesto "surveyed 'the notable record of achievement' of the farmers' administration in many fields, outlined the social dividends being paid to the people of Alberta, and concluded by setting forth in sixteen clauses the further steps that were necessary for the realization of the ultimate objectives of the U.F.A. movement. Replying to the challenge of the Social Credit movement, the government claimed that it had brought Alberta through the greatest depression in the world's history to better advantage than any other government anywhere" (Irving 1959, 352). Regarding the possibility of more radical change, the UFA declared that it was hamstrung by limitations on Alberta's sovereign powers and by the province's economic dependence on the rest of Canada. The voters were clearly not impressed by these excuses. After his final campaign rally, UFA Premier

34 A pamphlet issued by the Economic Safety League (quoted by Irving 1959, 361–362) sheds light both on the flavor of the Social Credit plan and on the exasperation of its opponents at its apparent illogic: "Social Credit proposes to issue toy or make-believe money (which it calls credit) at the rate of $10,000,000 a month. It does not disclose any method by which this toy money can be given the same purchasing power as Canadian money.... Existing provincial taxes are about $15,000,000 a year. Dividend payments alone would require $120,000,000, which is eight times this revenue.... Mr. Aberhart himself admits the need for revenue, but does not show how it can be obtained. His attempts to do so are childish.... Social Credit claims to be able to pay $120,000,000 a year with a much smaller sum (such as $10,000,000) if the toy-money is turned over fast enough. This is a crude fallacy. $120,000,000 a year can be paid with 10,000,000 dollar coins, notes, or even dollar-certificates if these are used over and over again (12 times a year is the example chosen). But the Government cannot use the dollars a second time till it gets them back from the public. The process of getting them back is called taxation.... Since continued inflation will make the toy-money valueless; and since the means for raising $120,000,000 a year are absurd, the whole Social Credit scheme is impracticable."

35 The combined vote for Liberals and Conservatives in the 1930 provincial election had totaled less than 40%. Irving (1959, 230) cited "a continuous tradition of great dissatisfaction with the conventional party system.... The operation of democracy in Alberta in terms of the two-party system had therefore been tenuous and uncertain."

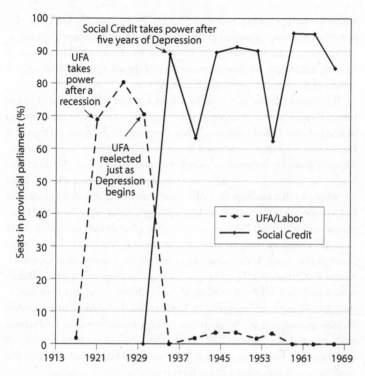

Figure 7.5. The Legacy of the Great Depression in Alberta Provincial Politics

R. G. Reid overheard a young man "say, to nobody in particular, 'Well, I guess Social Credit's no darn good, but who's there to vote for anyway—I guess I'll vote for Social Credit anyway'" (Irving 1959, 330–331). Many others did the same.

The result was a startling political earthquake, even by Depression-era standards. The fledgling Social Credit Party won 56 of the 63 seats in the provincial parliament; the incumbent UFA won none. Voters who lined up to receive their $25 bonuses on the morning after the election were to be disappointed. Nevertheless, as the timelines of party fortunes presented in figure 7.5 make clear, the critical election of 1935 precipitated a durable partisan realignment in Alberta. Social Credit would go on to dominate provincial politics for an entire generation, winning nine consecutive provincial elections (often with 90% or more of the seats in parliament) and governing without interruption for more than 35 years. By contrast, the UFA, the proponent of all the social welfare programs that one would suppose Depression-era voters needed, was destroyed forever as an effective political force in Alberta, never again winning as much as 5% of the seats (and seldom as much as 20% of the votes) in provincial elections.[36]

The remarkable rise of the Social Credit Party in Alberta is all the more remarkable when it is juxtaposed with the story of the adjacent Canadian prairie province of Saskatchewan. While the economic hardships of the Great Depression led Albertans to hand the reins of government to a charismatic preacher peddling funny-money economic policies, their neighbors in Saskatchewan followed a very different path, gravitating toward the very same left-wing populist ideology that Albertans abandoned. A provincial election in 1934 saw the utter collapse of the governing Conservative Party and its replacement with a new Liberal government. The Liberals were reelected in 1938 (Canada having averted the economic downturn that afflicted the United States in that year). At the same time, however, the Co-operative Commonwealth Federation (CCF)—the agrarian socialist party allied with Alberta's now-demolished UFA—flourished in Saskatchewan, first in opposition to the Liberals and later, beginning in 1944, as North America's first avowedly socialist government. As Seymour Martin Lipset acknowledged in his classic study of agrarian socialism (1968, xxii), "There has not yet been an adequate explanation, or even a detailed descriptive account of the factors involved that resulted in such different reactions from two quite similar social units."

Despite their drastic ideological differences, the Social Credit Party in Alberta and the CCF in Saskatchewan both managed to build durable electoral pluralities in the years following the Depression. In Saskatchewan, the socialists won five consecutive elections and governed the province without interruption from 1944 through 1964. The Liberal Party survived in opposition and won two elections during the 1960s, but never regained the share of seats it held in the provincial legislature in virtually every election before 1944. The Conservative Party, swept from office in 1934, won a total of one seat in all elections thereafter until 1975, despite carrying the province repeatedly in federal elections.

According to John Bennett and Cynthia Krueger (1968, 359), "the prevailing pattern of Saskatchewan voting can be summarized by the remark: 'They vote CCF in provincial elections, and Conservative in Federal. It

---

36 A quasi-successor, the New Democratic Party (NDP), enjoyed its first-ever victory in an Alberta election in 2015.

makes sense only if you live here.'" They added, "The sense in this situation is clear enough; the farmers voted for those parties that furnished or were associated with solutions to their problems, regardless of ideological doctrine." We would add that those parties were "associated with solutions" only in the sense that they happened to be in office when economic conditions improved.

CONCLUSION

John Irving (1959, ix–x) suggested that "the functioning of the democratic process in Alberta during the rise of the Social Credit movement provides a much needed corrective to the abstract concepts of the classical philosophers of democracy from John Locke to John Dewey." We agree, at least, that the rise of Social Credit—and the responses of a variety of democratic electorates to the stresses of the Great Depression—cast profound doubts on the romantic image of "the people" incorporated in the folk theory of democracy.

Looking at evidence from the United States, along with an array of election outcomes in Europe, Canada, and elsewhere, we have argued for an understanding of the politics of the Great Depression that is radically different from the usual contemporary views. Most voters, we argue, are busy with their lives in the best of times, and doubly so when they are under great economic pressure in recessions and depressions. Politics is full of complexities and uncertainties, even for those who can devote full time to it. The voters, not knowing what the best policies are, content themselves with asking at election time whether events have gone well or badly lately. Then they vote that myopic judgment. [myopic def]

These facts make sense of such otherwise perplexing electoral outcomes as Winston Churchill's loss of the British prime minister's office in 1945. He may well have asked, "What? Saving you from death in the concentration camps wasn't enough?" But once victory in Europe was achieved, the voters lost interest in that topic. What was on their minds at election time seems to have been the housing shortage (McCallum and Readman 1947, 203–204), to which no competent government would have diverted money during the war. The voters didn't care. They voted for a change.

When the state of the election-year economy is particularly dreadful, as it surely was during the depths of the Great Depression, voters are likely to feel more strongly about their retrospections, forming strong partisan aversions to the incumbents, and—if times improve—strong attachments to the parties that replace them. The resulting preferences endure in less stressful periods and are eventually passed on to children, imposing a long-term stamp on the party system. Voters will adopt more or less coherent "ideological" explanations for their behavior, the policies of the lucky party will be enacted, and a country may be substantially remade. The resulting political realignment may appear to political scientists and historians as a momentous ideological judgment by the electorate. But we find in the cases we have examined that the evidence for such interpretations is weak. Political insiders debate policy alternatives, but the electorate votes on a very different basis.

CHAPTER EIGHT

The Very Basis of Reasons: Groups, Social Identities, and Political Psychology

> What, then, is a "group"? How does it acquire the capacity for exercising such a decisive influence over the mental life of the individual?
>
> —Sigmund Freud, *Group Psychology and the Analysis of the Ego* (1921, 6)

In the preceding parts of this book, we took up two broad classes of democratic theory. The first class we called "populist," conveying the notion that the political preferences of ordinary people should be the foundation of good government. In the simplest folk theory version, those preferences are taken at face value, and the majority should rule. In more sophisticated doctrines, preferences might need to be enlightened by education or deliberation. But in all versions of this style of democratic thinking, preferences are the starting point and the foundation. Hence this category of democratic theory is variously called "liberal" (in the 19th-century sense deriving from utilitarianism), or sometimes "individualist" or "intellectualist," for it is founded on and relies on careful thought by individuals in their role as democratic citizens (Mannheim 1936, 219–225; de Grazia 1951, 172–175).[1] As we have seen, this is a role that people struggle to fulfill in everyday political life. The attentive, judicious, unprejudiced individuals attuned to the

---

1 In the British context, Beer (1966, 39–43) called this category of democratic thought "Radical," and he traced its origins to the 17th-century Levellers movement. He noted that it has never been as influential in Britain as in the United States.

common good that populate the folk theory appear only too rarely in real life, and the barriers to erecting a satisfactory democratic theory on that foundation are formidable indeed.

The second class of theories we have considered focus less on policy choices and more on good management. In a Schumpeterian vein, they look for tools by which citizens with modest information can control the actions of their leaders. This retrospective theory of voting once seemed to offer great promise as a democratic theory responsive to the findings of modern social science. But as we have seen, this theory, too, asks too much of ordinary people. They cannot meet its demands, and the result is capricious judgments at election time.

Then what remains? In this chapter we outline an alternative view of political psychology. We argue that it provides a more scientifically accurate and politically realistic foundation for democratic theory. In one sense, not much of this chapter will be new. Indeed, we will argue that most of it was better understood by the Founders, and certainly by the social scientists of a century ago, than it is today. How was it lost? Alas, folk-democratic thinking and myopic retrospection afflict political science, too. As we will show, those forces have proven stronger than our strongest theories. Particularly when the popular research tools of the day have fit bad ideas better than good ones, we have readily exchanged our powerful intellectual inheritance for a mess of folk thinking.

THE REALIST POLITICAL TRADITION IN THE WEST

Realist thinking about politics can be found in the Hebrew Bible, in Aristotle and Thucydides, and in many other sources from the earliest years of Western thought. Its application to democracy appears prominently in the Federalist Papers. With respect to political psychology, here is Madison in Federalist Number 10:

> A zeal for different opinions concerning religion, concerning govern-
> ment, and many other points, as well of speculation as of practice; an at-
> tachment to different leaders ambitiously contending for pre-eminence
> and power; or to persons of other descriptions whose fortunes have
> been interesting to the human passions, have, in turn, divided mankind
> into parties, inflamed them with mutual animosity, and rendered them
> much more disposed to vex and oppress each other than to co-operate

for the common good. So strong is this propensity of mankind to fall into animosities that where no substantial occasion presents itself the most frivolous and fanciful distinctions have been sufficient to kindle their unfriendly passions and excite their most violent conflicts.

As we will show, that passage prefigures most of the key psychological ideas of the group theory of politics—the powerful tendency of people to form groups, the ensuing construction of "us" and "them," and the powerful role of emotion rather than reason in directing group activity. Madison also anticipated the experimental finding of 20th-century psychologists that group attachments are easily generated and profoundly felt. People are naturally group-oriented.

The subsequent theoretical development of group theory derives from a great achievement of 19th- and early 20th-century social science—the explicit recognition as a foundational principle that human beings everywhere live in groups and that human thought is deeply conditioned by culture, including group subcultures. Of course, national cultures had long been recognized: the Israelites were not like the Canaanites, the Athenians were not like the Spartans, and none of them resembled the Romans. Then, too, within civil society, 18th-century writers had already pointed out the profusion of groups, each with their demands on government. For example, decades before Madison, the Scottish Enlightenment figure Adam Ferguson (1767) emphasized the importance of "civil society" for thinking about government.

The group-theoretic strand of 19th-century thought went further, however, breaking from the rationalistic liberalism that underpins the folk theory of democracy. Karl Marx saw that while entire societies possessed a culture, economic classes within a society generated subcultures, too, and that those subcultures influenced what members of each class believed, what they valued, and what actions they were willing to take in defense of their class. Other scholars soon extended the argument to competing, conflictual civil groups of all kinds—national, racial, ethnic, religious, and professional. In Europe, Gabriel de Tarde (1890) emphasized individuals' widespread imitation of others, not just in manners and dress, but in their ideas as well. Gustave Le Bon (1895) pointed to the ubiquity of groups and their frequently irrational psychology. Georg Simmel (1908) focused on the inevitability of group conflict, and he identified overlapping and crosscutting group memberships as possible exacerbating or moderating influences. In the United States, Edward Ross (1905) and especially Albion Small (1905) brought this European tradition to the attention of their fellow citizens, emphasizing the central role of groups in sociological theory, the limitations of individual rationality, and the omnipresence of group conflict. And before any of these, the great Polish sociologist Ludwig Gumplowicz (1885) pioneered most of the central ideas.[2]

For all these scholars, mental life was group life. Human beings are cultural animals, and they spend their years absorbing in great detail the various subcultures in which they participate. From this viewpoint, all the great issues of life—religion, nationality, gender roles, popular scientific ideas, partisan loyalties, the value of different occupations, the appeal of different foods—are taught to the vast majority of people by their family, their culture, and their subcultures. At a slower pace, socialization to group norms continues throughout adulthood. Indeed, it is a commonplace that what passes for "going your own way" or "thinking for yourself" turns out to be, in practice, just switching from one set of culturally conditioned ideas to another, equally preformulated set. "Between the cradle and the grave . . . , a chain is extended whose every link is wrought into the preceding. Man may choose to break it by violence, but not to re-weld it" (Gumplowicz 1885, 160).

By the early 20th century, then, a powerful realist tradition in social science had arisen in opposition to the rationalistic Enlightenment assumptions of liberalism. It is that realist tradition that we adopt and extend in the remainder of this book. We argue that liberalism is simply too shallow to bear the weight put on it in conventional democratic theorizing. Put another way, for thinking about democracy, rational choice liberalism is a scientific error.

This is not to say, of course, that 19th-century liberal ideas have no uses. When people choose between receiving more or less money for similar tasks, or between cheap or expensive food of the same quality, the liberal assumption of rational choice will work well. Much of economics is a highly elaborated structure for dealing with situations of that kind. But, as Joseph Schumpeter (1942, 262–263) observed, once one leaves economics for politics, the choices take on a completely different character. Most people have little or no direct experience with the complexities of politics, and their thinking is far from the folk-democratic ideal, as Graham Wallas (1908) pointed out long ago. In consequence, when economics is carted into political science without attention to the evidence in the new field, as with the spatial model of elections, those foreign ideas will perform very poorly empirically, as we

2 This intellectual history was insightfully interpreted by James Aho (1975).

saw in chapter 2.[3] Much the same logic applies to the theory of deliberative democracy, which is an idealistic version of liberalism proposed by political theorists (Habermas 1994; Gutmann and Thompson 1996; Macedo 1999; Cohen 2003).

The limitations of rationalistic liberalism were clear to early 20th-century political scientists, and yet the implications for democracy and for its study were only slowly realized. For the early sociological theorists had spoken to politics only in part. They were intent on showing that states arose from violent conquest, not from some imaginary social agreement. And they argued that domestic social conflict arose as soon as states were formed. But the work of government—the policy-making process—got little attention from sociologists.

American political scientists of the 19th century were no different. They also ignored the role of group forces in government in spite of the omnipresence of "the lobby," the powerful collection of interest groups that so appalled observers of 19th-century American national and state politics. To take just three classic examples of this oversight, in volumes that are still in print, John Burgess (1933, 145) complained only briefly at the end of his important book that "everywhere, a designing class or group" deflects government to "the profit and privilege of the few." Woodrow Wilson's 333-page classic, *Congressional Government* (1900, 189–190), dedicated just a page and a half to interest groups, and then only to condemn their influence in general terms. And James Bryce's thousand-page second volume of *The American Commonwealth* gave just one chapter to an interest group—the railroads—a chapter that, he said, "No one will expect to find in a book like this" (Bryce 1894, 643).

It was left to Arthur Bentley, a journalist who had seen the rough and tumble of Chicago politics close up and who had taught at the University of Chicago for part of one year, to lay out the detailed implications for politics of the new ideas in social theory. Bentley had studied in Europe, and he explicitly acknowledged his deep debt to the Continental European sociologists who

---

3 As we have already noted, we have no dispute with rational choice per se, which is nearly tautological in content. What matters is what the citizen's starting point in politics is assumed to be. The Federalist Papers, supported and enhanced by 19th-century sociology, make it clear that preferences over policies or outcomes are not where citizens start. Instead, they begin from group affiliations. From that basis, group theory can be given a rational-choice microfoundation, outlined in Truman (1951, 18–21) and developed in different ways by Hechter (1987) and Hardin (1995), among others. Thus the issue is not rational *whether*, but rational *how*. Self-interested individualistic rational choice is the wrong "how" for understanding most of politics.

had preceded him. For him as for them, groups were fundamental to politics. Yet Bentley pushed well past those who came before him.

In *The Process of Government*, Bentley (1908) emphasized the importance of groups in politics—all sorts of groups, including organized interest groups, self-conscious but politically unorganized social groups, potential groups not yet self-conscious, and governmental actors.[4] He saw most governmental decisions as decisively influenced by the power and intensity of rival groups. He also described the ability of intense minorities to get their way when the majority is apathetic, uninterested, or unorganized. The strategic choice of techniques by pressure groups, the legal and normative rules structuring group conflict, the role of parties as group coalitions, and the impact of government as both referee and independent actor—all these are discussed. Indeed, there is not much of theoretical import in subsequent group theories of the policymaking process that is not anticipated in Bentley's book. Though not an easy read, it is a monument of creative thought, in our estimation the most important book of 20th-century political science.

In chapter 11 we return to the policy-making process, which was Bentley's central focus. For now, our key point is that he portrayed groups not just as vehicles for pressuring government, but as the mainsprings of political attitudes and interests. "When we go down to the group statement," he wrote (1908, 241), "we get down below mere reasoning to the very basis of reasons." However, he had little to say about the *processes* by which groups shape individuals' political opinions. He took the previous sociological treatises, which he discussed at considerable length, as having established the profound impact of groups on individuals, and he moved on.

For the next few decades, other scholars of public opinion followed Bentley's lead. They oriented themselves to group influences on public opinion, but paid little attention to the underlying causal mechanisms. For example, W. Brooke Graves's (1928) reader on public opinion took an explicitly group-theoretic approach. It contained selections from Freud, A. Lawrence Lowell, and Walter Lippmann. Other readings explained how the schools, religion, the press and radio, the arts, business, political parties, and pressure groups each affected citizens' thinking and their political preferences. Conceptually speaking, this was a more sophisticated book than virtually all modern readers on public opinion, which pay little attention to group attempts to

---

4 This description departs from many stereotypical summaries of Bentley (1908) in the literature, but it is faithful to the book itself.

influence the citizenry or to the processes by which people absorb their ideas from the subcultures to which they belong.

The arguments of the public opinion specialists of this period, like the analyses of the pioneering sociologists who preceded them, were primarily humanistic, illustrated by colorful, even compelling examples from the politics of the time, it is true, but with none of the inferential rigor that social scientists began to expect under the growing influence of empiricism. The theoretical arguments were quite general and undifferentiated, too. Considerable scope was left for subsequent scholars to fill in the mechanisms, using close observation and laboratory experiments to expand and validate group theory in a more systematic way. And that they proceeded to do.

In monumental multivolume studies of "Middletown" by Robert and Helen Lynd (1929; 1937) and of "Yankee City" by W. Lloyd Warner and his associates (1963), ethnic, gender, and religious memberships were studied in great detail, with attention to each of the corresponding subcultures, and to "training the young" into their roles. Participant observation in these towns (Muncie, Indiana, and Newburyport, Massachusetts, respectively) confirmed just what the 19th-century sociologists had said: groups are fundamental to social life. People took their views from the groups to which they belonged, often because the people around them made it difficult not to do so. Ideas that individuals had picked up elsewhere were disapproved of, and most people were eventually convinced to discard them. One Middletown attorney told the Lynds, "Why, when I was in the university I believed all the professors told me. . . . Now I realize it was downright wrong for them to talk to us the way they did" (Lynd and Lynd 1929, 493).[5]

These findings regarding the power of groups to shape thinking have been reinforced by the results of multiple studies in the decades since. For example, the impact of families and schools in the first years of life has been extensively documented. The work of Herbert Hyman (1959), Fred Greenstein (1965), Robert Hess and Judith Torney (1968), Kenneth Langton (1969), and M. Kent Jennings and Richard Niemi (1974; 1981), among others, established empirically the powerful effects of early socialization on adult political allegiances. The effects were not immutable, but neither were they easily

---

5 The Lynds do not say which topics—evolution? socialism?—or which college. If the institution in question was Indiana University, as seems probable, then unfortunately for the student, Alfred Kinsey had not yet arrived there to offend small-town sensibilities in more thrilling fashion.

changed. Most adults felt the same ties to nation, religion, race, ethnicity, and political party as their parents.

Researchers also took to the laboratory to demonstrate the power of group norms to override individuals' own judgments. Muzafer Sherif (1936, chap. 6) and Solomon Asch (1951) carried out famous experiments showing that even ad hoc groups of strangers who announced a faulty factual judgment could induce people to go along. For example, Asch (1951) asked a group of previously unacquainted male undergraduates to judge which of three line segments was closest in length to a fourth reference line. Left to themselves, more than 99% of students gave the correct answer. But in groups, the outcome was quite different. Unbeknownst to the experimental subjects, the other group members were confederates of the experimenter, instructed to give wrong answers at some points in a sequence of trials. The confederates were seated so that they spoke first, leaving the remaining student to either give the correct answer in defiance of everyone else, or to go along. A large majority of the experimental subjects conformed on at least some of the trials, and some conformed all the time. In debriefings afterward, the conformists ranged from those who knew their answers were wrong but thought they should go along, to those who felt their eyes must be deceiving them and so adopted the group's perception. A few subjects conformed so completely that they professed not even to have noticed the evidence from their own eyes.

Outcomes of this kind would have come as no surprise to James Madison, nor to the thinkers who pioneered group theory, nor indeed to any thoughtful observer of group life, but they confirmed central sociological arguments within the new framework of experimental validation. Backed by a great many similar studies, the results were widely influential. Theorizing, too, became more sophisticated in this period. For example, Peter Blau (1964) set out a proto-formal theory of individuals' search for approval, status, and power, the formation of groups, and their exchange and conflict in society and politics.

Further dramatic evidence of the affinity of human beings for groups was developed by Henri Tajfel (1970; 1981). In his experiments, people arbitrarily assigned to meaningless groups quickly began to favor their fellow group members against others, even when they knew nothing about anyone else involved, they themselves did not profit from their bias, and no prior group conflict had occurred. This "minimal group" paradigm demonstrated that the human capacity for joining groups and disliking other groups was close to the surface and easily mobilized, a phenomenon particularly familiar in competitive situations.

The great similarity to each other of undergraduate populations in most American college football conferences, for example, does not prevent students and alumni of each university from entertaining elaborate and emotionally felt theories about how dramatically they differ from the unfortunates at the other institutions, particularly those at their main rival school. Hard-fought, "dirty" college games have long been fodder for social psychologists studying out-group stereotyping (Hastorf and Cantril 1954). The psychological processes at work are familiar to anyone who has attended sports events.[6] At this level, it is usually harmless.

Out-group stereotyping has deeper and more consequential effects when the stakes are larger. Racial and ethnic prejudices are endemic in all societies, as is nationalism in every country. Particularly when conflict arises, as in ethnic violence or in war, the stereotyping can lead to seeing the "other" as evil or even subhuman. In less dramatic conflict, such as election campaigns, group tensions can be mobilized to benefit a political party at the expense of a stereotyped minority. Gordon Allport (1954) pioneered the study of prejudice and its roots in individual and group psychology. He found that drawing boundaries between a good "us" and a bad "them" occurs widely in social life. Subsequent students of political psychology have found repeatedly that many, perhaps most, individuals organize their political thinking around social groups and their role in competing political parties. They see political and racial clashes as group conflict, and they engage in the same kind of stereotyping and moralizing that Allport had found (for example, Converse 1964; Kinder and Kam 2010).

In sum, an enormous body of experimental, quantitative, and qualitative evidence has accumulated that validates the realist understanding of how people think. Precise causal mechanisms remain in dispute. Are group attachments dark irrationalities or simply an often misguided attempt to pursue rational self-interest? Do people's group-related ideas and attachments derive primarily from their own needs or from elite cues and messages? Much remains to be learned. But in our judgment, the argument that people typically think as the realists say they do, and not as theorists in the Enlightenment

---

6 About 15 years ago, one of us attended with his wife a football game in Ann Arbor in which the town's two principal high schools played each other. Both schools were similar in racial and social class composition. His children attended the school with green football uniforms; the bitter cross-town rivals wore purple. The fans of each school sat on opposite sides of the stadium. About halfway through the game, his soft-spoken wife said under her breath, "I know that if we had bought the first house we considered, we'd be sitting on the other side of this field. But I just can't stand those purple people."

tradition claim—that much is beyond serious dispute. But what about politics? And what about elections in particular?

THE HIGH POINT OF GROUP THEORY
INFLUENCE AND ITS DECLINE

In the 1950s and 1960s, political scientists were well aware of the intellectual developments of the preceding century in psychology and sociology. The key statements from that period about American politics (Truman 1951), about empirical political theory (Easton 1953; 1965), and about comparative politics (Almond and Powell 1966) all took their starting point to be groups making demands on government, constrained by the institutional structure and the political culture. Government, in turn, had its own agenda, and it reacted back upon the society. Individuals played little role; elections received little attention except as a "feedback loop" in the informal systems-theory language popular at the time (Richardson 1991).

When elections were studied in greater detail, the findings matched group theory, too. The pioneering Columbia University studies (Lazarsfeld, Berelson, and Gaudet 1948; Berelson, Lazarsfeld, and McPhee 1954) took group forces as fundamental. The Columbia scholars showed that group memberships—being a Protestant rather than a Catholic, a union member rather than not, or a white person rather than an African American or other minority—powerfully shaped vote choices. People adapted their ideas to those of the presidential candidate they favored, or if they were less informed, they simply assumed (sometimes incorrectly) that his ideas matched their own.

The Columbia studies were subject to the criticism that group memberships might be proxying for attitudes or ideology. Thus, subsequent survey research often employed far more elaborate batteries of attitudinal questions and devoted substantial effort to disentangling the relationships among them. Critics also worried that the particular locales the Columbia researchers investigated might not be representative. Thus, most subsequent researchers have sampled the national electorate rather than specific communities, achieving greater representativeness at the cost of a much-diminished grasp of community context and social group action.[7] National surveys of unrelated individuals were all too congenial for folk theory thinking.

---

7 The work of Robert Huckfeldt and his colleagues (Huckfeldt and Sprague 1995; Ahn, Huckfeldt, and Ryan forthcoming) represents a prominent exception to this trend, and it provides ample discussion and illustration of the benefits of understanding local context.

Nonetheless, the first (and still the best) of these studies, *The American Voter* (Campbell et al. 1960), achieved a new depth of understanding. As we saw in chapter 2, in most respects it came to conclusions similar to those of the Columbia studies. The authors reported that the typical person lacked clear, stable attitudes toward major political issues. Most conceptualized politics in terms of groups, not ideology. But *The American Voter* departed from previous work in stressing that a particular political *identity*, party identification, proved fundamental to vote choice. Party loyalty powerfully shaped issue positions as well: again, group memberships largely drove policy views, not vice versa.

We address the group-theoretic understanding of the policy-making process in greater depth in chapter 11. Here, we simply note that one offshoot of group theory—"pluralism"—lent itself to a rosy view of American politics. Pluralists conceded the prominent role of groups in both the voters' thinking and the process of government, and the inequalities of power among those groups, but they attempted to defend the resulting peaceful equilibrium of group pressures, managed by political leadership, as tolerably "democratic." For example, in his classic pluralist study of politics in New Haven, Robert Dahl (1961, 228) argued that the democratic process worked reasonably well. While resources were by no means equal, almost everyone had at least some resources, those with many resources of one kind often were badly off with respect to other resources, and no one resource worked well in all or even most aspects of city politics; thus, no one group dominated all aspects of city life. Edward Banfield's study of Chicago politics took a similar view, with a more explicit normative defense of the equilibrium of group interests. "Where there exists no concretely meaningful criterion of the public interest," Banfield (1961, 339) wrote, "the competition of interested parties supplies a criterion—the distribution of 'real' influence—which may be both generally acceptable and, since it puts a premium upon effort to acquire influence, serviceable to the society."

In short, by the early 1960s pluralist ideas had come to dominate how prominent American political scientists thought about domestic politics. But pluralism was in many respects a heretical departure from the earlier group theorists' vision of politics as inevitably conflictual and violence-prone. Writing in the wake of the Depression and the Second World War, the pluralists put a powerful emphasis on political stability. Truman's (1951, 535) final paragraph emphasized "stability"; Dahl's (1961) concluding chapter was titled "Stability, Change, and the Democratic Creed." In their view, the United States was not like Nazi Germany or Soviet Russia; it was capable of solving its problems using regular elections and peaceful policy compromises. Thus, the pluralist perspective on the American political system was largely supportive of its basic institutional framework and of its status as a constitutional democracy. Not without criticisms of American politics, nor Pollyannaish about the potential for disaster, these gifted scholars nonetheless thought that with skilled leadership and devotion to democratic norms, needed changes could be achieved in much the same way that the New Deal had reshaped American politics. They were realists in their view of people, and meliorists in their view of American democracy—then and now, an appealing vision in many respects. They had gotten well past the folk theory. But at their weakest, there was a certain 1950s complacency in their thinking.

Then a reaction set in. In 1960s America, African-Americans engaged in widespread peaceful demonstrations to insist on their long-denied civil rights, particularly in the South. They were met by violent resistance from police forces and from white vigilantes. Violence broke into politics at the national level, too, first with the assassination of a president, and then the fatal shootings of the country's most prominent black leader and a presidential candidate, plus the serious wounding of another candidate. Most large American cities experienced at least one summer of violent unrest. The increasingly unpopular, unwinnable, and morally questionable Vietnam War inspired campus demonstrations, which were often met by violent police suppression. Sporadic incidents of violence and political murder by fringe groups inflamed the situation further. It seemed to many that the country was coming apart.

None of this would have surprised Arthur Bentley or his realist predecessors. Bentley (1908, 259) wrote, "Pressure is broad enough to include all forms of the group influence upon group, from battle and riot to abstract reasoning and sensitive morality."[8] But the standing and scholarly reputation of the pluralists was shaken by the events of the 1960s. The academic establishment was suddenly seen as overly satisfied with status quo politics and out of touch with the forces bubbling up from civil society (Walker 1966). In the view of critics, peaceful interest group conflict tending to an equilibrium did not seem to be what was going on. Instead, left-wing perspectives of various stripes were called into service, and theories of popular mobilization

8 Bentley (1908, 216, 241, 371, 433) explicitly took note of a spectrum of political action ranging from discussion through voting to bribery and, when satisfaction of grievances was blocked, assassination, terrorism, and revolutionary violence. Contrary to claims from some opponents of pluralism, the racial demonstrations and riots of the 1960s fit his arguments perfectly, if not always those of the pluralists who claimed his mantle.

and moral resistance got more attention. The demands and ideas of ordinary people were taken as morally compelling (Garson 1978).

In the American politics of this period, the Democratic Party became divided between an old guard dedicated to Cold War anticommunism and big-government social welfare policies versus an antiwar New Left that wanted more direct popular participation in politics. These divisions played into the academic politics of the time, with the tired and ineffectual national political establishment identified with the tired and ineffectual pluralists. Truman (1971, xl) complained about careless critics treating the failures of the political system as criticisms of pluralism. But in other respects, the critics had a point. Times were bad. The academic establishment was associated with pluralism, and pluralism had little place or sympathy for the kind of politics that had arisen. The powerful group theories that would have made sense of the 1960s had been forgotten, or blurrily misremembered as early pluralism. An academic version of collective guilt resulted: the offending party and its innocent relatives were all convicted. Pluralism and group theory went into decline.

The ideas that replaced pluralism, after an initial period of uncertainty, debate, and eclecticism, were in most respects the old-time American political religion. That is, the folk theory of democracy returned with a new lease on life. The accumulated science against it was not refuted; indeed, it continued to accumulate, as we have seen. But it was ignored in the schizophrenic fashion we documented in chapter 2. To younger authors in the folk theory tradition, group theory seemed to be *terra incognita*: *Hic dracones*. Groups were implicitly moved offstage; the structure of civil society disappeared from view.

For one group of authors, direct participation in politics by individual citizens became a new ideal, as in the work of Carole Pateman (1970) and her successors.[9] Another widely influential group of scholars rediscovered Anthony Downs's (1957) attempt to inject economistic thinking into political science. For them, as we saw in chapter 2, people's preferences were to be taken as given; there was no accounting for ideological tastes. When a basis for ideology was posited in this tradition, it was self-interest, usually economic self-interest. Social groups were absent. Citizens were rational individuals with an ideological viewpoint but no group identities, much as in a high school civics course.

---

9 We do not attempt to review this voluminous literature here except to note that, in spite of its tensions with rational choice, participatory theory descends from the same liberal tradition.

The notion that our own thoughts and feelings are rational, or should become so, is always superficially appealing, of course. The liberal tradition celebrates that doctrine as foundational for politics, as Karl Mannheim (1936, 122–126, 219–229, and passim) pointed out long ago. Thus, following Downs, an entire field of collective choice and political economy was developed to play out the implications of rational individualism, often with relatively sophisticated applied mathematics. Adopting that viewpoint was sometimes just a modeling convenience for the political economists; more often it powerfully affected their conclusions, as we have seen in chapter 2. They wrote as if the "crisis of reason" that formed the modern mind a century ago had never occurred (Burrow 2000). The result was a body of work that was simultaneously advanced in its methods and antiquated in its ideas.

The political economists' school of thought had devotees, but it had strictly limited impact on the rest of the discipline. In model after model, the assumptions were too uninformed about well-established social science findings, and the implications were too naive about politics and about people, to make much lasting contribution to understanding democracy. Indeed, as we discussed in chapter 2, the two big results from this tradition—Downs's demonstration that competing political parties would converge to the ideological center, making polarization impossible, and Kenneth Arrow's theorem establishing that no voting rule would satisfy a simple and appealing-looking list of ethical postulates—embroiled the field in empirical oversimplifications and deep conceptual tangles, respectively. Obviously, both results were substantial theoretical achievements, and subsequent work in this tradition sometimes achieved valuable insights. Any serious theory of democracy must wrestle with them. But in our view, this approach is not foundational. Rather, it underlines the need for theorists of democracy to look elsewhere for more fruitful starting points.

DEVELOPMENTS IN POLITICAL PSYCHOLOGY

In this same period, psychology, too, moved away from group studies. The field underwent a "cognitive turn." Influenced by experimental findings that simple stimulus-response models of attitude formation and change were inadequate, psychologists placed more emphasis on the mental processing that their experimental subjects undertook. In social psychology, "social cognition"—focused primarily on individual thinking—became the central focus of the field (Fiske and Taylor 1991).

In addition, the experimental paradigm became ever more powerful in psychology, including among cognitive psychologists. Randomizing gender, religious affiliation, or social class was impossible.[10] Thus when groups appeared in experiments, they were usually ad hoc groups created in the laboratory, not races, religions, or interest groups. In consequence, external validity came into question, and even more so, external relevance. As Tajfel (1981, 23) put it, "There are few social psychologists who have not at one time or another felt uneasy about the social vacuum in which most of their experiments were conducted." Did the stated effects hold outside the artificial environment of the university laboratory, typically populated only by undergraduates? No one knew for certain. Many of the same concerns arose about experiments embedded in public opinion surveys, which also became popular in political science and sociology. Did isolated individuals answering survey questions respond as they would in realistic political circumstances? It was often difficult to be sure. But the preferred social science tools worked best for studying artificially isolated individuals, not the consequential groups functioning in the society outside the lab, and so the study of individuals is where psychology focused.

For a macro–social science like political science, therefore, borrowing from an increasingly micro–social science like psychology became more difficult. Most psychologists addressed political groups only indirectly, and making use of their results in analyzing everyday politics required complex chains of auxiliary reasoning. Some political scientists mastered the cognitive psychology literature and employed it in studies of public opinion and voting, arriving at a skeptical view of human cognitive capacities in politics (for example, Lodge and Taber 2013). Most students of politics, though, went their own way, using an informal, eclectic psychologism as the main, and not very powerful, alternative to the economists' rational choice theories. Modern treatments of how individuals acquire their ideas from the social world continued to sell well, impress, and even shock undergraduates (notably Berger and Luckmann 1967). But it was hard to know what to do with them. A few political scientists carried out sophisticated empirical studies exploring the influence of national political culture on ordinary citizens (for example, McClosky and Zaller 1984) or the impact of party elites on the attitudes of their partisans (Zaller 1992). But for most, the group theory inheritance had little effect on their day-to-day practice of political science. Liberal individualism

---

10 Of course, political group affiliations can be made experimentally more or less salient to subjects, but that is not the same as altering the affiliations themselves.

fit our theoretical and empirical tools all too well. Thus, when pressed about democracy, we fell back on the familiar and congenial folk theory, with occasional nods to retrospective voting.

IDENTITY THEORY IN POLITICS
AND THE ROAD FORWARD

In recent decades, as always in politics, new realities have intervened to disturb the conventional wisdom and reinvigorate scholarship. Beginning in the 1980s, evangelical Christians and other religious conservatives began playing an important electoral role in American politics. The terrorist attacks of September 11, 2001, themselves a consequence of religious fanaticism, also made American nationalism a potent force in elections. The increase of Latinos and Asians in the American population directed additional academic attention to the politics of racial and ethnic diversity.

In each of these areas of political science, the concept of *identity* became central (Tajfel 1982).[11] This concept serves to distinguish groups to which an individual belongs that are not central to his or her self-concept from those that are a more integral part of the personality. Different people in the same group may differ. Thus some Catholics have a purely nominal attachment to the denomination. Others think of it as central to who they are, so that a disparaging remark about Catholics is an attack on *them*. The latter group have a Catholic identity. As Cantril (1941, 35) put it in an earlier period before the term "identity" had been coined, "When a person's national flag is torn down, *he* is insulted; when disparaging remarks are made of his parents, *he* is involved; when his football team or political party loses a contest, *he* has been defeated. Certain standards, frames and attitudes the individual feels are a part of him."

Identities are not primarily about adherence to a group ideology or creed. They are emotional attachments that transcend thinking. The Irish poet Seamus Heaney once spoke at a University of Michigan event that one of us attended. Northern Ireland was undergoing "The Troubles," with bitter Protestant-Catholic tensions punctuated by terrorist violence on both sides. Heaney told of an Irish visitor to the North who was asked whether he was a Protestant or a Catholic. The man said he was an atheist. "Yes, yes, we un-

---

11 The literature on identity is vast—far too extensive to cite here. Monroe, Hankin, and Bukovchik Van Vechten (2000) provided a helpful review emphasizing political identity and group behavior. Huddy (2001) is also an important source.

derstand," his hosts replied. "But are you a Protestant atheist or a Catholic atheist?" Theology was not the issue.

Identity theory made sense of why people adopt the opinions of their group, as group theory had emphasized but not explained. Thus, for example, the quixotic but powerful temperance movement in American history, so difficult to understand as rational self-interest, became understandable once it was seen as a "symbolic crusade," that is, as an attempt to reinforce Protestant identity as that identity came under threat from extensive Catholic immigration (Gusfield 1963). Self-sacrifice for the group's mission also became understandable; in some sense, people were doing it in their own interest. Subsequent theoretical development extended identity theory in many directions and fit it more closely within the framework of cognitive psychology, as in John Turner's (1991, chap. 6) self-categorization theory.

The concept of identity was widely adopted within political science. Thus, decades after group concepts from sociology had been abandoned and replaced by 19th-century liberal perspectives on human behavior, groups regained a central role in political psychology. A vast quantity of important work has been produced, far too much to cite here. Some of the most powerful work in this vein has focused on the single most powerful social cleavage in contemporary American politics—race. Michael Dawson (1994, 204–205), for example, showed that the political behavior of African-Americans is "powerfully influenced" by their sense of "shared fate"—their "perceptions of group interests. What is perceived as good for the group . . . plays a dominant role in shaping African-American partisanship, political choice, and public opinion" despite significant disagreements regarding specific racial and economic policy issues. In the same spirit, Vincent Hutchings and Hakeem Jefferson (2014) showed that racial identity is a key predictor of Democratic Party identification among African-Americans, well beyond the impact of policy views.

Of course, political scientists have also studied other identity groups grounded in ethnicity, social class, religion, nationality, or region. For example, Katherine Cramer's (forthcoming) in-depth examination of "the politics of resentment" traced the crucial role of rural consciousness in shaping the political views of working-class whites in upstate Wisconsin. Much of what has been said in studies of this sort tracks closely with the perspectives of the Founding Fathers and 19th-century sociologists; but the new scholarship has produced far deeper evidence and more sophisticated conceptual differentiation. It represents a genuine intellectual advance.

Yet even now, the concept of identity is too often imperfectly integrated into the study of political behavior. Much political science research mentions the concept but fails to measure it. Group memberships are substituted for group identities, as if every group member were interchangeable. Hence degrees of identity cannot be used to explain differences in opinions and behavior within the group. Nor, without careful measurement, can its effects be separated from those of attitudes correlated with it (Abdelal et al. 2009). Do the attitudes motivate the identity, or does the identity produce the attitudes? The same inferential challenges that bedeviled the Columbia studies of voting behavior in the 1940s are still with us.

In our view, a realist theory of democracy must be founded on a realistic theory of political psychology. At present, nothing of that kind exists. Step one, therefore, is to begin building a framework for thinking about voters that escapes from the populist liberalism that has constrained so much recent thought. Madison pointed the way, and 19th- and 20th-century scholars advanced the subject considerably. But we have too often stalled in recent decades. It is time to set Jeremy Bentham aside and bring James Madison back in.

To accomplish that, identity theory will have to be brought into the macrosocial world of politics. The role of political elites in structuring politically relevant cleavages needs to be understood better. It is popular now to treat identities as malleable and socially constructed, as indeed they are. We agree that politicians make their own cleavages, but we would add: not just as they please. The limits of malleability need to be spelled out.

Equally important, the impacts of identities need to be demonstrated, not only in the lab, but in the real political world. For example, when a presidential candidate draws surprising support in polls and primaries, we need sophisticated survey research tools that allow us to trace that support to identity groups, and not just to the preferences, attitudes, and ideology that the folk theory holds dear.

In addition, the political science version of identity theory needs to become more cognitive, just as social psychology has. Predictive power emerges from theoretical differentiation, and an implicit stimulus-response theory of identity acquisition will not do. Formalization and close empirical investigation of how people acquire an identity and how they use it to adopt ideas and make decisions is critical to further progress.

We can make no more than a start on this agenda in the remaining chapters of this book. Thus, just as births have a less finished quality than funerals, the succeeding chapters have a less finished quality than those preceding. The work of a great many scholars will be needed to complete the project we outline. What we do hope to achieve is to lay out a preliminary version of what a modern group-theoretic understanding of political attitudes and behavior might look like. Thus, in chapter 9 we argue in detail that social identities have trumped policy reasoning in shaping the politics of religion, race, and abortion in contemporary America. Hence in thinking about politics, it makes no sense to start from issue positions—they are generally derivative from something else. And that something else is identity.

In chapter 10 we turn from empirical investigation of identity politics to offer an account of how partisan identity shapes perceptions, not just of candidates and issues but also of simple facts. Instead of beginning from fanciful assumptions about what people know, we begin instead from realistic postulates that allow for differing levels of exposure to factual information and differing levels of partisan attachment. The result is a framework that can account with considerable accuracy for the complex differences in opinions and beliefs between Democrats and Republicans across the entire spectrum of political expertise, from the most uninformed and disengaged to the most (supposedly) knowledgeable.

Together, chapters 9 and 10 attempt to make the case that "groupiness" (Stenner 2005, 18) is fundamental to thinking about the beliefs, preferences, and political behavior of democratic citizens. In our concluding chapter, we sketch the implications of that fact for normative theories of democracy and for models of the policy-making process.

Partisan Hearts and Spleens: Social Identities and Political Change

> Consider the parallels between political preferences and general cultural tastes. Both have their origin in ethnic, sectional, class, and family traditions. Both exhibit stability and resistance to change for individuals but flexibility and adjustment over generations for the society as a whole. Both seem to be matters of sentiment and disposition rather than "reasoned preferences." While both are responsive to changed conditions and unusual stimuli, they are relatively invulnerable to direct argumentation and vulnerable to indirect social influences.
>
> —Bernard Berelson, Paul Lazarsfeld, and William McPhee,
> *Voting* (1954, 311)

Voters' political choices are grounded in all sorts of considerations, ranging from economic conditions to foreign policy mishaps to the personalities of competing candidates. However, the group theory of politics outlined in chapter 8 provides a framework for understanding and analyzing what we take to be the most important factor in voters' judgments, their social and psychological attachments to groups (Campbell et al. 1960, chap. 12). The favorability or antagonism of candidates and parties toward various ethnic, religious, and other social groups is much easier to learn than the intricacies of foreign affairs, and human nature makes group attachments powerful forces in political thinking. Because political parties are the most salient groups in democratic politics, group theory also helps to make sense of the central role of parties and partisanship in contemporary democracies and the role of group attachments and social identities in accounting for partisan change.

Most American voters identify with a political party, and their party identifications profoundly shape their choices at the polls (Campbell et al. 1960, chap. 6). Turbulence in the American party system in the 1960s and 1970s was interpreted by some scholars as evidence of "partisan dealignment" (Norpoth and Rusk 1982; Carmines, McIver, and Stimson 1987); but the turbulence proved to be temporary, and partisan voting has subsequently rebounded to more typical high levels (Bartels 1998; 2000). Moreover, once some initial conceptual and methodological challenges were overcome, behavioral partisanship—a tendency to vote consistently for one party or bloc of related parties—has also been found to play an important role in France (Converse and Pierce 1985), Britain (Heath and Pierce 1992), and other established democracies. And in new or reestablished democracies, the development of partisan attachments in the electorate is often taken as an indicator of democratic consolidation (Barnes, McDonough, and López Pina 1985; Brader and Tucker 2001; Lupu and Stokes 2010).

Proponents of "party government" (Schattschneider 1942; Ranney 1962) have interpreted partisan loyalties as providing a meaningful basis for democracy. In their view, the parties "stand for something." Voters know that and choose accordingly. Even those who may lack broad, coherent ideologies can form politically meaningful partisan loyalties on the basis of specific issue preferences. Surely, we think, gays and lesbians are Democrats for good policy-related reasons, just as evangelical Christians adhere to the Republican Party because of agreement on social issues.

In fact, issue group and political party leaders, along with other professional insiders like journalists, do mostly behave that way, because politics is their profession. Like doctors talking about medicine or airline pilots discussing airplanes, they know more than the rest of us. In the political realm, the professionals dominate political discourse and media coverage. Thus, we slip into thinking that ideology and policy preferences drive partisanship more broadly. However, the story is quite different when one looks closely at the rank and file. There, group loyalties matter a great deal and the details of policy positions not very much. As a result, as we saw in chapter 2, the policies espoused by political parties are often at odds with what the people who are voting for them favor (Esaiasson and Holmberg 1996; Pierce 1999).

This chastened, group-centric view of political parties helps explain why partisan loyalties often carry across generations. As we saw in the previous chapter, children tend to adopt the partisanship of their parents, and those attachments tend to persist into adulthood (Jennings and Niemi 1981). Even when the children of left-wing, working-class parents become middle-class business people, their inherited party loyalties often persist (Butler and Stokes 1974, chap. 3). Partisanship, like religious identification, tends to be inherited, durable, and not about ideology or theology. In some cases the durability is remarkable. For example, V. O. Key, Jr. (1949, chap. 4; Key and Munger 1959) found U.S. counties in the mid-20th century persisting in partisan voting patterns traceable to the Civil War a century earlier.

Of course, such stability is by no means universal. Groups of voters may gradually change their loyalties over time, and rare events—"party realignments"—may even shift the balance quickly and dramatically. As group theory suggests, these instances of significant political change usually stem from significant shifts in the political resonance of group identities. But absent such shifts, as with religion, people are often adherents of a particular political party because their great-grandparents favored it for entirely different reasons. That in turn helps to explain why partisan leanings are often only modestly correlated with policy preferences.

Some political scientists have disputed this social interpretation of partisanship. For example, Alan Abramowitz and Kyle Saunders (2006) showed that voters' party identifications are much more strongly correlated with their ideological self-descriptions than with their group memberships, and concluded that partisanship is rooted in ideology rather than social identity after all. But this sort of inference is unpersuasive in at least two respects. First, it greatly oversimplifies social identity by supposing that its partisan ramifications can be captured by adding up the statistical "effects" of a battery of simple demographic indicators—married, female, union member, and so on. For some people in those categories the demographic characteristic is the basis of an identity; for others it is not. And many people have strong identities not captured by the usual survey demographics—being Cuban-American, transgender, or a college professor. Political analyses of identity have to go beyond rounding up the usual demographic suspects.

The second problem with the argument that ideology trumps identity is that it implausibly assumes that any observed correlation between ideology and party identification must reflect the impact of ideology on partisanship. While some people's ideological commitments affect their party identification to some degree, careful efforts to disentangle their reciprocal effects (Miller 2000; Goren 2005) suggest that ideology is more often an *effect* of partisanship than its *cause*.

Most scholars of political behavior seem to agree that partisanship is both a *form* of social identity and, in significant part, a *product* of social identity

(Greene 1999; Green, Palmquist, and Schickler 2002; Greene 2004; Iyengar, Sood, and Lelkes 2012). However, it is surprisingly difficult to provide clear empirical evidence for these propositions. Occasionally, the interconnection of politics and identity is clear, as when a popular president inspires a vogue for babies named "Reagan."[1] However, as a general matter, social identities are diverse, complex, and profoundly interwoven with other politically relevant attitudes and opinions. How can we tell, in any given case, that *identity* is the key moving force?

Scholars of voting behavior have recognized and wrestled with these problems for decades, attempting to trace the social and political processes by which group memberships get translated into social identities and imbued with partisan political significance. The landmark study of *Voting* by Paul Lazarsfeld and his colleagues (Berelson, Lazarsfeld, and McPhee 1954) examined the political role of labor unions and other organized groups, individuals' perceptions of group voting norms, the reinforcement of those norms through social interaction and political discussion over the course of the campaign, and the political consequences of cross-cutting group attachments. The authors of *The American Voter* (Campbell et al. 1960, chap. 12) took a different tack, measuring identification with a variety of the most politically prominent groups of their day and showing in each instance that partisan loyalties and voting behavior were significantly conditioned by psychological attachment to the group. However, neither of these approaches—nor any other that we know of—offers a reliable way to gauge the *overall* impact of social identities on partisanship and voting behavior.

In light of these difficulties, we focus in this chapter on a series of instances in which political circumstances (and available data) provide unusual opportunities to isolate the impact of social identities. A key implication of our argument is that major shifts in the group alliances within parties should precipitate significant partisan realignments for the group members affected. We therefore focus on some of the most momentous instances of partisan change in American political history, including the New Deal realignment of the 1930s, the collapse of the Democratic Party's political hegemony in the Solid South following the Jim Crow era, and the emergence of abortion as a powerful partisan issue in the 1980s and 1990s. By illustrating the importance

---

1 According to Urbatsch (2014, 464), the given name "Reagan" was "virtually unknown before President Reagan's tenure in office," but by 2012 it had become one of the hundred most popular names for newborn girls in the United States. We suspect that most of these new Reagans grew up in Republican households.

of group attachments in these momentous political shifts, we hope to shed broader light on the pervasive political importance of social identities.

ETHNIC POLITICS AND PARTISAN
CHANGE IN THE NEW DEAL ERA

The complexity of translating social identities into political loyalties is handsomely demonstrated in *The Making of New Deal Democrats*, Gerald Gamm's (1989) detailed examination of voting patterns in ethnically homogeneous precincts of Boston from 1920 to 1940. Gamm devoted separate chapters of his study to the political behavior of five distinct ethnic groups—Jews, Italian-Americans, African-Americans, Yankees, and Irish-Americans—over these crucial two decades. He concluded that "each cluster of precincts responded in its own peculiar way to the events of the era," and indeed that there were "many realignments" involving these five groups occurring "at different times in response to different stimuli and through different behavioral mechanisms" (Gamm 1989, 190, 199). Variation of this sort is very hard to account for on the assumption that the New Deal realignment was, fundamentally, a verdict on Roosevelt's policies or their economic ramifications. But it makes much more sense as a reflection of the varying social circumstances and political experiences of these distinct ethnic groups.

Public opinion polls were extremely rare in the period studied by Gamm, making the interpretation of voting patterns even more challenging than for the modern era. In some instances, the political behavior of specific ethnic groups can be plausibly explained in *either* ideological or social terms. However, other groups provide clearer tests of the relative weight of these forces, and in those cases group-based explanations generally look more compelling.

Boston's socially dominant ethnic group, the Yankees, offer a striking but, for our purposes, ambiguous instance of political stability. According to Gamm (1989, 126), "Republican candidates consistently received the support of the Yankees of Beacon Hill and the Back Bay" throughout the 1920s and 1930s, with the Democratic share of the presidential vote in prosperous Yankee precincts peaking at 29% in 1928.[2] Roosevelt's vote share in these precincts never budged above 22% in three successive presidential elections,

---

2 Gamm (1989, 127–130) attributed the modest Democratic surge in 1928 partly to "Smith's appeal as a cultural liberal" on the issue of Prohibition and partly to the votes of (mostly female) Irish Catholic domestic servants, who made up a sizable portion of the adult population of the Back Bay and Beacon Hill at the time.

while turnout increased only modestly (from 47% of the eligible electorate in 1932 to 54% in 1940).[3] The dramatic economic collapse and recovery that produced national landslides for Roosevelt in 1932 and 1936 left this group entirely unmoved. Was that because they were unusually insulated from economic distress? Because they objected on ideological grounds to Roosevelt's policy initiatives? Or simply because they could not abide being politically aligned with Boston's less prosperous, lower status (and heavily Democratic) ethnic groups?[4] Much more detailed data would be necessary to assess these alternative explanations.

While the steadfast Republican loyalty of the prosperous Yankees of Beacon Hill and the Back Bay throughout the 1920s and 1930s seems interpretable in economic or even ideological terms, the voting patterns of other ethnic groups confound any such interpretation. Boston's Jewish community, for example, shifted substantially toward the Democrats between 1928 and 1936. This shift occurred disproportionately not in working-class precincts, as a class-based response to New Deal policies would suggest, but in upper-middle-class precincts that were previously less Democratic (Gamm 1989, 57).

Boston's Jews were somewhat slow converts to the Democrats, due to discrimination against them by the Irish Catholics who dominated the Boston Democratic organization. In New York, Jewish Republican loyalties began to collapse in 1924 when the Catholic Al Smith ran successfully for governor, and Smith's candidacy for the presidency in 1928 led to widespread abandonment of the Republicans by Jews in most large cities (Fuchs 1956, 64–69). Substantial, though smaller, defections took place in those cities, like Boston, controlled by Irish machines. But by 1936 and 1940, Jews had become overwhelmingly Democratic nearly everywhere. Thus, "beginning in 1936 and continuing to this day, Jews, regardless of their income, have subsumed their supposed class interests and voted instead with a singular degree of ethnic solidarity" (Gamm 1989, 55).

A devotee of the folk theory might imagine that the change in Jewish voting patterns was due to Hitler's rise and Roosevelt's opposition to him. Undoubtedly the ultimate consolidation of the Jewish vote to near unanimity owed much to the growing American antagonism toward Germany. But as an explanation of the origins of the Jewish realignment, that gets the timing

3 The turnout and vote figures in this paragraph are calculated from Gamm's (1989, 126, 129) tables 5.2 and 5.3.

4 Democratic candidates for Congress and state and local offices received even less support than FDR did in Boston's Yankee precincts, and Democratic Party registration never exceeded about 5% of the eligible electorate.

wrong. Hitler's party received just 6% of the vote in 1924, the most recent German national election held before 1928. The two main American political parties paid no attention. Roosevelt's election as president and his wartime activities were far in the future. "In this pre-Hitlerian age it must have seemed to most Jews that there were no crucial issues dividing the major parties" (Fuchs 1956, 63). Yet by 1928, a very substantial majority of Jews had abandoned their Republican loyalties and begun voting for the Democrats. What had changed was not foreign policy, but rather the social status of Jews within one of America's major political parties. In a very visible way, the Democrats had begun fully accepting and incorporating religious minorities, both Catholics and Jews. The result was a durable Jewish partisan realignment grounded in "ethnic solidarity," in Gamm's characterization.[5]

Ethnic solidarity may also account for the realignment of Boston's African-Americans, though the evidence in this case is less clear-cut. The Democratic share of the presidential vote in predominantly black precincts increased enormously over the course of the New Deal era, from 32% in 1928 to 70% in 1940. This massive partisan realignment occurred fairly steadily over the whole period, suggesting no obvious correlation with specific policy initiatives, though *turnout* in black precincts did surge in 1936, to 46% of the eligible electorate from 26% in 1932.[6] Was that sudden political mobilization inspired by support for New Deal policies, or by the Roosevelt administration's cautious outreach to African-Americans, signaling that they, too, would be a welcome part of the Democratic coalition? Or were there purely local political factors behind the surge in black turnout in Boston? Gamm's account provides no clear evidence one way or the other. However, the fact that there was no consistent statistical relationship between black populations and Democratic presidential or congressional vote gains across the non-southern states in the 1930s—as we showed in chapter 7—may suggest that local factors played a substantial role in the partisan realignment of Boston's African-American community.

Finally, and perhaps most important for our purposes, Gamm found remarkably little additional surge to Roosevelt in Boston's heavily Democratic

5 Gamm (1989, 58–73) regarded 1928 as solely a deviating election for Jews, a result of their enthusiasm for Smith personally, and he noted that Republican Party registration figures in Boston did not begin to decline and Democratic registrations to rise until 1932. But as he noted, party registration figures often lag behind vote choices, and in any case, one has to ask *why* Smith was so popular.

6 About half of these new voters seem to have supported Democratic candidates in congressional and state senate elections as well, with the rest about evenly split between Republican candidates and roll-off. The turnout and vote figures in this paragraph are calculated from Gamm's (1989, 97) table 4.1.

Italian and Irish precincts. Much as with the Jews, for these Catholic groups the "New Deal realignment" occurred before the Great Depression began. The historic economic recovery during Roosevelt's first term in the White House had no discernible impact on their partisan loyalties. The key figure in their strong attachment to the Democratic Party was Al Smith, its 1928 presidential candidate, who was the first Catholic to win a major-party presidential nomination.

According to Gamm, Smith racked up a remarkable 94% of presidential votes in Boston's Italian precincts in 1928. Turnout also increased substantially, from 13% of the eligible electorate in 1924 to 24% in 1928. The gradual mobilization of new voters in Italian precincts, including many recent immigrants, continued thereafter, with turnout increasing to 27% in 1932 and to 40% in 1936. As a result, Roosevelt racked up even larger vote totals in Boston's Italian precincts in 1936 than Smith had in 1928; but he actually won a smaller *share* of the vote, 85%. Turnout in Italian precincts continued to swell in 1940, reaching 46%, even as Roosevelt's share of the Italian vote plummeted to 57% in the run-up to world war.[7] Thus, the historic political mobilization of Boston's Italian-American community in this era cannot plausibly be interpreted as a response to economic recovery or to New Deal policies.

Similarly, most of Boston's Irish precincts were overwhelmingly Democratic regardless of their socioeconomic composition—a pattern dating back to the 19th century, but intensified by Smith's presidential candidacy.[8] However, the Democratic share of the presidential vote *declined* steadily from 1928 to 1932 to 1936 to 1940, and Roosevelt, unlike Smith, generally ran even with or behind Democratic congressional and state senate candidates in Boston's Irish precincts.[9] Gamm (1989, 156) suggested that "the Irish were responding strictly to the personal appeal of Al Smith, an Irish and a Catholic with whom they could identify, and to his subsequent endorsement of

7 The turnout and vote figures in this paragraph are calculated from Gamm's (1989, 83) table 3.2, averaging the (generally similar) figures for East Boston and North End precincts.

8 Smith's ancestry was mixed, but he identified as Irish.

9 The party registration figures in Gamm's (1989, 148–149) table 6.2 show Democratic registration (as a share of the eligible electorate, averaging separate figures for men and women) increasing from 1928 to 1936 by 10 percentage points in poor Irish precincts, 11 percentage points in lower-class precincts, 10 percentage points in working-class precincts, and 7 percentage points in lower-middle-class precincts. Over the same period, according to Gamm's (1989, 151–152) table 6.3, the Democratic share of the presidential vote declined by 15 percentage points in poor Irish precincts, 16 percentage points in lower-class precincts, and 20 percentage points in working-class and lower-middle-class precincts.

Roosevelt. . . . Perhaps there was no permanent attachment to Roosevelt himself or to his New Deal."

The relative unimportance of issues and ideology is underlined by the fact that Gamm found no significant social class differences one way or the other in the political responses of Boston's Irish community to the events of the 1920s and 1930s. Isolating four sets of Irish precincts varying in socioeconomic status from "poor" to "lower middle class," he found that all four "moved together in direction and degree during the entire two decades" (Gamm 1989, 137). While "the wealthier were consistently more likely to register and to vote Republican . . . that slight cleavage remained static and did not increase in the late 1930s, when appeals to class were supposedly at a historic high in American politics." Again, the simplest interpretation of these voting patterns is that ethnic and religious identities—not class or political ideology—were shaping the political choices of Boston's Irish.

Of course, even Gamm's unusually detailed and skillful analysis of party registration and voting patterns cannot demonstrate conclusively *why* Boston's major ethnic groups responded so differently to the economic and political events of the New Deal era. His tentative explanations for the observed patterns range from more or less pure social identity ("the candidacy of Al Smith, the first Catholic to run for the presidency and a powerful symbol for the urban masses with recent immigrant pasts") to intergroup tensions ("antagonism toward the Irish-dominated machine" among Boston Jews) to group-specific concerns regarding policy and personnel (Gamm 1989, 201, 178, 155).[10] Whatever combination of these and other considerations shaped the partisanship and voting behavior of specific ethnic groups, it seems clear from Gamm's analysis that Bostonians responded to the New Deal in very different ways, and that these distinctive responses were significantly shaped by ethnic group attachments.

RELIGIOUS IDENTITY IN THE 1960 ELECTION

Gamm's detailed study of Irish and Italian precincts in Boston demonstrated that their inhabitants were overwhelmingly Democratic even before the New Deal. These and other Catholic immigrant groups had found a home in the

---

10 For example, Gamm (1989, 155) noted that "as their great leaders, Al Smith and William Cardinal O'Connell, rebelled against Roosevelt's policies, many Irish grew wary of the president whom they had supported with such vigor in 1932." He added that "many Irish prominent in the administration—Joseph P. Kennedy, James A. Farley, Thomas G. Corcoran, and Frank Murphy, for example—had begun to leave their positions, further undermining the president's popularity with Irish voters."

Democratic Party organizations that came to dominate urban politics in many parts of the country in the late 19th and early 20th centuries. Their Democratic loyalties were strongly reinforced by Al Smith's presidential candidacy in 1928 (Key 1955; but see Lichtman 1979). Catholics would remain more Democratic than non-Catholics through the rest of the 20th century. However, one moment in the post–New Deal era provides unique insight regarding the political ramifications of Catholicism, and of religious identity more broadly—John Kennedy's presidential candidacy in 1960.

Kennedy was the first Catholic since Smith to win a major party's presidential nomination. From our current perspective, more than half a century later, it is easy to forget how important that fact was to both Catholics and non-Catholics at the time.[11] According to the pioneering political reporter Theodore White (1961, 70), Kennedy's strategy for winning the nomination was shaped by the need to demonstrate popular appeal among Protestants in order to impress "the bosses and the brokers of the Northeast who regarded him fondly as a fellow Catholic but, as a Catholic, hopelessly doomed to defeat."

In the key primary state of West Virginia, Kennedy's support declined disastrously in the months leading up to the voting. Challenged to explain the erosion, local advisers observed that "no one in West Virginia knew you were a Catholic in December. Now they know" (White 1961, 121). However, a late television advertising blitz—with a heavy emphasis on the separation of church and state—helped pull out a crucial victory for Kennedy, and he went on to win the nomination.

In the general election campaign, Kennedy again found "the old echo of fear" among "gut-Democrats" around the country "disturbed by this candidate of Roman Catholic faith" (White 1961, 295–296). He addressed the issue head-on in a speech at a meeting of Protestant ministers in Houston. Once again, he declared that "the separation of Church and State is absolute" and that "no Catholic prelate would tell the President (should he be a Catholic) how to act." He patiently responded to questions about his relationship with Cardinal Cushing of Boston, the persecution of Protestant missionaries in South America (which he opposed), and the possibility of government support for Catholic schools (which he also opposed). "I do not speak for my church on public matters," Kennedy insisted, "and the church does not speak for me."

11 Donald Kinder and Allison Dale-Riddle's (2012) book-length study of the election of Barack Obama helpfully bridges the decades (and the social specificities) by systematically comparing the role of "religious attachments and antagonisms" in the 1960 presidential race to the role of "racial attachments and antagonisms" in 2008.

According to White (1961, 298), excerpts from Kennedy's remarks in Houston were broadcast by the national television networks and circulated by his campaign team "over and over again in both Catholic and Protestant areas of the country for the next seven weeks; it was to be their basic document; no measure is available of how many millions saw the film played and replayed, still less is there a measure available of its effect." For his part, Kennedy's opponent, Richard Nixon, carefully avoided any appearance of cultivating an anti-Catholic vote. "Both candidates were to denounce the prejudice," White wrote (1961, 110); "but neither could erase the intrusion of religious feeling."

White's assessment is quite consistent with Philip Converse's (1966b) detailed analysis of voting patterns in the 1960 election, which documented both the distinctive appeal of Kennedy's candidacy among Catholics and "the old echo of fear" among Protestant voters. Converse noted that "Protestants in 1960 were remarkably preoccupied by the fact that Kennedy was a Catholic," with nearly half spontaneously raising the issue in pre-election interviews. Their comments "varied widely in sophistication from moderate discussions of a Catholic's primary commitment to his faith to dark beliefs that Catholicism lay somewhere on the road to Communism" (Converse 1966b, 112–113). Converse estimated that the Democratic presidential vote was 7% below its "normal" level among white Protestants who seldom or never attended church and 21% below its "normal" level among churchgoing white Protestants.[12]

Contrary to prejudiced Protestant charges at the time, Kennedy's public declaration of independence from the dictates of Catholic prelates was a familiar and comfortable stance for Catholics; certainly it did not erase the significance of his religion among Catholic voters. Converse estimated that churchgoing Catholics (the substantial majority) were 15% more Democratic in their presidential voting behavior in 1960 than normal, while even those who seldom or never attended church were 10% more Democratic than normal.[13] Thus, the religious identities of both Catholics and Protestants were strongly engaged by Kennedy's historic presidential candidacy. While many voters at the time provided more or less cogent political explanations for their behavior, it seems farfetched in historical perspective to attribute

---

12 These estimated vote losses combine Converse's (1966b, 119) separate figures for white-collar and blue-collar white Protestants in the South and non-South. The separate estimates range from 2% (for nonattenders in clerical or blue-collar households outside the South) to 36% (for regular churchgoers in clerical or blue-collar households in the South).

13 The former figure combines Converse's (1966b, 108) separate estimates for Catholics who reported attending church "regularly" (72% of Catholic respondents) or "often" (12%). The remaining 16% of Catholic respondents said they seldom or never attended church.

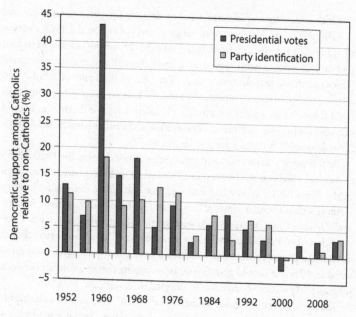

Figure 9.1. Catholic Support for Democrats, 1952–2012

these remarkable defections from traditional voting patterns to anything other than social group loyalties.

Figure 9.1 puts the impact of Kennedy's candidacy on the partisan religious cleavage in historical context. In the 1950s, Catholics were more Democratic than non-Catholics by about 10 percentage points in both party identification and presidential voting behavior—the continuation of a long-standing attachment to the Democratic Party dating to the Republicans' embrace of the anti-Catholic "Know Nothings" in the 1850s. But in 1960, a stunning 83% of Catholic voters in the American National Election Studies (ANES) survey reported voting for Kennedy, while only 39% of non-Catholics did so.[14] Democratic Party identification among Catholics also spiked, albeit much more modestly.[15]

14 Data from ANES surveys and information about the design and implementation of the studies are available from the ANES website, http://www.electionstudies.org.

15 From 1952 through 1958, 53% of Catholics in ANES surveys called themselves strong or weak Democrats; in 1960, 60% did so.

Of course, religious identity was not decisive for every voter. Converse (1966b, 96) began his account of religion and politics in the 1960 election by quoting a respondent from that year's ANES survey, a cross-pressured 34-year-old woman who served as a local Republican committeewoman: "I'm so confused this election year.... I'm a Republican and a Catholic, and religion and politics are important to me. I'll have to make a decision, looks like I'll have to go against my church.... [Kennedy] is a Democrat. I could not vote for him for that reason. I *couldn't*. On the other hand he is a Catholic—oh, dear! Why does it have to be that way?"

As it happens, this woman and many other respondents in the 1960 ANES survey had also been interviewed in 1956 and 1958. In response to a question in the 1956 ANES survey, she had said that she didn't feel much closer to Catholics than to other kinds of people and that she had "not much interest at all" in how Catholics as a whole were "getting along." Moreover, while Converse described her as "unusually devout in religion," her self-reported church attendance in three interviews conducted over a four-year period was quite variable.[16] Thus, it should perhaps not be surprising that in a conflict between religion and politics, she reluctantly decided to "go against" her church.

The survey question about interest in other Catholics proved to be highly indicative of voting behavior in 1960, over and above church attendance— exactly as one might expect on the basis of social identity theory. Fifteen Republican Catholics in the 1956 ANES survey, including the woman quoted by Converse, expressed "not much interest at all" in how Catholics were getting along. Ten of them reported voting for Nixon four years later, while only two reported voting for Kennedy. Conversely, only 4 of the 18 Republican Catholics who expressed "a good deal of interest" in how Catholics were getting along stuck with Nixon, while 12 defected to Kennedy. Even with small numbers of survey respondents, this strong correlation suggests that the strength of Catholic identity (measured four years earlier) was a significant factor in determining whether Republican Catholics would "go against" their church when the nomination of a Catholic presidential candidate posed a conflict between religion and partisanship. It is hard to imagine a clearer demonstration of the political impact of group attachments and the trade-offs among them.

16 In the three waves of the 1956–1958–1960 ANES panel survey, this respondent reported attending church "regularly," "seldom," and "often." In 1956, she was one of only 21% of Catholic respondents who said they had "not much interest at all" in "how Catholics as a whole are getting along in this country." (The rest were roughly evenly split between "some interest" and "a good deal of interest.")

Stokes's (1966, 24) analysis of attitudes toward Kennedy based on 1960 measurements of partisanship and religious identification similarly found that "the biasing tendencies of party identification were generally effective among the mildly religious" (weak Catholics and weak Protestants) while "party loyalty could have a marked impact on the strongly religious only if a party faith were itself strongly held." Converse's (1966b) analysis of vote choices echoed Stokes's finding that Protestant identity mattered, too. White Protestants classified as "high" in identification with the Protestant community were 22% less Democratic in their presidential voting behavior than expected in 1960, while the corresponding deviation among those classified as "low" in Protestant identification was only 10%.[17] Clearly, religious identity cut both ways. In a separate analysis, Converse and his colleagues (1961) attempted to estimate the net impact of Catholic and Protestant group attachments on the outcome of the 1960 election. They estimated that Kennedy's national vote share was 2.2% lower due to "the Catholic issue" than it would otherwise have been. However, Kennedy's net losses were concentrated in southern states, most of which he carried anyway due to the overwhelming Democratic loyalty of southern voters at the time. Outside the South, Converse and his colleagues estimated that Kennedy's "unexpected" gains among Catholics outweighed his losses among Protestant Democrats and Independents, producing a net gain of 1.6% of the two-party vote. Given his narrow margins of victory in several key non-southern states, it seems likely that "the Catholic issue" (which was not a political issue at all in the usual ideological sense) was crucial to his victory.[18]

As figure 9.1 makes clear, the impact of Kennedy's candidacy on Catholic support for the Democratic Party was temporary. By 1964, the Democratic edge in party identification among Catholics (relative to non-Catholics) was back to its 1950s level, and it remained relatively stable through the 1970s before eroding in the 1980s and 1990s. The Democratic presidential vote among Catholics (again, relative to non-Catholics) remained slightly elevated in 1964 and 1968; but it, too, eroded substantially thereafter. By the time another Catholic Massachusetts Democrat, John Kerry, ran for president in 2004, Catholics were no more likely than non-Catholics to identify as Democrats—and Kerry's vote share was only 2 percentage points greater

17 These figures combine Converse's (1966b, 119) separate estimates for white-collar and blue-collar households in the South and outside the South.

18 Kennedy carried Pennsylvania by 2.3%, Michigan by 2.0%, Minnesota by 1.4%, New Jersey by 0.8%, Missouri by 0.5%, and Illinois by 0.2%. Losing just the three closest of these states would have cost him his Electoral College majority.

among Catholics than among non-Catholics. His religion arose in the campaign only as an intra-denominational issue, when Catholic bishops criticized his position on abortion. Four decades after Kennedy's death, the social significance of a Catholic presidential candidacy was no longer sufficient to produce substantial deviations from accustomed voting behavior.

While Catholics have become less politically distinctive over the past half century, evangelical Christians have become prominent within the Republican Party's electoral coalition (Wilcox 1992; Layman 2001). Recent scholarly work has documented the ramifications of these changes in party-group ties for citizens' assessments of politicians and political issues. For example, identifying a hypothetical candidate as a Catholic has no impact on partisan voting patterns in the contemporary political environment—while identifying a candidate as an evangelical Christians increases support for the candidate among Republican identifiers and decreases support among Democratic identifiers (Campbell, Green, and Layman 2011). Similarly, associating issue positions with evangelical religious leaders makes those positions less popular among Democrats (Adkins et al. 2013). And evangelical Christians in Congress are viewed by their constituents as more conservative than mainline Protestants whose actual voting records are ideologically indistinguishable (Jacobsmeier 2013). These findings nicely demonstrate that the association of political candidates with salient social groups both *shapes* and *mobilizes* voters' partisan loyalties.

RACE, SOCIAL IDENTITY, AND REALIGNMENT IN THE SOUTH

We have argued that social identities play a key role in shaping responses to political candidates and events. In the remainder of this chapter, we apply this perspective to two momentous cases of long-term partisan change in the post–New Deal era—the realignment of white southerners in the second half of the 20th century and of moral conservatives and liberals around the issue of abortion in the 1980s and 1990s. In each case, we argue that voters' social identities mattered as much or more than the parties' policy differences in triggering and reinforcing the process of partisan realignment.

The gradual but massive migration of white southerners from the Democratic Party to the Republican Party undoubtedly had its roots in America's complex and troubled history of racial politics. Race has always been central to American politics, both southern and northern, from the shaping of the Constitution through the Civil War, the Jim Crow era, and the civil rights revolution of the 1960s, down to the present day. In the wake of the Civil

War and Reconstruction, the states of the former Confederacy became the Solid South—a virtual one-party regime in which a hegemonic white Democratic Party enforced an elaborate and effective system of racial segregation and political exclusion. As V. O. Key, Jr. (1949, 664–665) put it in his monumental account of mid-20th-century *Southern Politics in State and Nation*, "the question of race overshadows all other factors conditioning the politics of the South. . . . The one-party system, suffrage restrictions departing from democratic norms, low levels of voting and of political interest, and all the consequences of these political arrangements and practices must be traced ultimately to this one factor. . . . The predominant consideration in the architecture of southern political institutions has been to assure locally a subordination of the Negro population and, externally, to block threatened interferences from the outside with these local arrangements."

The system described by Key was already beginning to erode when he wrote, and only two decades later it was largely swept away, thanks in part to decades of struggle by southern blacks (and some white allies) and in part to just the sort of "interferences from the outside" long feared by the beneficiaries of the Jim Crow regime. Sit-ins, protest marches, and freedom rides provided the moral spark, and the landmark federal Civil Rights Act of 1964 and Voting Rights Act of 1965 provided the legislative foundation, for a "second reconstruction" (Valelly 2004) resulting in the demise of legally mandated racial segregation and the political enfranchisement of millions of African-Americans—and the mobilization of an even greater number of white southerners (Stanley 1987).

The prominent role of the national Democratic Party in these events precipitated large-scale shifts in partisan loyalties among both African-Americans and white southerners. Southern blacks were already predominantly Democratic identifiers in the 1950s, but they became overwhelmingly Democratic in 1964 and thereafter.[19] Conversely, southern whites moved gradually but

---

19 Bruce Campbell (1977, 743) interpreted the "sharp alteration of the pre-1964 cleavage of black partisanship" as an instance of V. O. Key's (1955) concept of a "critical election." Harold Stanley's (1987, 107) tabulations of survey data from American National Election Studies indicate that Democratic identification among southern blacks increased from an average of 56% in 1952–1960 to 82% in 1964–1972, while Republican identification declined from 17% to 6%. The share of "apolitical" southern blacks declined even more substantially, from 25% in 1952–1960 to 4% in 1964–1972. Unlike southern whites, southern blacks showed little further partisan change after the 1960s; the comparable average party identification figures for 1976–1984 were 79% Democratic, 8% Republican, and 2% apolitical. Unfortunately, there are too few southern blacks in these surveys to analyze their realignment in detail.

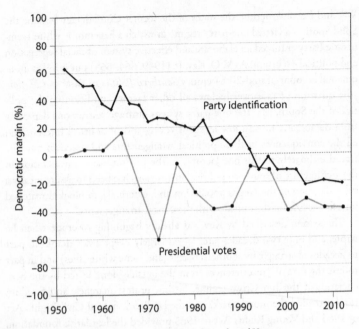

Figure 9.2. Southern White Party Identification and Presidential Votes

decisively from being overwhelmingly Democratic in the 1950s to being predominantly Republican today. It is the latter shift we analyze here, focusing specifically on the extent to which the partisan realignment of southern whites was driven by group identity.

Figure 9.2 displays trends in Democratic margins (the difference between the percentage Democratic and the percentage Republican) in presidential voting behavior and party identification among southern whites over the past six decades using data from ANES surveys. The figure shows a rapid and substantial shift in the presidential voting behavior of southern whites after 1964, facilitated by George Wallace's third-party candidacy in 1968 and the Republican Party's "southern strategy" under Richard Nixon. However, the *party identification* of southern whites evolved much more slowly. Indeed, Republicans did not outnumber Democrats among southern white party identifiers until the 1990s—more than a quarter century after this group began

Figure 9.3. Southern White Party Identification by Birth Cohort

voting solidly and consistently for Republican presidential candidates. As Donald Green, Bradley Palmquist, and Eric Schickler (2002, 162) put it, "political disruption expressed itself immediately at the voting booth but altered self-conceptions much more gradually."

This long process of partisan change was partly, but by no means wholly, a matter of generational replacement. Figure 9.3 shows that younger cohorts entered the electorate as less Democratic than their elders. On average, the Democratic identification margin in any given year was 7 points lower in the middle cohort of white southerners in figure 9.3 (born between 1921 and 1945) than in the older cohort (born before 1921); the average margin in the younger cohort (born after 1945) was another 13 points lower than in the middle cohort. But even white southerners who grew up in the Jim Crow era were changing. They called themselves Democrats by overwhelming 60-point margins in the early 1950s, but by the 1970s the Democratic margins in these same cohorts had eroded by half or more. A substantial partisan shift was occurring in all cohorts.[20] But why?

The conventional interpretation of the dramatic partisan realignment of white southerners is that it reflected an "issue evolution" (Carmines and Stimson 1989) precipitated by dramatic shifts in the positions of Democratic and Republican political leaders on the issue of civil rights. We believe that elite cues played an important role, but in a somewhat different way than the "issue evolution" perspective suggests. Other scholars who have looked closely at the evidence have found that signals about where one's group belonged made a big difference to individual voters, while racial policy issues played a less central role (Beck 1977; Campbell 1977).[21] Our reading of the evidence suggests a similar interpretation.

For one thing, as the trend shown in figure 9.2 makes clear, the process of partisan change among white southerners was well under way *before* Democratic Party elites took a clear stand in support of civil rights for African-Americans in the 1960s. Second, a closer look at the available survey data suggests—contrary to the conventional view, but just as we would expect—that these shifts in party identification were only weakly related to white southerners' views about specific policy issues.

The most fraught racial policy issue in this period was also the focus of the question asked most consistently in ANES surveys—whether the government

20 Beck (1977, 484–488) assessed the impact of generational replacement and partisan conversion among native white southerners from 1952 through 1972. He concluded (Beck 1977, 488) that partisan change was "largely a tale of the entry into the electorate and the changing partisan dispositions of a new generation of native whites" reaching adulthood after World War II. This cohort (corresponding roughly to the middle cohort in figure 9.3) accounted for a 7-point decline in overall Democratic identification among native white southerners through pure generational replacement and an additional 12-point decline through within-cohort partisan change. Campbell's (1977, 755) independent analysis of native white southerners over the same 20-year period likewise found that "change was strongest among the youngest members of the electorate. However, there was also significant change among both transitionals and adults."

21 Beck (1977, 489–491) examined the impact of perceptions of the parties' stands on racial integration among native white southern segregationists from 1960 to 1968. He found considerable change in party images, with the Democratic Party increasingly seen as pro-integration, but concluded that the effect of this "image alteration" on party identification was "negligible." Campbell (1977, 750–751) presented an analysis more nearly similar to ours, assessing the impact of racial policy views on partisan change among native white southerners through 1972. He combined responses to the question employed here regarding school integration and a separate question regarding fair employment practices, and analyzed an "expected Democratic vote" derived from Converse's (1966a) "normal vote" framework rather than party identification per se. He concluded that "no change in partisanship [among native white southerners] can be attributed to the events surrounding the civil rights controversy."

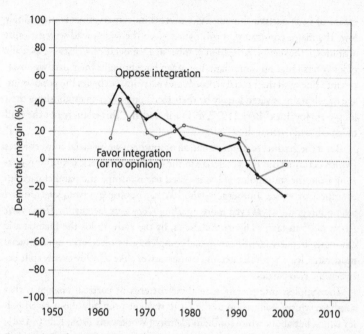

Figure 9.4. Southern White Party Identification by Views about Government-Enforced School Integration

should enforce racial integration of public schools. When this question was first asked, in the early 1960s, the substantial majority of southern whites who opposed government-enforced racial integration overwhelmingly identified as Democrats. By 2000, the remaining opponents of integration (still about 40%) were solidly *Republican*. However, as figure 9.4 shows, their partisan conversion was remarkably gradual; as late as the 1980s, opponents of school integration were still more likely to think of themselves as Democrats than as Republicans.

Paul Beck (1977, 491–494), focusing on the early stages of this evolution, argued that voters' willful misperceptions of the parties' policy stands were a key factor limiting issue-based partisan change. He found "a surprisingly high amount of what might be labeled misperception" accounting for "a fair portion of the staying power of Democratic loyalties" among native white southerners who were themselves racial conservatives. "On the whole," he wrote, "the extent of issue partisanship among native white conservatives is surprisingly low. The major constraint on this figure, given the widespread segregationist attitudes in the region, is the high number of Democratic loyalists—especially older voters. That no more than one of ten have brought their partisan loyalties into line with their racial attitudes and party images belies the popular image of whites motivated largely by their racial prejudices in establishing their long-term loyalties." Beck (1977, 491) concluded, "This is surely not the stuff of issue-based partisanship!"

But if the gradual partisan evolution of southern white racial conservatives (which certainly did not accelerate in the decades after Beck wrote) was puzzling from the standpoint of "issue-based partisanship," the parallel partisan evolution of white southerners who *did not* oppose government-enforced school integration was even more puzzling. *They were leaving the Democratic Party, too.*[22] In fact, as figure 9.4 shows, by the early 1990s the Democratic advantage in party identification had completely dissolved even among racial moderates, leaving moderates and conservatives alike roughly evenly split between the two parties.

The simplest interpretation of these patterns of partisan change is that southern whites' conversion to the GOP was not primarily about racial policy issues, but about white southern identity (Woodward 1968; Killian 1985; Reed 1986), a powerful force in southern culture at least since the antebellum period (Sydnor 1948; Craven 1953; McCardell 1981). Green, Palmquist, and Schickler (2002, 162) noted that "the maintenance of a one-party system hinged on the psychological connection between Democrats and white supremacy." As southern blacks became mobilized as Democrats, that psychological connection was broken, and southern whites increasingly came to think of the Republican Party first as a potential home and then as their natural home.

Of course, the opposing partisan shifts among blacks and whites had consequences for the distribution of racial policy views in each party, and policy and social identity eventually became mutually reinforcing. According to Green, Palmquist, and Schickler (2002, 159–160), "Once a critical mass of people begin to shift parties, change in the parties' social imagery gains momentum. As conservative, devout Southerners became reticent about calling themselves

22 Opposition to school integration among white southerners declined somewhat over this period; for that reason among others, the trend lines portrayed in figure 9.4 do not really represent fixed groups of people. However, the important point for our purposes is that the similarity of the two trend lines over much of this period is inconsistent with the view that opinions, or changes in opinions, about school integration were a significant driver of partisan change.

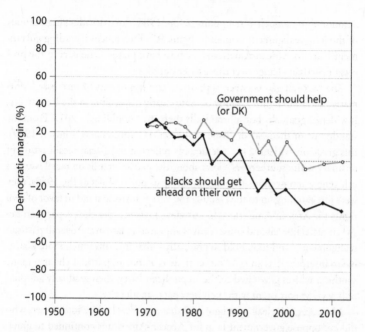

Figure 9.5. Southern White Party Identification by Views about Government Aid to Blacks

Democrats, they less and less defined the social imagery of the party. As older party stereotypes faded, self-designated conservatives in the South gravitated steadily toward Republican affiliation." While racial attitudes and policy preferences no doubt had some causal impact, racial and regional *identity* was the more important factor. Southern whites judged the parties primarily as collections of social groups, not as packages of policy positions.

This conclusion is strengthened when we consider another ANES survey item focusing more generally on government assistance to African-Americans. Beginning in 1970, ANES surveys regularly asked whether "the government in Washington should make every possible effort to improve the social and economic position of blacks" or "not make any special effort" because blacks "should help themselves." Figure 9.5 shows trends in party identification among white southerners differentiated by their responses to this question. Throughout the 1970s, there were only minor differences in partisanship between supporters and opponents of race-based affirmative action; indeed, the gap in party identification between the two groups never amounted to as much as ten points before 1984, three decades after the start of the long realignment evident in figure 9.2. Preferences regarding government help for African-Americans seem to have played little part in the process of partisan change over those three decades.

The partisan gap between supporters and opponents of race-based affirmative action in figure 9.5 only became clearly discernible in the Reagan era. It widened gradually but substantially thereafter, doubling by 2012. From the standpoint of theorists of "issue evolution" (Carmines and Stimson 1989), this gradually widening gap presumably reflected the glacial recalibration of ordinary white southerners' views about the parties' stands on racial issues: a full generation or more after the momentous policy shifts of the 1960s, they were just catching on to the Democratic Party's historic stand in favor of civil rights for African-Americans. In our view, however, the clear separation between racial liberals and conservatives appeared so late in the overall partisan realignment—and took hold so gradually—that it seems much more plausible to interpret it as an *effect* rather than as a *cause* of partisan change: many southern whites gravitated to the Republican Party, then gradually adopted policy views consistent with their new partisan identity.

Moreover, it is clear from figure 9.5 that even those white southerners who did *not* oppose government help for African-Americans continued to gravitate toward the Republican Party throughout this period, despite the party's strong stand in opposition to affirmative action. By 2004, the Democratic Party's massive edge in party identification had entirely eroded even among those white southerners who shared the Democratic Party's position on the central issue of the long partisan realignment. *Their* partisan evolution cannot plausibly be attributed to racial conservatism; but it does make sense in social identity terms, as a growing preponderance of their fellow white southerners increasingly came to identify as Republicans, gradually but steadily shifting the balance of group loyalties affecting even those who were not themselves racial conservatives.[23]

23 The widening gap in partisan loyalties evident in figure 9.5 appears even more strongly when southern whites are distinguished on the basis of general ideological views. White southerners who considered themselves conservatives identified as Democrats by an 18-point margin in 1972, but as Republicans by a 57-point margin in 2008. Those who considered themselves moderates or (rarely) liberals were, not surprisingly, more likely to remain Democrats; but even their Democratic partisan attachments eroded significantly over this period, from a 33-point margin in the 1970s to a 16-point margin in the 2000s. Again, policy calculations alone seem insufficient to account for these shifts in partisan loyalty, while social identity provides a more promising alternative explanation.

Our argument for the importance of social identity in the partisan re-alignment of white southerners is bolstered by some more direct evidence from the ANES surveys. At several points over the past half century, ANES respondents were asked to express their feelings toward southerners using a "feeling thermometer" running from zero for very cold feelings through 50 for neutral feelings to 100 for very warm feelings. The group-related attitudes captured by these thermometer ratings are theoretically distinct from social identity; nonetheless, it seems quite plausible to suppose that white southern-ers who felt especially warmly toward "southerners" as a group were also more likely to think of *themselves* as southerners, to think of southerners as white, and to think and act politically in ways that seemed to them to be consistent with that group attachment. Thus, tracing the changing partisan resonance of feelings toward southerners since the 1960s can shed some more specific light on the role of southern identity in the erosion of white southerners' attach-ment to the Democratic Party.[24]

The statistical analysis presented in the top panel of table 9.1 shows how changes in the Democratic Party's identification advantage among white southerners varied with their attitudes toward "southerners."[25] The results indicate that the Democratic partisan advantage in 1964 among white south-erners who expressed neutral attitudes toward "southerners" was almost 25 percentage points, while the corresponding advantage among those who expressed very warm feelings toward "southerners" was more than twice as large, almost 55 percentage points.[26] This very significant difference provides support for the notion that southern identity played an important role in the Democratic Solid South of the mid-20th century.

Over the subsequent 40 years, of course, the Democratic Solid South disap-peared. However, the decline in Democratic attachment among white south-erners was far from uniform. Those with high levels of southern identity, who

24 The "feeling thermometer" for southerners was included in the 1964, 1968, 1972, 1976, 1980, 1992, 2004, and 2008 ANES surveys. We are grateful to Marc Hetherington for suggesting an analysis of these data.

25 The analyses reported in table 9.1 impose linear trends in partisanship over the entire period from 1964 through 2008. The overall trend in southern white partisanship displayed in figure 9.2 is sufficiently linear to make that assumption seem reasonable here. In any case, there are too few white southerners in each survey to analyze separately (about 340, on average).

26 We have recoded the 100-point "feeling thermometer" ratings to range from −1 to +1, so that a neutral rating corresponds to a score of 0 and a very positive rating to a score of +1. Thus, the intercepts in table 9.1 represent Democratic identification margins among white southerners with neutral attitudes toward southerners, while the parameter estimates for attitudes toward southerners represent the incremental margin among those with very positive attitudes toward southerners.

Table 9.1. Southern Regional and Racial Identity and Democratic Partisanship, 1964–2008

	1964	2008	Change
Attitudes toward southerners	29.3	−12.2	−41.5
(−1 to +1)	(6.2)	(6.6)	(10.4)
Intercept	24.6	−15.2	−39.7
	(4.3)	(4.5)	(7.2)
Standard error of regression	75.1		
Adjusted R^2	.09		
N	2,751 (white southerners)		
Attitudes toward southerners	23.7	−19.9	−43.6
(−1 to +1)	(6.9)	(7.8)	(12.0)
Attitudes toward whites	15.2	10.0	−5.2
(−1 to +1)	(7.7)	(8.5)	(13.1)
Attitudes toward blacks	1.5	7.8	+6.2
(−1 to +1)	(5.8)	(7.4)	(10.8)
Intercept	16.9	−18.1	−35.0
	(5.7)	(4.9)	(8.7)
Standard error of regression	75.1		
Adjusted R^2	.09		
N	2,743 (white southerners)		

Dependent variable is the Democratic Party identification margin (−100 to +100) among white southerners. Ordinary least squares regression parameter estimates (with standard errors in parentheses) for linear change model.

were most strongly attached to the Democratic Party in 1964, were most likely to have left by 2008. Indeed, by 2008 southern identity cut the other way, making white southerners more likely to identify as *Republicans*. The cumulative partisan shift among white southerners with neutral attitudes toward "southerners" amounted to about 20 percentage points, whereas the corresponding shift among those with very warm feelings toward "southerners" was twice that large.

Was *southern* identity really the basis of these very different responses to the political events of the long southern realignment era? The ANES surveys that elicited feeling thermometer ratings of "southerners" also elicited ratings of "whites" and "blacks." The analysis reported in the bottom panel of table 9.1 traces the impact of attitudes toward these groups on Democratic partisanship among white southerners from 1964 through 2008. At the beginning of this period, warm feelings toward "whites" were positively related to Democratic partisanship, though somewhat less politically potent than feelings toward "southerners." On the other hand, feelings toward "blacks" had no apparent partisan resonance one way or the other. This striking non-finding reinforces our interpretation of Democratic loyalties among rank-and-file white southerners in the 1960s as resting primarily on (positive) social identities rather than on racial animus.

By 2008, attitudes toward *both* "whites" and "blacks" were positively correlated with Democratic partisanship among white southerners, though in both cases the relationships were modest in magnitude and statistically uncertain. By comparison, the estimated effect of feelings toward "southerners"—which by 2008 were pushing white southerners toward the Republican Party—was twice as large. The estimated *change* in that effect between 1964 and 2008 was massive, implying a cumulative shift of almost 40 percentage points in the partisanship of white southerners who felt very warmly toward "southerners," again more than twice as large as the shift observed among those with neutral feelings toward "southerners."

The apparent importance of southern identity in shaping the partisan loyalties of white southerners underlines the limitations of the conventional interpretation of the southern realignment. The racial issues of the civil rights era—and the parties' stands on those issues—were clearly important in precipitating the realignment, as the "issue evolution" perspective (Carmines and Stimson 1989) suggests. However, for most white southerners, policy preferences were probably of secondary importance. White southern loyalty to the Democratic Party was eroding well before the parties clearly split on civil rights for African-Americans, and continued to erode thereafter among proponents as well as opponents of government efforts to eradicate racial segregation and improve the lot of African-Americans. Eventually, white southern Democrats and Republicans came to differ substantially on these and other issues; but those partisan policy divisions clearly emerged only decades after the dramatic political events of the early and mid-1960s. By comparison, feelings toward "southerners"—a plausible proxy for white southern social identity—mattered substantially both in accounting for the strong

Democratic loyalties of white southerners in the 1960s and in accounting for the dramatic erosion of those loyalties over the course of the subsequent half century.

ISSUES AND PARTISAN CHANGE: THE CASE OF ABORTION

Our final example of the power of social identity in shaping attitudes gives us an opportunity to examine more closely what happens when identities conflict. In 1973, the U.S. Supreme Court ruled that American states could not forbid a woman to have an abortion during the first trimester of her pregnancy. The Court also declared that states could regulate abortion during the second trimester and could forbid it during the final three months. This famous case, *Roe v. Wade*, and related court rulings ratified what many states had already done (Rosenberg 1991), but were well ahead of public opinion and existing public policy in some parts of the country.

Liberalized abortion laws set off a backlash among cultural and moral traditionalists, including many conservative Catholics, and eventually among many Protestant evangelicals as well (Hanna 1979, chap. 5; Balmer 2006). A countermobilization by abortion liberals ensued. Bitter struggles in courts and legislatures began, along with struggles to win over public opinion. By its very nature, the abortion debate evoked profound disagreements regarding "our most cherished beliefs about the world, about motherhood, and about what it means to be human" (Luker 1984, 10).

Initially, the Democratic and Republican parties were both internally divided on the issue. However, the legal battles began to polarize the parties' leaders and activists in the late 1970s (Adams 1997; Carmines and Woods 1997). By 1980, the Republican platform clearly declared its opposition to abortion. Subsequent GOP platforms strengthened the language.[27] By the

27 The 1976 Republican platform favored "a continuance of the public dialogue on abortion and supports the efforts of those who seek enactment of a constitutional amendment to restore protection of the right to life for unborn children." In 1980, "While we recognize differing views on this question among Americans in general—and in our own Party—we affirm our support of a constitutional amendment to restore protection of the right to life for unborn children. We also support the Congressional efforts to restrict the use of taxpayers' dollars for abortion." In 1984, "The unborn child has a fundamental individual right to life which cannot be infringed. We therefore reaffirm our support for a human life amendment to the Constitution, and we endorse legislation to make clear that the Fourteenth Amendment's protections apply to unborn children. We oppose the use of public revenues for abortion and will eliminate funding for organizations which advocate or support abortion." Subsequent Republican platforms have included language close to that of 1984.

late 1990s, the abortion opinions of ordinary Democrats and Republicans diverged as well (Jelen and Wilcox 2003). For example, in a long-term study led by M. Kent Jennings of people who were high school seniors in 1965, the Youth-Parent Socialization Panel Study, the correlation between abortion attitudes and party identification was only .07 in 1982, but it rose to .22 in 1997. Among the best informed citizens during the same period, the correlation rose from .04 to .36.[28]

Almost uniquely among issues, abortion attitudes are quite stable over time. In the Youth-Parent Socialization Panel Study, for example, the correlation between abortion attitudes over the tumultuous 15-year period from 1982 to 1997 is .59.[29] Moreover, of the 935 people in the study, just 9 lacked abortion opinions in 1982 and 12 in 1997, remarkably low levels of non-opinion for political attitudes. Where abortion is concerned, the overwhelming majority of people know what they think and drastic changes in opinion are rare.

Clearly, abortion is a familiar and morally fraught issue for most Americans. Thus, the notion that abortion attitudes shape party identification and voting behavior seems obvious to observers of contemporary American politics, and many of the customary tests seem to confirm it (Jelen and Wilcox 2003, 494–496). However, as we noted in chapter 2, most tests of this sort confound issue voting and partisan persuasion. Do people vote Republican because they are conservative on abortion? Or are they conservative on abortion because they are Republicans? No one doubts that there is some issue voting where abortion is concerned—but how much, after allowing for partisan persuasion?

Few scholars have considered the possibility that abortion attitudes, like other political attitudes, are significantly shaped by partisan loyalties. Geoffrey Layman and Thomas Carsey (2002) are a prominent exception. However, they focused on short-term rather than long-term responses to elite partisan polarization and on cognitive rather than social bases of differential

---

28 Party identification is measured using the standard ANES 7-point scale. Views about abortion are measured on a 4-point scale ranging from forbidding abortion entirely to allowing abortion on demand. (The original coding of the abortion scale is reversed here, so that positive correlations indicate that respondents' abortion positions tended to be compatible with their party identifications.) The "best-informed citizens" are those who scored in either of the top two categories on a 6-point assessment of political knowledge made by the interviewer at the end of each interview.

29 The corresponding correlation of party identification over the same 15-year period is only slightly higher, .63. In both cases, correction for measurement error would produce significantly higher estimates of underlying attitude stability.

responsiveness. Moreover, their analysis relied on complex statistical specifications with multiple variables assumed to have the same linear, additive effects for every individual. While much can be learned from explorations of this sort, they obscure the fact that causal processes may work quite differently in different groups. Hence, our preference here is for simpler and more flexible data analysis.

Before beginning, we mention two important considerations in studying abortion attitudes. The first is that Catholics differ from other Christians on this issue. The Roman Catholic Church has long opposed abortion, and when *Roe v. Wade* was handed down, most Catholics were more conservative on the issue than the average Protestant.[30] Well-defined theological and political left and right wings have developed within Catholicism—a division that standard survey questions about denominational membership fail to capture. Moreover, views about abortion are correlated with departures from Catholicism: pro-choice Catholics have disproportionately dropped out of that denomination, whether for that reason or for reasons correlated with it.[31] Thus, the relationships between Catholicism and abortion attitudes are unique and complex, requiring separate study. Hence we focus here on non-Catholics only.[32]

Second, identity as a woman is a powerful force in shaping attitudes toward women's health, pregnancy, and childbirth. Whether liberal or conservative, women's ideas on these issues are tied to strong views about what it means to be a woman. For men, what it means to be a man is much less directly tied to these topics. Thus many women have two potentially competing identities where abortion attitudes are concerned—their gender and their partisanship. Men have both identities as well, but human biology ensures that abortion does not affect men as deeply and personally as it does women.

Consequently, even a cursory look at abortion attitudes quickly uncovers the greater reliability of women's opinions relative to men's. Even among the best-informed, women's responses to abortion questions exhibit much less random variation, according to the Wiley-Wiley (1970) model for measurement

30 As evangelicals have taken up the abortion issue the average Protestant has moved somewhat to the right, while many Catholics have moved to the left; thus, the two groups have become similar in their distributions of abortion views over time (Jelen and Wilcox 2003, 492).

31 In the Jennings sample, almost half of 1965 Catholic identifiers who said in 1982 that abortion was always permissible had ceased to call themselves Catholics by the latter date.

32 We found much weaker selection effects for evangelicals ("neo-fundamentalists," as the Jennings study labels them). Thus we have grouped them with other non-Catholics. Similarly, although many African-American Democrats expressed firm pro-life attitudes, we found that excluding them generally made little difference.

error in over-time attitudes. In the 1992–1994–1996 ANES panel study, for example, the estimated reliability of abortion attitudes among non-Catholic men who were in the best informed 30% of the population was .84. The corresponding estimated reliability for well-informed women was .97.[33] Hence, we analyze women and men separately.

Given these differences in the likely significance of abortion between women and men, we expect the increasingly salient partisan divisions over abortion during the 1980s to have produced greater movement between parties among women than among men. By contrast, we expect changes in abortion views to accord with party positions more frequently among men than among women, since women tend to care more about the issue and thus are better able to resist partisan persuasion. In both cases, we expect these gender differences to be more pronounced among well-informed people than among the poorly informed, who are less likely to recognize any tension between their own view and their party's.

We begin by setting out the simple bivariate relationships between party identification and abortion attitudes in the Youth-Parent Socialization Panel Study. Since abortion opinions were asked only in the 1982 and 1997 waves, we analyze those years exclusively. Figure 9.6 shows the percentage of 1982 non-Catholic Republicans (strong or weak identifiers on the classic seven-point party identification scale) who remained Republican in 1997, displayed as a function of their 1982 abortion attitudes. Men and women are shown separately. The two most conservative positions on the abortion scale ("never" and "rarely") have been combined because "never" was chosen by just 4% of this group.[34]

The figure suggests a simple interpretation: both male and female Republicans were more likely to leave the party if they held liberal abortion views, but the partisan shift was only substantial among women, whose abortion views were more likely to be fundamentally bound up in their identity as women. Indeed, more than one-third of the non-Catholic Republican women who expressed pro-choice views in 1982 had left the party by 1997. This movement of pro-choice women to the Democrats is a key aspect of party polarization on abortion in this period.

33 Gender differences are smaller at lower levels of political information.

34 There are 98 women and 87 men represented in figure 9.6, roughly equally distributed across the three categories of abortion opinion. This implies that as a rule of thumb, differences in percentages are statistically significant at conventional levels when they reach 7 percentage points or more.

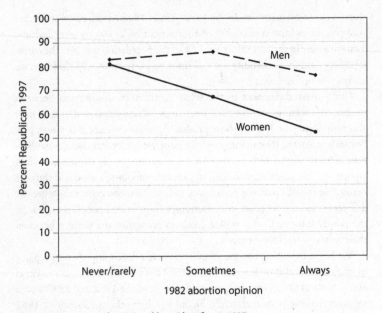

Figure 9.6. Retention of 1982 Republican Identifiers in 1997

An equally interesting but less obvious question concerns the reverse effect: how does party membership affect abortion attitudes? With attitudes generally trending to the left in the society as a whole during this period, we expect those who were already pro-choice in 1982 to have stayed put. That is especially true for Democrats, whose opinions were reinforced by both their party and the broader society.[35]

By contrast, those who were pro-life in 1982 were more likely to feel social pressure to convert as the balance of opinion shifted in a pro-choice direction. Here, too, we expect partisan differences. Pro-life Republicans had their party reinforcing their views, but pro-life Democrats faced liberalizing pressures from both the society and their party. Thus, among 1982 pro-life citizens, we expect Democrats to have become substantially more pro-choice by 1997,

35 There is some movement among 1982 pro-choice Republican women toward pro-life positions by 1997, as one would expect if our argument is correct that partisanship causes issue positions, but this may be just the response error in these women's 1982 views averaging out in subsequent years.

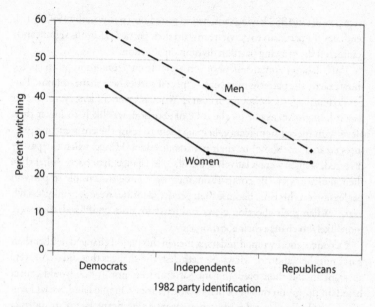

Figure 9.7. Conversion to 1997 Pro-Choice Views by 1982 Pro-Life Respondents

with Republicans remaining largely unmoved and Independents in between. Less obviously, if our reasoning is correct, the liberalizing movement for Democratic men should have been larger than that for Democratic women, since men generally had weaker gender-grounded commitments on this issue, cared less about it, and thus were more susceptible to partisan persuasion. Of course, we would also expect individual deviations for idiosyncratic reasons, and some pseudo-movement due to measurement error. No group would be expected to show perfect stability. But the basic pattern should hold.

Figure 9.7 tests these predictions. It shows opinion change to pro-choice views ("sometimes" or "always") among those with 1982 pro-life opinions ("never" or "rarely") expressed as a function of their 1982 party identification. The figure shows exactly what one would expect from the logic we have described: Democrats changed their views the most, then Independents, and Republicans the least. Again, the effects are substantial. About half of 1982 pro-life Democrats had become pro-choice by 1997—twice as much change as among pro-life Republicans. As expected, the effect was larger for men than for women, with more than half of the Democratic men who said they were pro-life in 1982 having switched to pro-choice positions by 1997.[36] This tendency for partisans to gravitate toward their parties' positions significantly reinforced the growing partisan division on abortion.

Thus, data on Americans' abortion views from a long-term panel survey show exactly the patterns one would expect if parties help shape opinion. Parties do not shape *all* opinions, of course. Women's gender identity, whichever way it brought them out on the issue of abortion, was likely to invest their views with special significance, helping them to resist the cross-cutting pressures created (for some) by their partisan loyalties. Hence, when the parties diverged, women were relatively more likely to change their party rather than their abortion view. By comparison, men were more susceptible to partisan persuasion on this issue because their gender identities were generally less relevant. When their abortion views and party loyalties conflicted, they were more likely to change their abortion views.

Of course, most women and most men in this period changed neither their party nor their abortion views. Nonetheless, the changes that did occur were substantial, and their predominant patterns were just as one would expect based on the group theory of democratic politics. On one hand, social identities—in this case, gender identities—were a significant factor in spurring partisan change. On the other hand, preexisting partisan identities and partisan persuasion played a substantial role in shaping people's political views, even on a momentous and highly salient policy issue.

CONCLUSION

In this chapter, we have attempted to trace the political impact of social identities at a variety of crucial points in the evolution of American party politics using various kinds of data and modes of analysis. The combined weight of the evidence suggests that in these instances, and presumably many others as well, partisan preferences and voting patterns were powerfully shaped by group loyalties and social identities. Even in the context of hot button issues like race and abortion, it appears that most people make their party choices based on who they are rather than on what they think—just as Berelson, Lazarsfeld, and McPhee (1954, 311) concluded more than six decades ago.

36 There are few 1982 non-Catholic, non-African-American Democrats in the pro-life categories—just 14 men and 14 women. Hence, percentages for Democrats must be interpreted as suggestive rather than definitive.

Our interpretation of the evidence provided by these crucial historical cases is bolstered by recent experimental work illustrating the political impact of group attachments. For example, two recent experiments conducted by psychologists Maureen Craig and Jennifer Richeson (2014) provide insights regarding the current and possible future implications of white racial identity in American politics. In one experiment, a nationally representative sample of white political Independents was asked "if they had heard that California had become a majority-minority state." An otherwise similar control group was asked "if they had heard that Hispanics had become roughly equal in number to Blacks nationally." Both groups were then asked which political party they leaned toward. The people who had been informed (or simply reminded) of the potentially threatening demographic shift in California were significantly more likely to lean Republican. This effect was twice as strong in the West as in the nation as a whole, producing a substantial 11-point increase in Republican leaning (and a 15-point decrease in Democratic leaning).

In a follow-up study, white subjects who were randomly assigned to read a press release about "projections that racial minorities will constitute a majority of the U.S. populace by 2042" subsequently expressed more conservative policy views than those who read about "the growth in geographic mobility in the United States." Being prompted to consider the prospect of demographic change produced more conservative views not only on plausibly relevant issues like immigration and affirmative action, but also on seemingly unrelated issues like defense spending and health care reform. The most natural interpretation of these effects, in our view, is that contemplating threats to the numerical dominance of white Americans triggered defensive reactions among some white people, heightening their sense of white identity and—crucially— associated (Republican) partisan attachments and (conservative) policy views.

An experimental study by Alexander Kuo, Neil Malhotra, and Cecilia Hyunjung Mo (2014) provided an even more subtle demonstration of the political impact of social identity. As part of a broader examination of growing Democratic Party identification among Asian-Americans, Kuo, Malhotra, and Mo randomly subjected Asian-American college students to a seemingly incidental but carefully staged "microaggression"—having their U.S. citizenship questioned by the research assistant supervising an experiment. This minor but socially charged interaction boosted Democratic partisanship by 13 percentage points. (The corresponding effect among white students was only 3 percentage points.)

Asian-Americans who experienced the insensitive questioning were also "more likely to view Republicans generally as closed-minded and ignorant" and to express more negative feelings toward them. These political effects are striking in light of the fact that Republicans were never mentioned by the experimenter or connected in any way to the microaggression. As the authors put it, their findings "suggest that Asian Americans associate feelings of social exclusion based on their ethnic background with the Republican Party." That sort of spontaneous association of social identity with partisan politics illustrates a key psychological mechanism underlying the group theory of politics.

For most people, partisanship is not a carrier of ideology but a reflection of judgments about where "people like me" belong. They do not always get that right, but they have much more success than they would constructing their political loyalties on the basis of ideology and policy convictions. Then, often enough, they let their party tell them what to think about the issues of the day. As a result, self-described liberals mostly wind up with the Democrats and conservatives with the Republicans. But the usual interpretation of that relationship supplied by the folk theory of democracy is quite misleading. If election outcomes have policy content, it comes primarily, not from voters, but from the relationships between parties and social groups (Bawn et al. 2012).

Parties are coalitions of groups, albeit coalitions with loose edges and indeterminate centers. Some of the groups in each coalition are included for purely historical or idiosyncratic reasons. Beer distributors and evangelicals are now in the same party; a century ago they were bitter political enemies. When coalitions shift, politicians scramble to adjust their policy positions accordingly (Karol 2009). Intellectuals and policy subcommunities strive to define and defend what each party stands for (Noel 2013), imposing a certain coherence on their constituent groups' various policy demands. The result is that when party elites gain office they endeavor, subject to a little pragmatism, to implement a predictable "ideological" agenda—but *not* because rank-and-file partisans are unified proponents of a coherent set of policy positions.

We explore the implications of that fact in our final chapter. First, however, we turn to a more detailed look at the role of political parties in structuring the political opinions and perceptions of their rank-and-file supporters. Our analysis of abortion attitudes implies that people, especially men, consciously or unconsciously take ethical advice on that topic from the politicians of their party—hardly an obvious source for wisdom of that kind. If our party leaders are shaping our views even about painfully difficult moral issues, how much of the rest of our political worldviews are similarly constructed on partisan foundations?

CHAPTER TEN

It Feels Like We're Thinking:
The Rationalizing Voter

> Every voter is more or less attracted or repelled by some political
> party, and usually to such an extent that he is unable to form an
> entirely unbiased judgment either on questions of policy or on
> the merits of candidates.
>
> —A. Lawrence Lowell, *Public Opinion and Popular Government*
> (1913, 86)

> The primary use of party is to create public opinion.
>
> —Philip C. Friese, *An Essay on Party* (1856, 7)

The primary sources of partisan loyalties and voting behavior, in our account, are social identities, group attachments, and myopic retrospections, not policy preferences or ideological principles. We showed in the previous chapter that particular identities—being a Catholic, a white southerner, or a woman—may have dramatic effects on party identification or on the choice of a candidate in an election. When political events make a particular identity salient or threatened, powerful psychological forces can be evoked, with effects that go well beyond the impact of the issues involved.

In this chapter we take up the most important political identity of all, party identification. Partisan loyalty is a common, uniquely powerful feature of mass political behavior in most established democracies.[1] The importance

---

1 We recognize that the classic University of Michigan version of the concept (Campbell et al. 1960, chaps. 6–7) is not applicable everywhere. However, the complexities involved in applying the American concept of party identification in other settings are irrelevant to our argument here. For example, during particular periods in some countries, party names were in flux, and the party system was instead primarily organized around support for a particular

of party identification reflects the fact that—unlike particular social identities, which may come and go as electoral forces—partisanship is relevant in nearly all elections. It shapes voting behavior, of course. But beyond that, each party organizes the thinking of its adherents. A party constructs a conceptual viewpoint by which its voters can make sense of the political world. Sympathetic newspapers, magazines, websites, and television channels convey the framework to partisans. That framework identifies friends and enemies, it supplies talking points, and it tells people how to think and what to believe. Thus, unlike particular social identities tied to the special interests of groups, the reach of partisanship is very broad. For the voters who identify with a party, partisanship pulls together conceptually nearly every aspect of electoral politics.

Once inside the conceptual framework, the voter finds herself inhabiting a relatively coherent universe. Her preferred candidates, her political opinions, and even her view of the facts will all tend to go together nicely. The arguments of the "other side," if they get any attention at all, will seem obviously dismissible. The fact that none of the opinions propping up her party loyalty are really hers will be quite invisible to her. It will feel like she's thinking.

Even among unusually well-informed and politically engaged people, the political preferences and judgments that look and feel like the bases of partisanship and voting behavior are, in reality, often *consequences* of party and group loyalties. In fact, the more information the voter has, often the better able she is to bolster her identities with rational-sounding reasons. All the appropriate partisan chimes will be rung, and the voter may sound quite impressive. Converse (1964) might put her at the top of his informational pyramid and anoint her as an "ideologue." But she may be just as impervious to evidence as anyone else, as the everyday connotation of the word "ideologue" suggests.

This fundamental disjuncture between our subjective experience of thinking about the political world and the reality of group and party influences on us is a testament to the remarkable ability of human beings to misconstrue the bases of our own attitudes and behavior. As Wendy Rahn, Jon Krosnick, and Marijke Breuning (1994, 592) wrote, summarizing the voluminous

---

leader or opposition to him, such as Charles de Gaulle in France or Juan Perón in Argentina. In South Korea, the same parties continue in political life, but they change their names at every presidential election. But in all these cases, most voters have had little trouble finding "their party" and staying loyal to it at most elections. For our purposes, such systems have "party identification" in the sense that we use the term.

psychological literature on this point, "when asked to explain their preferences, people are biased toward mentioning reasons that sound rational and systematic and that emphasize the object being evaluated, while overlooking more emotional reasons and factors other than the object's qualities." In other words, "people *rationalize* their pre-existing preferences."

In this chapter we examine the psychology of political belief-construction and its implications for democratic citizenship. We focus on party identification, in part because of its ubiquity in elections, and in part because the evidence for its political effects is far broader and deeper than for the impact of any other identity. Thus we can give far more extensive evidence for its effect than was available for any one of our examples in the previous chapter. Indeed, the evidence is overwhelming. We find that partisan loyalties strongly color citizens' views about candidates, issues, and even "objective" facts. Citizens' political preferences and beliefs are constructed from emotional or cognitive commitments whose real bases lie elsewhere. We take up three different aspects of partisan beliefs—perceptions of where the parties stand on issues, beliefs about purely factual matters in politics, and the ricochet effect on other issues when an exogenous shock moves partisanship.

PARTISAN PERCEPTION AND MISPERCEPTION

An important function of partisan rationalization is to minimize "cognitive dissonance" (Festinger 1957)—in this case, the unpleasant feeling that candidates of my party do not share my issue preferences. In the face of that discrepancy, one way to feel better is to change my mind and adopt my party's position, as men often do with respect to abortion policy (see chapter 9). But an even simpler route to relief is to ignore or resist learning my party's views, and to imagine that their opinions are the same as my own. This phenomenon of "cognitive balancing" is far more common than many political observers realize.

For example, a question about the trade-off between taxes and government services has been asked repeatedly in American National Election Studies (ANES) surveys since 1982.[2] Respondents are asked to place themselves on a seven-point scale ranging from "many more services" on the left to "reduce

---

2 "Some people think the government should provide fewer services, even in areas such as health and education, in order to reduce spending. Other people feel that it is important for the government to provide many more services even if it means an increase in spending. Where would you place yourself on this scale, or haven't you thought much about this?"

spending a lot" on the right. They are also asked to place the two political parties on the same scale. This allows a researcher to calculate how close the respondent thinks each party is to her own position on the issue. Suppose that on the seven-point scale, a respondent sees the GOP as one unit away from her own position and the Democrats as four units away. Then we will say that she favors the Republicans by three points, which is the difference in those two distances. We refer to differences of this kind as "issue proximities." If the respondent sees herself as closer to the Republicans, our measure of relative issue proximity is coded as a positive number; if she sees herself as closer to the Democrats, the resulting issue proximity score is coded as a negative number.

Data of that kind allow a simple test of whether voters are engaged in rationalizing how close their party is to their own views. To see this, suppose that no rationalization were occurring. Then consider a Democrat and a Republican, both of whom placed themselves at 2 on a 7-point scale. If they both see the parties accurately, they will each be exactly the same distance from each party, and thus they will each have exactly the same relative issue proximity. Their partisanship should be irrelevant. On the other hand, if rationalization is occurring, each respondent may perceive her own party as closer to her than it really is, and perhaps also perceive the other party as further away than it is. Thus Republican respondents will pull their proximities upward toward the positive numbers favoring the GOP, while Democrats will pull theirs downward toward negative numbers that favor their party.

Over the years, more than 22,000 ANES survey respondents have been asked this question. About 15% of those people declined to place themselves on the scale—they said they didn't know or "hadn't thought much about" the central domestic policy issue of the past three decades. Another 14% placed themselves on the scale but declined to place one or both of the political parties. Thus, despite the centrality of this issue in contemporary partisan debate, about 30% of the public could not possibly make a calculation of relative "issue proximity" of the sort taken for granted in the spatial model of voting described in chapter 2.

But what of the remaining 70%? Figure 10.1 provides a simple tabulation of Republicans' and Democrats' perceptions of relative issue proximity—which major party was closer to their own position—on the taxing and spending question. The figure shows the average perception of relative proximity for Republican and Democratic partisans at each point on the issue scale.

If respondents' perceptions of the parties' issue positions were unbiased, the curves in figure 10.1 for Republican and Democratic identifiers would overlap perfectly. Instead, they are markedly divergent. Among the 24% of

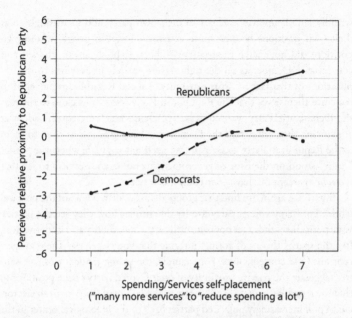

Figure 10.1. Party Identification and Perceptions of Issue Proximity for Spending/Services, 1982–2012

these respondents in figure 10.1 who placed themselves in the middle of the seven-point issue scale, Republicans and Democrats differed by a full point in their assessments of issue proximity.[3] That is, Republicans believed their party was more than half a point closer to the middle of the scale, on average, while Democrats believed *their* party was almost half a point closer to the same midpoint. Obviously, both could not be right.[4]

The partisan disparities were even larger for people whose own positions did not happen to fall at the midpoint of the seven-point scale. Liberal Democrats (on the left) and conservative Republicans (on the right) each quite

3 With 2,803 partisan identifiers who placed themselves at the middle of the scale, the *t*-statistic for this difference is 25.6; the customary standard for "statistical significance" is 1.96.

4 In principle, Republicans could have been right in some years and Democrats in other years. However, allowing for movement in the actual positions of the parties on the spending and services scale by adding year-specific intercepts to the analysis does very little to alter the picture; the partisan difference in perceived proximity is virtually unchanged.

sensibly saw themselves as closer to their own party, and increasingly so as their own positions became more extreme. However, people whose own positions did not match their party's—liberal Republicans on the left and conservative Democrats on the right—were entirely impervious to the implications of that fact for issue proximity.[5] Liberal Republicans managed to convince themselves that the Republican Party was just as close to them as the Democratic Party was; conservative Democrats were equally adept at convincing themselves that the Democratic Party was just as close to them as the Republican Party was. Again, we need not stipulate where the parties "really" stood on the issue of government spending and services to see that *someone's* perceptions have gone badly astray here.

Thus, once again, we find that group identities drive views of the political world. For many voters, party loyalty determines how they see the parties' issue positions—the exact opposite of how the folk theory and its derivatives, like the spatial theory of voting, imagine that voters behave. These misperceptions have consequences. For example, the strong tendency of partisans to exaggerate the relative proximity of their favored party's issue positions to their own may contribute significantly to the failure of the American electorate to pull increasingly polarized parties back to the ideological center in the manner posited by the spatial model of elections (Sood and Iyengar 2014).

Figure 10.1 is no isolated example.[6] Indeed, for more than half a century students of public opinion and voting behavior have been documenting the role of party and group loyalties in shaping political perceptions. For example, Bernard Berelson, Paul Lazarsfeld, and William McPhee (1954, chap. 10) were among the first to show that partisanship colored perceptions of candidates' issue positions.

In the light of this well-verified finding, some scholars have proposed formal models of how the perceptual process works. Henry Brady and Paul

5 Given the political salience of government spending and services in this era, only 20% of Republican identifiers and 15% of Democratic identifiers took positions on the issue contrary to those conventionally assigned to their respective parties (while 46% of Republicans took positions to the right of the midpoint and 44% of Democrats took positions to the left of the midpoint). Dissonance between partisanship and issue positions has been more common on most of the other issues included in the ANES surveys.

6 Not every issue produces errors in perception as large as those displayed in figure 10.1. On the issue of abortion, for example, most pro-choice Republicans and (by a narrower margin) most pro-life Democrats have managed to recognize that their views put them closer to the opposing party than to their own party. However, analogous figures for most of the issues included in ANES surveys over the years look much more similar to the pattern for spending and services presented in figure 10.1 than to the pattern for abortion. Partisan misperception is the rule, not the exception.

Sniderman (1985) proposed that people's attributions of policy positions to political groups balanced two distinct psychological objectives: a desire for accuracy and "a strain to consistency" between perceptions and feelings (Brady and Sniderman 1985, 1068). On one hand, people were assumed to want to be accurate in their perception of where a group actually stood. On the other hand, if they liked the group, they wanted its views to be near their own; and if they disliked it, they wanted its views to be far away from theirs. As a result, actual perceptions represented weighted averages of the group's actual and hoped-for positions, with the weights reflecting the relative psychological importance of accuracy and cognitive consistency.

Models like that proposed by Brady and Sniderman are non-rational. They take account of the extensive empirical evidence that people value certain kinds of inaccuracy because adopting those fallacious perceptions makes them feel better. However, another explanatory tradition has arisen in which the same people are seen as perfectly rational, but simply poorly informed. Long ago, A. Lawrence Lowell (1913, 87) observed that "for a man to follow blindly in national politics a national party that he has learned to trust is not wholly without justification, because there is a strong chance that it stands for the opinions he would himself hold if he studied the issues involved." Thus *partisan inference* is an effort by citizens to "fill in the blanks" using what they do know (their views about the parties) to make plausible guesses about what they do not know (where candidates stand on the issues). On this view, using parties to infer issue proximities is completely sensible.

In this rational spirit, Stanley Feldman and Pamela Conover (1983) proposed "an inference model of political perception." They noted that the patterns of rationalization typically interpreted as reflecting cognitive dissonance reduction could also be interpreted as rational inferences in the face of uncertainty: "Rather than being motivated by a need to reduce inconsistency, people may simply learn that certain aspects of the social and political world are, in fact, constructed in a consistent fashion . . . In the absence of information to the contrary, an individual's assumption that certain types of consistency exist may be an efficient way of perceiving the world."

Feldman and Conover (1983, 813) argued that "a theoretical focus on cognitive inference provides more than just a reinterpretation of consistency effects; it suggests a basis for developing a more general explanation of political perception." Their more general explanation involved accounting for perceptions of candidates' issue stands by reference to a variety of plausibly relevant political cues, including respondents' own issue positions and their perceptions of political parties and ideological groups. In subsequent work

(Conover and Feldman 1989), they put a similar framework to good effect in accounting for the crystallization of perceptions of Democratic presidential candidate Jimmy Carter over the course of the 1976 campaign. Using repeated interviews with the same people over the course of the election year, they showed that most people were quite uncertain of Carter's issue positions during the primary season, but shifted markedly toward associating him with the positions of the Democratic Party after he became the Democratic nominee.

But how much comfort should we take from this rationalistic reinterpretation of voter errors? Perceptual biases may be "efficient" in the sense of minimizing psychological stress. If I am a Democrat who favors cutting spending, my customary Democratic vote will engender no unease; I can manage to convince myself that Barack Obama is just as committed as I am to cutting spending. The result may even represent a "reasonable response to ambiguity," as Feldman and Conover (1983, 837) put it—at least, for someone who has paid no attention to Obama's statements and actions over the course of his presidency or to party platforms or policies over the past three decades. But we see no reason to suppose that it is conducive to effective electoral democracy.

As we have seen, the same pervasive impact of partisanship on the perceived issue positions of the parties can be interpreted as either cognitive balancing or partisan inference. For the purposes of our argument, this is a distinction without a difference. In this chapter, as elsewhere in this volume, we resist getting too caught up in debates about the specific psychological mechanisms underlying people's political preferences and beliefs. Much of the best contemporary work in the field of political psychology focuses on "powerful affective and cognitive forces that motivate and direct deliberation and political action outside of conscious awareness and control" (Lodge and Taber 2013, 1; see also see Payne et al. 2010; Pérez 2010; Albertson 2011; Erisen, Lodge, and Taber 2014).[7] From that perspective, a subconscious impulse to minimize cognitive dissonance seems like a pretty good bet to be the central force at work. However, as Feldman and Conover observed, it is quite possible to account for essentially similar patterns of preference and belief on

---

7 The subtitle of this chapter is an accidental homage to Lodge and Taber's book, *The Rationalizing Voter*, which examined specific psychological mechanisms of political attitude formation in considerable detail. The same phrase appeared independently in the subtitle of the 2006 conference paper from which this chapter derives and in the title of a 2007 conference paper by Lodge and Taber subsequently incorporated into their book.

the basis of the more stylized assumptions underlying rational choice theory (Achen and Bartels 2006; Lauderdale 2012).

As with the broader literature on political cues and heuristics surveyed in chapter 2, the literature on partisan perception generally conveys a good deal of enthusiasm for the "efficiency," "consistency," "reasonableness," and "rationality" of whatever it is that citizens are doing. For example, despite important differences in their theoretical perspectives, Feldman and Conover (1983) and Brady and Sniderman (1985) seemed similarly heartened by the implications of their findings for electoral democracy. Feldman and Conover (1983, 837) concluded that voters "do the best they can," and that "the general contribution of inference processes to vote choice is a positive one." For their part, Brady and Sniderman (1985, 1075) concluded that "affect can be a quite efficient way of encoding and storing what is after all the most vital political information: who and what one is for or against."

Efficient, perhaps. What is striking, though, is that Brady and Sniderman had very little to say about the implications of this efficiency for the *accuracy* of people's perceptions of the political landscape. At one point (1985, 1076) they asserted that "the mass public is remarkably accurate in attributing positions to strategic groups on major issues"; but that assertion seems to have referred to the *average* attributions of the public as a whole rather than to the judgments of any particular individual. In any case, it is unclear what contribution, if any, their "likeability heuristic" made to the accuracy of the issue perceptions they examined.

Brady and Sniderman's results from 34 separate statistical analyses, each focusing on perceptions of a particular group on a particular issue, suggested that people's perceptions of disliked groups were relatively accurate, on average, but that their perceptions of favored groups were strongly biased by their desire to see those groups as close to themselves. Indeed, for a typical favored group, people's *own* issue positions received about one-third as much weight as the group's *actual* position in shaping perceptions of where the group stood.[8] And this was for perceptions of very salient groups—liberals

---

8 Brady and Sniderman's model included two terms measuring projection: a "false consensus" effect applying to all groups regardless of whether they were liked or disliked, and a "more focused, or partisan, effect" pulling perceptions of favored groups toward one's own position and pushing perceptions of disfavored groups away from that position. The average magnitudes of Brady and Sniderman's statistical estimates were .185 for the false consensus effect and .550 for the differential projection effect. Assuming a difference of 25 points between favored and disfavored groups on the ANES feeling thermometer (roughly the observed average difference between the groups Brady and Sniderman considered), the combined effect is

and conservatives, blacks and whites, Republicans and Democrats—on major political issues of the day. It seems safe to assume that projection effects would loom even larger for less familiar groups or candidates and for less prominent issues.

Indeed, an analysis along similar lines of perceived issue positions of candidates in presidential primaries (Bartels 1988, 98–107) did find even larger projection effects, especially early in the primary season and for candidates who were relatively unknown. For example, Democrats in the 1984 primary campaign perceived well-known frontrunner Walter Mondale as about 20% closer, on average, to their own issue positions than he really was; but the corresponding distortion for little-known challenger Gary Hart was about 40% at the beginning of the campaign, only gradually declining to a similar 20% level. For people who were particularly enthusiastic about Hart, for whatever reason, the estimated projection effect was even larger. People who gave Hart the warmest possible rating on a 100-point "feeling thermometer" at the beginning of the primary season managed to see him as almost 75% closer than he actually was to their own issue positions.

Thus, voters may "do the best they can," as Feldman and Conover insisted, but still be depressingly far from having realistic perceptions of the political world. Their patent inaccuracy seems to us to belie the "encouraging" conclusion that "the general contribution of inference processes to vote choice is a positive one" (Feldman and Conover 1983, 837).[9]

OUR OWN FACTS

Thus far we have seen that voters use their own preferences and their partisanship to help construct their ideas of what the parties stand for. That is bad enough. But it gets worse: They use their partisanship to construct "objective" facts, too, as we now demonstrate.

---

minimal for disfavored groups (+.05) but considerable for favored groups (+.31) by comparison with the effect of groups' actual positions, which is normalized to 1.0.

9 Of course, the effects of partisan inference will be even less "encouraging" if partisan surmise crowds out real information. Wendy Rahn's (1993) experimental study of the role of partisan stereotypes in information processing suggests that it does. She found that in the absence of party labels, voters furnished with "particular information" about candidates' policy stands used that information in evaluating candidates and making inferences about their issue positions. "However, when voters have both particular information and party stereotypes available . . . they prefer to rely on heuristic-based processing. They neglect policy information in reaching evaluations; they use the label rather than policy attributes in drawing inferences; and they are perceptually less responsive to inconsistent information" (Rahn 1993, 492).

"Everyone is entitled to his own opinions," Daniel Patrick Moynihan is supposed to have said, "but not to his own facts." In the folk theory of democracy, objective facts about the political world transcend whatever disagreements arise from our differing moral commitments. Thus, in principle, people with differing policy views may nonetheless come to agreement regarding matters of fact—for example, that raising the minimum wage increases unemployment (or not), that crime is on the rise (or not), that a foreign adversary possesses weapons of mass destruction (or not)—and agreement about relevant facts may in turn contribute to reaching agreement about whether to raise the minimum wage, build more prisons, or invade Iraq.

Of course, people do not know all the facts that would be relevant to know about the political world. Nonetheless, the folk theory tells us, they can *learn* what they need to know in order to translate their moral commitments into cogent political preferences and effective political action. Indeed, on this view, the surest route to democratic improvement is to increase the level of political engagement and awareness among ordinary citizens. The implicit epistemology of the folk theory comes straight from the 18th-century Enlightenment, as we have seen.

One obvious problem with all of this, as we remarked in chapter 2, is the sheer magnitude of most people's ignorance about politics. Another, slightly less obvious problem—as Jennifer Hochschild and Katherine Einstein (2015, vii) suggested, channeling Will Rogers or Mark Twain or Satchel Paige (actually, Josh Billings)—is how much they *do* know that ain't so. Political misinformation has many potential sources, but prominent among them are the same processes of partisan perception we have found at work in the realm of political issues.

For example, the 1988 ANES survey asked respondents whether, "compared to 1980, the level of inflation in the country has gotten better, stayed about the same, or gotten worse." The correct answer to this question was clearly "much better"—the inflation rate had fallen from 13.5% in 1980 to 4.1% in 1988. Almost half (47%) of "strong" Republicans gave that correct answer, while only 13% said inflation had gotten worse. However, fewer than 8% of "strong" Democrats acknowledged that inflation had gotten "much better" on President Reagan's watch, while more than half claimed that it had gotten worse (Bartels 2002a).

Mistaken beliefs, even about highly salient facts, can persist over long periods of time. More than 18 months after the 2003 U.S.-led invasion of Iraq, for example, 47% of Republicans (but only 9% of Democrats) said they believed that Iraq had possessed weapons of mass destruction on the eve of the invasion; 71% of Republicans (but only 37% of Democrats) believed that Iraq was directly involved in the 9/11 attacks or had provided substantial support to al-Qaeda. Another 18 months later, both of these beliefs had eroded, but only slightly: 41% of Republicans (and 7% of Democrats) still believed that Iraq had had weapons of mass destruction, while 63% of Republicans (and 35% of Democrats) still believed that Iraq was linked to al-Qaeda (Program on International Policy Attitudes 2006).[10]

Partisan bias may even creep into *interpretations* of agreed-upon facts. Thus, Brian Gaines and his colleagues (2007) found in a series of repeated interviews with college students in late 2003 and 2004 that "all partisan groups, strong Republicans included, held reasonably accurate beliefs" about the Iraq War and updated those beliefs as circumstances changed; however, Democratic and Republican students differed greatly in their *interpretations* of pertinent facts, causing the authors to conclude that partisans "effectively used interpretations to rationalize their existing opinions" rather than to rationally revise those opinions (Gaines et al. 2007, 961, 969).

Why do people adopt such different views even about straightforward matters of judgment? On one hand, just as a desire to minimize cognitive dissonance may lead people to adopt their preferred party's issue positions as their own, it may lead them to adopt their preferred party's views about whether the crime rate is rising or falling. On the other hand, people may be doing the best they can. After all, very few politically consequential facts are subject to direct, personal verification. Just as Lowell's (1913, 87) rational partisan was "not wholly without justification" in guessing that his preferred party "stands for the opinions he would himself hold if he studied the issues involved," he may be justified in guessing that his preferred party's accepted views about factual controversies of the day are more likely than not to be the views he would himself come to if he devoted significant time and attention to those matters. In either case, the result will be a marked tendency toward partisan consistency in the realm of political beliefs, just as in the realm of political attitudes. But the dangers of this kind of thinking should be even more obvious where facts are concerned than they are with respect to other kinds of political perceptions.

---

10 Gary Jacobson (2008) cited even larger partisan disparities in responses to similar questions in CBS News/*New York Times* polls in late 2004 and early 2005: around 80% of Republicans, but fewer than 40% of Democrats, said that Iraq had possessed weapons of mass destruction.

People's factual judgments are often cobbled together from various more or less pertinent and trustworthy sources, including news accounts, water-cooler conversation, campaign propaganda, and folk wisdom about the way the world works. In some cases, accurate information will trump partisanship, and the most engaged and politically aware citizens will have the firmest hold on reality, just as the folk theory of democracy would lead us to expect. Thus, many observers assume that "rationalization is probably greater for less informed citizens" (Aldrich, Sullivan, and Borgida 1989, 132). However, Danielle Shani's analysis of responses to a wide variety of factual questions produced a good deal of evidence to the contrary, leading her to conclude that "political knowledge does not correct for partisan bias in perception of 'objective' conditions, nor does it mitigate the bias. Instead, and unfortunately, it enhances the bias; party identification colors the perceptions of the most politically informed citizens far more than the relatively less informed citizens" (Shani 2006, 31).[11]

How should we understand these patterns? If we follow Lowell (1913) or Feldman and Conover (1983) in trying to make sense of voters' thinking as rational inference, we might begin with a formal model of fully rational decision-making. Elsewhere (Achen and Bartels 2006) we have developed a model of just that sort. It implies that citizens' opinions represent weighted averages of three distinct quantities—first, background opinions representing what they already "know" before encountering any specific information about an issue (in the terminology of Bayesian decision-making, a *prior belief*); second, what they hear from party leaders and co-partisans or infer from their own partisanship; and third, actual factual knowledge regarding the matter at hand. The relative weight of these three quantities for any given citizen will depend upon the reliability of her information about them, which is determined in turn by her levels of political information and experience.[12]

---

11 Shani analyzed eight factual questions in the 2000 ANES survey, including the budget deficit and national economy questions examined here. In seven of the eight cases she found substantial (and statistically significant) increases in partisan bias among well-informed respondents. These differences were largely unaffected by the introduction of statistical controls for differing political values or plausible demographic correlates of differing personal experiences.

12 As is commonly the case in Bayesian learning models of this sort (Achen 1992), weighting each of these three factors by its reliability produces complex nonlinear relationships between political information and experience (for which our proxy is age) and observed judgments within each partisan group. Thus, our model implies that one should not generally expect to find linear relationships between "cues" and judgments, or between levels of political information and the extent of partisan bias in perceptions.

Citizens who are very sure of the facts will base their judgments largely on those facts. Those who know only the partisan talking points will parrot their party's view or simply assume that if the other party is in office, the times must be bad. And those who know neither the facts nor the party line will tend to formulate guesses based on folk wisdom about "how things always are" or other aspects of the prevailing zeitgeist.

Here, we illustrate the application of this model to the study of objective factual beliefs using responses to a question in the 1996 ANES survey asking whether "the size of the yearly budget deficit increased, decreased, or stayed about the same during Clinton's time as President?" The question is straight-forwardly factual. It would be very hard to argue that Republicans and Democrats had different views about the meaning of the phrase "yearly budget deficit" or different standards for assessing whether the deficit had increased or decreased. Thus, any difference in responses must logically be attributable to some process of rationalization or partisan inference rather than to differences in ideologies or values.

Moreover, the actual trend in the budget deficit was remarkably clear and politically salient in 1996. The deficit had increased substantially under Bill Clinton's Republican predecessor, George H. W. Bush, and Ross Perot had made it the centerpiece of his historic independent presidential campaign in 1992.[13] However, once Clinton became president in 1993 the deficit began to fall steadily and substantially—from $255 billion in FY 1993 to $203 billion in FY 1994, $164 billion in FY 1995, and $107 billion in FY 1996. Thus, the correct answer was clearly that the budget deficit had decreased a lot during Clinton's first term.[14] The president trumpeted this success on the campaign

---

13 Perot supporters in 1992 were very likely to express concern about the budget deficit. However, this too was in large part a matter of rationalization. In the 1990 ANES survey, the same people who would later become Perot supporters were only slightly more likely than other people were to express concern about the budget deficit; their concern seems to have been a *consequence* of Perot's campaign as much as it was a *reason* to support him (Zaller and Hunt 1995).

14 The federal fiscal year ends on September 30, and official annual deficit figures are re-leased in late October. However, the fact that the budget deficit was continuing to decline rapidly in FY 1996 was clear well before the end of the fiscal year (and before the ANES survey got under way in September). For example, the Congressional Budget Office had estimated in its August update of "The Economic and Budget Outlook" that the FY 1996 deficit would be $116 billion, almost 30% lower than in FY 1995 and 55% lower than in FY 1993 (https://cbo.gov/sites/default/files/cbofiles/ftpdocs/0xx/doc1/eb08-96.pdf).

Table 10.1. Perceptions of the Budget Deficit by Party Identification, 1996

	1992 Democrats (%)	1992 Independents (%)	1992 Republicans (%)	Total (%)
Increased a lot (−50)	6.7	15.8	22.6	14.8
Increased a little (−25)	25.6	22.1	29.7	25.2
Stayed about the same (0)	28.5	29.7	23.5	27.7
Decreased a little (+25)	32.0	24.2	20.4	25.6
Decreased a lot (+50)	7.3	8.1	3.8	6.7
N	185	235	156	576

"Would you say that the size of the yearly budget deficit increased, decreased, or stayed about the same during Clinton's time as President? Would you say it has increased [decreased] a lot or a little?"

trail, while congressional Republicans demanded their share of the credit for the "common-sense belt-tightening" in Washington (Richter 1996).

Despite the clarity, salience, media coverage, and political significance of the declining budget deficit, the improvement in the nation's fiscal health went nearly unnoticed by the public. Information about it was highly concentrated among the best-informed people. The result was widespread public misperception of a fundamental fact about American politics and public policy. The summary of survey responses presented in table 10.1 shows that only one-third of the public recognized that the deficit had decreased, while 40% said it had increased. Republicans were especially inaccurate; more than half said that the deficit had increased, while only one-fourth said that it had decreased. This evidence of partisan bias is consistent with the findings of a good deal of previous research on perceptions and evaluations of political figures, issues, and conditions (Fischle 2000; Bartels 2002a; 2002b; Erikson 2004; Gerber and Huber 2010; Hetherington, Long, and Rudolph 2014). In

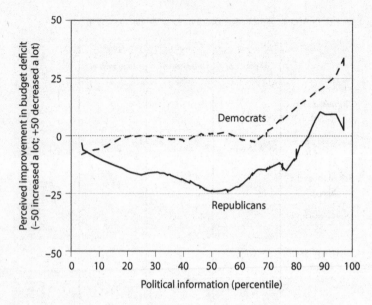

Figure 10.2. Perceptions of Budget Deficit by Party and Information Level, 1996

this case, however, even most Democrats were quite wrong, with fewer than 10% recognizing that the deficit had decreased a lot.[15]

Figure 10.2 traces the role of political information in shaping these perceptions of the budget deficit.[16] Among the least well-informed respondents, neither objective reality nor partisan bias seems to have provided much structure to perceptions of the budget deficit. Uninformed Republicans and Democrats were slightly, and about equally, more likely to say that the deficit

15 We categorize people as Democrats or Republicans based on partisan attachments expressed in 1992, before Clinton even took office—thus ruling out the possibility that their partisanship was somehow an *effect* rather than a *cause* of their perceptions about how the budget deficit had changed on Clinton's watch.

16 The curves presented in figure 10.2 are derived from locally weighted (lowess) regressions using 30% of the data (50–60 survey responses) at each point along the information scale. Our measure of political information cumulates responses to a variety of factual questions (identifying prominent political figures, knowing which party controlled Congress, and so on) in each wave of the 1992–1996 ANES survey. Classifying respondents on the basis of party identification measured in 1996 produces very similar curves, suggesting that parallel analyses with cross-sectional data are unlikely to go too far astray in this case.

had increased than that it had decreased. Perhaps this tendency reflected a murky understanding that the budget deficit increased at some point in the past; perhaps it was a bit of prejudice based on folk wisdom about profligate politicians.

The beliefs of somewhat better-informed Republicans and Democrats did diverge significantly. However, among people in the bottom two-thirds of the national distribution of political information, this partisan divergence was entirely attributable to moderately informed Republicans being *less* likely than the least-informed to give the correct answer to the budget deficit question. They knew that a Democrat was in office and that the president was in some way responsible for the deficit. They did not know the actual progress of the deficit, but they did know that Democrats do a poor job by their standards. They inferred that Clinton was probably doing a poor job on the deficit, too.

Thus a modicum of political information was enough for Republicans to figure out what ought to be true, but not to learn what was in fact true. They were likely to recognize the partisan relevance of a factual question of this sort, and to answer it in decidedly partisan terms. Partisanship is likely to trump reality in this way when the issue, however vital, is the least bit arcane or divorced from personal experience, as in the case of the budget deficit.

The best-informed Republicans presumably had as much or more stake in resisting the notion that a Democratic president had produced a dramatic improvement in the deficit. However, they were also much more likely to have been exposed to objective information about the dramatic downward trend in the deficit. The result was a substantial uptick in recognition of the improved deficit situation among the best-informed Republicans—though even they were only slightly more likely to say that the deficit had decreased than that it had increased.

In contrast, well-informed Democrats—untroubled by any contradiction between the reality and their partisan hopes or expectations—were very likely to recognize at least some improvement in the budget deficit. However, it is worth noting that "well-informed" in this case refers to just the best-informed quarter or so of the citizenry. More typical Democrats, in the middle third of the distribution, were no more likely to say that the deficit had decreased than to say that it had increased.[17]

17 We also investigated another question from the same survey asking respondents whether "over the past year the nation's economy has gotten better, stayed the same or gotten worse." This is the question most frequently employed in individual-level analyses of

Again, our point is *not* that citizens are irrational. Indeed, our formal model of partisan inference (Achen and Bartels 2006) gives rationality every benefit of the doubt by assuming that people make perfectly rational use of whatever information they happen to have. That model, applied to the budget deficit question, reproduces the nonlinear patterns in figure 10.2 very well, and it predicts that moderately informed Republicans will be the group most likely to be mistaken, just as figure 10.2 demonstrates. Thus the problem is not that voters are necessarily irrational, but that most voters have very little real information, even about crucially important aspects of national political life. Thus, even when they "do the best they can," as Feldman and Conover (1983, 837) put it, their beliefs on issues like the deficit are likely to be made up in large part of folk wisdom and partisan supposition. That is, partisanship shapes people's worldviews in a deep way, right down to "their own facts."

THE RAMIFICATIONS OF A PARTISAN SHOCK: REACTIONS TO WATERGATE

Our account of partisan perception implies that people's political views and factual judgments are likely to be significantly and pervasively influenced by their partisan predispositions. Thus far, however, we have ignored the *process* by which preferences and perceptions come into equilibrium. As with any snapshot of an individual's political views at a single point in time, the evidence we have presented thus far is consistent with a variety of distinct dynamic processes whose theoretical and normative implications may be quite different.

Carefully designed experiments may shed light on these alternative dynamic processes.[18] So, too, may repeated observations of people exposed to real political change. However, considerable care is required to provide cogent

---

retrospective economic voting (e.g., Kinder and Kiewiet 1981; Duch and Stevenson 2008). There were substantial partisan biases in the responses, but less dramatically so than in the question about the deficit (Achen and Bartels 2006).

18 Alan Gerber, Gregory Huber, and Ebonya Washington (2010) randomly assigned registered voters with no party affiliation to receive a mailing noting that only voters registered with a party would be eligible to participate in an upcoming primary election. A follow-up survey showed that the mailing stimulated an increase in party identification and corresponding shifts in candidate preferences and evaluations of salient political figures. Auxiliary analysis of potential alternative mechanisms bolstered the authors' (2010, 742) interpretation "that the change in attitudes we observe was due to a change in partisan identity" rather than vice versa.

causal interpretations of observed change in partisanship and political views (Miller 2000), especially since both partisanship and specific political views are likely to be quite stable over months or even years, aside from measurement error. As our analysis of partisanship and abortion attitudes in chapter 9 showed, studies of the same people over much longer periods of time— decades rather than months or years—can mitigate these limitations, providing clearer understandings of political change; but studies of that sort are time-consuming, expensive, and rare.

An alternative approach is to focus on unusual moments in which dramatic political events change people's partisanship. In the aftermath of such moments we may be able to observe with unusual clarity whether and how the various aspects of people's political worldviews reequilibrate. The account of partisan perception offered in this chapter implies that if citizens' partisan loyalties change due to some dramatic external shock, the reverberations should include changes in a variety of political preferences and beliefs logically unrelated to the shock. That is, if Watergate was bad, then the government should do more to help everyone get a job. Again, this effect need not require citizens to be irrational in the technical sense: peculiar behavior of this kind is a logical implication of the Bayesian model presented by Achen and Bartels (2006). Indeed, it is an implication of the model that the reverberations of changing partisanship may well be most far-reaching among people who are sufficiently engaged and well-informed to recognize a wide variety of specific implications of their altered partisan loyalties.

In this section, we examine one such set of dramatic political shocks—the Watergate scandal of the early 1970s. Fortuitously, for our purposes, the Watergate scandal was largely unrelated to substantive political issues of the day. There was no obvious reason, aside from partisanship, for people's responses to Watergate to alter (or be altered by) their views about school busing or government employment programs. Equally fortuitously, a large-scale ANES survey bracketed the major events of the Watergate era, allowing us to observe how people's perceptions and preferences regarding a variety of specific political issues evolved in response to the escalating scandal, beginning with the run-up to the 1972 presidential election, continuing in the immediate aftermath of President Nixon's resignation in 1974, and ending with the 1976 election cycle.

The 1974 ANES survey included a variety of questions tapping respondents' reactions to the Watergate scandal, including whether they were pleased or displeased by President Nixon's resignation,[19] whether they viewed the House Judiciary Committee's impeachment hearings as fair or unfair,[20] whether the media's coverage of Watergate was fair or unfair,[21] and whether the president's resignation was good or bad for the country.[22] We used responses to these four questions to construct a simple additive scale of Watergate attitudes, with scores ranging from −50 (for the most extreme pro-Nixon responses to all four questions) to +50 (for the most extreme anti-Nixon responses to all four questions).[23]

Not surprisingly, these reactions to the Watergate scandal were shaped in significant part by preexisting partisan attachments. The average score on the Watergate scale (in 1974) for people who had called themselves strong Republicans in the fall of 1972, when the origins of the break-in were still quite murky and the broader outlines of the scandal were not yet evident, was essentially neutral—0.6. By comparison, people who called themselves strong Democrats in 1972 were strongly critical of Nixon in 1974, with an average score of 29.3. Nevertheless, there was also a good deal of variation in responses within each partisan camp. For example, almost one-third of the people who were strong Republican identifiers in 1972 expressed considerable sympathy for Nixon and antipathy toward his attackers (with Watergate scale scores below −20) in 1974, while another one-third were critical of Nixon and supportive of the media and the impeachment process (with Watergate scale scores above 20). Thus, it should be possible to distinguish the specific effects of reactions to the scandal from the effects of more general partisan predispositions.

We begin by examining the impact of Watergate attitudes on perceptions of relative proximity to the Democratic and Republican parties on a variety of political issues included in the 1972–1976 ANES survey—a summary

19 "Thinking back a few months to when Richard Nixon resigned from office, do you remember if you were *pleased* or *displeased* about his resignation, or didn't you care very much one way or the other?"

20 "As you probably know, before Richard Nixon resigned, the Judiciary Committee was holding hearings to decide whether he should be impeached, that is, brought to trial in the Senate for possible wrongdoings. Would you say that these hearings were very fair, somewhat fair, somewhat unfair, or very unfair, or didn't you pay much attention to this?"

21 "How fair would you say that the television and newspaper coverage of the Nixon administration's involvement in the Watergate affair was? Would you say it was very fair, somewhat fair or not very fair, or didn't you follow this very closely?"

22 "Do you think that President Nixon's resignation was a good thing or a bad thing for the country?"

23 The scale has a mean value of 20.1, a standard deviation of 26.9, and an alpha reliability coefficient of .68.

liberal-conservative scale,[24] government jobs and income maintenance,[25] school busing,[26] rights of accused criminals,[27] and government aid to minorities.[28] We focus on these issues because self-placements and party placements were included in each wave of the three-wave survey.[29] Thus, rather than simply observing the extent to which people's perceptions of relative proximity seem to make sense at any given moment, as in figure 10.1, we can explore how they change when the political environment shifts.

In order to test our assertion that such changes should be concentrated among people sufficiently well-informed to recognize the broad potential ramifications of their partisan predispositions, table 10.2 reports separate

24 "We hear a lot of talk these days about liberals and conservatives. I'm going to show you a 7-point scale on which the political views that people might hold are arranged from extremely liberal to extremely conservative. Where would you place yourself on this scale, or haven't you thought much about this?"

25 "Some people feel that the government in Washington should see to it that every person has a job and a good standard of living. Others think the government should just let each person get ahead on his own. And, of course, other people have opinions somewhere in between. Where would you place yourself on this scale, or haven't you thought much about this?"

26 "There is much discussion about the best way to deal with racial problems. Some people think achieving racial integration of schools is so important that it justifies busing children to schools out of their own neighborhoods. Others think letting children go to their neighborhood schools is so important that they oppose busing. Where would you place yourself on this scale, or haven't you thought much about this?"

27 "Some people are primarily concerned with doing everything possible to protect the legal rights of those accused of committing crimes. Others feel that it is more important to stop criminal activity even at the risk of reducing the rights of the accused. Where would you place yourself on this scale, or haven't you thought much about this?"

28 "Some people feel that the government in Washington should make every possible effort to improve the social and economic position of blacks and other minority groups. Others feel that the government should not make any special effort to help minorities because they should help themselves. Where would you place yourself on this scale, or haven't you though much about it?"

29 Our research design requires that we be able to compare responses before and after the Watergate scandal. In addition, the fact that these items were included in all three waves of the ANES panel survey facilitates estimation of the statistical reliability of the responses. The estimates of the effects of Watergate attitudes in tables 10.2 and 10.3 are derived from errors-in-variables regression models using estimates of the reliability of each explanatory factor within each information group. Our estimates of the reliability of party identification, perceived issue proximity, and respondents' own issue positions are based on the correlations among responses to each item in the three waves of the survey using the measurement error model proposed by Wiley and Wiley (1970). For Watergate attitudes, which were measured only in 1974, our estimates of reliability are the alpha reliability coefficients derived from the correlations among responses to the four distinct survey items making up our Watergate scale.

Table 10.2. The Impact of Watergate Attitudes on Perceptions of Issue Proximity, 1972–1976

	Liberal-conservative	Government jobs	School busing	Rights of accused	Aid to minorities	Weighted average
HIGH INFORMATION						
Watergate attitudes	−0.153 (0.061)	−0.060 (0.079)	−0.174 (0.083)	−0.180 (0.064)	−0.080 (0.073)	−0.134 (0.070)
1972 party identification	0.108 (0.043)	0.059 (0.048)	0.027 (0.044)	0.044 (0.035)	0.049 (0.036)	0.056 (0.040)
1972 issue proximity	0.648 (0.095)	0.829 (0.152)	0.490 (0.096)	0.627 (0.127)	0.855 (0.139)	0.648 (0.113)
Intercept	7.50 (1.57)	5.41 (2.28)	5.04 (2.44)	4.21 (1.61)	2.99 (1.83)	5.13 (1.83)
Standard error of regression	13.02	14.97	16.07	12.38	13.29	—
R^2	.54	.44	.31	.40	.45	—
N	316	309	279	268	313	—
LOW INFORMATION						
Watergate attitudes	−0.032 (0.054)	−0.049 (0.057)	0.131 (0.066)	−0.041 (0.050)	−0.004 (0.051)	−0.008 (0.055)
1972 party identification	0.163 (0.043)	0.091 (0.051)	0.206 (0.045)	0.102 (0.037)	0.129 (0.036)	0.137 (0.041)
1972 issue proximity	0.590 (0.116)	0.491 (0.117)	0.467 (0.096)	0.447 (0.127)	0.397 (0.128)	0.481 (0.114)
Intercept	0.87 (1.47)	1.41 (1.54)	−3.71 (1.79)	0.52 (1.24)	1.33 (1.29)	0.40 (1.42)
Standard error of regression	13.81	16.39	15.54	13.14	13.43	—
R^2	.42	.24	.32	.22	.19	—
N	286	323	268	275	303	—

Errors-in-variables regression parameter estimates (with standard errors in parentheses) for survey respondents in the top one-third and bottom two-thirds of the distribution of political information, respectively. Dependent variables are 1976 perceived issue proximities (−50 = closer to Democratic Party; +50 = closer to Republican Party).

analyses of the effects of Watergate attitudes on changing perceptions of issue proximity among respondents in the upper one-third of the overall distribution of political information (in the upper panel) and those in the lower two-thirds of the distribution (in the lower panel).[30] To facilitate interpretation of the results, we also present averages of the estimates for all five issues.[31]

The results presented in the first row of table 10.2 represent the estimated impact of Watergate attitudes on perceived issue proximity among high-information respondents. Our measure of perceived proximity ranges from −50 for people who perceived the Democratic Party's position as identical to their own and the Republican Party's position at the opposite end of the seven-point issue scale to +50 for people who perceived the Republican Party's position as identical to their own and the Democratic Party's position at the opposite end of the scale. We relate perceived proximity in 1976 to perceived proximity on the same issue scale in 1972, party identification in 1972, and Watergate attitudes.[32]

The negative estimated effects of Watergate attitudes in the top panel of table 10.2 indicate that, as expected, well-informed people who reacted especially strongly to the scandal tended to see themselves as further from the Republican Party (and closer to the Democratic Party) on every issue by 1976, other things being equal. On the other hand, people who were sympathetic to President Nixon and critical of his attackers tended to see themselves closer to the Republican Party (and further from the Democratic Party) as a result.[33] These estimates are fairly consistent across the five issues for which

30 This division of the sample reflects both our sense of the difficulty of the partisan inferences we are attempting to document here and the limitations of the ANES data. Less-informed people were less likely to answer the issue questions we are analyzing here, and they were significantly more likely to drop out of the panel between 1972 and 1976. Thus, a more natural-looking division of the sample into two equal halves would leave too few usable cases in the bottom half to provide any realistic hope of finding Watergate effects among less-informed people.

31 In order to reflect differences in the statistical uncertainty of the separate issue-specific parameter estimates, we report weighted averages in which each parameter estimate and standard error are weighted by the precision (the reciprocal of the squared standard error) of the relevant parameter estimate.

32 We include lagged party identification to allow for the possibility that partisan predispositions in place by the time of the 1972 survey produced partisan rationalization on specific issues between 1972 and 1976. However, since our model does not specify the timing of the inferential processes we posit, we have no strong reason to expect such effects. In contrast, the timing of the Watergate scandal virtually ensures that its effects, if any, will be visible within the compass of the four-year ANES survey.

33 The positive intercepts in these regression models imply that people with scores of zero on the Watergate scale generally saw themselves as increasingly close to the Republican Party

data are available, and in three of the five cases they are too large to be plausibly attributable to sampling error. Moreover, the implied effects are large enough to be politically consequential. For example, a difference of 35 points on the Watergate scale—roughly the difference between respondents at the 25th and 75th percentiles of the distribution—would imply a reduction in perceived distance from the Democratic Party of between two and six points on each of the 100-point issue proximity scales. (By comparison, the average total shifts on these scales from 1972 to 1976, including measurement error, ranged from 11 to 17 points.)

The bottom panel of table 10.2 presents analogous results for respondents in the bottom two-thirds of the distribution of political information. In marked contrast to the top panel, there is very little evidence here of changing perceptions of issue proximity in the wake of the Watergate scandal. Only one of the five separate estimates (for school busing) is comparable in magnitude to the average estimated effect for well-informed respondents, and it has the "wrong" sign (that is, the people who were most critical of Nixon saw themselves as closer to the Republican position on school busing). The average estimated effect for all five issues is almost exactly zero.

The changes in perceived issue proximity documented in table 10.2 could be attributable to either or both of the two distinct processes of rationalization distinguished by Richard Brody and Benjamin Page (1972). On one hand, new (or more committed) Democrats may have *projected* their own preexisting issue preferences onto the party, while viewing Republican positions with a more critical eye. On the other hand, they may have been *persuaded* to change their own issue positions, bringing them into closer alignment with their revised partisan sensibilities. The analyses reported in table 10.3 focus specifically on the latter possibility, estimating the impact of Watergate attitudes on respondents' own positions on the various issue scales included in the 1972–1976 ANES panel survey. In each case, respondents' issue positions are coded to range from −50 for the most conservative position on the 7-point ANES issue scale to +50 for the most liberal position. We relate respondents' positions on each issue in 1976 to their positions on the same issue in 1972, party identification in 1972, and Watergate attitudes.

---

by 1976. That may seem odd, given that the Democratic presidential nominee in 1972 was widely viewed as being more ideologically extreme than usual. However, it is worth bearing in mind that a score of zero on the Watergate scale actually represents a relatively sympathetic response; only one-fifth of all survey respondents, and only half of strong Republicans, had negative scale values.

Here, too, there is surprisingly strong evidence that Watergate attitudes reverberated in seemingly unrelated corners of the political landscape, at least for well-informed respondents. Those who were most critical of Nixon shifted to the left on government job guarantees, the rights of accused criminals, and school busing, while those who sympathized with him (or were critical of his critics in Congress and the media) became more conservative on those issues. As with the shifts in perceptions of issue proximity, the magnitudes of these shifts are considerable; a typical difference in Watergate attitudes translated into a difference of from two to six points in 1976 issue positions. (By comparison, the average total shifts on these scales from 1972 to 1976, including measurement error, ranged from 12 to 25 points.)[34]

Parallel analyses for less-informed people (reported in the bottom panel of table 10.3) produce one sizable negative estimate (for aid to minorities), but the average estimated effect across all five issues is only about one-third as large as the corresponding average estimated effect for better-informed people (and even that effect is too imprecisely estimated to be considered reliable). We attribute this difference to the fact that less-informed people lacked the contextual knowledge necessary to translate the partisan shock of Watergate into new positions on the range of logically unrelated issues examined here. Whereas the best-informed people were likely to associate views about the president and the parties with views about government jobs, school busing, and criminal justice procedures, most Americans failed to make those connections, and so their views about specific political issues were largely unaffected by the unmaking of the president.

The most obvious potential objection to the evidence presented in tables 10.2 and 10.3 is that the same people who were most affected by the Watergate scandal might have become more liberal between 1972 and 1976 for entirely different reasons. Reactions to the scandal were correlated with a variety of characteristics beyond partisanship and ideology; for example, better educated people were especially pleased to see President Nixon go, whereas southerners were somewhat more critical than non-southerners

---

34 As the estimated effects of 1972 issue positions in table 10.3 make clear, well-informed respondents' views about government jobs were considerably less stable than their views about other issue positions between 1972 and 1976. We interpret this instability as reflecting a shift in the debate about whether the government should try to provide every person with "a job and a good standard of living," from McGovern's controversial proposal to give $1,000 annual grants to every man, woman, and child in 1972 to discussions of more modest public works programs in 1976.

Table 10.3. The Impact of Watergate Attitudes on Issue Preferences, 1972–1976

	Liberal-conservative	Government jobs	School busing	Rights of accused	Aid to minorities	Weighted average
HIGH INFORMATION						
Watergate attitudes	−0.085 (0.063)	−0.228 (0.104)	−0.125 (0.064)	−0.161 (0.110)	−0.077 (0.101)	−0.122 (0.078)
1972 party identification	0.017 (0.038)	0.100 (0.056)	−0.040 (0.036)	−0.165 (0.059)	−0.018 (0.047)	−0.017 (0.044)
1972 issue position	0.850 (0.062)	0.458 (0.070)	0.807 (0.042)	0.897 (0.091)	0.840 (0.074)	0.775 (0.059)
Intercept	7.38 (1.60)	12.13 (2.71)	7.67 (2.21)	9.40 (2.64)	8.00 (2.36)	8.43 (2.13)
Standard error of regression	13.34	23.97	15.63	24.29	20.98	—
R^2	.66	.29	.63	.42	.48	—
N	325	348	356	344	353	—
LOW INFORMATION						
Watergate attitudes	0.085 (0.061)	−0.040 (0.076)	−0.078 (0.055)	−0.076 (0.079)	−0.155 (0.077)	−0.044 (0.067)
1972 party identification	0.079 (0.039)	0.098 (0.054)	−0.021 (0.040)	−0.061 (0.056)	0.006 (0.054)	0.024 (0.046)
1972 issue position	0.832 (0.096)	0.660 (0.074)	0.830 (0.069)	0.881 (0.078)	0.705 (0.068)	0.774 (0.075)
Intercept	−0.47 (1.69)	6.53 (2.06)	4.44 (3.27)	3.98 (2.05)	8.76 (2.02)	4.20 (2.04)
Standard error of regression	16.61	26.79	21.27	27.56	26.36	—
R^2	.38	.28	.36	.39	.33	—
N	343	456	509	451	448	—

Errors-in-variables regression parameter estimates (with standard errors in parentheses) for survey respondents in the top one-third and bottom two-thirds of the distribution of political information, respectively. Dependent variables are 1976 issue positions (−50 = extreme liberal; +50 = extreme conservative).

were of the House Judiciary Committee and the news media. If, for reasons unrelated to Watergate, better educated people were becoming more liberal during this period or southerners were becoming more conservative, those policy shifts may have been only spuriously related to their views about the Watergate scandal.

To assess that possibility, we replicated the analyses presented in tables 10.2 and 10.3 including a variety of demographic characteristics—including age, education, income, race, region, gender, marital status, home ownership, union membership, and church attendance—as additional explanatory factors. The results of those analyses generally confirmed the results presented in tables 10.2 and 10.3. Not surprisingly, the results of the more elaborate statistical analyses were somewhat less precise; nevertheless, both the magnitude and the consistency of our apparent Watergate effects held up quite well, with substantial effects detected among well-informed respondents but rather little evidence of changes in issue positions or perceived issue proximity among those in the bottom two-thirds of the distribution of political expertise.

Our data are not sufficiently powerful to rule out the possibility that even the views of relatively uninformed people were altered to some modest extent by their reactions to the Watergate scandal. For the most part, however, the contextual grasp of politics necessary to make an inferential leap from the scandal to economic and social policy issues seems to have eluded them. On the other hand, there is a good deal of evidence that well-informed people changed both their perceptions of issue proximity and their own views about a diverse assortment of issues in the wake of the Watergate scandal.

In summary, just as our theoretical expectations imply, the shock to established partisan attachments generated by the Watergate scandal altered people's views about a variety of specific political issues logically unrelated to the scandal. Moreover, these effects were concentrated among people who were especially well-informed about politics—in the top one-third of the national distribution of political expertise. Those who responded most negatively to Watergate moved significantly to the left, and saw themselves significantly closer to the Democratic Party, on a variety of issues by 1976.

If anyone had asked these well-informed citizens to explain the changes in their thinking about school busing or government employment programs between 1972 and 1976, we suspect that they would have provided rationalizations of exactly the sort posited by Rahn, Krosnick, and Breuning (1994, 592), "mentioning reasons that sound rational and systematic and that emphasize the object being evaluated, while overlooking more emotional reasons and factors other than the object's qualities." The overlooked factor in this case, we argue, was the essentially random partisan shock of a Republican president's disgrace and forced resignation. The observable ramifications of that shock among politically attentive people were surprisingly broad and consistent, and thus provide considerable empirical support for the account of partisan perception we have set out here.

CONCLUSION

Most of the time, voting behavior merely reaffirms voters' partisan and group identities. They do not rethink their fundamental political commitments with every election cycle. Insofar as they do consider new issues or circumstances, they often do so not in order to challenge and revise their fundamental commitments, but in order to bolster those commitments by constructing preferences or beliefs consistent with them. They sound like they are thinking, and they feel like they are thinking. We all do. The unwary scholarly devotee of democratic romanticism is thereby easily misled.

When proponents of the folk theory do recognize such pseudo-thinking, they tend to attribute it to political ignorance and inattention—a failure to live up to the high ideals of democratic citizenship. But that view misunderstands the nature of the problem. In fact, political rationalization is often most powerful among people who are well-informed and politically engaged, since their fundamental political commitments tend to be most consistent and strongly held. The result is that the political behavior of well-informed people often displays a sort of stasis grounded in the consistency of their partisan commitments. John Zaller (2004, 166), in a detailed study of voting behavior in U.S. presidential elections, found well-informed voters "resisting short-term forces," while the less-informed were "typically more responsive to the content of individual elections," "more apt to reward incumbents who preside over strong national economies and punish those who do not," "more reactive to changes in the ideological location of the candidates," and "at least as likely . . . to respond to presidential success or failure in foreign affairs." In short, political sophistication *dampened* voters' responsiveness to the very considerations that the folk theory of democracy portrays as the appropriate bases of electoral choice.

Better-informed voters may be logically consistent and even "rational" in the thin technical sense of that term, but the truth of the matter is that they— and all of us, most of the time—exist in what Walter Lippmann (1922, 10) referred to as a "pseudo-environment" only loosely connected to the real environment where action eventuates. If the behavior is not a practical act, but what we call roughly thought and emotion, it may be a long time before there is any noticeable break in the texture of the fictitious world. But when the stimulus of the pseudo-fact results in action on things or other people, contradiction soon develops. Then comes the sensation of butting one's head against a stone wall, of learning by experience, . . . of the murder of a Beautiful Theory by a Gang of Brutal Facts, the discomfort in short of a maladjustment.

For many people, of course, the discomfort of maladjustment never comes, either because they never emerge from the world of thought and emotion into the world of practical action, or because the concrete consequences of their misperceptions are too indirect for them to apprehend. They exist comfortably in their false but efficient pseudo-environments. Thin rationality of this sort is a far cry from "the notion of a competent citizenry" set out (and criticized) by James Kuklinski and Paul Quirk (2000). Democratic competence requires not only logical consistency and cognitive efficiency, but also some modicum of accuracy in perception and receptiveness to new and, perhaps, disconfirming evidence. In Amartya Sen's (1977) phrase, it is perfectly possible to be a rational fool.

Consider, once again, the example of the federal budget deficit. John Mark Hansen (1998) provided a detailed analysis of data from a 1995 ANES pilot study in which people were invited to favor or oppose a variety of possible departures from current fiscal policy—raising taxes to reduce the budget deficit, increasing the budget deficit to fund increases in spending on domestic programs, and so forth. The series of questions was carefully designed to allow people to provide logically inconsistent responses—for example, wanting to increase the budget deficit in order to increase domestic spending, but then in a separate question wanting to cut domestic spending in order to reduce the budget deficit. Hansen found very few logical inconsistencies of this sort. On the basis of his analysis, he concluded (1998, 519) that "the public has the ability to make budget policy choices with reasonable discernment. . . . They have well-formed and well-behaved preferences."

One would hardly guess that these are the same people who, one year later, were largely oblivious to the fact that the federal budget deficit had declined by more than half over the preceding few years. Could people so blatantly unaware of such a salient and politically consequential fact possibly "make budget policy choices with reasonable discernment"? Hansen's (1998, 526) assertion that "American democracy does not want for the competence of its citizens" seems hasty, if not wishful.

In sum, we have suggested here that the average citizen's perception of the federal budget deficit is constructed mostly of folk wisdom and partisan surmise, with a trace element of reality.[35] Viewed from the perspective of the folk theory, that is not a promising basis for wise political thinking, nor for sensible voting. Ordinary citizens may indeed do their best to construct consistent, subjectively plausible perceptions of a complex political world. And in practice, they may often succeed in making their beliefs, their policy preferences, and their vote choices fit together coherently. They sound like they're thinking. But their consistency is often driven by group loyalties and partisan biases, even when it comes to straightforward matters of fact. Thus, while the political psychology depicted in this chapter may be interpreted as remarkably efficient low-information rationality, it is a sort of rationality that should be deeply troubling to enthusiasts of democracy—especially when, as Lippmann (1922, 14) asserted almost a century ago, "these fictions determine a very great part of men's political behavior."

The characterization of human thought in politics that we have set out in this chapter may seem shocking, cynical, implausible, or at least exaggerated. But it follows naturally from the power of group loyalties. Of course, politics is no different from other domains of life in this respect. More than a century ago, Lowell (1913, 87) observed that "the influence of membership in an organized body is a force to be reckoned with, and its effect on men's judgments in all the relations of life is too obvious to require elaboration." Indeed, isolated or deviant individuals tend to be ignored, shunted aside, and discriminated against in group activities. Thus, most people are powerfully attracted to group membership and to the ideological self-justifications that sustain group life.

In the political sphere, the most salient groups are parties, and the self-justifications that sustain group life are primarily grounded in—and constructed to maintain—partisan loyalties. People tend to adopt beliefs, attitudes, and values that reinforce and rationalize their partisan loyalties. But those loyalties, not beliefs or ideologies or policy commitments, are fundamental to understanding how they think and act.

35 The relative weights of these ingredients are assessed much more exactly by Achen and Bartels (2006).

Groups and Power: Toward a Realist Theory of Democracy

> One consequence of our reliance on old definitions is that the modern American does not look at democracy before he defines it; he defines it first and then is confused by what he sees.... We become cynical about democracy because the public does not act the way the simplistic definition of democracy says that it should act, or we try to whip the public into doing things it does not want to do, is unable to do, and has too much sense to do. The crisis here is not a crisis in democracy but a crisis in theory.
>
> —E. E. Schattschneider, *The Semisovereign People* (1960, 127, 131)

Proponents of democracy have long thought that human dignity required self-government. People should choose their leaders at the polls and hold them accountable. Voters should be *represented*, not just governed. Reflecting Enlightenment optimism about human nature, along with skepticism about tradition and hierarchy, the argument for democracy supposed that good citizens would engage in thoughtful monitoring of their government. The abuses of kings, aristocrats, commissars, and dictators would be eliminated. Democratic norms would be enforced by the shared values of an enlightened populace. Mistakes would occur, of course, but they would be the people's own mistakes, and thus susceptible to quick recognition and reversal. Most of the time, democratic government would be very good government indeed.

As we have seen, this folk theory of democracy came to dominate American thinking, both popular and scholarly. Sovereignty rests with the people. A government derives its just powers not merely from the *consent* of the governed, but from their political *judgments*. That foundational logic now constitutes the accepted popular wisdom in virtually every established democracy, even in those whose original logic was quite different, such as parliamentary systems.

Widespread consensus for more than a century about the best form of government and its justification has impeded thought. "*Why* is democracy the best form of government?" has not struck most democratic citizens as a challenging question. And when that question *has* been asked, bromides and platitudes have generally sufficed as answers. Proponents of democracy have seldom found hard-nosed critics scrutinizing their logic and evidence, line by line.

Despite the cultural centrality of the folk theory of democracy, a few thoughtful observers in every era have recognized the limitations of conventional democratic thought and of the 19th-century liberal conceptual framework on which it is based, as we saw in chapter 1. Thus, a critical tradition is by no means lacking. Indeed, our observation in this book that Fourth of July rhetoric is a poor guide to understanding public opinion and elections in contemporary democracies breaks little genuinely new ground. For more than a century after the rise of mass democracy, skeptical commentators pointed out gaps between romanticized democratic theory and the actually workings of democracy, a tradition that continues to the present day (Milne and Mackenzie 1958, chap. 13; Riker 1982; Mueller 1999; Przeworski 2010). Every few years, another book, perhaps employing new data and the fashionable scientific methodology of the season, announces similar findings. In most cases, the authors examine the evidence, find the foundations of popular democratic theories inadequate, approach the edge of the critical abyss, and then skittishly back off, finding one or another reason why all must be—or soon will be—well after all. Defenses of the conventional faith, conceding a few difficulties but affirming the fundamental verities, generally predominate in both popular and scholarly conversation.

Those defenses, never very plausible to begin with, are by now in tatters. Few scholars of political behavior take them seriously as an empirical account of democracy. However, many thinkers implicitly or explicitly continue to embrace the folk theory as a normative benchmark, and few draw the seemingly logical conclusion that a new and distinctively different theory is needed.

Unfortunately, we are not prepared to supply, in this concluding chapter, a well-worked-out, new theory of democracy. However, we do summarize our evidence regarding the failures of existing theories of democracy, clear some of the intellectual ground on which a more realistic theory might be built, and highlight some of the key concepts and concerns that are likely to loom large in it. For example, we show that our framework best fits the evidence from the greatest electoral disaster of the 20th century, the victory of Adolf Hitler in the final free elections of Weimar Germany. And, for readers who may be more interested in *democracy* than in *democratic theory*, we also consider some of the practical implications of our analysis for efforts to construct a truly "more democratic" political system. But first we review the argument and evidence presented in this book and where they have brought us out.

DEMOCRATIC CITIZENS AND THE POPULIST IDEAL OF DEMOCRACY

The assumptions underlying the folk theory of democracy are very stringent. Can ordinary people, busy with their lives and with no firsthand experience of policy-making or public administration, do what the theory expects them to do? Can they formulate policy preferences, assess where candidates stand on the issues, set aside cognitive biases and group prejudices, and then choose a candidate who embodies an uplifting version of their own policy views? Can human nature meet those demands? Aristotle famously said that "a human being is by nature a political animal." But what kind of animal is that? The promise and the limits of democracy turn on the answer to that question.

As we showed in chapter 2, the answer is that real people are not much like the citizens imagined by the folk theory. Numerous studies have demonstrated that most residents of democratic countries have little interest in politics and do not follow news of public affairs beyond browsing the headlines. They do not know the details of even salient policy debates, they do not have a firm understanding of what the political parties stand for, and they often vote for parties whose long-standing issue positions are at odds with their own. Mostly, they identify with ethnic, racial, occupational, religious, or other sorts of groups, and often—whether through group ties or hereditary loyalties—with a political party. Even the more attentive citizens mostly adopt the policy positions of the parties as their own: they are mirrors of the parties, not masters. For most citizens most of the time, party and group loyalties are the primary drivers of vote choices.

Thus, the folk theory of democracy fails. For the same reasons, so do scholarly renditions of the folk theory, including mathematical versions like the spatial theory of voting, as we have seen. The folk theory is like the ether theory of electromagnetic and gravitational forces: it is based on 19th-century intellectual foundations, and the empirical evidence has passed it by. Moreover, the internal contradictions in that conceptual framework, illuminated by Arrow's theorem, cut off all obvious escape routes from the conclusion that the folk theory is fundamentally unworkable.

Chapter 2 also discussed the notion that voters can use "cues" to get the right political answers without following the news or understanding government policies. Some scholars have placed great stock in that idea (Popkin 1991; Lupia 1994; Lupia and McCubbins 1998). Unfortunately, as we saw in chapter 2, the idea works much less well in practice than in theory. Many voters pay no attention to the relevant cues; others find them hard to interpret—often because the cues are less informative than their proponents suppose. In any case, taking cues is no protection from thinking and voting wrong, and people do a great deal of that (Bartels 1996; Lau and Redlawsk 1997; Althaus 1998). The so-called miracle of aggregation—summing the choices of many citizens and hoping that their errors are offsetting—tends to dilute the resulting "errors," but certainly does not eliminate them, as we also saw in chapter 2. Thus, cues won't save populist theories of democracy.

Nor will party government, at least in its usual guise. As we discussed in chapter 9, many democratic citizens have durable partisan loyalties. Often those loyalties become part of the voter's social identity ("party identification").[1] If partisan loyalties reflected voters' considered ideological judgments, then the powerful impact of partisanship in elections would reflect thoughtful democratic citizenship, and voters would be electing representatives who reliably shared their political commitments. For historical reasons, this version of electoral theory has been most influential in Europe, but it is also reflected in American discussions of "the doctrine of responsible party government" (Schattschneider 1942; Committee on Political Parties 1950; Ranney 1962), and in some empirical studies of voting inspired by the "spatial model" of Anthony Downs (1957), which we examined in chapter 2.[2]

The main problem with this defense of democracy is that partisanship often has little real ideological content. As we have seen, while most voters do have at least a few more or less strongly held issue preferences, those preferences rarely cohere into consistent ideological positions. Nor need they neatly match the platform of any particular party. Most important, citizens often choose parties for reasons unrelated to ideology. As a result, the policies

1 As we noted in chapter 10, many democratic countries lack "party identification" in the American sense, but the great majority exhibit continuing voter loyalty to parties or party groupings at the ballot box.

2 Jeffrey Grynaviski (2010) provided a sophisticated, updated account of partisan voting and party government in the contemporary United States.

espoused by political parties are routinely at odds with the preferences of the people who vote for them, even after partisan loyalists adjust some of their ideas to match those of their party, as we saw in chapters 2 and 10. Whatever it is that partisan loyalties represent, it is mostly *not* ideology or issue congruence. The parties represent their voters, if they do, in some quite different way. Partisanship arises because a party presided over an economic recovery from a devastating depression, or because the party embodies bonds of racial or ethnic or class solidarity, or simply because we have been taught since childhood that a particular party represents "people like us." Issue congruence between parties and their voters, insofar as it exists, is largely a byproduct of these other connections, most of them lacking policy content.[3]

Academic theorists of democracy (with the notable exception of Rosenblum 2008) have shown little enthusiasm for political parties and partisanship. Indeed, they have often seemed unimpressed by mere electoral democracy, and thus uninterested in the pressing questions of institutional design and legitimacy raised by analyses like ours. Instead, much (and much of the best) contemporary political theory has focused on highly idealistic models of *participatory* or *deliberative* democracy (Pateman 1970; Barber 1984; Habermas 1994; Fishkin 1995; Benhabib 1996; Gutmann and Thompson 1996; Macedo 1999; Cohen 2003). These models of democracy emphasize—indeed, they often simply assume—rationality, mutual consideration, and the patient exchange of publicly justified reasons for supporting specific policies. Thus, they rest on essentially the same unrealistic expectations about human nature embodied in the folk theory. And like the folk theory, they are significantly undermined by what has been learned since the Enlightenment about human cognition and social life (Sanders 1997; Mendelberg and Oleske 2000).

Whatever else deliberation in its more refined and philosophically approved forms may have going for it, it is very likely to be distinctly *un*democratic in practice, since "many people do not have much desire to engage in political debate to begin with" (Mutz 2006, 10) and are intensely averse to political disagreement (Eliasoph 1998; Hibbing and Theiss-Morse 2002). Hence, they often fall silent in deliberative settings, letting better-educated and more prominent citizens dominate, as Mansbridge (1980, chaps. 9–11) found in New England town meetings. This is a telling indication that

---

3 Of course, as we saw in chapter 2, voters' expressed views during political campaigns often match those of their party, but that correlation mostly occurs because the parties and candidates teach their voters what to say, not vice versa (Lenz 2012).

theorists of deliberative democracy are "try[ing] to whip the public into doing things it does not want to do, is unable to do, and has too much sense to do" (Schattschneider 1960, 131). Most ordinary citizens do not *want* politics to be more like a philosophy seminar.

Perhaps for that reason, the practical impact of deliberative theory has been quite modest. The most cited and studied attempts to "scale up" these idealized models of democratic decision-making were large-scale, government-sponsored "citizens' assemblies" intended to consider changes in the election laws of the Canadian provinces of British Columbia and Ontario (Warren and Pearse 2008; Fournier et al. 2011). In each case, a body of ordinary citizens engaged in an elaborately funded year-long process of education, consultation, and deliberation aimed at recommending a new voting rule to be employed in provincial elections. And in each case, their nearly unanimous recommendation was decisively rejected by their fellow citizens in a subsequent referendum.[4] We do not know what combination of deliberative shortcomings, public inattention, and partisan conflict may have been to blame; but if the point of the assemblies was to shape the judgment of the broader electorate, this seemingly worthwhile Canadian initiative was an expensive, dramatic failure.

While political theories grounded in misguided assumptions about human nature are usually of little practical import, the dispute over the folk theory and its alternatives is not just an academic squabble, a tempest in a classroom teapot. The folk theory has also structured how everyday citizens and important political figures have understood American government and American ideals. In consequence, foolish reform movements have relied on its teachings, giving us flat-earth pronouncements about how government should work. As we saw in chapter 3, the results in American politics—excessive reliance on referendums at the state level and the dilution of the influence of knowledgeable party officials in the choice of presidential candidates—have strengthened the hand of narrow interest groups and often resulted in self-defeating choices by the electorate. We argued, for example, that voters' choices made a mess of car insurance, damaged their children's dental health, and even let homes be burned down. In the same way, every presidential primary season exposes the

---

4 In British Columbia, the final report of the citizen assembly was issued in the midst of the holiday season and put to a vote in a provincial general election five months later, with very little coverage of the proposed electoral reform. The proposal received 58% of the vote, with 60% needed for enactment. When a second referendum was held four years later with much greater media coverage, support for the proposed reform fell to 39%. Ontario had only a single referendum, scheduled two years after the report of the citizen assembly was issued. It, too, produced less than 40% support for the citizen assembly's recommendation.

dangers of voter fatigue with familiar, experienced politicians and their enthusiasm for hopelessly unqualified but clever demagogues known only from a few television appearances.

As we have seen, effective democracy requires an appropriate balance between popular preferences and elite expertise. The point of reform should not simply be to maximize popular influence in the political process, but to facilitate *more effective* popular influence. We need to learn to let political parties and political leaders do their jobs, too. Simple-minded attempts to thwart or control political elites through initiatives, direct primaries, and term limits will often be counterproductive. Far from empowering the citizenry, the plebiscitary implications of the folk theory have often damaged people's real interests.

In this book, we have argued that citizens in contemporary democracies exhibit profound limitations, just as human beings always have. But too much thinking about democracy takes at face value the self-justifying rationalizations we supply for ourselves, papering over the reality of how we actually think and act. In the theory, as in our self-images, we are well-informed, thoughtful, fair-minded people dedicated to the good of all. In reality, as Schattschneider (1960, 131) observed, "the public does not act the way the simplistic definition of democracy says that it should act."

DEMOCRATIC CITIZENS AND THE RETROSPECTIVE THEORY OF DEMOCRACY

Mountains of evidence have accumulated establishing the limitations of people's thinking about political issues and ideology. From the viewpoint of the naive folk theory, it is all quite depressing. In consequence, contemporary scholars of public opinion and electoral politics have sought to rethink the role of citizens in democratic systems. Many of them have turned to evaluations of political leaders and governmental performance as the primary basis of ordinary citizens' political thinking and behavior. As we saw in chapter 4, the resulting theory of *retrospective voting* offers more scope for political leadership than the conventional populist theory does, and it takes more realistic account of the limits of citizens' political knowledge. It requires only that voters know whether times have been good or bad under the current administration. If times have been good, voters should reelect the incumbents; if times have been bad, voters should throw the bums out.

However, as we also saw in chapter 4, for this mechanism to work effectively, voters must do two things well. First, they must be able to discern the specific role of the government's diligence and competence in producing the pain or pleasure they experience. Punishing the incumbents for events beyond their control makes no more sense than kicking the dog to get back at a difficult boss at work. And second, they must be able to evaluate sensibly whether times have been good or bad under the incumbent government. This may sound simple, but it is not. Citizens are unlikely to know whether crime has gone up or down, only whether gruesome murders appear in the local news. Their judgments about the seriousness of environmental threats are virtually uncorrelated with those of experts. Even in the domain of the economy, where detailed statistical information is plentiful and retrospective voting is a powerful electoral force, voters may fixate on current conditions to the neglect of the incumbent's full record.

Hence, as we have shown, citizens routinely fail in both these respects. Our analyses in chapter 5 of "blind retrospection" show that governments are punished willy-nilly for bad times, including bad times clearly due to events beyond the government's control. Voters along the Jersey Shore punished the incumbent president, Woodrow Wilson, for the panic and economic dislocation stemming from a dramatic series of shark attacks in 1916, reducing his vote share there by as much as 10 percentage points. Wilson was not responsible for the shark attacks; there was nothing he or his administration could have done to prevent them; remediation in the form of disaster assistance or unemployment benefits would have required legislation, bureaucratic capacity, and a conception of the role of government that did not exist at the time. Yet the voters punished anyway.

Even if some concrete dereliction on the part of Wilson's administration might have justified the political disaffection along the Jersey Shore in 1916, it would not account for the fact that incumbents are *routinely* punished for conditions beyond their control. We showed in chapter 5 that over the course of the entire 20th century, the president's party suffered at the polls in times and places that were too wet or too dry. Presidents do not cause droughts, and there is nothing they can do to prevent them. Nowadays, they can do something to ameliorate their effects, but that in itself does not account for the electoral pattern we discerned. If some incumbents were being punished for worse-than-average *responses* to droughts and floods, then just as many should have been rewarded for better-than-average responses. Yet, over the course of an entire century, the voters punished incumbents much more often than they rewarded them.

These findings suggest that voters have great difficulty making sensible attributions of responsibility for hard times. However, it is still more troubling to find that voters have great difficulty simply assessing whether times have been good or bad over the course of an incumbent's term in office. In chapter 6 we examined electoral responses to economic conditions—the most familiar and intensively studied instance of retrospective voting. We found, as other scholars have, that voters are extremely sensitive to income growth in the months leading up to elections. However, rather than simply celebrating this consistent electoral response to objective economic conditions, we proceeded to explore its implications for effective political accountability. The downside of sensitivity to short-term income growth is a remarkable *in*sensitivity to long-term economic performance. Our analyses indicated that income growth before the election year had little effect on the incumbent party's prospects at the polls. Jimmy Carter in the 1980 presidential election was punished for an election-year recession, despite considerable economic growth earlier in his term; Ronald Reagan in 1984 was reelected in a landslide thanks to an election-year boom, despite lackluster growth earlier in his term.

Because economic conditions fluctuate substantially over time, this myopic quirk in voters' assessments of economic performance induces substantial randomness in electoral rewards and punishments, in the sense that voters will reward and punish for reasons unrelated to competence. One implication is that myopic voters are unlikely to succeed in selecting competent economic managers; and indeed we find no evidence that their assessments of incumbent administrations predict subsequent economic performance. Another implication is that myopic voters are unlikely to succeed in motivating incumbents to pursue sustained economic growth, since there is little electoral payoff for growth outside the election year; and indeed we find a substantial "electoral cycle" in economic performance, with real income growth peaking in election years and falling substantially after the polls close.

In ordinary times, the foibles we have identified in retrospective voting significantly hamper prospects for effective political accountability. That is a substantial blow to the view that retrospection might provide an attractive alternative to the populist understanding of elections. However, one might still think that moments of crisis focus voters' minds, allowing for more sensible retrospective verdicts or even for meaningful collective judgments about the appropriate course of public policy. Thus, in chapter 7 we turned to the Great Depression, the greatest domestic crisis in modern American history. Did voters in the 1930s transcend the pattern of myopic retrospective voting evident in chapter 6?

Our conclusion is that they did not. Whereas previous scholars have characterized Franklin Roosevelt's landslide reelection in 1936 as a popular ratification of his New Deal agenda, we found that his electoral support in 1936 was grounded in the same sensitivity to election-year income growth we documented in chapter 6. Indeed, our analysis suggests that if the recession of 1938 had occurred two years earlier, FDR would not have been reelected, bringing the New Deal (and the New Deal realignment of the American party system) to a shrieking halt, long before the many achievements of his subsequent terms.

Our interpretation of U.S. voting behavior in the 1930s as myopically retrospective rather than ideological is bolstered by considering Depression-era election outcomes elsewhere. Simply put, the American notion of an ideological realignment does not travel well. Where conservatives were in power when the Depression hit, as in the United States, they were generally replaced by more liberal parties. But where relatively leftist governments were in power they were often replaced by more conservative parties, as in Britain and Australia. When coalition politics or successive failures in office discredited all the viable mainstream parties, unhappy citizens turned to extremist parties or to violent protest. Thus, for example, the Canadian prairie province of Alberta replaced its agrarian socialist government with the Social Credit Party, an untried funny-money party led by a charismatic radio preacher. The economy revived (as it did in other parts of Canada, the United States, and elsewhere at the same time), and the Social Credit Party became the dominant force in provincial politics for decades thereafter.

Academic theorists of democracy sometimes dismiss the retrospective theory of political accountability as a hopelessly thin and uninspiring account of democracy. Our concern is different—that it simply does not work. Our analyses cast profound doubt on retrospective voting as a reliable basis for good government. Thus, the retrospective theory of democracy will not bear the normative weight that its enthusiastic proponents want to place on it. Politics is a complex subject. Voters may indeed find retrospective judgment "easier" than sophisticated ideological reasoning, but not easy enough.

Where does this leave the current state of democratic theory? The short answer is: in a shambles. *All* the conventional defenses of democratic government are at odds with demonstrable, centrally important facts of political life. One has to believe six impossible things before breakfast to take real comfort in any of them. Some of the standard defenses romanticize human nature, some mathematize it, and others bowdlerize it, but they all have one thing in common: they do not portray human beings realistically, nor take honest account of our human limitations. For democratic theorists, that is the central challenge, which we addressed in the final third of this book.

DEMOCRATIC CITIZENS AND SOCIAL GROUPS

James Madison argued in Federalist Number 10 and Number 51 that in politics, human beings are not angels. We care more about ourselves than about the common good, and we are prone to faction. Madison's insights have been extended and deepened in the two centuries since he wrote, as we reviewed in chapter 8. Factions are visible in group attachments of all kinds—kinship, ethnic, racial, religious, occupational, and national—and they are powerful in political life (Bentley 1908). Contemporary understandings of "identity" in politics have reinforced and deepened this long-standing intellectual tradition of seeing people as embedded in human groups that are meaningful to them. Religious, ethnic, occupational, and other affiliations all range from nominal to central in people's lives. When people define themselves in terms of one of these categories, they have an identity.

The most important "factions" in politics are the parties, and they are central to any realist view of electoral politics. We have argued that voters choose political parties, first and foremost, in order to align themselves with the appropriate coalition of social groups.[5] Most citizens support a party not because they have carefully calculated that its policy positions are closest to their own, but rather because "their kind" of person belongs to that party. When people are asked what they like and dislike about political parties, or what characterizes the different parties, they often talk about perceived ties between the parties and prominent social groups (Campbell et al. 1960, chap. 10). Their own partisan identities are likewise frequently bound up in their social identities and commitments.

Thus, we found in chapter 9 that ethnic groups in Boston responded to the New Deal in quite different ways, and that group politics rather than policy calculations seemed to account most satisfactorily for those differences. Similarly, Catholics and Protestants in 1960 responded to John F. Kennedy quite differently than they had to previous (and subsequent) Democratic presidential candidates—not because his policy platform departed significantly from his party's traditional stances, but because his own identity as a Catholic activated powerful cultural loyalties and antipathies. And, most dramatically, we interpreted the monumental partisan realignment of southern whites in the second half of the 20th century as primarily driven not by changes in the

---

5 Note that this formulation is different from the older notion that parties are coalitions of *interest* groups. Social groups may or may not have organized interest groups representing them.

party's racial policy commitments but by changes in the political resonance of (white) southern identity. Thus, white southerners who felt most warmly about "southerners" as a group were the biggest contributors to the massive partisan shift; their attachment to the Democratic Party declined by almost 40 points over the course of four decades, while the corresponding decline among those with neutral feelings toward "southerners" was less than half as large. By comparison, policy preferences seem to have been much less important; Democratic support declined at fairly similar rates among supporters and opponents of racial integration, while views about government aid to blacks only sharply distinguished Democrats and Republicans beginning in the 1980s, well into the long process of realignment.

We also explored in chapter 9 how people balance multiple group identities, focusing in particular on the case of abortion. Changes in the party's policy stands over the course of the 1980s and 1990s produced significant conflicts for pro-choice Republicans and pro-life Democrats. Both were increasingly faced with a contradiction between their own views about abortion and those of their party. As a result, almost half of pro-choice Republican women in 1982 abandoned the party by 1997; but the effect was much smaller among men—a difference we attribute to the greater significance of abortion in the gender identities of women than of men. Conversely, and perhaps more surprisingly, we also found substantial changes in views about abortion in response to partisan influence, especially among men. For example, more than half of pro-life men who were Democrats in 1982 adopted pro-choice views by 1997, while only about one-fourth of pro-life men who were Republicans in 1982 did so. The difference reflects the impact of partisan loyalties and rhetoric on people's views about one of the most salient and wrenching moral issues of the era.

Our analysis of abortion politics sheds useful light on a common circumstance—friction between politically inconsistent social identities. A career military officer whose military service is central to his life may gravitate to his country's conservative nationalist party, even if his union family background makes him uncomfortable with the party's frequent pro-business stands. A member of the clergy whose vocation is defined by service to the poor may identify with the left-leaning social democratic party, even if that party is often lukewarm about religious groups. People sort out their group loyalties in ways that are meaningful to them, giving priority to some commitments while downplaying others. The result is that no group's members belong exclusively to one party. But that is an *implication* of our account, not a disconfirmation of it. Partisan loyalties reflect the way people understand their own lives, jobs, religious views, ancestral identities, family traditions, and personal ties. For ordinary citizens, parties make sense—if they make sense at all—in social identity terms, not as ideological frameworks.

When political candidates court the support of groups, they are judged in part on whether they can "speak our language." Small-business owners, union members, evangelical Christians, international corporations—each of these has a set of ongoing concerns and challenges, and a vocabulary for discussing them. Knowing those concerns, using that vocabulary, and making commitments to take them seriously is likely to be crucial for a politician to win their support (Fenno 1978).

Of course, talk is not the same thing as action. The problem of holding politicians accountable for pursuing group interests involves significant difficulties. The task may be simplified when the politicians themselves are members of the relevant groups. For example, David Broockman (2013) found that African-American legislators were considerably more likely than comparable white legislators to provide assistance to African-American citizens living outside their districts. And Nicholas Carnes (2013) showed that members of Congress with personal experience working in blue-collar jobs took significantly more liberal positions on economic policy issues as a result, even after allowing for the effects of party, district characteristics, and other factors. Similarly, Barry Burden (2007) showed that a variety of personal characteristics of American legislators sometimes cause them to deviate from party orthodoxy.

Thus, the familiar tendency for voters to gravitate toward political leaders of their own stripe—a backward, tribal dereliction of duty in some high-brow versions of the folk theory—may have concrete payoffs. More often, however, the party does not or cannot do much for the group. Usually, that seems not to matter (Egan 2013). That fact underlines the point that group politics does not automatically mitigate the challenges to effective political accountability we examined in chapter 4.

VOTER RATIONALITY AND RATIONALIZATION

In interviews, citizens often sound more ideological and conventionally "rational" than our description of them would suggest. That fact has led some scholars, particularly those who do fieldwork with extensive personal interviews, to suppose that somehow all the other scientific evidence is misleading. People make good sense: just listen to them!

Alas, as we showed in chapter 10, the apparent rationality is itself often misleading—a byproduct rather than the foundation of group politics.

Citizens tend to adopt the views of the parties and groups they favor. If they are unusually highly engaged in politics, they may even develop ideological frameworks rationalizing their group loyalties and denigrating those of their political opponents. Sometimes they even construct convenient "facts" to help support their group loyalties. The reasoned explanations they provide for their own beliefs and behavior are often just post hoc justifications of their social or partisan loyalties. Well-informed citizens are likely to have more elaborate and internally consistent worldviews than inattentive people do, but that just reflects the fact that their rationalizations are better rehearsed. For example, as we saw in the case of the budget deficit, the political beliefs of more attentive, knowledgeable citizens are often *more* subject to partisan bias than those of their less attentive neighbors. For most people most of the time, social identities and partisan loyalties color political *perceptions* as well as political *opinions*.

The role of political "sophistication" in analyses of this sort underlines the fact that the task of being a good citizen by the standards of conventional democratic theory is too hard for *everyone*. Attentive readers will already have surmised our view of intellectuals in politics, but for clarity, we spell it out here. The historical record leaves little doubt that the educated, including the highly educated, have gone astray in their moral and political judgments as often as anyone else. In the antebellum era, prominent southern professors and university administrators often defended slavery (Faust 1981). Brilliant 19th-century German professors helped give shape to German nationalism and the racial identity theories that led to Nazism, and German university students in the 1930s were often enthusiastic supporters of Hitler (Meinecke 1925, esp. 377–433; Kershaw 1998, 76, 80). Protestant and secular professors backed Otto von Bismarck's campaign to suppress the civil liberties of Catholics in 19th-century Germany (Gross 2004). Crude prejudice against Catholics, Jews, and others was common among American intellectuals until recent decades, too (Billington 1938; McGreevy 2003).

More recently, 20th-century communism attracted many highly educated people around the world. Numerous French intellectuals supported Russian communism well after its crimes had been exposed (Aron 1957; Caute 1964). Radical Chinese intellectuals backed Mao Zedong's campaign to establish his regime and keep it in power—a regime that eventually became, not just a relentless oppressor of intellectuals, but the most murderous government in the history of the world (Goldman 1981; Townsend and Womack 1986, 58–62). In the United States, prominent political science professors became advisors to the American government during the disastrous Vietnam

War, while others naively favored Ho Chi Minh in his ultimately successful effort to establish a repressive communist state in that country (Halberstam 1972).

Of course, a great many other people in each of these countries made the same or other equally appalling judgments. The point is simply that, as Gustave Le Bon (1895, 122) put it more than a century ago, "It does not follow because an individual knows Greek or mathematics, is an architect, a veterinary surgeon, a doctor, or a barrister, that he is endowed with a special intelligence of social questions. . . . Were the electorate solely composed of persons stuffed with sciences their votes would be no better than those emitted at present." Gifted in their own spheres, artists and intellectuals have no special expertise in politics. In our political judgments and actions, we all make mistakes, sometimes even morally indefensible errors. Thus, when we say that voters routinely err, we mean *all* voters. This is not a book about the political misjudgments of people with modest educations. It is a book about the conceptual limitations of human beings—including the authors of this book and its readers. As Walter Lippmann (1925, 10–11) remarked, "I have not happened to meet anybody, from a President of the United States to a professor of political science, who came anywhere near to embodying the accepted ideal of the sovereign and omnicompetent citizen."

A REALIST VIEW OF ELECTIONS

How, then, do elections actually work? In the contemporary United States, Democrats, Republicans, and Independents make up roughly equal shares of the population. Political campaigns consist in large part of reminding voters of their partisan identities—"mobilizing" them to support their group at the polls. Formal communications by the groups and informal communication networks among group members also help citizens understand how their identity groups connect to the candidates and parties (Harris-Lacewell 2004).

In consequence, the great majority of Democrats and Republicans consistently support their party in each election. As the first American political scientist, Francis Lieber (1839, 427–430), observed long ago, political parties teach us what to think about politics much more often than we teach them. Thus, at election time, voters choose a party validating their social and political identities, then rationalize their decisions with appropriate party-supplied reasons. The specific circumstances of a given election may occasionally inspire significant defections from standing partisan loyalties; but those, too, often reflect the heightened salience of specific religious, racial, or gender identities rather than voters' issue preferences. Many self-described "Independents" disdain party labels but admit to "leaning" toward one party or the other. They are subject to many of the same forces, and end up acting more or less like partisans at the polls (Keith et al. 1992). And because the parties are of approximately equal size, all these effects approximately cancel out at the ballot box.

Vote choices by "pure" Independents are different. While they, too, have group ties and social identities, they are often quite unclear about which groups "belong" in which party. Typically less-informed, they may fail to grasp what is at stake in the choice of one party or another, much less where their overall interests lie. Thus, they are often swept along by the familiarity of an incumbent, the charisma of a fresh challenger, or a sense that it is "time for a change," even when the government did not cause the current unsatisfactory situation and cannot greatly alter it. When the party balance is close—and there seems to be a "law of the pendulum" ensuring that it usually will be close in two-party systems (Lowell 1898; Munro 1928, chap. 3; Stokes and Iversen 1962; Bartels 1998)—election outcomes turn on how these "swing voters" happen to feel when they go to the polls. As Philip Converse (1962, 578) put it, "Not only is the electorate as a whole quite uninformed, but it is the least informed members within the electorate who seem to hold the critical balance of power, in the sense that alternations in governing party depend disproportionately on shifts in their sentiment."

The result is that, from the viewpoint of governmental representativeness and accountability, election outcomes are essentially random choices among the available parties—musical chairs.[6] Elections that "throw the bums out" typically do not produce genuine policy mandates, not even when they are landslides. They simply put a different elite coalition in charge. This bloodless change of government is a great deal better than bloody revolution, but it is not deliberate policy change. The parties have policy views and they carry them out when in office, but most voters are not listening, or are simply thinking what their party tells them they should be thinking. This is what an honest view of electoral democracy looks like. It is a blunder to expect elections to deliver more.

---

6 Exceptions occur when coalition politics make it impossible to assign clear responsibility for the performance of the government or when alternatives to the incumbent government are themselves uncertain or not credible, as in Japan throughout most of the post-war period (Powell and Whitten 1993; Anderson 2007).

Thus, the policy views of elected officials tend to be only roughly similar to the views of the people who elected them. The politicians belong to the parties, and the parties and other groups try to shape people's policy views, sometimes successfully and sometimes not.[7] Hence politicians will be—very imperfectly, sometimes only erratically—"representative" of their constituents' policy views. But the relationship between constituents' opinions and their representative's policy choices is correlation, not causation.[8] And in any case, as Miller and Stokes (1963) discovered long ago, the correlations are often quite modest—much smaller than those one would expect from the folk theory of democracy.

Findings of this sort imply that issue congruence is not the heart and soul of democratic representation. Rather, voters primarily look for politicians who match their identities.[9] If we are right about that, then the correlations should be powerful between the identities of politicians and the identities of their electorates. In contemporary American politics, perhaps the most powerful social identity is race. Thus, our argument implies that heavily African-American districts will elect African-Americans and heavily white districts will elect white representatives. And they should do so nearly all the time. Indeed they do. In the 2014–2015 U.S. House of Representatives, for example, 98% of the districts with black majorities elected black representatives. Conversely, just 5% of the districts with white majorities elected African-Americans.[10] This overwhelming correlation provides a powerful illustration of the importance of identity congruence in electoral politics. By comparison, as we showed in chapter 2, moderately liberal districts elected Republicans 46% of the time, while moderately conservative districts elected Democrats 25% of the time. Clearly in this case, and more subtly in many others, democratic representation is more about identities than about issue congruence.

7 Party ideologies, developed to help their coalition cohere, can also take on a life of their own and lead parties away from the interests of their coalition. We do not pursue this important topic here.

8 We have both worked in the tradition pioneered by Miller and Stokes (1963), in which the policy choices of legislators are compared with those of their constituents (Achen 1978; Bartels 1991). However, we now believe that those relationships are primarily of descriptive interest—that is, not causal.

9 Of course, most people have more than one politically meaningful group membership, an important topic in group theory for more than a century (Simmel 1908).

10 The data were assembled by Stephen Wolf for the Daily Kos, and accessed July 18, 2015 at https://docs.google.com/spreadsheets/d/1lGZQi9AxPHjE0RllvhNEBHFvrJGln mC43AXnR8dwHMc/edit?pli=1#gid=1978064869, which lists his sources.

The power of this viewpoint is appallingly illustrated by the most spectacular failure of 20th-century democratic politics, Hitler's rise to power via the ballot box. The observer in the grip of the folk theory asks, how could Germans have favored those policies? Indeed, anti-Semitism was common in Germany, as it was in most other European countries at the time. But in the view of most scholars, German voters first decided whether they liked Hitler as a potential leader, and then if they did, they adopted his policy views, including his views about "the Jewish question." They would have agreed with whatever he proposed. "[People] were drawn to anti-Semitism because they were drawn to Nazism, not the other way round" (Allen 1984, 77; for similar judgments, see Hamilton 1982, chap. 13; Fritzsche 1998, passim; Kershaw 2002, chap. 6).

Of course, Hitler's anti-Semitism was undoubtedly crucial to a minority of voters, but its appeal was limited. As detailed studies of Nazi election propaganda show, "Antisemitism had not been a top priority issue for the Nazis in the last elections of the Weimar Republic" (Gellately 2001, 24). The policy preferences of Hitler's voters are the wrong place to look for the mainsprings of his rise, just as the platforms of candidates and the ideologies of voters are the wrong place to look for the mainsprings of more typical democratic elections.

Many observers have also invoked retrospective voting to account for Hitler's electoral success, suggesting that Germans voted for the Nazis because times were hard and because the mainstream political parties had been discredited by prolonged economic distress.[11] In consequence, the Nazi vote, especially in the early elections, had a "catchall" quality, as protest voters in all regions and social classes were swept into Hitler's coalition (Falter 1990). After Hitler attained power, unemployment declined and Hitler's popularity rose. Speaking as many Germans did after the war, one woman said of Hitler's rise to the chancellorship in the midst of protests over unemployment and food shortages, "And naturally all that changed with one blow. My husband immediately got a job, too, and everyone got a job and bread and therefore people were naturally pro-Hitler" (Owings 1993, 177). It is not easy to imagine a clearer example of blind retrospection, nor a more damaging blow to retrospection as a defense of democracy.

---

11 The supporting literature is far too extensive to cite here. Kershaw (1998, chaps. 9 and 10, esp. 333–336 and 389–391) provided a comprehensive review. Hamilton's (1982) is the most knowledgeable English-language treatment of Weimar elections and the most conversant with political science theory and evidence, though he focuses primarily on religion and social class rather than economic retrospection.

Retrospection in hard times affects nearly everyone, and thus it tends to produce "uniform swing," a similar shift of all electoral districts against the incumbents and toward the out parties (Butler and Stokes 1974, 140–151). Retrospection in this simple sense, however, does not account well for Hitler's vote. Many voters in areas dominated by the Socialist and Communist parties resisted him, and Catholics, especially in rural areas, were nearly immune to his appeal (see, for example, Hamilton 1982, chap. 13). Those two identity groups each had very nearly the same percentage of the vote in the 1932 Reichstag elections as they had had in 1924—a notable anomaly from the standpoint of conventional retrospective explanations. What had collapsed were the old Protestant nationalist parties, the third identity grouping defining German electoral politics since the Wilhelmine period (Lepsius 1966; Burnham 1972; Rohe 1990a; 1990b). The Nazis largely replaced those parties. In the last more or less honest elections of the Weimar era, in 1932, the parties of the right got almost exactly the same total proportion of the vote that they had received in 1924. The difference was that the Nazis were now by far the largest among them, averaging just over a third of the total vote.

Thus, Hitler's electoral success is a story of identity groups, just as elections virtually always are, but identity groups of a certain kind—not, for example, social classes.[12] Hitler spoke the language of German nationalism in a period of post-war humiliation. Protestant nationalists recognized him as one of their own, though initially not a very respectable exemplar. However, as the horrors of the Depression deepened and made them desperate, they abandoned other parties of the same kind for the sort of strong leadership that Hitler promised. Other parts of the electorate were almost unmoved: Hitler was clearly and decisively anti-socialist and non-Catholic, and thus not one of theirs. Hence economic retrospection mattered, but not in the blanket way that many have supposed. It changed the votes of only a fraction of the electorate, and its impact was sharply channeled by Weimar's political identity groups.

When an economy fails, explanations of all kinds will be put forward, some of them simultaneously ugly and popular, as happened in the United States in the Great Depression (Brinkley 1982) and has happened repeatedly

12 Social class has received vast attention in the literature on Weimar, particularly in the first decades after the war. An extensive debate ensued over which classes were more important to Hitler (Hamilton 1982, chaps. 2–3). Unfortunately, most scholars in this tradition paid little or no attention to detailed election returns. In our view, subsequent scholarship has established that traditional social class analysis is, at best, of secondary causal relevance for understanding Hitler's electoral appeal.

in post-war France (Shields 2007) and many other places. Scapegoats are often proposed. Hitler's anti-Semitism is a particularly frightening example. But the actual causal explanations for left- and right-wing populist extremism lie elsewhere than in ideology. As we argued in chapter 5, to be successful, popular movements need a crisis, blind retrospection, and a message that plays to the identity and self-understanding of a substantial group in the population (Cantril 1941, chap. 3). The epidemic of support for Hitler is a case in point. The comforting view that there was something particularly evil about Germans and that the rest of us are immune will always have appeal for some. In truth, however, the desire for a strong leader who can identify domestic enemies and who promises to do something about them without worrying overmuch about legalities—those germs, mutated to fit the particular local subcultures, are latent in every democratic electorate, waiting for sufficiently widespread human suffering to provide conditions for their explosive spread.

WHAT IS GOOD ABOUT DEMOCRACY?

Having argued that the most prominent popular and scholarly intellectual defenses of democracy are incompatible with the empirical evidence, we can easily imagine (and indeed, have already heard) some irritated readers asking pointedly, "Well, would you rather live in *a dictatorship*?" The answer, for the record, is no. We, too, are inspired and heartened when a government of torturers collapses, when the Berlin Wall comes down, or when an unarmed young man faces down a tank during the Tiananmen demonstrations in China. But that does not make our argument any less persuasive. It merely demonstrates that actual democratic processes have quite real practical virtues unrelated to the idealistic virtues ascribed to them in the folk theory of democracy.

As we noted in chapter 1, proponents of the folk theory faced with its unrealism often fall back on Winston Churchill's pragmatic argument that contemporary democratic procedures are generally better than anything else that has been tried. We agree with that assessment. But if the folk theory cannot account for the pragmatic successes of democratic politics, other factors must make the difference. But *which* other factors? Getting a clearer picture of *why* democracy is a good political system—what it does or doesn't accomplish, which features and processes are essential to its success, which are not, and how it could be made to work more fairly—seems important as an intellectual challenge, as a practical guide, and as an ethical imperative.

An independent judiciary, freedom of speech and assembly, and other features of democratic institutions and culture are undoubtedly important; but our primary focus here is on the central mechanism in the folk theory of democracy, elections.[13] In our view, the most concrete and potentially important benefits of elections are not those envisioned in the folk theory. First, and perhaps most obviously, elections generally provide authoritative, widely accepted agreement about who shall rule. In the United States, for example, even the bitterly contested 2000 presidential election—which turned on a few hundred votes in a single state and a much-criticized five-to-four Supreme Court decision—was widely accepted as legitimate. A few Democratic partisans continued to grumble that the election had been "stolen"; but the winner, George W. Bush, took office without bloodshed, or even significant protest, and public attention quickly turned to other matters. As V. O. Key, Jr. (1961b, 487) once wrote, elections "have within themselves more than a trace of the lottery. That, of course, is not necessarily undesirable so long as all concerned abide by the toss of the coin."

Moreover, in well-functioning democratic systems, parties that win office are inevitably defeated at a subsequent election. They may be defeated more or less randomly, due to droughts, floods, or untimely economic slumps, but they are defeated nonetheless. Moreover, voters seem increasingly likely to reject the incumbent party the longer it has held office, reinforcing the tendency for governmental power to change hands. This turnover is a key indicator of democratic health and stability. It implies that no one group or coalition can become entrenched in power, unlike in dictatorships or one-party states where power is often exercised persistently by a single privileged segment of society. And because the losers in each election can reasonably expect the wheel of political fortune to turn in the not-too-distant future, they are more likely to accept the outcome than to take to the streets.

Third, electoral competition also provides some incentives for rulers at any given moment to tolerate opposition. The notion that citizens can oppose the incumbent rulers and organize to replace them, yet remain loyal to the

13 Systematic attempts to distinguish the specific effect of electoral processes from other aspects of democracy are surprisingly rare. John Mueller (1999, 140–145) deemed elections "useful, but not essential," pointing to Mexico and British Hong Kong as "cases of what might be called democracies without elections." Matthew Cleary (2010, 188) provided a detailed examination of the impact of a substantial increase in electoral competition in Mexico; he concluded that "electoral competition does not make Mexican municipal governments more responsive to the interests of their citizens," and that direct, informal participation in municipal governance is a far more important spur to responsiveness.

nation, is fundamental both to real democracy and to social harmony. But it is a very difficult concept, one that arrived surprisingly late in democratic theorizing. The Founders of the American Constitution warned against faction and did not foresee the importance of political parties. The concept of "His Majesty's Loyal Opposition" developed gradually over the course of the 19th century, as experience with party conflict in the world's oldest large-scale democracies demonstrated the importance and legitimacy of parties, especially opposition parties (Lieber 1839, 427–430; Hofstadter 1969).

Unfortunately, even many citizens in well-functioning democracies fail to see the importance of organized political opposition. Freedom is to faction what air is to fire, Madison said. But ordinary citizens often dislike the conflict and bickering that comes with freedom (Eliasoph 1998). They wish their elected officials would just do the people's work without so much squabbling amongst themselves (Hibbing and Theiss-Morse 2002). They dislike the compromises that result when many different groups are free to propose alternative policies, leaving politicians to adjust their differences. Voters want "a real leader, not a politician," by which they generally mean that their own ideas should be adopted and other people's opinions disregarded, because views different from their own are obviously self-interested and erroneous. To the contrary, politicians with vision who are also skilled at creative compromise are the soul of successful democracy, and they exemplify real leadership (see for example, Hargrove 2014). But this way of thinking about leadership is not much taught in schools nor emphasized in Fourth of July speeches. Hence, where this central aspect of democracy is concerned, many voters just do not get it.

Fourth, a long tradition in political theory stemming from John Stuart Mill (1861, chap. 3) has emphasized the potential benefits of democratic citizenship for the development of human character (Pateman 1970). Empirical scholarship focusing squarely on effects of this sort is scant, but it suggests that democratic political engagement may indeed have important implications for civic competence and other virtues (Finkel 1985; 1987; Campbell 2003; Mettler 2005). Thus, participation in democratic processes may contribute to better citizenship, producing both self-reinforcing improvements in "civic culture" (Almond and Verba 1963) and broader contributions to human development.

Finally, reelection-seeking politicians in well-functioning democracies will strive to avoid being caught violating consensual ethical norms in their society. As Key (1961a, 282) put it, public opinion in a democracy "establishes vague limits of permissiveness within which governmental action may occur without arousing a commotion." Thus, no president will strangle a kitten on the White House lawn in view of the television cameras. Easily managed governmental tasks will get taken care of, too. Chicago mayors will either get the snow cleared or be replaced, as Mayor Michael Bilandic learned in the winter of 1979. Openly taking bribes will generally be punished. When the causal chain is clear, the outcome is unambiguous, and the evaluation is widely shared, accountability will be enforced (Arnold 1990, chap. 3). So long as a free press can report dubious goings-on and a literate public can learn about them, politicians have strong incentives to avoid doing what is widely despised. Violations occur, of course, but they are expensive; removal from office is likely. By contrast, in dictatorships, moral or financial corruption is more common because public outrage has no obvious, organized outlet. This is a modest victory for political accountability.

Real as these benefits are, however, they have relatively little to do with the day-to-day workings of a national government, which only rarely concern kittens, snow removal, or anything similar. The causal chain for most important social events is complex and untraceable. As we have seen throughout this book, even the most attentive citizens mostly cannot figure it out. This is the flaw in John Dewey's (1927, 207) clever analogy for the role of public opinion in representative government, that the cobbler can repair a shoe but only the wearer can say where it pinches. That is a good model for dealing with cobblers and dentists, but a poor one for dealing with presidents. In politics, thousands of cobblers are at work, and pinches come and go, many with nobody at fault. Ordinary citizens with limited free hours in their day are very unlikely to learn who deserves credit or blame for the pains they suffer.

Thus, it should come as no surprise that the real benefits of democracy are mostly quite different from those envisioned in the folk theory of democracy. They are real benefits nonetheless, and constitute a substantial, albeit limited argument in favor of democratic systems compared to their authoritarian alternatives. However, they do little to answer the broader questions of whether and how everyday democratic policy-making promotes people's interests when they are judging politicians on entirely different grounds.

POWER AND IDENTITY GROUPS

If we are correct in claiming that group ties and social identities are the most important bases of political commitments and behavior, and that election outcomes have little real policy content, what are the implications for democracy and for democratic theory? Once the folk theory and retrospective voting theory are discarded, the answer is not obvious. The optimistic notion that policy-making is sharply constrained by public preferences runs aground on the fact that pressures from parties, interest groups, and the wealthy routinely trump broad left-leaning majorities on issues like the minimum wage and social spending, while pressures from parties, interest groups, and educated elites trump broad right-leaning majorities on issues like silent prayer in schools and parental notification for minors seeking an abortion (Bartels 2008; Gilens 2012; Page, Bartels, and Seawright 2013).

In every society, policy-making is a job for specialists. Policies are made by political elites of one kind or another, including elected officials, government bureaucrats, interest groups, and judges (Hansen 1985; 1991; Rothenberg 1992; Baumgartner et al. 2009). As we noted in chapter 3, "Politics has been, is, and always will be carried on by politicians, just as art is carried on by artists, engineering by engineers, business by businessmen" (Ford 1909, 2).

One need not spend much time in Washington, D.C., or any other capital city of a democracy to learn that, for the great majority of issues that the government decides, no "ordinary citizens" are actually involved in the policy-making process. Occasionally, politically engaged and well-financed groups of citizens do manage to bend democratic governments to some of their wishes, but such movements are rare. Day to day, few such influences exist, as close observers of the policy-making process have long noted (Lindblom 1968, chap. 6). For example, Jacobs and Page (2005) found that the views of U.S. foreign-policy-makers were strongly responsive to elite and expert opinion, but not to the opinions of ordinary citizens.

A broader empirical study of American policy-making by Matt Grossmann came to a similar conclusion. Drawing on 268 policy histories covering 790 notable policy enactments in 14 distinct domestic policy domains, Grossmann (2014, 12–13) found that presidents, agency heads, influential members of Congress, and relevant advocacy groups made policy—in other words, parties and interest groups. He wrote that "American policymaking is rarely responsive to the public; the role of opinion and elections is limited and inconsistent. . . . The patterns do not comport with the textbook view of political institutions, macro-level theories, or the hopeful image of government 'by the people.'" The complexity of modern societies ensures that the policy-making process cannot be organized like a New England town meeting.

Descriptions of the actual policy-making process return repeatedly to the same concepts—power and influence. Some officials, groups, and organizations are powerful; others are not, as classic studies of the policy-making process have emphasized (Truman 1951; Dahl 1956; 1961; Banfield 1961; Lindblom 1965).[14] The resulting differences between them in getting their way are enormous. Sheer group size helps, but wealth, social prestige, and access to media of communication and persuasion often bring greater power, both in their own right and as resources facilitating organization. Thus, it is hardly surprising that, as E. E. Schattschneider (1960, 34–35) famously put it, "The flaw in the pluralist heaven is that the heavenly chorus sings with a strong upper-class accent." Similarly, contemporary political scientists (e.g., Schlozman, Verba, and Brady 2012) have provided detailed analyses of the dramatic socioeconomic biases in group politics.

Understanding group conflict in power terms is not a new idea: "Whatever social problem we confront, whatever persons come into our field of view, the first questions involved will always be: *To what groups do these persons belong? What are the interests of these groups? What sort of means do the groups use to promote their interests? How strong are these groups, as compared with groups that have conflicting interests?* These questions go to the tap root of all social interpretation" (Small 1905, 497, emphasis original). In the same way, prominent political scientists have long thought that power was central to the discipline, and they have written about it frequently in books with titles like *Political Power* (Merriam 1934), *Power and Society* (Lasswell and Kaplan, 1950), and (again) *Political Power* (Bell, Edwards, and Wagner 1969). But in more recent years, and especially in democratic theory, the topic is too often neglected. In the folk theory and in retrospective voting models, every citizen is equal by assumption. Voting is supposed to equalize power: The rich and the poor all have one vote apiece, and they can listen to arguments and vote their interests equally well. But as we have shown, that naive view flies in the face of a great deal of social-scientific evidence.

If voters are to have their interests represented in the policy-making process, then, interest groups and parties have to do the work. And the organizations representing different interests have to have power in the policy-making process proportional to their presence in the electorate. The rich, the well-placed, and the well-organized cannot have extra power to advance their interests. Too often, as we have seen, naive reformers have imagined that the pseudo-democratization bestowed by plebiscites would solve all these problems cheaply and easily. To the contrary, spelling out the simple normative perspective of equal power in the context of an honest description of

14 Of course, not everything in politics reduces to power and raw competition among groups and parties. Nonetheless, they are central to understanding policy outcomes.

the policy-making process makes it only too clear how far we have to go to become seriously democratic. It also makes clear how hard the conceptual task will be of devising the right institutional arrangements, and how bitterly those reforms will be opposed by the groups that profit from the current inequalities and the ensuing injustices.

What are the mechanisms that would lead to more democracy in a realist sense? We have already mentioned the biases stemming from differences in resources among organized groups, but assessing the political and policy *implications* of those biases is still largely a matter of rough extrapolation and guesswork (Baumgartner et al. 2009; Gilens 2012, chap. 5). So is the role of unorganized groups. While "potential interest groups" (Truman 1951, chap. 2) are not entirely powerless, they are at a distinct disadvantage vis-à-vis organized groups. But not nearly enough is known about how much and why.

Thus, the implications of group politics for democracy depend in substantial part on the extent to which relevant political interests are, in fact, organized and active in elections and in the policy-making process. Does the roster of interest group headquarters on K Street in Washington adequately reflect the range of group interests in American society? That seems unlikely. As Matt Grossmann (2012, 15–16) summarized his study of national advocacy organizations, "a few ideological, occupational, and ethnic groups have a great deal of political representation, but most public groups in each of these categories have minimal representation." A great deal has been written about American interest groups, but detailed studies of their overall representativeness and differences in their relative power are in short supply.

We also need to know more about how interest groups acquire their clout. Presumably they influence their members to vote in ways that advance their interests, which in turn makes politicians listen to their policy proposals. But how, and how effectively, do groups actually do that? Peter Odegard (1928) studied the Anti-Saloon League's communications with its supporters, and Oliver Garceau (1941) wrote about the American Medical Association, but recent studies of political influence using modern research tools and data are exceedingly rare. How successful are interest groups' attempts to influence their followers' opinions and votes? David Truman (1949) studied labor unions' influence attempts and Christopher Kenny, Michael McBurnett, and David Bordua (2004) investigated the National Rifle Association, but again the evidence is uncomfortably thin.

The representation of group interests in the policy-making process also hinges significantly on the extent to which political entrepreneurs and activists are faithful agents of their groups. The problems of monitoring and accountability that we explored in our analysis of retrospective voting in chapters 4 to 7 also arise in the relationship between citizens and group leaders. Groups are relatively homogeneous: Does that make it easier for citizens to monitor the leadership? And how much does group organization matter to responsiveness? In a classic study of the internal politics of a progressive labor union, the International Typographical Union, sociologists Seymour Martin Lipset, Martin Trow, and James S. Coleman (1956) argued that favorable social circumstances produced a rare exception to the usual pattern of oligarchic leadership (Michels 1915). Unfortunately, we know of no comparably detailed contemporary studies of the internal politics of politically significant groups.[15]

Finally, the political influence of group interests is likely to vary considerably with the nature of the party system. Scholars of party politics have recently revived the notion that parties are, first and foremost, coalitions of groups (Bawn et al. 2012); but they have offered no simple formula for predicting how a given constellation of social groups will coalesce into a specific configuration of partisan conflict, how coalitions made up of groups with distinct interests will manage their internal tensions, or how political institutions will shape the processes of intra- and interparty bargaining that translate group interests into public policy. In systems where parliamentary representation is allocated in proportion to party strength, small parties representing isolated social groups may hold outsized power in the making or breaking of governments, as has sometimes been the case with ultra-conservative religious parties in Israel. On the other hand, political leaders in majoritarian systems may organize party coalitions and partisan conflict in ways that, for better or worse, effectively submerge certain group interests.

At its best, the process of interest aggregation in majoritarian systems may involve shearing off the more self-interested or damaging or wicked demands of component groups, resulting in a stronger and more coherent electoral coalition. We argued in chapter 3 that competent leadership is critical; from the viewpoint of group theory, what that requires is forging effective political coalitions that serve people's real interests. Franklin Roosevelt accomplished

---

15 John Gaventa (1980) devoted one chapter of his book on quiescence and rebellion in Appalachia to the failure of the United Mine Workers union to represent the interests of Appalachian coal miners. Lawrence Rothenberg (1992) used data on the members of the good-government lobbying group Common Cause to ask whether "joining, activism, or the threat of departure" by group members affected "the behavior of group leaders in determining organizational goals." In neither case was the fidelity of group leaders to the interests of group members a primary focus of analysis.

exactly that, overcoming the prior failures of the Populists and the Progressives (Hofstadter 1955). On the other hand, the "second party system" in the antebellum U.S. united "the plain Republicans of the North with Southern planters" in a national Democratic Party whose primary effect was to paper over the explosive issue of slavery. Indeed, Martin Van Buren recommended the cross-sectional alliance to his prospective southern allies on the grounds that it would stifle "the clamor against the Southern Influence and African Slavery" (Remini 1959; Cohen et al. 2008, 65–70).

We know too little about how parties shape their governing ideas and policy platforms.[16] With a few important exceptions (notably, Gerring 2001 and Noel 2013), contemporary political scientists have devoted little attention to this topic, despite the obvious importance of party ideologies as vehicles for composing, rationalizing, and (perhaps) elevating group interests. Herbert Croly's (1909) impact on the development of the American welfare state is an important illustration of how new ideologies change party policy. As Hans Noel (2013, 3) puts it, "Croly was among the first to articulate the importance of large-scale government intervention on behalf of the less fortunate," a position that was "not so supported, even by progressives, at the end of the nineteenth century." Of course, "Croly's position is widely held today by liberals in the United States" (Noel 2013, 3), and the policies of Democratic presidents since Franklin Roosevelt have been profoundly affected by that ideology.

What, then, can we say about the implications of group politics for democracy? As we noted in chapter 2, John Zaller (2012, 623) has pointed out the simple, appealing implication of the economic theory of democracy proposed by Anthony Downs: "The rationally ignorant median voter gets what he wants without much effort." In contrast, according to Zaller, "What might be called the group-politics view of democracy is not so optimistic: Organized policy demanders routinely get what they want at the expense of the unorganized; but groups of ordinary voters—if sufficiently numerous, cohesive, attentive, and pivotal—also get some of what they want."

Evaluations of the policies produced by group politics are often, knowingly or unknowingly, grounded in the normative framework inherited from

16 Exemplary historical treatments touching upon these issues include Sombart's (1906) study of the failure of American socialism, Schorske's (1955) analysis of the early 20th-century split in German socialist parties, Rossiter's (1955) investigation of the evolution of American conservative thought, and Beer's (1966) treatment of the self-understanding of British political parties, to name just a few.

the folk theory of democracy. Every victory of popular preferences over organized groups is celebrated. From that perspective, Zaller's tempered assessment of actual patterns of political influence is unlikely to inspire much optimistic Fourth of July rhetoric. But it is a realistic characterization of the actual workings of democratic government.

From a broader perspective, taking the psychology underlying the group theory of democracy seriously might lead to quite different normative conclusions. Giving groups of ordinary voters "some of what they want" may not always be so desirable if what they want is a byproduct of affective tribal loyalties. The politics of new democracies in developing countries provide sobering examples—but then, so do the politics of 20th-century Germany and many other wealthy, cultured democratic countries. A more compelling normative assessment will require a clearer empirical understanding of how group politics works. At present, normative thinking about democracy and democratic reform is hopelessly entangled with the unrealistic empirical assumptions of the folk theory.

WHAT WOULD IT MEAN TO HAVE "MORE DEMOCRACY"?

One of the most deleterious consequences of adherence to unrealistic ideas about democracy is that it keeps us from seeing what a truer and deeper democracy would be like. As we saw in chapter 3, the default assumption among proponents of the folk theory has long been that "the cure for the ills of democracy is more democracy." The empirical evidence presented in this book seems to us to make their notion of what that means untenable. For example, by the normative standards enshrined in the folk theory, the point of democracy is to reflect ordinary citizens' preferences in the policy-making process on an egalitarian basis. Given the empirical assumptions of the folk theory, a system with universal enfranchisement should lead more or less automatically to that end. In fact, anyone who looks at actual democratic processes finds a very different reality.

New thinking about both ideals and realities will be required if democracies are to become truly more democratic. Our account of group politics points to a variety of potentially significant reforms, but we will focus on just one here. In our view, more effective democracy would require a greater degree of *economic and social equality*. The most powerful players in the policy game are the educated, the wealthy, and the well-connected. Corporations have more clout than workers; major media outlets are more powerful than independent bloggers; affluent citizens' views matter more than those of the poor; and members of ethnic and racial majority groups are policy "winners" more often than members of minority groups. For decades, no informed observer has imagined otherwise, but in recent years quantitative evidence has begun to provide a somewhat more precise sense of the magnitudes of these imbalances (Bartels 2008, chap. 9; Griffin and Newman 2008; Gilens 2012; Gilens and Page 2014). This work has shown that, whether we assess the influence of the poor and minorities in terms of their expressed preferences or their apparent interests, the power imbalances are very large, and the resulting policy outcomes are far from those implied by any appealing democratic ideal.

The theory of group politics provides a clearer explanation for why a more egalitarian society would result in a more egalitarian political process. The result would be an increase in the real political power of a variety of currently underrepresented groups, not all of them approved of by the editorial pages of either the *New York Times* or the *Wall Street Journal*. The policy views of both corporate interests and college professors would get less weight in a fairer process.

The problem, of course, is how to accomplish such a change. At the moment, Americans lack the ideas, the will, and the political organization. Protest groups come along regularly; but because their political thinking is so bound up in the folk theory of democracy, they resist the leadership, organization, and coalition-building that would give them clout and staying power. They quickly fade, leaving everything much as it was.

A (somewhat) less daunting aim would be simply to reduce the most direct effects of existing differences in wealth in the democratic process. Rich people, large corporations, and business associations everywhere spend considerable sums financing politicians' campaigns and lobbying them between elections. But few established democracies do as little as the United States does to limit the distorting effects of money in the democratic process. Congress has made periodic attempts to regulate lobbying and campaign contributions, usually in ways that tend to protect the interests of incumbent politicians regardless of party or ideology, but sometimes in ways that would have helped level the playing field. However, in recent years conservative majorities on the Supreme Court have increasingly employed 19th-century liberalism's logic that buying elections is a form of free speech, and therefore protected under the Constitution, to gut restrictions on political contributions.

Most of the time, the big contributors are Republicans, and so this set of rules advantages the Republican Party, causing a predictable enthusiasm for the undemocratic status quo in that party. But the biases are not unique to Republicans. Because money, access, and intensity matter, both parties—and, for that matter, most political groups—privilege the affluent relative to the poor, sophisticated insiders relative to ordinary people, and intense minorities relative to more complacent and inattentive majorities. Those biases grease the squeaking wheels and help minimize protest. But reducing the influence of money in American elections is a clear implication of the vision of democracy we have set out. Thinking of campaign spending as free speech is naive when it is not disingenuous.

Of course, many proponents of the folk theory of democracy also argue for campaign finance reform and a more egalitarian society. But their interest in those reforms does more to contradict than to reflect their faith in the folk theory. By the logic of populism, universal suffrage in itself should be sufficient to mitigate the inequalities of political influence that we have identified. If campaign spending sways election outcomes, it does so because voters are not the principled "issue voters" envisioned in the folk theory. If campaign contributions influence policy, they do so because elections fail to enforce the allegiance of real flesh-and-blood policy-makers to the policy preferences of the median voter. Real politics is much more complex—and much more strongly shaped by unequal clout—than the fastidious vision of the folk theory suggests. Serious political reform must face that fact squarely.

We do not mean to suggest that these or any other reforms would correct all the problems of American democracy or of any other democracy. Government remains an all-too-human enterprise, not so different from business, religion, education, and every other aspect of public life. But misleading theories are not neutral, and they are not costless. In current thinking about democracy, bad ideas dominate public discourse. Romantic notions of democracy sound good and have emotion on their side. Let the people rule! Generations of thoughtful Americans have promoted with genuine sincerity reforms deriving from the folk theory of democracy. But they tend to be badly flawed in practice, primarily because they make life all too easy for special interests. Especially at the state level, proponents of mind-numbing clichés about giving power to ordinary people bear considerable responsibility for the domination of government by narrowly self-interested groups. In reforming government, good intentions and high-sounding rhetoric are not enough. In the end, it is the folk theory that props up elite rule, and it is unrepresentative elites that most profit from the convenient justifications it provides for their activities.

At the moment, America is a democracy, but it is not very democratic. In this book, we have tried to face without flinching the logical consequences of what democracy's most thoughtful observers have long seen, and what political scientists over the past several decades have demonstrated in meticulous detail. Democratic citizens—all of us—have to think differently. All too often, we bring rose-colored glasses when we look at democracy, glasses handed to us from the dead hands of Enlightenment thinkers. In consequence, we not only propose bad solutions; often enough, we cannot even see the problems. The gross inequalities of political power in contemporary America are the most obvious instance. The daunting challenge of altering a deeply entrenched and powerfully defended status quo that embodies those inequalities is often obscured by simplistic folk-theoretic faith in the responsiveness of the current system to its citizens.

We recognize that the view of democracy offered in this book is less cheery than the romantic alternatives, and thus less appealing—at least initially. Moreover, as we have acknowledged, our approach raises a host of problems and questions for which political scientists—ourselves very much included—have no ready answers. Nevertheless, just as a critical step toward democracy occurred when people lost faith in the notion that the king had been anointed by God, we believe that abandoning the folk theory of democracy is a prerequisite to both greater intellectual clarity and real political change. Too many democratic reformers have squandered their energy on misguided or quixotic ideas. Further political and social progress will require thinking more clearly about the contributions and limitations of citizens, groups, and political parties in the actual process of government. We have attempted to take steps in that direction; but there is a great deal more to do.

Appendix:
Retrospective Voting as
Selection and Sanctioning

This appendix sets out the formal models of retrospective *selection* and *sanctioning* described in the text.

RETROSPECTIVE VOTING AS SELECTION

In our model of retrospective *selection*, a representative voter's electorally relevant subjective well-being under the incumbent party in any given period t is determined by a simple combination of the incumbent party's intrinsic competence and random factors outside the incumbent's control—good or bad luck.[1] Using ω_t, θ_t, and δ_t to denote subjective well-being, competence, and luck, respectively,

$$\text{A.1} \qquad\qquad \omega_t = \theta_t + \delta_t, \qquad \delta_t \sim N(0, \sigma^2).$$

For the sake of concreteness, we assume that δ_t is normally distributed with mean zero and variance σ^2. We assume that the distribution of δ_t is known to the voter, but that the actual value of δ_t in any given period is not; thus, he must use good or bad experience under the incumbent (ω_t) to estimate her intrinsic competence (θ_t).[2]

---

1 The direct relationship between competence and well-being posited in equation A.1 rules out the possibility that incumbents may be tempted to demonstrate competence in ways that do not actually promote voters' well-being (Ashworth 2012, 188–189)—for example, by running impressive reelection campaigns rather than improving public policies (Daley and Snowberg 2011).

2 The simple assumption that δ_t has the same distribution in each time period rules out "so-called 'rational retrospective' models" in which voters "understand the stochastic structure

Our prospectively rational voter cares not about the incumbent's competence in the current period, θ_T, but about her competence in the *next* period if she is reelected, θ_{T+1}. If her expected competence in the next period exceeds that of his best alternative, he reelects the incumbent; if not, not.[3] However, in order to implement this rule he needs some strategy for inferring θ_{T+1}. The simplest possible assumption is that the incumbent's intrinsic competence does not vary over time: $\theta_1 = \theta_2 = \ldots \theta_T = \theta_{T+1} = \theta$. In that case the voter's task is simply to estimate the constant parameter θ. He might do so based solely on his subjective well-being in period T, ω_T; however, there is additional information to be gleaned from his earlier history of good or bad experiences with the incumbent, $\omega_1, \omega_2, \ldots \omega_{T-1}$.

Given the assumptions of this model, assessing the incumbent's competence is formally equivalent to estimating the unknown mean of a distribution with variance σ^2 from a sample of size T (Achen 1992).[4] The best estimate is simply the average well-being experienced in each period under the incumbent,

A.2
$$\hat{\theta}_{T+1} = \Sigma_t \, \omega_t \, / T.$$

The uncertainty of that estimate depends upon the extent of the voter's experience (T) and the extent to which good or bad luck obscures intrinsic competence in each period (σ):

A.3
$$\mathrm{var}(\hat{\theta}_{T+1}) = \sigma^2 / T.$$

---

of the real macroeconomy" and its implications for well-being unrelated to incumbent competence (Hibbs 2006, 571, 573). According to Hibbs (2006, 574), models of this sort "are quite ingenious but their influence has been confined wholly to the realm of detached theory. Such models have received no support in data." Duch and Stevenson (2008) argue that they do receive support in data; Achen (2012) argues that they are not theoretically robust and do not imply standard retrospective results if minor modifications are made to their most implausible assumptions.

3 We can simplify the analysis—without loss of generality in a two-party system—by defining the competence of the incumbent *relative* to that of the out-party. Thus, surprisingly good experiences under the incumbent party and surprisingly bad experiences under the out-party both increase the probability of voting to reelect the incumbent; surprisingly bad experiences under the incumbent party and surprisingly good experiences under the out-party both decrease that probability.

4 We assume here that the random variables $\delta_1, \delta_2, \ldots \delta_T$ are statistically independent. If good or bad luck is correlated from one period to the next, our voter's observed experience is less informative and he must adjust his inferences accordingly.

Thus, a rational voter's assessment of the incumbent's competence will take into account performance in every relevant period, not just in the current period. How many periods are "relevant" depends on the party system. If the parties' leadership and commitments are quite stable, performance in several previous periods may be informative regarding likely future performance. In a less stable system, only one or a few previous periods may be informative.

Figure 4.1 shows how the efficacy of selection in this model varies with the incumbent's true competence, θ, and with the magnitude of random forces obscuring the incumbent's true competence. (Since the impact of random forces on the uncertainty of the voter's estimate of incumbent competence declines with relevant experience, it is convenient to gauge the "blindness" of retrospection by $\sigma/\sqrt{T}$—the square root of the variance in equation A.3—rather than σ alone.)

RETROSPECTIVE VOTING AS SANCTIONING

Our alternative model of retrospective *sanctioning* assumes that all potential leaders are identical (so that it is impossible for voters to *select* a more competent leader on the basis of past performance). Each voter's electorally relevant subjective well-being in each period depends solely on the amount of effort devoted by the incumbent leader to increasing the voter's well-being and on the net effect of random forces beyond the incumbent's control. In particular, we assume that

$$\text{A.4} \qquad \omega_t = \gamma_t + \varepsilon_t, \qquad \varepsilon_t \sim N(0, \psi^2),$$

where $\gamma_t \, (\geq 0)$ represents the incumbent's level of diligence in furthering the voter's subjective well-being.

The random variable ε_t in this model plays much the same role as the random variable δ_t played in our model of selection on the basis of incumbent competence, representing the impact on the voter's subjective well-being of factors unrelated to the incumbent's effort. For the sake of concreteness, we assume that ε_t is normally distributed with mean zero and variance ψ^2, and that this *distribution* is known both to the voter and to the incumbent. However, we assume that the actual value of ε_t is unknown by the incumbent when she chooses her level of effort, and unobserved by the voter even after the fact.

Following the usual rule in principal-agent models,[5] our voter reelects the incumbent leader if and only if his subjective well-being in the period before the election exceeds some threshold value τ_t. Thus, the probability of reelection is:

A.5 $$\pi_t = \text{prob}(\omega_t \geq \tau_t).$$

Substituting A.4 into A.5 and rearranging,

A.6 $$\pi_t = \text{prob}(-\varepsilon_t \leq (\gamma_t - \tau_t))$$

$$= \Phi((\gamma_t - \tau_t)/\psi),$$

where $\Phi(\cdot)$ represents the cumulative normal distribution function.

The part of equation A.6 that is under the incumbent's control is her level of effort, γ_t. Other things being equal, higher values of γ_t produce higher probabilities of reelection. However, since effort devoted to increasing the voter's subjective well-being may be costly, we assume that the incumbent maximizes[6]

A.7 $$\nu_t = \pi_t - \gamma_t^2/2$$

$$= \Phi((\gamma_t - \tau_t)/\psi) - \gamma_t^2/2.$$

The equilibrium relationship implied by this objective function is

A.8 $$\gamma_t^* = \phi((\gamma_t^* - \tau_t^*)/\psi)/\psi,$$

5 In principle, one might imagine alternative equilibria in which voters employ, and incumbents anticipate, more complex strategies of reward and punishment contingent on experienced well-being in previous periods as well as in the most recent period. Since unaddressed problems of coordination are already rampant in models of this sort, we limit our analysis to the simple case in which incentives are created and enforced on a term-by-term basis.

6 Since the scale of γ_t is arbitrary, there is no loss of generality in choosing the coefficient 1/2 for the cost of effort in equation A.7, simplifying the exposition. However, the assumption that cost varies with γ_t^2 rather than γ_t (so that the marginal cost of effort is greater at higher levels of effort) has a substantively important impact on equilibrium behavior in our model.

where γ_t^* and τ_t^* are the equilibrium choices of effort and the reelection threshold, respectively, and $\phi(\cdot)$ represents the normal density function.

This equilibrium relationship implies that the incumbent's choice of effort level, γ_t^*, depends in part on the voter's choice of reelection threshold, τ_t^*. How will our voter choose τ_t^*? If his aim is to maximize his electorally relevant subjective well-being, he will choose a reelection threshold that maximizes equation A.4. His choice can have no effect on the second term in equation A.4; luck is random. Only the first term in equation A.4, the incumbent's level of effort, γ_t, is subject to influence. Thus, the voter will want to choose a reelection threshold that elicits as much effort as possible from the incumbent, and his expected well-being will vary directly with that level of effort.

It is clear from the equilibrium relationship in equation A.8 that the incumbent's effort is maximized when the voter chooses $\tau_t^* = \gamma_t^*$, because in that case the expression on the right-hand side of equation A.8 is maximized.[7] In light of that fact, equation A.8 simplifies to

A.9 $$\gamma_t^* = \phi(0)/\psi,$$

which expresses the incumbent's optimal level of effort as a simple function of the parameter ψ—the standard deviation of random factors affecting the voter's subjective well-being.

There is one additional constraint to bear in mind in this analysis. Since we have seen that the voter will always choose $\tau_t^* = \gamma_t^*$, the incumbent's probability of reelection in equilibrium (substituting $(\gamma_t - \tau_t) = 0$ in equation A.6) will be .5. Given that fact, and the incumbent's objective function in equation A.7, it will never be worthwhile for the incumbent to choose a level of effort greater than 1.0, since if she did her expected payoff would be negative.[8] Thus, the equilibrium level of effort (and the equilibrium reelection threshold) will be *either* 1.0 (for sufficiently small values of ψ) *or* the value implied by equation A.9.

Figure 4.2 shows how the efficacy of sanctioning in this model—as measured by the incumbent's equilibrium level of effort on the voter's behalf, γ_t^*— varies with the magnitude of random forces influencing the voter's electorally relevant subjective well-being, ψ. Clearly, increasing randomness produces less effective sanctioning, and thus less subjective well-being for voters.

---

7 Recall that the normal density function $\phi(x)$ takes its maximum value at $x = 0$.

8 The incumbent can always assure herself of a nonnegative payoff by exerting no effort.

Afterword to the Paperback Edition

When we submitted the foregoing pages to Princeton University Press in September 2015, Donald Trump was just a few months into his seemingly quixotic campaign for the presidency. As we write this postscript, he is president. Few foresaw that outcome, and certainly we did not. Yet the social and electoral forces that we have pointed to in this book were as much in evidence in the 2016 election as always, even if the precise nature and magnitude of their impacts were unknowable in advance.[1]

SOCIAL IDENTITIES IN THE 2016 ELECTION

Much commentary during and after the 2016 presidential election pointed to Trump's appeal to white "working class" voters, especially men. Sample surveys also showed Hillary Clinton's relative strength among educated voters, especially women. These are examples of identity-based voting of just the sort we emphasized in the book.

Many non-college white voters saw Trump as a strong leader, a man who spoke his mind without respect for elitist proprieties. Like themselves, he saw life in terms of group antagonisms—ethnic, racial, religious, and national. If speaking the truth meant violating conventional norms of politeness and respect for others, so be it. A great many of his supporters were thrilled to hear white Christian America forcefully defended against its perceived enemies. Those were their identities. He was their hero. Whether he got the facts right did not matter. Like every hero before him, he was quickly and easily forgiven for all that, as well as for ethical failures in his personal, business, and political life, some of which would have doomed an ordinary politician.

---

[1] Parts of this chapter are adapted from our op-eds, "The Presidential Primaries Are Out of Control—and the Party Conventions Are Broken," which appeared in *The Los Angeles Times* print version on May 2, 2016, and "Do Sanders Supporters Favor His Policies?" in Campaign Stops, *The New York Times* online, May 23, 2016.

Clinton, too, was a heroine to her strongest supporters. She had been a successful lawyer, First Lady, Senator from New York, and Secretary of State. She was a long-time, firm supporter of gender equality and women's rights, including the right to an abortion. For educated older women in particular, those who had come through the same battles she had and shared her view of women's roles, the prospect of Clinton becoming the first woman president was appealing indeed. Clinton also had strong support from a variety of ethnic, racial, and religious minorities whom she had championed over the course of her long public life. For most voters in these groups, the lapses of judgment in office that infuriated Clinton's opponents and her stiffness on the campaign trail seemed minor or irrelevant considerations. Identity mattered far more.

The impact of social, religious, racial, and national identities was more obvious in 2016 than in most election years. So, too, was the voters' relative lack of interest in the candidates' policy proposals. Because our book summarized a good deal of prior research on both these points, and added more, some reviewers found us a helpful guide to the presidential contest. But our broader argument, that *every* election is more about social, ethnic, racial, occupational, religious, and partisan identities than about policy judgments, may have been overlooked in the rush to "explain" what happened in 2016. Witness the post-election calls in the Democratic Party for de-emphasizing "identity politics"—as if policy-based appeals could be persuasive in a social vacuum.

The role of identities was even more frequently overlooked in commentary on the Bernie Sanders campaign. Adopting left-wing, populist themes, Sanders mounted a strong challenge to Clinton for the Democratic nomination. In primaries and caucuses, he offered anti-establishment rhetoric and themes of economic renewal, similar in some respects to Trump's. Many political observers saw Sanders as the leader of a new mass movement that would push the Democratic Party leftward, toward firm opposition to both corporate capitalism and the neoliberal international trade order. In their minds, this was an *ideological* campaign, firmly in the Old Left style, focused on economic changes that would benefit ordinary people of all races and ethnicities. Identities, with the possible exception of class identities, were not seen as central to the Sanders campaign.

This view of Sanders' voters was mostly illusory. To the extent that exit polls can be trusted, those conducted in primary and caucus states revealed ample evidence of the importance of group loyalties to the Sanders vote. He did just nine points better, on average, among liberals than he did among moderates. By comparison, he did eleven points worse among women than among men, eighteen points worse among nonwhites than among whites, and a whopping twenty-eight points worse among those who identified as Democrats than among independents. It is very hard to point to differences between Clinton and Sanders's proposed policies that could plausibly account for such substantial cleavages. They are reflections of social identities, symbolic commitments, and partisan loyalties.

Nor is there much evidence that support for Sanders reflected a shift to the left in the policy preferences of Democrats. In a survey conducted for the American National Election Studies in late January, supporters of Sanders were *less* likely than Clinton's supporters to favor concrete policies that Sanders offered as remedies for these ills, including a higher minimum wage, increased government spending on health care, and an expansion of government services financed by higher taxes. It is quite a stretch to view Sanders fans as the vanguard of a new, ideologically left-wing Democratic Party.

In short, Sanders was a convenient vehicle for anti-Clinton sentiment among Democratic primary voters, especially white men. Sanders also drew enthusiastic support from young people and others disaffected from political parties and conventional politics—a common pattern for outsider candidates of all stripes.[2] But none of these supportive groups was a hotbed of left-wing ideology. Sanders' support, too, was primarily rooted in the social identities and group attachments that we emphasized in the book.

AN EXTRAORDINARY ORDINARY ELECTION

In chapter 6, we showed that the outcomes of contemporary presidential elections can be surprisingly well accounted for on the basis of two simple factors: the state of the election-year economy and how long the incumbent party has held the White House. (Figure 6.1 provides a graphical summary of the historical relationship.) In 2016, those factors suggested a narrow victory for the incumbent party: with eight years in office and real income growth at a moderate 2.2% annual rate over the second and third quarters of the election year (according to the most recent data from the Bureau of

---

[2] As the authors of The *American Voter* noted, "Young people not only vote less, then, but appear less securely bound to the existing party system as well. . . . They have little base for the suspicion with which older voters may view the lineage of the *parvenus* among political parties . . ." (Campbell et al. 1960, 497). On youth and partisan independence as factors augmenting support for "outsider" candidates more generally, see John Zaller and Mark Hunt, "The Rise and Fall of Candidate Perot: The Outsider Versus the Political System—Part II," *Political Communication* 12 (1995): 97-123, and Steven J. Rosenstone, Roy L. Behr, and Edward H. Lazarus, *Third Parties in America*, 2nd ed. (Princeton, NJ: Princeton University Press, 1996), chapters 6 and 9.

Economic Analysis), our statistical analysis implied that the Democrats should have been expected to win the popular vote by about 2.2 percentage points. As it turned out, Hillary Clinton's popular vote margin was 2.1 percentage points—an impressive validation in statistical terms. Of course, from the Democrats' viewpoint her support was unfortunately distributed in the Electoral College, and Trump became the second Republican in the 21st century to win the presidency while losing the popular vote.[3]

Had Trump been a typical presidential candidate, the striking adherence of the 2016 popular vote to the historical pattern might have counted as a confirmation of political scientists' understanding of American electoral politics, notwithstanding the anomalous outcome of the Electoral College vote. But Donald J. Trump was far from being a typical presidential candidate. He was a political neophyte whose intemperate rhetoric was decried by members of his own party as offensive and riddled with falsehoods. He feuded with the Republican speaker of the House and was disavowed by dozens of prominent party leaders, including four of the last five Republican presidential nominees. Conservative intellectuals rejected him in droves.

In light of Trump's manifest weaknesses as a candidate, many election analysts, ourselves included, expected him to garner significantly less support than the "fundamentals" implied. Dylan Matthews of *Vox* created a running tally through the general election campaign of the "Trump Tax"—the gap between Trump's standing in the polls and an average of academic forecasts based on the "fundamentals."[4] In the end, the "Trump Tax" turned out to be remarkably modest: his popular vote share fell about two percentage points short of Matthews' consensus forecast from the academic models, and almost exactly matched the historical benchmark implied by figure 6.1.[5]

The biggest surprise of the 2016 election—far bigger than the endlessly discussed defection of white working class voters to Trump—was that, once Trump became the Republican nominee, the vast majority of Republicans brought themselves to vote for him in spite of everything. Long-term panel data collected by the firm YouGov suggest that more than 90% of people

---

[3] Neither we nor any responsible sources we are aware of attach credence to the president's claim that millions of fraudulent votes robbed him of a popular majority.

[4] Dylan Matthews, "We Set Out to Measure Just How Much Trump is Hurting the GOP This Cycle. Here's How." *Vox*, August 17, 2016.

[5] Matthews' consensus forecast was skewed by economist Ray Fair's prediction of a Republican landslide. The other five forecasts used to assess the "Trump Tax" overestimated his actual share of the two-party popular vote by an average of 1.2 percentage points. Dylan Matthews, "The Trump Tax." *Vox*, November 8, 2016.

who thought of themselves as Republicans or Republican leaners *in 2011*, well before Trump emerged as a significant political figure, voted for him in 2016[6]—about the same proportion as for other recent Republican nominees, according to the American National Election Study.[7] Add in some less-educated Democrats and (especially) Independents who were more relaxed than the *New York Times* thought they should be about Trump's various violations of democratic and ethical norms, and it is not hard to get to 46% of the popular vote, Trump's share. Thus an extraordinary campaign produced a remarkably ordinary election outcome.

In most competitive democratic elections, we said in chapter 1, "the choice between the candidates is essentially a coin toss." That claim provoked complaints from readers even before the book appeared in print. It is deeply unsettling to think that something as important as the outcome of a presidential election hinges on factors that are, from the standpoint of the folk theory of democracy, irrelevant. Thus, in the wake of Trump's unlikely victory, political observers scrambled to interpret the "message" of the election. Indeed, in 2016 some groups deviated a bit from their customary habits, as happens in every election, and those deviations were not random or meaningless. But we are struck by how modest they were, given the choices on offer. In 2012, the "fundamentals" had predicted a close election and the Democrats won narrowly. In 2016, the "fundamentals" predicted a close election and the Republicans lost narrowly but were saved—thanks to the Electoral College—by minuscule margins in three states that could easily have gone the other way. That's how coin tosses go. Most of the time, as we put it in chapter 11, "It is a blunder to expect elections to deliver more."

PARTIES AND NOMINATIONS

Trump's overwhelming support from Republican voters in the general election underscores the importance of partisanship in contemporary American politics, but it also underscores the importance of the parties' nomination

[6] The collection of these data was underwritten by the Democracy Fund. We thank John Sides for supplying us with this finding.

[7] The ANES cumulative time series (available from www.electionstudies.org) shows 91% support for George W. Bush among Republicans in 2000, and 93% in 2004. The corresponding figures for John McCain in 2008 and Mitt Romney in 2012 are 87% and 92%, respectively. These ANES rates average a bit more than Trump's 90%, but they are undoubtedly inflated slightly because, unlike the YouGov result, they are based on election-year partisanship. A few voters choose their partisanship to match their current vote intention, which makes election-year party loyalty look higher than it actually is.

processes. It mattered a great deal that those Republicans were voting for Donald Trump rather than Ted Cruz, John Kasich, or some other Republican nominee. Majoritarian electoral systems paper over the complexities of collective choice discussed in chapter 2 by relying on nomination processes to effectively winnow a vast number of potential choices down to just two. The problem is that in a crowded primary field, fringe candidates can win, as the presidential primary process has demonstrated more than once. Trump was the first choice of a plurality of Republicans almost as soon as he announced his candidacy. But his support mostly hovered around 25% in early polls and never reached as much as 40% until after most of his opponents had dropped out of the race. Trump's nomination was a classic illustration of the danger of relying solely on primary elections to choose nominees.

What would a more "democratic" nomination process look like? As we saw in chapter 2, E. E. Schattschneider (1942, 60) attempted to sidestep that question by declaring that "Democracy is not to be found *in* the parties but *between* the parties." Writing in an era when party elites controlled presidential nominations, Schattschneider had faith in their ability to pick nominees who could appeal to voters in the general election and govern effectively if they won. But today, leaving party nominations in the hands of professional politicians rather than "the people" seems fundamentally undemocratic by the standards of the folk theory. Direct election through primaries is thought to be the only legitimate way to choose a party's candidates.

Party elites have tried to regain effective control over the presidential nominating process by coordinating their support and resources behind a broadly acceptable candidate before the primaries (Cohen et al. 2008). But they do not always come to agreement; and even when they do, primary voters may not follow their lead. The 2016 Republican nomination campaign was both a spectacular instance of party leaders failing to coordinate and a spectacular instance of "the people" eschewing the judgment of the professionals.

Ironically, given the Democratic Party's rhetorical commitment to popular control, its nomination rules retain a somewhat more robust layer of professional oversight than the GOP's. Having been stung by the improbable nominations of outsiders George McGovern and Jimmy Carter, Democrats since the 1980s have reserved a block of votes at their convention for "superdelegates"—top party leaders and elected officials who can choose for themselves whom to support. But having superdelegates sounds so undemocratic by the standards of the folk theory that it is unclear whether they could really bring themselves to overturn the choice of "the people." In 2016, about 15% of the delegates at the Democratic convention were super-delegates, and they tilted sharply toward Hillary Clinton. However, many political commentators charged that it would be thoroughly undemocratic for them to determine the outcome. Unsurprisingly, Bernie Sanders agreed. Yet is it really so far-fetched to suppose that professional politicians—many of whom had known Clinton and Sanders personally for many years, and whose careers hinged on the party's performance at the polls and in government—might usefully supplement the judgment of primary voters whose impressions of the candidates stemmed only from television and the Internet?

Abraham Lincoln promised Americans "government of the people, by the people, for the people"—if taken literally, a notable departure from the republican system set up by the architects of the Constitution. In the 150 years since Lincoln, the ideal of government "by the people" has re-shaped Americans' democratic aspirations and their political practices—for example, in the Progressive Era introductions of direct primary elections and referendums and initiatives. That ideal makes sense, descriptively and normatively, only if citizens understand politics in terms of issues and ide-ologies, and if their votes convey coherent collective judgments regarding the course of public policy. Americans' commitment to the folk theory of democracy may make them wish that primary elections worked that way. But the truth is that they do not.

Neither do referendums, as Britain's recent experience reiterates. In vio-lation of his Conservative Party's longstanding devotion to parliamentary supremacy, Prime Minister David Cameron put British membership in the European Union to a national vote in 2016. The electorate voted narrowly to leave, mostly for reasons unrelated to the relevant economics. In conse-quence, they may have put at risk, not only their country's economic stand-ing, but the unity of Great Britain as well, as Scotland may vote to go its own way within the European Union.

In the United States, we have drifted far from the view of the Founders that popular sentiment needs to be respected, but also tempered and refined by experienced, well-informed political judgment. The Founders were nei-ther elitists nor populists; they sought a balance. In the current presidential primary system, that balance has tilted too far toward empowering popular sentiment. But we, the people, like the power, and we are resistant to sharing it with those more knowledgeable than ourselves.

DEMOCRACY IN CRISIS—OR JUST DEMOCRACY?

Political developments in recent decades, and especially in recent months, have fueled renewed interest in the perennial notion of a "crisis of democracy."[8] Partisan polarization, declining trust in government, economic stagnation, the rise of populist movements in Europe and the United States, and an apparent fraying of democratic norms of civility and self-restraint have punctured any illusion of having reached "the end point of mankind's ideological evolution and the universalization of Western liberal democracy as the final form of human government."[9] But while these developments are real, and alarming, they are not really new. Indeed, the current political environment is probably more typical in the broad sweep of history than the mid-20th-century period that contemporary observers often think of as "normal."

American politics in the decades after World War II was quite unusual in a variety of ways, shaped by sustained economic prosperity, a major external threat in the form of communism, a media system dominated by three essentially similar television networks and several dozen essentially similar big-city newspapers, and a party system depending for its survival on the submersion of both racial and ideological conflict. But further back in American history, it is not hard to find numerous parallels to the current political situation in the early 19th century, the antebellum period, the Gilded Age, and even the New Deal era. True, we have never had a president as remarkable as Trump; but he is an accident of a sort that could have happened at various points in American history—or, for that matter, in other democratic systems, as our description in chapter 7 of the not-dissimilar Social Credit movement in Depression-era Alberta shows.

Populist candidates of all ideologies are often impatient with democratic procedures and constitutional norms, which they see as tools of the corrupt establishment. For their part, most ordinary citizens have never been all that

---

[8] See, for example, "What's Gone Wrong with Democracy," *The Economist* (March 1, 2014); Mohamed A. El-Erian, "How Political Polarisation is Crippling Western Democracies," World Economic Forum (May 12, 2015); Marc J. Hetherington and Thomas J. Rudolph, *Why Washington Won't Work: Polarization, Political Trust, and the Governing Crisis* (Chicago: University of Chicago Press, 2015); Steven Levitsky and Daniel Ziblatt, "Is Donald Trump a Threat to Democracy?" *New York Times* (December 16, 2016); Ed Miliband, "Trump, Brexit—The West in Crisis," *Democracy* (Winter 2017). As for "perennial," see Michel Crozier, Samuel P. Huntington, and Joji Watanuki, *The Crisis of Democracy: Report on the Governability of Democracies to the Trilateral Commision* (New York: New York University Press, 1975).

[9] Francis Fukuyama, "The End of History?" *The National Interest* 16 (1989), 3-18, at page 3.

strongly devoted to democratic norms and civil liberties. Political scientists have long recognized that most people have only a tenuous grasp of "the pre-suppositions and complex obligations of democracy, the rights it grants and the self-restraints it imposes," as Herbert McClosky put it.[10] The evidence on this point goes back to the 1950s and '60s, when social scientists shaken by the rise of fascism in Europe began studying American public opinion. They discovered that well-informed commitment to democratic values was largely limited to the most active and best-informed sliver of the population, though it was by no means universal among them. Below that stratum, large major-ities expressed strong support at the level of broad generalities but quickly abandoned their principles or simply became confused when it came to (even slightly difficult) concrete cases.

Not much seems to have changed on this score over the past half-century. When the Latin American Public Opinion Project's 2014 AmericasBarom-eter surveys asked people in 23 countries whether "it would be justified for the military of this country to take power by a coup d'état (military coup)" in response to high unemployment, crime, or corruption, one-third of U.S. respondents said that a military coup would be justified "when there is a lot of corruption"—a higher proportion than in Panama, Bolivia, and Haiti, among other places. The investigators, surprised by this finding, tried re-writing the question to explain what a military coup meant, but the result persisted.[11]

Thus, political elites—politicians, civil servants, judges, and journalists—"serve as the major repositories of the public conscience," if anyone does.[12] But Americans have little faith in political elites. The same AmericasBarom-eter survey found that U.S. respondents were also much less likely than Latin Americans (and Canadians) to agree that "Those who govern this country are interested in what people like you think." Add in an attachment to an unre-alistic "folk theory" of democracy, and the influence of political elites quickly

[10] Herbert McClosky, "Consensus and Ideology in American Politics," *American Political Science Review* 58 (1964): 361-382, at page 375. See also David Truman (1951, 512) on "the rules of the game" and Robert Dahl (1961, 311-325) on "the democratic creed."

[11] "Some people say that under some circumstances it would be justified for the mili-tary of this country to take power by a coup d'état (military coup). In your opinion would a military coup be justified under the following circumstances?" "When there is high unem-ployment"—6.2%. "When there is a lot of crime"—29.2%. "When there is a lot of corrup-tion"—33.6%. Mitchell A. Seligson, "The Americas Upside Down: The Decline of Civic Culture in the USA," keynote lecture, symposium on Values and Value Change in the Americas, Monk School of Global Affairs, University of Toronto, April 17, 2015.

[12] McClosky, "Consensus and Ideology in American Politics," 374.

becomes untenable, increasing the risks of demagogic candidates, constitutional crises, or worse.

In the current political environment, as we noted in chapter 10, most politically engaged citizens are firmly committed to one party or the other, and they are willing to overlook a lot in order to feel good about "their" politicians and opinion leaders. Moreover, given the enormous prominence of the presidency, any leader or faction controlling the White House can exert substantial pressure on co-partisans in Congress and elsewhere. So they, too, often fall into line in spite of knowing better.

As the depressing history of the 20th century demonstrates, preserving constitutional democracy requires sound institutional structures and unfailing vigilance. At the moment, carelessness abounds, fueled in part by the folk theory of democracy. Foolish referendums and a slipshod procedure for choosing presidential candidates have had real consequences.

Will democratic citizens outgrow the comforting fiction of the folk theory? Will they adopt a more sophisticated understanding of the importance of competent political leadership in making policy decisions and in choosing nominees? Will they regain the realistic understanding of human nature embraced by the Founders, or will they continue to indulge in dangerous populist fantasies? We do not know. We do know that in a world of widespread human suffering and widespread nuclear weapons, a great deal may hinge on the answers to those questions.

Christopher H. Achen
Larry M. Bartels

References

Abdelal, Rawi, Yoshiko M. Herrera, Alastair Iain Johnston, and Rose McDermott. 2009. *Measuring Identity: A Guide for Social Scientists*. New York: Cambridge University Press.

Abney, F. Glenn, and Larry B. Hill. 1966. "Natural Disasters as a Political Variable: The Effect of a Hurricane on an Urban Election." *American Political Science Review 60*: 974–981.

Abramowitz, Alan. 1988. "An Improved Model of Predicting Presidential Outcomes." *PS: Political Science & Politics 21*: 843–847.

———. 2012. "Forecasting in a Polarized Era: The Time for Change Model and the 2012 Presidential Election." *PS: Political Science & Politics 45*: 618–619.

Abramowitz, Alan, and Kyle L. Saunders. 2006. "Exploring the Bases of Partisanship in the American Electorate: Social Identity vs. Ideology." *Political Research Quarterly 59*: 175–187.

Achen, Christopher H. 1975. "Mass Political Attitudes and the Survey Response." *American Political Science Review 69*: 1218–1231.

———. 1978. "Measuring Representation." *American Journal of Political Science 22*: 475–510.

———. 1992. "Social Psychology, Demographic Variables, and Linear Regression: Breaking the Iron Triangle in Voting Research." *Political Behavior 14*: 195–211.

———. 2002. "Parental Socialization and Rational Party Identification." *Political Behavior 24*: 151–170.

———. 2006a. "Evaluating Political Decisionmaking Models." In Robert Thomson, Frans N. Stokman, Christopher H. Achen, and Thomas Koenig, eds., *The European Union Decides*, 264–298. Cambridge: Cambridge University Press.

———. 2006b. "Institutional Realism and Bargaining Models." In Robert Thomson, Frans N. Stokman, Christopher H. Achen, and Thomas Koenig, eds., *The European Union Decides*, 86–123. Cambridge: Cambridge University Press.

———. 2012. "When Is Myopic Retrospection Rational?" Prepared for presentation at the Annual Meeting of the American Political Science Association, New Orleans.

———. 2016. "A Baseline for Incumbency Effects." In Alan Gerber and Eric Schickler, eds., *Governing in a Polarized Age: Elections, Parties, and Political Representation in America*. New York: Cambridge University Press.

Achen, Christopher H., and Larry M. Bartels. 2002. "Blind Retrospection: Electoral Responses to Drought, Flu, and Shark Attacks." Prepared for presentation at the Annual Meeting of the American Political Science Association, Boston.

———. 2004. "Musical Chairs: Pocketbook Voting and the Limits of Democratic Accountability." Prepared for presentation at the Annual Meeting of the American Political Science Association, Chicago.

———. 2006. "It Feels like We're Thinking: The Rationalizing Voter and Electoral Democracy." Prepared for presentation at the Annual Meeting of the American Political Science Association, Philadelphia.

———. 2007. "Tumbling Down into a Democratical Republick." Prepared for presentation at the Annual Meeting of the Midwest Political Science Association, Chicago.

Adams, Greg D. 1997. "Abortion: Evidence of an Issue Evolution." *American Journal of Political Science* 41: 718–737.

Addams, Jane. 1902. *Democracy and Social Ethics*. New York: Macmillan.

Adkins, Todd, Geoffrey C. Layman, David E. Campbell, and John C. Green. 2013. "Religious Group Cues and Citizen Policy Attitudes in the United States." *Politics and Religion* 6: 235–263.

Ahler, Douglas J., Jack Citrin, and Gabriel S. Lenz. 2013. "Do Open Primaries Help Moderate Candidates? An Experimental Test on the 2012 California Primary." Prepared for presentation at the Annual Meeting of the Western Political Science Association, Los Angeles.

Ahn, T. K., Robert Huckfeldt, and John Barry Ryan. Forthcoming. *Experts, Activists, and Democratic Politics: Are Electorates Self-Educating?* New York: Cambridge University Press.

Aho, James Alfred. 1975. *German Realpolitik and American Sociology*. Cranbury, NJ: Associated University Presses.

Albertson, Bethany L. 2011. "Religious Appeals and Implicit Attitudes." *Political Psychology* 32: 109–130.

Aldrich, John H., John L. Sullivan, and Eugene Borgida. 1989. "Foreign Affairs and Issue Voting: Do Presidential Candidates 'Waltz Before a Blind Audience?'" *American Political Science Review* 83: 123–141.

Allen, William S. 1984. *The Nazi Seizure of Power*. Revised ed. Danbury, CT: Franklin Watts.

Allport, Gordon W. 1954. *The Nature of Prejudice*. Reading, MA: Addison-Wesley.

Almond, Gabriel A., and G. Bingham Powell, Jr. 1966. *Comparative Politics: A Developmental Approach*. Boston: Little, Brown.

Almond, Gabriel A., and Sidney Verba. 1963. *The Civic Culture: Political Attitudes and Democracy in Five Nations*. Princeton, NJ: Princeton University Press.

Althaus, Scott L. 1998. "Information Effects in Collective Preferences." *American Political Science Review* 92: 545–558.

Alvarez, R. Michael, and Jonathan Nagler. 1995. "Economics, Issues and the Perot Candidacy: Voter Choice in the 1992 Presidential Election." *American Journal of Political Science* 39: 714–740.

References

Anderson, Christopher J. 2007. "The End of Economic Voting? Contingency Dilemmas and the Limits of Democratic Accountability." *Annual Review of Political Science 10*: 271–296.

Anderson, Kristi. 1979. *The Creation of a Democratic Majority 1928–1936*. Chicago: University of Chicago Press.

Anderson, William. 1921. *A History of the Constitution of Minnesota*. Minneapolis: University of Minnesota.

Ansolabehere, Stephen, Jonathan Rodden, and James M. Snyder, Jr. 2008. "The Strength of Issues: Using Multiple Measures to Gauge Preference Stability, Ideological Constraint, and Issue Voting." *American Political Science Review 102*: 215–232.

Arceneaux, Kevin, and Robert M. Stein. 2006. "Who Is Held Responsible When Disaster Strikes? The Attribution of Responsibility for a Natural Disaster in an Urban Election." *Journal of Urban Affairs 28*: 43–53.

Arian, Asher, and Michal Shamir. 1983. "The Primarily Political Functions of the Left-Right Continuum." *Comparative Politics 15*: 139–158.

Aristotle. 1958. *The Politics of Aristotle*. Edited and translated by Ernest Barker. New York: Oxford University Press.

Arnold, Jason Ross. 2012. "The Electoral Consequences of Voter Ignorance." *Electoral Studies 31*: 796–815.

Arnold, R. Douglas. 1990. *The Logic of Congressional Action*. New Haven, CT: Yale University Press.

Aron, Raymond. 1957. *The Opium of the Intellectuals*. London: Secker and Warburg.

Arrow, Kenneth J. 1951. *Social Choice and Individual Values*. New Haven, CT: Yale University Press.

Asch, Solomon E. 1951. "Effects of Group Pressure upon the Modification and Distortion of Judgment." In Harold Guetzkow, ed., *Groups, Leadership, and Men*, 177–190. Pittsburgh: Carnegie Press.

Ashworth, Scott. 2012. "Electoral Accountability: Recent Theoretical and Empirical Work." *Annual Review of Political Science 15*: 183–201.

Austen-Smith, David, and Jeffrey S. Banks. 1996. "Information Aggregation, Rationality, and the Condorcet Jury Theorem." *American Political Science Review 90*: 34–45.

———. 1999. *Positive Political Theory I: Collective Preference*. Ann Arbor: University of Michigan Press.

Bachrach, Peter. 1967. *The Theory of Democratic Elitism: A Critique*. Boston: Little, Brown.

Bachrach, Peter, and Morton S. Baratz. 1962. "Two Faces of Power." *American Political Science Review 56*: 947–952.

Bafumi, Joseph, and Michael C. Herron. 2010. "Leapfrog Representation and Extremism: A Study of American Voters and Their Members in Congress." *American Political Science Review 104*: 519–542.

Balmer, Randall. 2006. *Mine Eyes Have Seen the Glory: A Journey into the Evangelical Subculture in America*. 4th ed. New York: Oxford University Press.

Banfield, Edward C. 1961. *Political Influence: A New Theory of Urban Politics*. Glencoe, IL: Free Press.

Banks, Jeffrey S., and Rangarajan K. Sundaram. 1993. "Adverse Selection and Moral Hazard in a Repeated Elections Model." In William A. Barnett, Melvin J. Hinich, and Norman J. Schofield, eds., *Political Economy: Institutions, Competition, and Representation*, 295–311. Cambridge: Cambridge University Press.

Barber, Benjamin R. 1984. *Strong Democracy: Participatory Politics for a New Age*. Berkeley: University of California Press.

Barnes, Samuel H. 1971. "Left, Right, and the Italian Voter." *Comparative Political Studies 4*: 157–175.

Barnes, Samuel H., Peter McDonough, and Antonio López Pina. 1985. "The Development of Partisanship in New Democracies: The Case of Spain." *American Journal of Political Science 29*: 695–720.

Barnhart, John D. 1925. "Rainfall and the Populist Party in Nebraska." *American Political Science Review 19*: 527–540.

Barry, Brian. 1970. *Sociologists, Economists and Democracy*. London: Collier-Macmillan.

Barry, John M. 2004. *The Great Influenza: The Story of the Deadliest Pandemic in History*. New York: Viking.

Bartels, Larry M. 1988. *Presidential Primaries and the Dynamics of Public Choice*. Princeton, NJ: Princeton University Press.

———. 1990. "Public Opinion and Political Interests." Paper presented at the Annual Meeting of the Midwest Political Science Association, Chicago.

———. 1991. "Constituency Opinion and Congressional Policy Making: The Reagan Defense Buildup." *American Political Science Review 85*: 457–474.

———. 1996. "Uninformed Votes: Information Effects in Presidential Elections." *American Journal of Political Science 40*: 194–230.

———. 1998. "Electoral Continuity and Change, 1868–1996." *Electoral Studies 17*: 301–326.

———. 2000. "Partisanship and Voting Behavior, 1952–1996." *American Journal of Political Science 44*: 35–50.

———. 2002a. "Beyond the Running Tally: Partisan Bias in Political Perceptions." *Political Behavior 24*: 117–150.

———. 2002b. "The Impact of Candidate Traits in American Presidential Elections." In Anthony King, ed., *Leaders' Personalities and the Outcomes of Democratic Elections*, 44–69. New York: Oxford University Press.

———. 2003. "Democracy with Attitudes." In George Rabinowitz and Michael B. MacKuen, eds., *Electoral Democracy*, 48–82. Ann Arbor: University of Michigan Press.

———. 2008. *Unequal Democracy: The Political Economy of the New Gilded Age*. New York and Princeton, NJ: Russell Sage Foundation and Princeton University Press.

———. 2010. "The Study of Electoral Behavior." In Jan E. Leighley, ed., *The Oxford Handbook of American Elections and Political Behavior*, 239–261. New York: Oxford University Press.

———. 2013. "Party Systems and Political Change in Europe." Prepared for presentation at the Annual Meeting of the American Political Science Association, Chicago.

———. 2014. "Ideology and Retrospection in Electoral Responses to the Great Recession." In Nancy Bermeo and Larry M. Bartels, eds., *Mass Politics in Tough Times: Opinions, Votes, and Protest in the Great Recession*, 185–223. New York: Oxford University Press.

———. 2015. "The Social Welfare Deficit: Public Opinion, Policy Responsiveness, and Political Inequality in Affluent Democracies." Paper presented at the 22nd International Conference of Europeanists, Paris.

Bartels, Larry M., Joshua D. Clinton, and John G. Geer. Forthcoming. "Representation." In Robert Lieberman, Suzanne Mettler, and Richard Valelly, eds., *The Oxford Handbook of American Political Development*. New York: Oxford University Press.

Bartels, Larry M., and John Zaller. 2001. "Presidential Vote Models: A Recount." *PS: Political Science & Politics 34*: 9–20.

Baum, Matthew A., and Samuel Kernell. 1999. "Has Cable Ended the Golden Age of Presidential Television?" *American Political Science Review 93*: 99–114.

Baumgartner, Frank R., Jeffrey M. Berry, Marie Hojnacki, David C. Kimball, and Beth L. Leech. 2009. *Lobbying and Policy Change: Who Wins, Who Loses, and Why*. Chicago: University of Chicago Press.

Bawn, Kathleen, Martin Cohen, David Karol, Seth Masket, Hans Noel, and John Zaller. 2012. "A Theory of Political Parties: Groups, Policy Demands and Nominations in American Politics." *Perspectives on Politics 10*: 571–597.

Beard, Charles A. 1912. "Introductory Note." In Charles A. Beard and Birl E. Shultz, eds., *Documents on the State-Wide Initiative, Referendum and Recall*, 1–70. New York: Macmillan.

———. 1913. *An Economic Interpretation of the Constitution*. New York: Macmillan.

Beck, Paul Allen. 1977. "Partisan Dealignment in the Postwar South." *American Political Science Review 71*: 477–496.

Beer, Samuel H. 1966. *British Politics in the Collectivist Age*. New York: Knopf.

Bell, Barbara. 1971. "The Dark Ages in Ancient History I: The First Dark Age in Egypt." *American Journal of Archaeology 75*: 1–26.

Bell, Roderick, David V. Edwards, and R. Harrison Wagner. 1969. *Political Power: A Reader in Theory and Research*. New York: Free Press.

Bendor, Jonathan, Sunil Kumar, and David A. Siegel. 2010. "Adaptively Rational Retrospective Voting." *Journal of Theoretical Politics 22*: 26–63.

Benhabib, Seyla. 1996. "Toward a Deliberative Model of Democratic Legitimacy." In Seyla Benhabib, ed., *Democracy and Difference: Contesting the Boundaries of the Political*, 67–94. Princeton, NJ: Princeton University Press.

Bennett, John W., and Cynthia Krueger. 1968. "Agrarian Pragmatism and Radical Politics." In Seymour Martin Lipset, *Agrarian Socialism*, updated ed., 347–363. Garden City, NY: Doubleday.

Bentley, Arthur F. 1908/2008. *The Process of Government: A Study of Social Pressures.* New Brunswick, NJ: Transaction.

Berelson, Bernard R., Paul F. Lazarsfeld, and William N. McPhee. 1954. *Voting: A Study of Opinion Formation in a Presidential Campaign.* Chicago: University of Chicago Press.

Berger, Peter L., and Thomas Luckmann. 1967. *The Social Construction of Reality: A Treatise in the Sociology of Knowledge.* New York: Anchor.

Billington, Ray Allen. 1938. *The Protestant Crusade.* New York: Macmillan.

Birkland, Thomas A. 1997. *After Disaster: Agenda Setting, Public Policy, and Focusing Events.* Washington, DC: Georgetown University Press.

Bishop, George F., Robert W. Oldendick, and Alfred J. Tuchfarber. 1978a. "Change in the Structure of American Political Attitudes: The Nagging Question of Question Wording." *American Journal of Political Science* 22: 250–269.

———. 1978b. "Effects of Question Wording and Format on Political Attitude Consistency." *Public Opinion Quarterly* 38: 81–92.

Black, Duncan. 1948. "On the Rationale of Group Decision Making." *Journal of Political Economy* 56: 23–34.

———. 1958. *The Theory of Committees and Elections.* Cambridge: Cambridge University Press.

Blais, André, Elisabeth Gidengil, Patrick Fournier, and Neil Nevitte. 2009. "Information, Visibility and Elections: Why Electoral Outcomes Differ When Voters Are Well Informed." *European Journal of Political Research* 48: 256–280.

Blanchard, Oliver J., and Roberto Perotti. 2002. "An Empirical Characterization of the Dynamic Effects of Changes in Government Spending and Taxes on Output." *Quarterly Journal of Economics* 117: 1329–1368.

Blau, Peter M. 1964. *Exchange and Power in Social Life.* New York: John Wiley.

Blum, John M. 1951. *Joe Tumulty and the Wilson Era.* Boston: Houghton Mifflin.

Bourne, Jonathan, Jr. 1912. "Functions of the Initiative, Referendum and Recall." *Annals of the American Academy of Political and Social Science 43–44*: 3–16.

Bowler, Shaun, and Todd Donovan. 1998. *Demanding Choices: Opinion, Voting, and Direct Democracy.* Ann Arbor: University of Michigan Press.

Brader, Ted. n.d. "Disasters and Reelection to Congress: A Natural Experiment on the Link between Constituency Service and Incumbency Advantage." Unpublished manuscript, Political Science Department, University of Michigan.

Brader, Ted, and Joshua A. Tucker. 2001. "The Emergence of Mass Partisanship in Russia, 1993–1996." *American Journal of Political Science* 45: 69–83.

Brady, Henry E., and Paul M. Sniderman. 1985. "Attitude Attribution: A Group Basis for Political Reasoning." *American Political Science Review 79*: 1061–1078.

Brinkley, Alan. 1982. *Voices of Protest: Huey Long, Father Coughlin, and the Great Depression*. New York: Random House.

Broder, David S. 2000. *Democracy Derailed: Initiative Campaigns and the Power of Money*. San Diego, CA: Houghton Mifflin Harcourt.

Brody, Richard A., and Benjamin I. Page. 1972. "Comment: The Assessment of Policy Voting." *American Political Science Review 66*: 450–458.

Broockman, David E. 2013. "Black Politicians Are More Intrinsically Motivated to Advance Blacks' Interests: A Field Experiment Manipulating Political Incentives." *American Journal of Political Science 57*: 521–536.

Brunk, Gregory G. 1978. "The 1964 Attitude Consistency Leap Reconsidered." *Political Methodology 5*: 347–359.

Bryan, Frank M. 2004. *Real Democracy: The New England Town Meeting and How It Works*. Chicago: University of Chicago Press.

Bryce, James. 1894. *The American Commonwealth*. 3rd ed., vol. 2. New York: Macmillan.

Brzezinski, Zbigniew, and Samuel P. Huntington. 1963. *Political Power USA/USSR*. New York: Viking.

Bullock, John G., Alan S. Gerber, Seth J. Hill, and Gregory A. Huber. 2013. "Partisan Bias in Factual Beliefs about Politics." NBER Working Paper No. 19080. http://www.nber.org/papers/w19080.

Bullock, Will, and Joshua D. Clinton. 2011. "More a Molehill Than a Mountain: The Effects of the Blanket Primary on Elected Officials' Behavior from California." *Journal of Politics 73* (3): 915–930.

Burden, Barry. 2007. *The Personal Roots of Representation*. Princeton, NJ: Princeton University Press.

Burgess, John W. 1933/1994. *The Foundations of Political Science*. New Brunswick, NJ: Transaction.

Burnham, Walter Dean. 1972. "Political Immunization and Political Confessionalism: The United States and Weimar Germany." *Journal of Interdisciplinary History 3*: 1–30.

Burrow, J. W. 2000. *The Crisis of Reason: European Thought, 1848–1914*. New Haven, CT: Yale University Press.

Butler, David, and Donald E. Stokes. 1974. *Political Change in Britain*. 2nd ed. London: Macmillan.

Cain, Bruce. 2015. *Democracy More or Less: America's Political Reform Quandary*. New York: Cambridge University Press.

Calvert, Randall L. 1995. "Rational Actors, Equilibrium, and Social Institutions." In Jack Knight and Itai Sened, eds., *Explaining Social Institutions*, 57–93. Ann Arbor: University of Michigan Press.

Campbell, Andrea Louise. 2003. *How Policies Make Citizens: Senior Political Activism and the American Welfare State*. Princeton, NJ: Princeton University Press.

Campbell, Angus, Philip E. Converse, Warren E. Miller, and Donald E. Stokes. 1960. *The American Voter*. New York: John Wiley.

Campbell, Bruce A. 1977. "Patterns of Change in the Partisan Loyalties of Native Southerners: 1952–1972." *Journal of Politics* 39: 730–761.

Campbell, David E., John C. Green, and Geoffrey C. Layman. 2011. "The Party Faithful: Partisan Images, Candidate Religion, and the Electoral Impact of Party Identification." *American Journal of Political Science* 55: 42–58.

Campbell, James E. 2001. "The Referendum That Didn't Happen: The Forecasts of the 2000 Presidential Election." *PS: Political Science & Politics* 34: 33–38.

Campello, Daniela, and Cesar Zucco. 2013. "Merit or Luck? International Determinants of Presidential Performance in Latin America." Unpublished manuscript, Princeton University and Rutgers University.

Canes-Wrone, Brandice, Michael C. Herron, and Kenneth W. Shotts. 2001. "Leadership and Pandering: A Theory of Executive Policymaking." *American Journal of Political Science* 45: 532–550.

Cantril, Hadley. 1941. *The Psychology of Social Movements*. New York: John Wiley.

———. 1958. *The Politics of Despair*. New York: Collier.

Capuzzo, Michael. 2001. *Close to Shore: A True Story of Terror in an Age of Innocence*. New York: Broadway Books.

Carey, John M., Richard G. Niemi, and Lynda W. Powell. 1998. "The Effects of Term Limits on State Legislatures." *Legislative Studies Quarterly* 23 (2): 271–300.

Carmines, Edward G., John P. McIver, and James A. Stimson. 1987. "Unrealized Partisanship: A Theory of Dealignment." *Journal of Politics* 49: 376–400.

Carmines, Edward G., and James A. Stimson. 1989. *Issue Evolution: Race and the Transformation of American Politics*. Princeton, NJ: Princeton University Press.

Carmines, Edward G., and James Woods. 1997. "The Role of Party Activists in the Evolution of the Abortion Issue." *Political Behavior* 24: 361–377.

Carnes, Nicholas. 2013. *White-Collar Government: The Hidden Role of Class in Economic Policy Making*. Chicago: University of Chicago Press.

Casey, Steven. 2001. *Cautious Crusade: Franklin D. Roosevelt, American Public Opinion, and the War Against Nazi Germany*. New York: Oxford University Press.

Caute, David. 1964. *Communism and the French Intellectuals*. New York: Macmillan.

Centers for Disease Control and Prevention. 2015. "State Vaccination Requirements." http://www.cdc.gov/vaccines/imz-managers/laws/state-reqs.html. Accessed July 25, 2015.

Christiano, Lawrence J., Martin Eichenbaum, and Charles L. Evans. 1999. "Monetary Policy Shocks: What Have We Learned and to What End?" In John B. Taylor and Michael Woodford, eds., *Handbook of Macroeconomics*, vol. 1A, 65–148. Amsterdam: North-Holland.

Cleary, Matthew R. 2010. *The Sources of Democratic Responsiveness in Mexico*. Notre Dame, IN: University of Notre Dame Press.

Clinch, Thomas A. 1970. *Urban Populism and Free Silver in Montana.* Missoula: University of Montana Press.

Clinton, Joshua D. 2006. "Representation in Congress: Constituents and Roll Calls in the 106th House." *Journal of Politics 68*: 397–409.

Clubb, Jerome M., William H. Flanigan, and Nancy H. Zingale. 1990. *Partisan Realignment: Voters, Parties and Government in American History.* Boulder, CO: Westview.

Cohen, Joshua. 2003. "Deliberation and Democratic Legitimacy." In Derek Matravers and Jon Pike, eds., *Debates in Contemporary Political Philosophy: An Anthology,* 342–360. London: Routledge.

Cohen, Marty, David Karol, Hans Noel, and John Zaller. 2008. *The Party Decides: Presidential Nominations Before and After Reform.* Chicago: University of Chicago Press.

Cohen, Marty, and John Zaller. 2012. "The Effect of Candidate and Party Extremism in U.S. Presidential Elections." Unpublished manuscript, James Madison University and UCLA.

Cole, G. D. H. 1920. *Guild Socialism Restated.* London: L. Parsons.

Commission on Party Structure and Delegate Selection. 1970. *Mandate for Reform.* Washington, DC: Democratic National Committee.

Committee on Political Parties. 1950. *Toward a More Responsible Two-Party System: A Report of the Committee on Political Parties, American Political Science Association.* New York: Rinehart.

Conley, Patrick T. 1988. "Rhode Island: First in War, Last in Peace." In Patrick T. Conley and John P. Kaminski, eds., *The Constitution and the States: The Role of the Original Thirteen in the Framing and Adoption of the Federal Constitution,* 269–294. Madison, WI: Madison House.

Connors, Richard J. 1971. *A Cycle of Power: The Career of Jersey City Mayor Frank Hague.* Metuchen, NJ: Scarecrow Press.

Conover, Pamela Johnston, and Stanley Feldman. 1989. "Candidate Perception in an Ambiguous World: Campaigns, Cues, and Inference Processes." *American Journal of Political Science 33*: 912–940.

Conover, Pamela Johnston, Stanley Feldman, and Kathleen Knight. 1987. "The Personal and Political Underpinnings of Economic Forecasts." *American Journal of Political Science 31*: 559–583.

Converse, Philip E. 1962. "Information Flow and the Stability of Partisan Attitudes." *Public Opinion Quarterly 26*: 578–599.

———. 1964. "The Nature of Belief Systems in Mass Publics." In David E. Apter, ed., *Ideology and Discontent,* 206–261. Glencoe, IL: Free Press.

———. 1966a. "The Concept of a Normal Vote." In Angus Campbell, Philip E. Converse, Warren E. Miller, and Donald E. Stokes, *Elections and the Political Order,* 9–39. New York: John Wiley.

———. 1966b. "Religion and Politics: The 1960 Election." In Angus Campbell, Philip E. Converse, Warren E. Miller, and Donald E. Stokes, *Elections and the Political Order*, 96–124. New York: John Wiley.

———. 1990. "Popular Representation and the Distribution of Information." In John A. Ferejohn and James H. Kuklinski, eds., *Information and Democratic Processes*, 369–388. Urbana: University of Illinois Press.

———. 2000. "Assessing the Capacity of Mass Electorates." *Annual Review of Political Science 3*: 331–353.

———. 2006. "Democratic Theory and Electoral Reality." *Critical Review 18*: 297–329.

Converse, Philip E., Angus Campbell, Warren E. Miller, and Donald E. Stokes. 1961. "Stability and Change in 1960: A Reinstating Election." *American Political Science Review 55*: 269–280.

Converse, Philip E., and Roy Pierce. 1985. "Measuring Partisanship." *Political Methodology 11*: 143–166.

———. 1986. *Political Representation in France*. Cambridge, MA: Belknap.

Craig, Maureen A., and Jennifer A. Richeson. 2014. "On the Precipice of a 'Majority-Minority' America: Perceived Status Threat from the Racial Demographic Shift Affects White Americans' Political Ideology." *Psychological Science 25*: 1189–1197.

Crain, Robert L., Elihu Katz, and Donald B. Rosenthal. 1969. *The Politics of Community Conflict: The Fluoridation Decision*. Indianapolis: Bobbs-Merrill.

Cramer, Katherine. Forthcoming. *The Politics of Resentment: Rural Consciousness in Wisconsin and the Rise of Scott Walker*. Chicago: University of Chicago Press.

Craven, Avery. 1953. *The Growth of Southern Nationalism, 1848–1861*. Baton Rouge: Louisiana State University Press.

Croly, Herbert D. 1909. *The Promise of American Life*. New York: Macmillan.

Crosby, Alfred W. 1989. *America's Forgotten Pandemic: The Influenza of 1918*. New York: Cambridge University Press.

Cuddy, Edward. 1969. "Irish-Americans and the 1916 Election: An Episode in Immigrant Adjustment." *American Quarterly 21*: 228–243.

Dahl, Robert A. 1956. *A Preface to Democratic Theory*. Chicago: University of Chicago Press.

———. 1961. *Who Governs? Democracy and Power in an American City*. New Haven, CT: Yale University Press.

———. 1971. *Polyarchy: Participation and Opposition*. New Haven, CT: Yale University Press.

———. 1989. *Democracy and Its Critics*. New Haven, CT: Yale University Press.

———. 1998. *On Democracy*. New Haven, CT: Yale University Press.

Daley, Brendan, and Erik Snowberg. 2011. "Even if It Is Not Bribery: The Case for Campaign Finance Reform." *Journal of Law and Economic Organization 27*: 301–323.

References

Davis, Otto A., and Melvin J. Hinich. 1966. "A Mathematical Model of Policy Formation in a Democratic Society." In Joseph Bernd, ed., *Mathematical Applications in Political Science II*, 175–208. Dallas: Southern Methodist University Press.

———. 1967. "Some Results Related to a Mathematical Model of Policy Formation in a Democratic Society." In Joseph Bernd, ed., *Mathematical Applications in Political Science III*, 14–38. Charlottesville: University of Virginia Press.

Davis, Otto A., Melvin J. Hinich, and Peter C. Ordeshook. 1970. "An Expository Development of a Mathematical Model of the Electoral Process." *American Political Science Review* 64: 426–448.

Dawson, Michael C. 1994. *Behind the Mule: Race and Class in African-American Politics*. Princeton, NJ: Princeton University Press.

de Grazia, Alfred. 1951. *Public and Republic: Political Representation in America*. New York: Knopf.

Delli Carpini, Michael X., and Scott Keeter. 1996. *What Americans Know about Politics and Why It Matters*. New Haven, CT: Yale University Press.

Dewey, John. 1927. *The Public and Its Problems*. New York: Henry Holt.

Dickinson, John. 1930. "Democratic Realities and Democratic Dogma." *American Political Science Review* 24: 283–309.

Dixon, Frank Haigh. 1898. "Railroad Control in Nebraska." *Political Science Quarterly* 13: 617–647.

Downs, Anthony. 1957. *An Economic Theory of Democracy*. New York: Harper & Row.

Duch, Raymond M., and Randolph T. Stevenson. 2008. *The Economic Vote: How Political and Economic Institutions Condition Election Results*. New York: Cambridge University Press.

Dunn, John. 1999. "Situating Democratic Political Accountability." In Adam Przeworski, Susan C. Stokes, and Bernard Manin, eds., *Democracy, Accountability, and Representation*, 329–344. New York: Cambridge University Press.

Easton, David. 1953. *The Political System: An Inquiry into the State of Political Science*. New York: Knopf.

———. 1965. *A Systems Analysis of Political Life*. Chicago: University of Chicago Press.

Egan, Patrick J. 2013. *Partisan Priorities: How Issue Ownership Drives and Distorts American Politics*. New York: Cambridge University Press.

Eliasoph, Nina. 1998. *Avoiding Politics: How Americans Produce Apathy in Everyday Life*. New York: Cambridge University Press.

Elkins, Stanley, and Eric McKitrick. 1993. *The Age of Federalism*. New York: Oxford University Press.

Enelow, James M., and Melvin J. Hinich. 1984. *The Spatial Theory of Voting: An Introduction*. New York: Cambridge University Press.

Erikson, Robert S. 1989. "Economic Conditions and the Presidential Vote." *American Political Science Review* 83: 567–573.

———. 1990. "Economic Conditions and the Congressional Vote: A Review of the Macrolevel Evidence." *American Journal of Political Science 34*: 373–399.

———. 2004. "Macro- vs. Micro-Level Perspectives on Economic Voting: Is the Micro-Level Evidence Endogenously Induced?" Prepared for presentation at the Annual Summer Meeting of the Society for Political Methodology, Stanford, CA.

Erikson, Robert S., Joseph Bafumi, and Bret Wilson. 2002. "Was the 2000 Presidential Election Predictable?" *PS: Political Science & Politics 35*: 815–819.

Erikson, Robert S., Michael B. MacKuen, and James A. Stimson. 2002. *The Macro Polity*. New York: Cambridge University Press.

Erikson, Robert S., and David W. Romero. 1990. "Candidate Equilibrium and the Behavioral Model of the Vote." *American Political Science Review 84*: 1103–1126.

Erikson, Robert S., and Christopher Wlezien. 2012. "The Objective and Subjective Economy and the Presidential Vote." *PS: Political Science & Politics 45*: 620–624.

Erisen, Cengiz, Milton Lodge, and Charles S. Taber. 2014. "Affective Contagion in Effortful Political Thinking." *Political Psychology 35*: 187–206.

Esaiasson, Peter, and Sören Holmberg. 1996. *Representation from Above: Members of Parliament and Representative Democracy in Sweden*. Aldershot, UK: Dartmouth.

Falter, Jürgen W. 1990. "The First German *Volkspartei* : The Social Foundations of the NSDAP." In Karl Rohe, ed., *Elections, Parties and Political Traditions: Social Foundations of German Parties and Party Systems, 1867–1987*, 53–81. New York: Berg.

Faust, Drew Gilpin, ed. 1981. *The Ideology of Slavery: Proslavery Thought in the Antebellum South, 1830–1860*. Baton Rouge: Louisiana State University Press.

Fearon, James. 1999. "Electoral Accountability and the Control of Politicians: Selecting Good Types versus Sanctioning Poor Performance." In Adam Przeworski, Susan C. Stokes, and Bernard Manin, eds., *Democracy, Accountability, and Representation*, 55–97. New York: Cambridge University Press.

Feddersen, Timothy, and Wolfgang Pesendorfer. 1998. "Convicting the Innocent: The Inferiority of Unanimous Jury Verdicts under Strategic Voting." *American Political Science Review 92*: 23–35.

Feldman, Stanley. 1988. "Structure and Consistency in Public Opinion: The Role of Core Beliefs and Values." *American Journal of Political Science 32*: 416–440.

Feldman, Stanley, and Pamela Johnston Conover. 1983. "Candidates, Issues and Voters: The Role of Inference in Political Perception." *Journal of Politics 45*: 810–839.

Fenno, Richard F., Jr. 1978. *Home Style: House Members in Their Districts*. Boston: Little, Brown.

Ferejohn, John. 1986. "Incumbent Performance and Electoral Control." *Public Choice 50*: 5–25.

Ferguson, Adam. 1767/1995. *An Essay on the History of Civil Society*. Cambridge: Cambridge University Press.

Fernicola, Richard G. 2001. *Twelve Days of Terror: A Definitive Investigation of the 1916 New Jersey Shark Attacks.* Guilford, CT: Lyons Press.

Festinger, Leon. 1957. *A Theory of Cognitive Dissonance.* Evanston, IL: Row, Peterson.

Finkel, Alvin. 1989. *The Social Credit Phenomenon in Alberta.* Toronto: University of Toronto Press.

Finkel, Steven E. 1985. "Reciprocal Effects of Participation and Political Efficacy: A Panel Analysis." *American Journal of Political Science 29*: 891–913.

———. 1987. "The Effects of Participation on Political Efficacy and Political Support: Evidence from a West German Panel." *Journal of Politics 49*: 441–464.

Fiorina, Morris P. 1977. "An Outline for a Model of Party Choice." *American Journal of Political Science 21*: 601–625.

———. 1981. *Retrospective Voting in American National Elections.* New Haven, CT: Yale University Press.

Fischle, Mark. 2000. "Mass Response to the Lewinsky Scandal: Motivated Reasoning or Bayesian Updating?" *Political Psychology 21*: 135–159.

Fishkin, James S. 1991. *Democracy and Deliberation: New Directions for Democratic Reform.* New Haven, CT: Yale University Press.

———. 1995. *The Voice of the People: Public Opinion and Democracy.* New Haven, CT: Yale University Press.

———. 2009. *When the People Speak: Deliberative Democracy and Public Consultation.* New York: Oxford University Press.

Fiske, Susan T., and Shelley E. Taylor. 1991. *Social Cognition.* 2nd ed. New York: McGraw-Hill.

Ford, Henry Jones. 1909. "The Direct Primary." *North American Review 190* (644): 1–14.

———. 1912. "Direct Legislation and the Recall." *Annals of the American Academy of Political and Social Science 43*: 65–77.

Foster, Christine. 2008. "Electoral Reform in Ontario and British Columbia." Junior Paper, Department of Politics, Princeton University.

Fournier, Patrick, Henk van der Kolk, R. Kenneth Carty, Andre Blais, and Jonathan Rose. 2011. *When Citizens Decide.* Oxford: Oxford University Press.

Franklin, Charles H., and John E. Jackson. 1983. "The Dynamics of Party Identification." *American Political Science Review 77*: 957–973.

Freeder, Sean, Gabriel S. Lenz, and Shad Turney. 2014. "The Importance of Knowing 'What Goes with What': Reinterpreting the Evidence on Policy Voting and Multi-Item Issue Scales." Prepared for the Annual Meeting of the American Political Science Association, Washington, DC.

Freud, Sigmund. 1921/1989. *Group Psychology and the Analysis of the Ego.* New York: Norton.

Friese, Philip C. 1856. *An Essay on Party.* New York: Fowler and Wells.

Fritzsche, Peter. 1998. *Germans into Nazis.* Cambridge, MA: Harvard University Press.

Fuchs, Lawrence H. 1956. *The Political Behavior of American Jews*. Glencoe, IL: Free Press.

Fung, Archon. 2004. *Empowered Participation: Reinventing Urban Democracy*. Princeton, NJ: Princeton University Press.

Gaines, Brian J. 2001. "Popular Myths about Popular Vote-Electoral College Splits." *PS: Political Science & Politics 34* (1): 70–75.

Gaines, Brian J., James H. Kuklinski, Paul J. Quirk, Buddy Peyton, and Jay Verkuilen. 2007. "Same Facts, Different Interpretations: Partisan Motivation and Opinion on Iraq." *Journal of Politics 69*: 957–974.

Gallup, George. 1940/1968. *The Pulse of Democracy: The Public Opinion Poll and How It Works*. New York: Greenwood.

Gamm, Gerald H. 1989. *The Making of New Deal Democrats: Voting Behavior and Realignment in Boston, 1920–1940*. Chicago: University of Chicago Press.

Garceau, Oliver. 1941. *The Political Life of the American Medical Association*. Cambridge, MA: Harvard University Press.

Garson, G. David. 1978. *Group Theories of Politics*. Beverly Hills, CA: Sage.

Gasper, John T., and Andrew Reeves. 2011. "Make It Rain? Retrospection and the Attentive Electorate in the Context of Natural Disasters." *American Journal of Political Science 55*: 340–355.

Gaventa, John. 1980. *Power and Powerlessness: Quiescence and Rebellion in an Appalachian Valley*. Urbana: University of Illinois Press.

Gellately, Robert. 2001. *Backing Hitler*. Oxford: Oxford University Press.

Gerber, Alan, and Donald P. Green. 1998. "Rational Learning and Partisan Attitudes." *American Journal of Political Science 42*: 794–818.

Gerber, Alan S., and Gregory A. Huber. 2010. "Partisanship, Political Control, and Economic Assessments." *American Journal of Political Science 54*: 153–173.

Gerber, Alan S., Gregory A. Huber, and Ebonya Washington. 2010. "Party Affiliation, Partisanship, and Political Beliefs: A Field Experiment." *American Political Science Review 104*: 720–744.

Gerring, John. 2001. *Party Ideologies in America 1828–1996*. New York: Cambridge University Press.

Gidwitz, Tom. 2004. "Secrets in the Cinders: How Native Americans in the Southwest Survived—and Even Profited from—an Eleventh-Century Volcanic Eruption." *Archaeology*, March/April, 46–52.

Gilens, Martin. 1999. *Why Americans Hate Welfare: Race, Media and the Politics of Antipoverty Policy*. Chicago: University of Chicago Press.

———. 2012. *Affluence and Influence: Economic Inequality and Political Power in America*. Princeton, NJ: Princeton University Press.

Gilens, Martin, and Benjamin I. Page. 2014. "Testing Theories of American Politics: Elites, Interest Groups, and Average Citizens." *Perspectives on Politics 12*: 564–581.

Goldman, Merle. 1981. *China's Intellectuals: Advise and Dissent*. Cambridge, MA: Harvard University Press.

Goodwin, Doris Kearns. 2013. *The Bully Pulpit: Theodore Roosevelt, William Howard Taft, and the Golden Age of Journalism*. New York: Simon & Schuster.

Goodwyn, Lawrence. 1976. *Democratic Promise: The Populist Movement in American Politics*. New York: Oxford University Press.

Goren, Paul. 2001. "Core Principles and Policy Reasoning in Mass Publics: A Test of Two Theories." *British Journal of Political Science* 31: 159–177.

———. 2005. "Party Identification and Core Political Values." *American Journal of Political Science* 49: 882–897.

Gosnell, Harold F. 1942. *Grass Roots Politics: National Voting Behavior of Typical States*. Washington, DC: American Council on Public Affairs.

Gosnell, Harold F., and Morris H. Cohen. 1940. "Progressive Politics: Wisconsin an Example." *American Political Science Review* 34: 920–935.

Gosnell, Harold F., and William G. Coleman. 1940. "Political Trends in Industrial America: Pennsylvania an Example." *Public Opinion Quarterly* 4: 473–486.

Gosnell, Harold F., and Norman N. Gill. 1935. "An Analysis of the 1932 Presidential Vote in Chicago." *American Political Science Review* 29: 967–984.

Gosnell, Harold F., and Norman Pearson. 1939. "The Study of Voting Behavior by Correlational Techniques." *American Sociological Review* 4: 809–815.

Gosnell, Harold F., and Margaret J. Schmidt. 1936. "Factorial and Correlational Analysis of the 1934 Vote in Chicago." *Journal of the American Statistical Association* 31: 507–518.

Graber, Dorris A. 1980. *Crime News and the Public*. New York: Praeger.

Graves, W. Brooke. 1928. *Readings in Public Opinion*. New York: Appleton-Century.

Green, Donald, Bradley Palmquist, and Eric Schickler. 2002. *Partisan Hearts and Minds: Political Parties and the Social Identities of Voters*. New Haven, CT: Yale University Press.

Greene, Steven. 1999. "Understanding Party Identification: A Social Identity Approach." *Political Psychology* 20: 393–403.

———. 2004. "Social Identity Theory and Party Identification." *Social Science Quarterly* 85: 136–153.

Greenstein, Fred I. 1965. *Children and Politics*. New Haven, CT: Yale University Press.

Griffin, John D., and Brian Newman. 2008. *Minority Report: Evaluating Political Equality in America*. Chicago: University of Chicago Press.

Grofman, Bernard. 2004. "Downs and Two-Party Convergence." *Annual Review of Political Science* 7: 25–46.

Gross, Michael B. 2004. *The War Against Catholicism: Liberalism and the Anti-Catholic Imagination in Nineteenth-Century Germany*. Ann Arbor: University of Michigan Press.

Grossmann, Matt. 2012. *The Not-So-Special Interests: Interest Groups, Public Representation, and American Governance.* Stanford, CA: Stanford University Press.

———. 2014. *Artists of the Possible: Governing Networks and American Policy Change since 1945.* New York: Oxford University Press.

Grynaviski, Jeffrey D. 2010. *Partisan Bonds: Political Reputations and Legislative Accountability.* New York: Cambridge University Press.

Guilfoyle, James H. 1933. *On the Trail of the Forgotten Man: A Journal of the Roosevelt Presidential Campaign.* Boston: Peabody.

Gumplowicz, Ludwig. 1885/1899. *The Outlines of Sociology.* Philadelphia: American Academy of Political and Social Science.

Gusfield, Joseph R. 1963. *Symbolic Crusade: Status Politics and the American Temperance Movement.* Urbana: University of Illinois Press.

Gutmann, Amy, and Dennis Thompson. 1996. *Democracy and Disagreement: Why Moral Conflict Cannot Be Avoided in Politics, and What Should Be Done about It.* Cambridge, MA: Belknap.

Habermas, Jürgen. 1994. "Three Normative Models of Democracy." *Constellations 1*: 1–10.

Halberstam, David. 1972. *The Best and the Brightest.* New York: Random House.

Hamilton, Richard F. 1982. *Who Voted for Hitler?* Princeton, NJ: Princeton University Press.

Hanna, Mary T. 1979. *Catholics and American Politics.* Cambridge, MA: Harvard University Press.

Hansen, John Mark. 1985. "The Political Economy of Group Membership." *American Political Science Review 79*: 79–96.

———. 1991. *Gaining Access: Congress and the Farm Lobby, 1919–1981.* Chicago: University of Chicago Press.

———. 1998. "Individuals, Institutions, and Public Preferences over Public Finance." *American Political Science Review 92*: 513–531.

Hansen, Kasper M. 2009. "Changing Patterns in the Impact of Information on Party Choice in a Multiparty System." *International Journal of Public Opinion Research 21*: 525–546.

Hardin, Russell. 1995. *One for All: The Logic of Group Conflict.* Princeton, NJ: Princeton University Press.

Hargrove, Erwin C. 2014. *The Effective Presidency: Lessons on Leadership from John F. Kennedy to Barack Obama.* 2nd ed. Boulder, CO: Paradigm.

Harris-Lacewell, Melissa V. 2004. *Barbershops, Bibles, and BET.* Princeton, NJ: Princeton University Press.

Hassan, Fekri A. 1994. "Nile Floods and Political Disorder in Early Egypt." In H. Nuzhet Dalfes et al., eds., *Third Millennium BC Climate Change and Old World Collapse*, 1–23. Berlin: Spring.

Hastorf, A. H., and Hadley Cantril. 1954. "They Saw a Game: A Case Study." *Journal of Abnormal and Social Psychology 49*: 129–134.

Hazan, Reuven Y., and Gideon Rahat. 2010. *Democracy within Parties: Candidates Selection Methods and Their Political Consequences.* New York: Oxford University Press.

Healy, Andrew, and Gabriel S. Lenz. 2014. "Substituting the End for the Whole: Why Voters Respond Primarily to the Election-Year Economy." *American Journal of Political Science 58*: 31–47.

Healy, Andrew, and Neil Malhotra. 2009. "Myopic Voters and Natural Disaster Policy." *American Political Science Review 103*: 387–406.

———. 2010. "Random Events, Economic Losses, and Retrospective Voting: Implications for Democratic Competence." *Quarterly Journal of Political Science 5*: 193–208.

Healy, Andrew J., Neil Malhotra, and Cecilia H. Mo. 2010. "Irrelevant Events Affect Voters' Evaluations of Government Performance." *Proceedings of the National Academy of Sciences 107*: 12804–12809.

Heath, Anthony, and Roy Pierce. 1992. "It Was Party Identification All Along: Question Order Effects on Reports of Party Identification in Britain." *Electoral Studies 11*: 93–105.

Hechter, Michael. 1987. *Principles of Group Solidarity.* Berkeley: University of California Press.

Herlihy, David. 1997. *The Black Death and the Transformation of the West.* Cambridge, MA: Harvard University Press.

Hershey, Marjorie Randon. 2011. *Party Politics in America.* 14th ed. New York: Longman.

Hess, Robert D., and Judith V. Torney. 1968. *The Development of Political Attitudes in Children.* Garden City, NY: Anchor.

Hetherington, Marc J. 1996. "The Media's Role in Forming Voters' National Economic Evaluations in 1992." *American Journal of Political Science 40*: 372–395.

———. 2001. "Resurgent Mass Partisanship: The Role of Elite Polarization." *American Political Science Review 95*: 619–631.

———. 2009. "Review Article: Putting Polarization in Perspective." *British Journal of Political Science 39*: 413–448.

Hetherington, Marc J., Meri Long, and Thomas J. Rudolph. 2014. "The Polarization in Perceptions of Presidential Candidate Traits, 1980–2012." Unpublished manuscript, Department of Political Science, Vanderbilt University.

Hibbing, John R., and Elizabeth Theiss-Morse. 2002. *Stealth Democracy.* New York: Cambridge University Press.

Hibbs, Douglas A., Jr. 1977. "Political Parties and Macroeconomic Policy." *American Political Science Review 71*, 1467–1487.

———. 1982. "President Reagan's Mandate from the 1980 Elections: A Shift to the Right?" *American Politics Research 10*: 387–420.

———. 1987. *The American Political Economy: Macroeconomics and Electoral Politics.* Cambridge, MA: Harvard University Press.

———. 2000. "Bread and Peace Voting in U.S. Presidential Elections." *Public Choice* 104: 149–180.

———. 2006. "Voting and the Macroeconomy." In Barry R. Weingast and Donald Wittman, eds., *The Oxford Handbook of Political Economy*, 565–586. New York: Oxford University Press.

———. 2012. "Obama's Reelection Prospects under 'Bread and Peace' Voting in the 2012 US Presidential Election." *PS: Political Science & Politics 45*: 635–639.

Hirst, Paul Q. 1989. "Introduction." In Paul Q. Hirst, ed., *The Pluralist Theory of the State: Selected Writings of G. D. H. Cole, J. N. Figgis, and H. J. Laski*, 1–45. London: Routledge.

Hochschild, Jennifer L. 2001. "Where You Stand Depends on What You See: Connections among Values, Perceptions of Fact, and Political Prescriptions." In James H. Kuklinski, ed., *Citizens and Politics: Perspectives from Political Psychology*, 313–340. New York: Cambridge University Press.

Hochschild, Jennifer L., and Katherine Levine Einstein. 2015. *Do Facts Matter? Information and Misinformation in American Politics*. Norman: University of Oklahoma Press.

Hofstadter, Richard. 1955. *The Age of Reform: From Bryan to F.D.R.* New York: Vintage.

———. 1969. *The Idea of a Party System: The Rise of Legitimate Opposition in the United States, 1780–1840*. Berkeley: University of California Press.

———. 1973. *The American Political Tradition and the Men Who Made It*. 2nd revised ed. New York: Knopf.

Hollingsworth, Charles M. 1912. "The So-Called Progressive Movement: Its Real Nature, Causes and Significance." *Annals of the American Academy of Political and Social Science 43*: 32–48.

Horack, F. E. 1910. "Primary Elections in Iowa." *Proceedings of the American Political Science Association 7*: 175–186.

Hotelling, Harold. 1929. "Stability in Competition." *Economic Journal 39*: 41–57.

Huber, Gregory A., Seth J. Hill, and Gabriel S. Lenz. 2012. "Sources of Bias in Retrospective Decision Making: Experimental Evidence on Voter's Limitations in Controlling Incumbents." *American Political Science Review 106*: 720–741.

Huckfeldt, Robert, and John Sprague. 1995. *Citizens, Politics and Social Communication: Information and Influence in an Election Campaign*. New York: Cambridge University Press.

Huddy, Leonie. 2001. "From Social to Political Identity: A Critical Examination of Social Identity Theory." *Political Psychology 22*: 127–156.

Huston, James L. 1987. *The Panic of 1857 and the Coming of the Civil War*. Baton Rouge: Louisiana State University Press.

Hutchings, Vincent L., and Hakeem Jefferson. 2014. "Out of Options? Blacks and Support for the Democratic Party." Paper presented at the 2014 World Congress of the International Political Science Association, Montreal.

Hyman, Herbert. 1959. *Political Socialization: A Study in the Psychology of Political Behavior.* Glencoe, IL: Free Press.

Inglehart, Ronald, and Hans Klingemann. 1976. "Party Identification, Ideological Preference and the Left-Right Dimension among Western Mass Publics." In Ian Budge, Ivor Crewe, and Dennis Fairlie, eds., *Party Identification and Beyond*, 243–273. London: Wiley.

Irving, John A. 1959. *The Social Credit Movement in Alberta.* Toronto: University of Toronto Press.

Iyengar, Shanto. 1991. *Is Anyone Responsible? How Television Frames Political Issues.* Chicago: University of Chicago Press.

Iyengar, Shanto, Gaurav Sood, and Yphtach Lelkes. 2012. "Affect, Not Ideology: A Social Identity Perspective on Polarization." *Public Opinion Quarterly 76*: 405–431.

Jackson, John E. 1975. "Issues, Party Choices, and Presidential Votes." *American Journal of Political Science 19*: 161–185.

Jacobs, Lawrence R., and Benjamin I. Page. 2005. "Who Influences U.S. Foreign Policy?" *American Political Science Review 99*: 107–123.

Jacobsmeier, Matthew L. 2013. "Religion and Perceptions of Candidates' Ideologies in United States House Elections." *Politics and Religion 6*: 342–372.

Jacobson, Gary C. 2008. *A Divider, Not a Uniter: George W. Bush and the American People.* New York: Pearson Longman.

———. 2011. "The Republican Resurgence in 2010." *Political Science Quarterly 126*: 27–52.

Jelen, Ted G., and Clyde Wilcox. 2003. "Causes and Consequences of Public Attitudes toward Abortion: A Review and Research Agenda." *Political Research Quarterly 56*: 489–500.

Jennings, M. Kent, and Richard G. Niemi. 1974. *The Political Character of Adolescence.* Princeton, NJ: Princeton University Press.

———. 1981. *Generations and Politics: A Panel Study of Young Adults and Their Parents.* Princeton, NJ: Princeton University Press.

Johnston, Richard, André Blais, Henry Brady, and Jean Crête. 1992. *Letting the People Decide: The Dynamics of a Canadian Election.* Stanford, CA: Stanford University Press.

Johnston, Richard, Michael G. Hagen, and Kathleen Hall Jamieson. 2004. *The 2000 Presidential Election and the Foundations of Party Politics.* New York: Cambridge University Press.

Jordan, William Chester. 1996. *The Great Famine: Northern Europe in the Early Fourteenth Century.* Princeton, NJ: Princeton University Press.

Kahneman, Daniel. 2000. "Evaluation by Moments: Past and Future." In Daniel Kahneman and Amos Tversky, eds., *Choice, Values and Frames*, 693–708. New York: Cambridge University Press and Russell Sage Foundation.

Kahneman, Daniel, Paul Slovic, and Amos Tversky, eds. 1982. *Judgment under Uncertainty: Heuristics and Biases.* New York: Cambridge University Press.

Kaminski, John P. 1989. "Rhode Island: Protecting State Interests." In Michael Allen Gillespie and Michael Lienesch, eds., *Ratifying the Constitution*, 368–390. Lawrence: University of Kansas Press.

Kang, Shin-Goo, and G. Bingham Powell, Jr. 2010. "Representation and Policy Responsiveness: The Median Voter, Election Rules and Redistributive Welfare Spending." *Journal of Politics 72*: 1014–1028.

Kantorowicz, Ernst H. 1957. *The King's Two Bodies: A Study in Mediaeval Political Theology*. Princeton, NJ: Princeton University Press.

Karol, David. 2009. *Party Position Change in American Politics: Coalition Management*. New York: Cambridge University Press.

Karpowitz, Christopher. 2006. "Having a Say: Public Hearings, Deliberation, and American Democracy." PhD dissertation, Department of Politics, Princeton University.

Katz, Elihu, and Paul F. Lazarsfeld. 1955. *Personal Influence: The Part Played by People in the Flow of Mass Communications*. New York: Free Press.

Katznelson, Ira. 2013. *Fear Itself: The New Deal and the Origins of Our Time*. New York: Norton.

Kedar, Orit. 2005. "When Moderate Voters Prefer Extreme Parties: Policy Balancing in Parliamentary Elections." *American Political Science Review 99*: 185–199.

Keech, William R. 2013. *Economic Politics in the United States*. 2nd ed. Cambridge: Cambridge University Press.

Keith, Bruce E., David B. Magleby, Candice J. Nelson, Elizabeth Orr, Mark C. Westlye, and Raymond E. Wolfinger. 1992. *The Myth of the Independent Voter*. Berkeley: University of California Press.

Kenny, Christopher, Michael McBurnett, and David Bordua. 2004. "The Impact of Political Interests in the 1994 and 1996 Congressional Elections: The Role of the National Rifle Association." *British Journal of Political Science 34*: 331–344.

Kershaw, Ian. 1998. *Hitler 1889–1936: Hubris*. New York: Norton.

———. 2002. *Popular Opinion and Political Dissent in the Third Reich,* 2nd ed. New York: Oxford University Press.

Key, V. O., Jr. 1942. *Politics, Parties, and Pressure Groups*. New York: Thomas Y. Crowell.

———. 1947. *Politics, Parties, and Pressure Groups*. 2nd ed. New York: Thomas Y. Crowell.

———. 1949. *Southern Politics in State and Nation*. New York: Knopf.

———. 1955. "A Theory of Critical Elections." *Journal of Politics 17*: 3–18.

———. 1958. *Politics, Parties, and Pressure Groups*. 4th ed. New York: Thomas Y. Crowell.

———. 1961a. *Public Opinion and American Democracy*. New York: Knopf.

———. 1961b. "Public Opinion and the Decay of Democracy." *Virginia Quarterly Review 37*: 481–494.

———. 1964. *Politics, Parties, and Pressure Groups.* 5th ed. New York: Thomas Y. Crowell.

———. 1966. *The Responsible Electorate: Rationality in Presidential Voting 1936–1960.* Cambridge, MA: Harvard University Press.

Key, V. O., Jr., and Winston W. Crouch. 1939. *The Initiative and Referendum in California.* Los Angeles: University of California Press.

Key, V. O., Jr., and Frank Munger. 1959. "Social Determinism and Electoral Decisions: The Case of Indiana." In Eugene Burdick and Arthur J. Brodbeck, eds., *American Voting Behavior*, 281–299. Glencoe, IL: Free Press.

Keyssar, Alexander. 2000. *The Right to Vote: The Contested History of Democracy in the United States.* New York: Basic Books.

Killian, Lewis M. 1985. *White Southerners.* Revised ed. Amherst: University of Massachusetts Press.

Kinder, Donald R. 1983. "Diversity and Complexity in American Public Opinion." In Ada Finifter, ed., *Political Science: The State of the Discipline*, 389–425. Washington, DC: American Political Science Association.

———. 1998. "Opinion and Action in the Realm of Politics." In Daniel Gilbert, Susan T. Fiske, and Gardner Lindzey, eds., *The Handbook of Social Psychology*, 778–867. Boston: McGraw-Hill.

———. 2003. "Belief Systems after Converse." In George Rabinowitz and Michael B. MacKuen, eds., *Electoral Democracy*, 13–47. Ann Arbor: University of Michigan Press.

Kinder, Donald R., and Allison Dale-Riddle. 2012. *The End of Race? Obama, 2008, and Racial Politics in America.* New Haven, CT: Yale University Press.

Kinder, Donald R., and Nathan Kalmoe. n.d. *Neither Liberal nor Conservative: Ideological Innocence in the American Electorate.* Unpublished manuscript.

Kinder, Donald R., and Cindy D. Kam. 2010. *Us Against Them: Ethnocentric Foundations of American Opinion.* Chicago: University of Chicago Press.

Kinder, Donald R., and D. Roderick Kiewiet. 1981. "Sociotropic Politics: The American Case." *British Journal of Political Science 11*: 129–161.

Knight, Jack, and James Johnson. 2011. *The Priority of Democracy: Political Consequences of Pragmatism.* New York and Princeton, NJ: Russell Sage Foundation and Princeton University Press.

Kolata, Gina. 1999. *Flu: The Story of the Great Influenza Pandemic of 1918 and the Search for the Virus That Caused It.* New York: Farrar, Straus and Giroux.

Kousser, Thad. 2005. *Term Limits and the Dismantling of State Legislative Professionalism.* New York: Cambridge University Press.

Kramer, Gerald H. 1971. "Short-Term Fluctuations in U.S. Voting Behavior, 1896–1964." *American Political Science Review 65*: 131–143.

———. 1973. "On a Class of Equilibrium Conditions for Majority Rule." *Econometrica 41*: 285–297.

———. 1983. "The Ecological Fallacy Revisited: Aggregate- versus Individual-Level Findings on Economics and Elections, and Sociotropic Voting." *American Political Science Review 77*: 92–111.

Krasno, Jonathan S. 1997. *Challengers, Competition, and Reelection: Comparing Senate and House Elections*. New Haven, CT: Yale University Press.

Krugman, Paul. 2014. "The Populist Imperative." *New York Times*, January 24, A27. http://www.nytimes.com/2014/01/24/opinion/krugman-the-populist-imperative.html.

Kuklinski, James H., and Paul J. Quirk. 2000. "Reconsidering the Rational Public: Cognition, Heuristics, and Mass Opinion." In Arthur Lupia, Mathew D. McCubbins, and Samuel L. Popkin, eds., *Elements of Reason: Cognition, Choice, and the Bounds of Rationality*, 153–182. New York: Cambridge University Press.

Kuo, Alexander, Neil A. Malhotra, and Cecilia Hyunjung Mo. 2014. "Why Do Asian Americans Identify as Democrats? Testing Theories of Social Exclusion and Intergroup Solidarity." Social Science Research Network No. 2423950.

Laffont, Jean-Jacques, and David Martimort. 2002. *The Theory of Incentives: The Principal-Agent Model*. Princeton, NJ: Princeton University Press.

Langton, Kenneth P. 1969. *Political Socialization*. New York: Oxford University Press.

Laski, Harold J. 1921. *The Foundations of Sovereignty and Other Essays*. New York: Harcourt, Brace.

Lasswell, Harold D., and Abraham Kaplan. 1950. *Power and Society: A Framework for Political Inquiry*. New Haven, CT: Yale University Press.

Lau, Richard R. 2013. "Correct Voting in the 2008 U.S. Presidential Nominating Elections." *Political Behavior 35*: 331–355.

Lau, Richard R., and David P. Redlawsk. 1997. "Voting Correctly." *American Political Science Review 91*: 585–598.

———. 2006. *How Voters Decide: Information Processing during Election Campaigns*. New York: Cambridge University Press.

Lauderdale, Benjamin E. 2012. "How to Generate Partisan Disagreement about Political Facts Without Misinformation." Unpublished manuscript, London School of Economics and Political Science.

Lawson, Chappell, Gabriel S. Lenz, Andy Baker, and Michael Myers. 2010. "Looking Like a Winner: Candidate Appearance and Electoral Success in New Democracies." *World Politics 62*: 561–593.

Layman, Geoffrey. 2001. *The Great Divide: Religious and Cultural Conflict in American Party Politics*. New York: Columbia University Press.

Layman, Geoffrey C., and Thomas M. Carsey. 2002. "Party Polarization and Party Structuring of Policy Attitudes: A Comparison of Three NES Panel Studies." *Political Behavior 24*: 199–236.

Layman, Geoffrey C., Thomas M. Carsey, and Juliana Menasce Horowitz. 2006. "Party Polarization in American Politics: Characteristics, Causes, and Consequences." *Annual Review of Political Science 9*: 83–110.

Lazarsfeld, Paul F., Bernard Berelson, and Hazel Gaudet. 1948. *The People's Choice: How the Voter Makes Up His Mind in a Presidential Campaign.* 2nd ed. New York: Columbia University Press.

Leary, William M., Jr. 1967. "Woodrow Wilson, Irish Americans, and the Election of 1916." *Journal of American History* 54: 57–72.

Le Bon, Gustave. 1895/2002. *The Crowd: A Study of the Popular Mind.* New York: Dover Books.

Lenz, Gabriel S. 2009. "Learning and Opinion Change, Not Priming: Reconsidering the Priming Hypothesis." *American Journal of Political Science* 53: 821–837.

———. 2012. *Follow the Leader? How Voters Respond to Politicians' Policies and Performance.* Chicago: University of Chicago Press.

Lenz, Gabriel S., and Chappell Lawson. 2011. "Looking the Part: Television Leads Less Informed Citizens to Vote Based on Candidates' Appearance." *American Journal of Political Science* 55: 574–589.

Leonard, John. 1982. "Funny Things to Think about and Eat." *New York Times*, July 4.

Lepsius, M. Rainier. 1966. *Extremer Nationalismus.* Stuttgart: W. Kohlhammer Verlag.

Levendusky, Matthew. 2009. *The Partisan Sort: How Liberals Became Democrats and Conservatives Became Republicans.* Chicago: University of Chicago Press.

Lewis-Beck, Michael S. 1988. *Economics and Elections: The Major Western Democracies.* Ann Arbor: University of Michigan Press.

Lewis-Beck, Michael S., William G. Jacoby, Helmut Norpoth, and Herbert F. Weisberg. 2008. *The American Voter Revisited.* Ann Arbor: University of Michigan Press.

Lewis-Beck, Michael S., and Mary Stegmaier. 2007. "Economic Models of Voting." In Russell Dalton and Hans-Dieter Klingemann, eds., *The Oxford Handbook of Political Behavior*, 518–537. New York: Oxford University Press.

Lewis-Beck, Michael S., and Charles Tien. 2001. "Modeling the Future: Lessons from the Gore Forecast." *PS: Political Science & Politics* 34: 21–23.

Lichtman, Allan J. 1979. *Prejudice and the Old Politics: The Presidential Election of 1928.* Chapel Hill: University of North Carolina Press.

Lieber, Francis. 1839. *Manual of Political Ethics.* Vol. 2. Philadelphia: Lippincott.

Lindblom, Charles E. 1965. *The Intelligence of Democracy.* New York: Free Press.

———. 1968. *The Policy-Making Process.* Englewood Cliffs, NJ: Prentice Hall.

Link, Arthur S. 1947. *Wilson: The Road to the White House.* Princeton, NJ: Princeton University Press.

———. 1954. *Woodrow Wilson and the Progressive Era 1910–1917.* New York: Harper and Brothers.

Lippmann, Walter. 1914. *A Preface to Politics.* New York: Mitchell Kennerley.

———. 1922/1946. *Public Opinion.* New York: Penguin.

———. 1925. *The Phantom Public.* New York: Harcourt, Brace.

Lipset, Seymour Martin. 1968. *Agrarian Socialism: The Cooperative Commonwealth Federation in Saskatchewan: A Study in Political Sociology*. Updated ed. Garden City, NY: Doubleday.

Lipset, Seymour Martin, Martin Trow, and James S. Coleman. 1956. *Union Democracy: The Internal Politics of the International Typographical Union*. New York: Free Press.

List, Christian, Robert C. Luskin, James S. Fishkin, and Iain McLean. 2013. "Deliberation, Single-Peakedness, and the Possibility of Meaningful Democracy: Evidence from Deliberative Polls." *Journal of Politics* 75: 80–95.

Lockwood, Jeffrey A. 2004. *Locust: The Devastating Rise and Mysterious Disappearance of the Inset That Shaped the American Frontier*. New York: Basic Books.

Lodge, Milton, and Charles S. Taber. 2013. *The Rationalizing Voter*. New York: Cambridge University Press.

Lowell, A. Lawrence. 1898. "Oscillations in Politics." *Annals of the American Academy of Political and Social Science* 12: 69–97.

———. 1913. *Public Opinion and Popular Government*. New York: Longmans, Green.

Luker, Kristin. 1984. *Abortion and the Politics of Motherhood*. Berkeley: University of California Press.

Lupia, Arthur. 1994. "Shortcuts versus Encyclopedias: Information and Voting Behavior in California Insurance Reform Elections." *American Political Science Review* 88 (1): 63–76.

Lupia, Arthur, and John G. Matsusaka. 2004. "Direct Democracy: New Approaches to Old Questions." *Annual Review of Political Science* 7: 463–482.

Lupia, Arthur, and Mathew D. McCubbins. 1998. *The Democratic Dilemma: Can Citizens Learn What They Need To Know?* New York: Cambridge University Press.

Lupu, Noam, and Susan C. Stokes. 2010. "Democracy, Interrupted: Regime Change and Partisanship in Twentieth-Century Argentina." *Electoral Studies* 29: 91–104.

Luskin, Robert. 2002. "From Denial to Extenuation (and Finally Beyond): Political Sophistication and Citizen Performance." In James Kuklinski, ed., *Thinking about Political Psychology*, 281–305. New York: Cambridge University Press.

Luskin, Robert C., James S. Fishkin, and Roger Jowell. 2002. "Considered Opinion: Deliberative Polling in Britain." *British Journal of Political Science* 32: 455–487.

Lynd, Robert S., and Helen Merrell Lynd. 1929. *Middletown: A Study in Modern American Culture*. New York: Harcourt, Brace & World.

———. 1937. *Middletown in Transition: A Study in Cultural Conflict*. New York: Harcourt Brace Jovanovich.

Macedo, Stephen, ed. 1999. *Deliberative Politics: Essays on Democracy and Disagreement*. New York: Oxford University Press.

Mackie, Gerry. 2003. *Democracy Defended*. New York: Cambridge University Press.

Maddison, Angus. 2004. *The World Economy: Economic Statistics*. Paris: OECD.

Maine, Henry Sumner. 1885. *Popular Government: Four Essays.* London: John Murray.

Mann, James. 1998. *About Face: A History of America's Curious Relationship with China, from Nixon to Clinton.* New York: Knopf.

Mann, Thomas E., and Norman J. Ornstein. 2012. *It's Even Worse Than It Looks: How the American Constitutional System Collided with the New Politics of Extremism.* New York: Basic Books.

Mannheim, Karl. 1936. *Ideology and Utopia: An Introduction to the Sociology of Knowledge.* New York: Harcourt, Brace & World.

Mansbridge, Jane J. 1980. *Beyond Adversary Democracy.* New York: Basic Books.

———. 2009. "A 'Selection Model' of Political Representation." *Journal of Political Philosophy 17*: 369–398.

Markus, Gregory. 1988. "The Impact of Personal and National Economic Conditions on the Presidential Vote: A Pooled Cross-Sectional Analysis." *American Journal of Political Science 32*: 137–154.

Markus, Gregory B., and Philip E. Converse. 1979. "A Dynamic Simultaneous Equation Model of Electoral Choice." *American Political Science Review 73*: 1055–1070.

Matsusaka, John G. 2004. *For the Many or the Few: The Initiative, Public Policy, and American Democracy.* Chicago: University of Chicago Press.

Mayhew, David R. 2002. *Electoral Realignments: A Critique of an American Genre.* New Haven, CT: Yale University Press.

———. 2008. "Incumbency Advantage in Presidential Elections: The Historical Record." *Political Science Quarterly 123*: 201–228.

McCallum, R. B., and Alison Readman. 1947. *The British General Election of 1945.* Oxford: Oxford University Press.

McCann, James A. 1997. "Electoral Choices and Core Value Change: The 1992 Presidential Campaign." *American Journal of Political Science 41*: 564–583.

McCardell, John. 1981. *The Idea of a Southern Nation: Southern Nationalists and Southern Nationalism, 1830–1860.* New York: Norton.

McClosky, Herbert. 1964. "Consensus and Ideology in American Politics." *American Political Science Review 58*: 361–382.

McClosky, Herbert, and John Zaller. 1984. *The American Ethos: Public Attitudes toward Capitalism and Democracy.* Cambridge, MA: Harvard University Press.

McGhee, Eric, Seth E. Masket, Boris Shor, Steven Rogers, and Nolan McCarty. 2014. "A Primary Cause of Partisanship? Nomination Systems and Legislator Ideology." *American Journal of Political Science 58*: 337–351.

McGraw, Kathleen M. 1991. "Managing Blame: An Experimental Test of the Effects of Political Accounts." *American Political Science Review 85*: 1133–1157.

McGreevy, John T. 2003. *Catholicism and American Freedom.* New York: Norton.

McKean, Dayton David. 1940. *The Boss: The Hague Machine in Action.* Boston: Houghton Mifflin.

McKelvey, Richard D. 1976. "Intransitivities in Multidimensional Voting Models and Some Implications for Agenda Control." *Journal of Economic Theory 12*: 472–482.

McKelvey, Richard D., and Peter C. Ordeshook. 1985. "Elections with Limited Information: A Fulfilled Expectations Model Using Contemporaneous Poll and Endorsement Data as Information Sources." *Journal of Economic Theory 36*: 55–85.

———. 1986. "Information, Electoral Equilibria, and the Democratic Ideal." *Journal of Politics 48*: 909–937.

Meinecke, Friedrich. 1925/1957. *Machiavellism: The Doctrine of Raison D'Etat and Its Place in Modern History*. New York: Praeger.

Mencken, H. L. 1916. *A Little Book in C Major*. New York: John Lane.

Mendelberg, Tali, and John Oleske. 2000. "Race and Public Deliberation." *Political Communication 17*: 169–191.

Merriam, Charles E. 1934. *Political Power: Its Composition and Incidence*. New York: McGraw-Hill.

Merriam, Charles Edward, and Louise Overacker. 1928. *Primary Elections*. Chicago: University of Chicago Press.

Mettler, Suzanne. 2005. *Soldiers to Citizens: The G.I. Bill and the Making of the Greatest Generation*. New York: Oxford University Press.

Michels, Robert. 1915. *Political Parties: A Sociological Study of the Oligarchical Tendencies of Modern Democracy*. New York: Hearst's International Library.

Middlekauff, Robert. 1982. *The Glorious Cause*. New York: Oxford University Press.

Mill, John Stuart. 1861. *Considerations on Representative Government*. London: Parker, Son, and Bourn.

Miller, David. 1992. "Social Choice and Deliberative Democracy." *Political Studies 40*: 54–68.

Miller, Raymond Curtis. 1925. "The Background of Populism in Kansas." *Mississippi Valley Historical Review 11*: 469–489.

Miller, Warren E. 1964. "Majority Rule and the Representative System of Government." In Erik Allardt and Yrjo Littunen, eds., *Cleavages, Ideologies and Party Systems*, 343–376. Helsinki: Academic Bookstore.

———. 2000. "Temporal Order and Causal Inference." *Political Analysis 8*: 119–140.

Miller, Warren E., and Donald E. Stokes. 1963. "Constituency Influence in Congress." *American Political Science Review 57*: 45–56.

Millspaugh, Arthur C. 1916. "The Operation of the Direct Primary in Michigan." *American Political Science Review 10*: 710–726.

Milne, Robert Stephen, and Hugh C. Mackenzie. 1958. *Marginal Seat, 1955: A Study of Voting Behaviour in the Constituency of Bristol North East at the General Election of 1955*. London: Hansard Society for Parliamentary Government.

Monroe, Kristen Renwick, James Hankin, and Renée Bukovchik Van Vechten. 2000. "The Psychological Foundations of Identity Politics." *Annual Review of Political Science 3*: 419–447.

Monypenny, William F., and George E. Buckle. 1929. *The Life of Benjamin Disraeli*. Vol. 2, revised ed. London: John Murray.

Morgan, Edmund S. 1988. *Inventing the People: The Rise of Popular Sovereignty in England and America*. New York: Norton.

Morton, W. L. 1950. *The Progressive Party in Canada*. Toronto: University of Toronto Press.

Mosca, Gaetano. 1939. *The Ruling Class*. New York: McGraw-Hill.

Mueller, John E. 1966. "The Politics of Fluoridation in Seven California Cities." *Western Political Quarterly* 19 (1): 54–67.

———. 1994. *Policy and Opinion in the Gulf War*. Chicago: University of Chicago Press.

———. 1999. *Capitalism, Democracy, and Ralph's Pretty Good Grocery*. Princeton, NJ: Princeton University Press.

Munro, William B. 1928. *The Invisible Government*. New York: Macmillan.

Mutz, Diana C. 2006. *Hearing the Other Side: Deliberative versus Participatory Democracy*. New York: Cambridge University Press.

Nathan, Andrew. 1986. *Chinese Democracy*. Berkeley: University of California Press.

Nebraska Legislative Reference Bureau. 1918. *The Nebraska Blue Book*. Lincoln: Nebraska Legislative Reference Bureau.

Neustadt, Richard E., and Harvey V. Fineberg. 1983. *The Epidemic That Never Was: Policymaking and the Swine Flu Scare*. New York: Vintage.

Nie, Norman H., Sidney Verba, and John R. Petrocik. 1976. *The Changing American Voter*. Cambridge, MA: Harvard University Press.

Niebuhr, Reinhold. 1932. *Moral Man and Immoral Society*. New York: Scribner's.

———. 1944. *The Children of Light and the Children of Darkness*. New York: Scribner's.

Nivola, Pietro S., and David W. Brady, eds. 2006. *Red and Blue Nation? Volume One: Characteristics and Causes of America's Polarized Politics*. Washington, DC: Brookings Institution Press.

———, eds. 2008. *Red and Blue Nation? Volume Two: Consequences and Correction of America's Polarized Politics*. Washington, DC: Brookings Institution Press.

Noel, Hans. 2013. *Political Ideologies and Political Parties in America*. New York: Cambridge University Press.

Nordhaus, William D. 1975. "The Political Business Cycle." *Review of Economic Studies* 42: 169–190.

Norpoth, Helmut. 2004. "Bush v. Gore: The Recount of Economic Voting." In Herbert F. Weisberg and Clyde Wilcox, eds., *Models of Voting in Presidential Elections: The 2000 U.S. Election*, 49–64. Stanford, CA: Stanford University Press.

Norpoth, Helmut, and Jerrold G. Rusk. 1982. "Partisan Dealignment in the American Electorate: Itemizing the Deductions since 1964." *American Political Science Review* 76: 522–537.

Odegard, Peter H. 1928. *Pressure Politics: The Story of the Anti-Saloon League*. New York: Columbia University Press.

Office of Policy Analysis, U.S. Environmental Protection Agency. 1987. *Unfinished Business: A Comparative Assessment of Environmental Problems*. Washington, DC: U.S. Environmental Protection Agency.

Olin, Spencer C. 1968. *California's Prodigal Sons: Hiram Johnson and the Progressives 1911–1917*. Berkeley: University of California Press.

Olivola, Christopher Y., and Alexander Todorov. 2010. "Elected in 100 Milliseconds: Appearance-Based Trait Inferences and Voting." *Journal of Nonverbal Behavior* 34: 83–110.

Oscarsson, Henrik. 2007. "A Matter of Fact? Knowledge Effects on the Vote in Swedish General Elections, 1985–2002." *Scandinavian Political Studies* 30: 301–322.

Owings, Alison. 1993. *Frauen: German Women Recall the Third Reich*. New Brunswick, NJ: Rutgers University Press.

Page, Benjamin I., Larry M. Bartels, and Jason Seawright. 2013. "Democracy and the Policy Preferences of Wealthy Americans." *Perspectives on Politics* 11: 51–73.

Page, Benjamin I., and Richard A. Brody. 1972. "Policy Voting and the Electoral Process: The Vietnam War Issue." *American Political Science Review* 66: 979–995.

Page, Benjamin I., and Calvin C. Jones. 1979. "Reciprocal Effects of Policy Preferences, Party Loyalties and the Vote." *American Political Science Review* 73: 1071–1089.

Page, Benjamin I., and Robert Y. Shapiro. 1992. *The Rational Public: Fifty Years of Trends in Americans' Policy Preferences*. Chicago: University of Chicago Press.

Pareto, Vilfredo. 1935. *The Mind and Society*. London: Jonathan Cape.

Pateman, Carole. 1970. *Participation and Democratic Theory*. Cambridge: Cambridge University Press.

Payne, B. Keith, Jon A. Krosnick, Josh Pasek, Yphtach Lelkes, Omair Akhtar, and Trevor Tompson. 2010. "Implicit and Explicit Prejudice in the 2008 American Presidential Election." *Journal of Experimental Social Psychology* 46: 367–374.

Pérez, Efrén O. 2010. "Explicit Evidence on the Import of Implicit Attitudes: The IAT and Immigration Policy Judgments." *Political Behavior* 32: 517–545.

Pernick, Martin S. 1972. "Politics, Parties, and Pestilence: Epidemic Yellow Fever in Philadelphia and the Rise of the First Party System." *William and Mary Quarterly*, Third Series, 29: 559–586.

Pierce, Roy. 1999. "Mass-Elite Issue Linkages and the Responsible Party Model." In Warren E. Miller, Roy Pierce, Jacques Thmassen, Richard Herrera, Soren Holmberg, Peter Esaisson, and Bernhard Wessels, eds., *Policy Representation in Western Democracies*, 9–32. New York: Oxford University Press.

Plott, Charles R. 1967. "A Notion of Equilibrium and Its Possibility under Majority Rule." *American Economic Review* 57: 787–806.

———. 1976. "Axiomatic Social Choice Theory: An Overview and Interpretation." *American Journal of Political Science* 20: 511–596.

Polsby, Nelson W. 1983. *Consequences of Party Reform*. New York: Oxford University Press.

———. 1990. "Limiting Terms: Is New Blood Really Better Than Old Blood?" *Los Angeles Times*, September 30.

Poole, Keith T., and Howard Rosenthal. 2007. *Ideology and Congress*. New Brunswick, NJ: Transaction.

Popkin, Samuel L. 1991. *The Reasoning Voter: Communication and Persuasion in Presidential Campaigns*. Chicago: University of Chicago Press.

Powell, G. Bingham, Jr. 2000. *Elections as Instruments of Democracy: Majoritarian and Proportional Visions*. New Haven, CT: Yale University Press.

Powell, G. Bingham, Jr., and Guy Whitten. 1993. "A Cross-National Analysis of Economic Voting: Taking Account of the Political Context." *American Journal of Political Science* 37: 391–414.

Prior, Markus. 2007. *Post-Broadcast Democracy: How Media Choice Increases Inequality in Political Involvement and Polarizes Elections*. New York: Cambridge University Press.

———. 2014. "Visual Political Knowledge: A Different Road to Competence?" *Journal of Politics* 76: 41–57.

Prior, Markus, and Arthur Lupia. 2008. "Money, Time, and Political Knowledge: Distinguishing Quick Recall and Political Learning Skills." *American Journal of Political Science* 52: 169–183.

Program on International Policy Attitudes. 2006. "Iraq: The Separate Realities of Republicans and Democrats." March 28. http://www.worldpublicopinion.org/pipa/.

Pruitt, Dean G. 1967. "Reward Structure and Cooperation: The Decomposed Prisoner's Dilemma Game." *Journal of Personality and Social Psychology* 71: 21–27.

Przeworski, Adam. 2010. *Democracy and the Limits of Self-Government*. New York: Cambridge University Press.

Przeworski, Adam, Michael E. Alvarez, José Antonio Cheibub, and Fernando Limongi. 2000. *Democracy and Development: Political Institutions and Well-Being in the World, 1950–1990*. New York: Cambridge University Press.

Putnam, Robert D. 1973. *The Beliefs of Politicians: Ideology, Conflict, and Democracy in Britain and Italy*. New Haven, CT: Yale University Press.

Pyle, Gerald F. 1986. *The Diffusion of Influenza: Patterns and Paradigms*. Lanham, MD: Rowman & Littlefield.

Rahn, Wendy M. 1993. "The Role of Partisan Stereotypes in Information Processing about Political Candidates." *American Journal of Political Science* 37: 472–496.

Rahn, Wendy M., Jon A. Krosnick, and Marijke Breuning. 1994. "Rationalization and Derivation Processes in Survey Studies of Political Candidate Evaluation." *American Journal of Political Science* 38: 582–600.

Ranney, Austin. 1962. *The Doctrine of Responsible Party Government*. Champaign: University of Illinois Press.

———. 1975. *Curing the Mischiefs of Faction: Party Reform in America*. Berkeley: University of California Press.

Rasinski, Kenneth A. 1989. "The Effect of Question Wording on Public Support for Government Spending." *Public Opinion Quarterly* 53: 388–394.

Redelmeier, Donald A., Joel Katz, and Daniel Kahneman. 2003. "Memories of Colonoscopy: A Randomized Trial." *Pain* 104: 187–194.

Reed, John Shelton. 1986. *The Enduring South: Subcultural Persistence in Mass Society*. Chapel Hill: University of North Carolina Press.

Rehm, Philipp, and Timothy Reilly. 2010. "United We Stand: Constituency Homogeneity and Comparative Party Polarization." *Electoral Studies* 29: 40–53.

Remini, Robert V. 1959. *Martin Van Buren and the Making of the Democratic Party*. New York: Columbia University Press.

Reynolds, John F. 2006. *The Demise of the American Convention System, 1880–1911*. New York: Cambridge University Press.

Richardson, George R. 1991. *Feedback Thought in Social Science and Systems Theory*. Philadelphia: University of Pennsylvania Press.

Richter, Paul. 1996. "Clinton Heralds Drop in Federal Budget Deficit." *Los Angeles Times*, October 29.

Riker, William H. 1953. *Democracy in the United States*. New York: Macmillan.

———. 1980. "Implications from the Disequilibrium of Majority Rule for the Study of Institutions." *American Political Science Review* 74: 432–446.

———. 1982. *Liberalism Against Populism: A Confrontation between the Theory of Democracy and the Theory of Social Choice*. San Francisco: W. H. Freeman.

Rogoff, Kenneth. 1990. "Equilibrium Political Budget Cycles." *American Economic Review* 80: 21–36.

Rogoff, Kenneth, and Anne Sibert. 1988. "Elections and Macroeconomic Policy Cycles." *Review of Economic Studies* 55: 1–16.

Rohe, Karl. 1990a. "German Elections and Party Systems in Historical and Regional Perspective." In Karl Rohe, ed., *Elections, Parties and Political Traditions: Social Foundations of German Parties and Party Systems, 1867–1987*, 1–25. New York: Bloomsbury.

———. 1990b. "Political Alignments and Re-alignments in the Ruhr 1867–1987." In Karl Rohe, ed., *Elections, Parties and Political Traditions: Social Foundations of German Parties and Party Systems, 1867–1987*, 107–144. New York: Bloomsbury.

Rosenberg, Gerald N. 1991. *The Hollow Hope: Can Courts Bring about Social Change?* Chicago: University of Chicago Press.

Rosenblum, Nancy. 2008. *On the Side of the Angels: An Appreciation of Parties and Partisanship*. Princeton, NJ: Princeton University Press.

Ross, Edward A. 1905. *The Foundations of Sociology*. New York: Macmillan.

Rossiter, Clinton. 1955. *Conservatism in America*. New York: Knopf.

Rothenberg, Lawrence S. 1992. *Linking Citizens to Government: Interest Group Politics at Common Cause*. New York: Cambridge University Press.

Rusk, Jerrold. 2001. *A Statistical History of the American Electorate*. Washington, DC: CQ Press.

Saad, Lydia. 2007. "Perceptions of Crime Problem Remain Curiously Negative." Gallup, October 22. http://www.gallup.com/poll/102262/perceptions-crime-problem-remain-curiously-negative.aspx.

Saloma, John S., III, and Frederick H. Sontag. 1972. *Parties: The Real Opportunity for Effective Citizen Politics*. New York: Knopf.

Sances, Michael W. 2015. "The Distributional Impact of Greater Responsiveness: Evidence from New York Towns." *Journal of Politics*.

Sandburg, Carl. 1936. *The People, Yes*. New York: Harcourt, Brace.

Sanders, Lynn M. 1997. "Against Deliberation." *Political Theory* 25: 347–376.

Schattschneider, E. E. 1942. *Party Government*. New York: Holt, Rinehart and Winston.

———. 1960. *The Semisovereign People: A Realist's View of Democracy in America*. New York: Holt, Rinehart and Winston.

Schlesinger, Arthur M., Jr. 1945. *The Age of Jackson*. Boston: Little, Brown.

———. 1997. "Rating the Presidents: Washington to Clinton." *Political Science Quarterly* 11: 179–190.

Schlozman, Kay Lehman, Sidney Verba, and Henry E. Brady. 2012. *The Unheavenly Chorus: Unequal Political Voice and the Broken Promise of American Democracy*. Princeton, NJ: Princeton University Press.

Schneider, Saundra K. 1995. *Flirting with Disaster: Public Management in Crisis Situations*. Armonk, NY: M. E. Sharpe.

Schofield, Norman. 1983. "Generic Instability of Majority Rule." *Review of Economic Studies* 50: 695–705.

Schorske, Carl E. 1955. *German Social Democracy 1905–1917*. Cambridge, MA: Harvard University Press.

Schultz, Kenneth A. 1995. "The Politics of the Political Business Cycle." *British Journal of Political Science* 25: 79–99.

Schuman, Howard, and Stanley Presser. 1981. *Questions and Answers in Attitude Surveys: Experiments on Question Form, Wording, and Context*. New York: Academic Press.

Schumpeter, Joseph A. 1942. *Capitalism, Socialism and Democracy*. New York: Harper & Brothers.

Science Advisory Board, U.S. Environmental Protection Agency. 1990. *Reducing Risk: Setting Priorities and Strategies for Environmental Protection*. Washington, DC: U.S. Environmental Protection Agency.

Sears, David O., and Jack Citrin. 1985. *Tax Revolt: Something for Nothing in California*. Enlarged ed. Cambridge, MA: Harvard University Press.

Sen, Amartya K. 1977. "Rational Fools: A Critique of the Behavioral Foundations of Economic Theory." *Philosophy & Public Affairs* 6: 317–344.

Shani, Danielle. 2006. "Knowing Your Colors: Can Knowledge Correct for Partisan Bias in Political Perceptions?" Paper presented at the Annual Meeting of the Midwest Political Science Association, Chicago.

Shepsle, Kenneth A. 1979. "Institutional Arrangements and Equilibrium in Multidimensional Voting Models." *American Journal of Political Science* 23: 27–59.

Sherif, Muzafer. 1936. *The Psychology of Social Norms*. New York: Harper.

Sherwood, Robert E. 1948. *Roosevelt and Hopkins: An Intimate History*. New York: Harper.

Shields, J. G. 2007. *The Extreme Right in France: From Pétain to Le Pen*. New York: Routledge.

Simmel, Georg. 1908/1964. *Conflict and The Web of Group Affiliations*. Glencoe, IL: Free Press.

Simon, Gregory L., and Sarah Dooling. 2013. "Flame and Fortune in California." *Global Environmental Change* 2: 1410–1423.

Sinclair, Barbara. 2006. *Party Wars: Polarization and the Politics of National Policy Making*. Norman: University of Oklahoma Press.

Skocpol, Theda. 2012. *Obama and America's Political Future*. Cambridge, MA: Harvard University Press.

Small, Albion. 1905. *General Sociology*. Chicago: University of Chicago Press.

Sniderman, Paul M., Richard A. Brody, and Philip E. Tetlock. 1991. *Reasoning and Choice: Explorations in Political Psychology*. New York: Cambridge University Press.

Sombart, Werner. 1906/1976. *Why Is There No Socialism in the United States?* New York: Macmillan.

Somin, Ilya. 2013. *Democracy and Political Ignorance: Why Smaller Government Is Smarter*. Stanford, CA: Stanford University Press.

Sood, Gaurav, and Shanto Iyengar. 2014. "All in the Eye of the Beholder: Partisan Affect and Ideological Accountability." Unpublished manuscript, Stanford University.

Spies, Dennis C., and André Kaiser. 2014. "Does the Mode of Candidate Selection Affect the Representativeness of Parties?" *Party Politics* 20: 576–590.

Stanley, Harold W. 1987. *Voter Mobilization and the Politics of Race: The South and Universal Suffrage, 1952–1984*. New York: Praeger.

Statistical Office of the United Nations. 1949. *United Nations Statistical Yearbook: 1948*. Lake Success, NY: Statistical Office of the United Nations.

Stenner, Karen. 2005. *The Authoritarian Dynamic*. New York: Cambridge University Press.

Stimson, James A. 1991. *Public Opinion in America: Moods, Cycles, and Swings*. Boulder, CO: Westview.

———. 2004. *Tides of Consent: How Public Opinion Shapes American Politics*. New York: Cambridge University Press.

Stokes, Donald E. 1963. "Spatial Models of Party Competition." *American Political Science Review 57*: 368–377.

———. 1966. "Some Dynamic Elements of Contests for the Presidency." *American Political Science Review 60*: 19–28.

Stokes, Donald E., and Gudmund R. Iversen. 1962. "On the Existence of Forces Restoring Party Competition." *Public Opinion Quarterly 26*: 159–171.

Stokes, Susan C. 2001. *Mandates and Democracy: Neoliberalism by Surprise in Latin America*. New York: Cambridge University Press.

Stone, Deborah A. 1989. "Causal Stories and the Formation of Policy Agendas." *Political Science Quarterly 104*: 281–300.

Sturgis, Patrick. 2003. "Knowledge and Collective Preferences: A Comparison of Two Approaches to Estimating the Opinions of a Better Informed Public." *Sociological Methods & Research 31*: 453–485.

Sugarman, Stephen D. 1990. "California's Insurance Regulation Revolution: The First Two Years of Proposition 103." *San Diego Law Review 27*: 683–714.

Sullivan, John L., James E. Piereson, George E. Marcus, and Stanley Feldman. 1979. "The More Things Change, the More They Stay the Same: The Stability of Mass Belief Systems." *American Journal of Political Science 23*: 176–186.

Sundquist, James L. 1983. *Dynamics of the Party System*. Revised ed. Washington, DC: Brookings.

Sydnor, Charles S. 1948. *The Development of Southern Sectionalism, 1819–1848*. Baton Rouge: Louisiana State University Press.

Tajfel, Henri. 1970. "Experiments in Intergroup Discrimination." *Scientific American 223*: 96–102.

———. 1981. *Human Groups and Social Categories*. Cambridge: Cambridge University Press.

———, ed. 1982. *Social Identity and Intergroup Relations*. Cambridge: Cambridge University Press.

Tarde, Gabriel de. 1890/1903. *The Laws of Imitation*. New York: Henry Holt.

Tessin, Jeff. 2009. "Representation and Government Performance." PhD dissertation, Department of Politics, Princeton University.

Theriault, Sean M. 2008. *Party Polarization in Congress*. New York: Cambridge University Press.

Tocqueville, A. de. 1848/1969. *Democracy in America*. Edited by J. P. Mayer. New York: Harper & Row.

Todorov, Alexander, Anesu N. Mandisodza, Amir Goren, and Crystal C. Hall. 2005. "Inferences of Competence from Faces Predict Election Outcomes." *Science 308*: 1623–1626.

Townsend, James R., and Brantly Womack. 1986. *Politics in China*. 3rd ed. Boston: Little, Brown.

Truman, David B. 1949. "Political Behavior and Voting." In Fredrick Mosteller, Herbert Hyman, Philip J. McCarthy, Eli S. Marks, and David B. Truman, eds.,

The Pre-Election Polls of 1948, 225–250. New York: Social Science Research Council.

———. 1951. *The Governmental Process: Political Interests and Public Opinion*. New York: Knopf.

———. 1971. *The Governmental Process: Political Interests and Public Opinion*. 2nd ed. New York: Knopf.

Tsou, Tang. 1991. "The Tiananmen Tragedy." In Brantly Womack, ed., *Contemporary Chinese Politics in Historical Perspective*, 265–327. New York: Cambridge University Press.

Tufte, Edward R. 1978. *Political Control of the Economy*. Princeton, NJ: Princeton University Press.

Turner, John C. 1991. *Social Influence*. Pacific Grove, CA: Brooks/Cole.

Tversky, Amos, and Daniel Kahneman. 1981. "The Framing of Decisions and the Psychology of Choice." *Science 211* (4481): 453–458.

Uchitelle, Louis. 2004. "Beyond a President's Control." *New York Times*, July 11.

Uras, Vedat. 2004. "Elections Fail to Surpass Four-Year Limit." *Turkpulse*, August 16. www.turkpulse.com.

Urbatsch, R. 2014. "Nominal Partisanship: Names as Political Identity Signals." *PS: Political Science & Politics 47*: 463–467.

Valelly, Richard M. 2004. *The Two Reconstructions: The Struggle for Black Enfranchisement*. Chicago: University of Chicago Press.

Vavreck, Lynn, and Douglas Rivers. 2008. "The 2006 Cooperative Congressional Election Study." *Journal of Elections, Public Opinion and Parties 18* (4): 355–366.

Verhovek, Sam Howe. 1997. "Houston Voters Maintain Affirmative-Action Policy." *New York Times*, November 6.

Walker, Jack L. 1966. "A Critique of the Elitist Theory of Democracy." *American Political Science Review 60*: 285–295.

Wallas, Graham. 1908. *Human Nature in Politics*. London: Archibald Constable.

Wand, Jonathan N., Kenneth W. Shotts, Jasjeet S. Sekhon, Walter R. Mebane, Jr., Michael C. Herron, and Henry E. Brady. 2001. "The Butterfly Did It: The Aberrant Vote for Buchanan in Palm Beach County, Florida." *American Political Science Review 95*: 793–810.

Warner, W. Lloyd, ed. 1963. *Yankee City*. One-vol. abridged ed. New Haven, CT: Yale University Press.

Warren, Mark E., and Hilary Pearse, eds. 2008. *Designing Deliberative Democracy*. Cambridge: Cambridge University Press.

White, Theodore H. 1961/1967. *The Making of the President 1960*. New York: New American Library.

White, William Allen. 1910. *The Old Order Changeth: A View of American Democracy*. New York: Macmillan.

Whiting, Theodore E. 1942. *Final Statistical Report of the Federal Emergency Relief Administration*. Washington, DC: Government Printing Office.

Whitman, Walt. 1847/1921. "The Democratic Spirit." *Brooklyn Daily Eagle*, April 20. Reprinted in Emory Holloway, ed., *The Uncollected Poetry and Prose of Walt Whitman*, vol. 1, 159–160. Garden City, NY: Doubleday, Page & Company.

———. 1871/2010. *Democratic Vistas*. Original edition in facsimile, edited by Ed Folsom. Iowa City: University of Iowa Press.

Wilcox, Clyde. 1992. *God's Warriors: The Christian Right in Twentieth-Century America*. Baltimore: Johns Hopkins University Press.

Wilentz, Sean. 2005. *The Rise of American Democracy: Jefferson to Lincoln*. New York: Norton.

Wiley, David E., and James A. Wiley. 1970. "The Estimation of Measurement Error in Panel Data." *American Sociological Review* 35: 112–117.

Wilson, Woodrow. 1900/2002. *Congressional Government: A Study in American Politics*. 15th ed. New Brunswick, NJ: Transaction.

Winchester, Simon. 2003. *Krakatoa*. New York: HarperCollins.

Wolfers, Justin. 2002. "Are Voters Rational? Evidence from Gubernatorial Elections." Research Paper No. 1730, Graduate School of Business, Stanford University.

Woodward, C. Vann. 1968. *The Burden of Southern History*. Enlarged ed. Baton Rouge: Louisiana State University Press.

Zaller, John R. 1992. *The Nature and Origins of Mass Opinion*. New York: Cambridge University Press.

———. 1994. "Strategic Politicians, Public Opinion, and the Gulf Crisis." In W. Lance Bennett and David L. Paletz, eds., *Taken by Storm: The Media, Public Opinion, and U.S. Foreign Policy in the Gulf War*, 250–274. Chicago: University of Chicago Press.

———. 2003. "Coming to Grips with V.O. Key's Concept of Latent Opinion." In Michael B. MacKuen and George Rabinowitz, eds., *Electoral Democracy*, 311–336. Ann Arbor: University of Michigan Press.

———. 2004. "Floating Voters in U.S. Presidential Elections, 1948–2000." In Willem E. Saris and Paul M. Sniderman, eds., *Studies in Public Opinion: Attitudes, Nonattitudes, Measurement Error, and Change*, 166–212. Princeton, NJ: Princeton University Press.

———. 2012. "What *Nature and Origins* Leaves Out." *Critical Review* 24: 569–642.

Zaller, John, and Mark Hunt. 1995. "The Rise and Fall of Candidate Perot: The Outsider versus the Political System—Part II." *Political Communication* 12: 97–123.

Zechmeister, Elizabeth. 2006. "What's Left and Who's Right? A Q-method Study of Individual and Contextual Influences on the Meaning of Ideological Labels." *Political Behavior* 28: 151–173.

———. 2010. "Left-Right Semantics as a Facilitator of Programmatic Structuration." In Herbert Kitschelt, Kirk A. Hawkins, Juan Pablo Luna, Guillermo Rosas, and Elizabeth J. Zechmeister, eds., *Latin American Party Systems*, 96–118. New York: Cambridge University Press.

Index

Italic pages refer to figures and tables.

381